HEARING THE CALL

Hearing the Call

LITURGY
JUSTICE
CHURCH
and
WORLD

Essays by

Nicholas Wolterstorff

Edited by

Mark R. Gornik and
Gregory Thompson

William B. Eerdmans Publishing Company
Grand Rapids, Michigan / Cambridge, U.K.

Published 2011 by
Wm. B. Eerdmans Publishing Co.
2140 Oak Industrial Drive N.E., Grand Rapids, Michigan 49505 /
P.O. Box 163, Cambridge CB3 9PU U.K.

Printed in the United States of America

17 16 15 14 13 12 11   7 6 5 4 3 2 1

Library of Congress Cataloging-in-Publication Data

Wolterstorff, Nicholas.
Hearing the call: liturgy, justice, church, and world: essays / by Nicholas Wolterstorff;
edited by Mark R. Gornik and Gregory Thompson.
p.   cm.
ISBN 978-0-8028-6525-0 (pbk.: alk. paper)
1. Christianity and justice.   I. Gornik, Mark R.
II. Thompson, Gregory, 1971-   III. Title.

BR115.J8W64   2011

261.8 — dc22

2010046674

www.eerdmans.com

Contents

Preface   ix

The Grace That Shaped My Life   1

Part One: Liturgy

Trumpets, Ashes, and Tears   19

The Tragedy of Liturgy in Protestantism   29

Justice as a Condition of Authentic Liturgy   39

Liturgy, Justice, and Holiness   59

If God Is Good and Sovereign, Why Lament?   80

Part Two: Justice

Why Care about Justice?   95

For Justice in Shalom   109

The Wounds of God: Calvin's Theology of Social Injustice   114

Lest Your Brother Be Degraded in Your Sight   133

An Evening in Amman   136

Death in Gaza   140

The Troubled Relationship between Christians
   and Human Rights   148

Six Days in South Africa   155

Seeking Justice in Hope   170

Hondurans Seek Justice   188

Part Three: Church

"When Did We See Thee?"   199

The Bible and Women: Another Look at the
   "Conservative" Position   202

Hearing the Cry   210

Letter to a Young Theologian   218

The Theological Significance of Going to Church and Leaving
   and the Architectural Expression of That Significance   228

The Light of God's Love   241

Thinking about Church Architecture   245

Thinking about Church Music   254

Playing with Snakes: A Word to Seminary Graduates   268

Part Four: World

Can a Calvinist Be Progressive?   275

The Moral Significance of Poverty   287

Love it or Leave It   297

Reflections on Patriotism   299

Contemporary Christian Views of the State: Some Major Issues 308

The Political Ethic of the Reformers   328

Theological Foundations for an Evangelical
   Political Philosophy   346

Contents

Has the Cloak Become a Cage?
　Love, Justice, and Economic Activity　　　　　　372

Justice, Not Charity: Social Work through the Eyes of Faith　　395

Afterword

An Interview with Nicholas Wolterstorff　　　　413

It's Tied Together by Shalom　　　　　　　　　423

How My Mind Has Changed: The Way to Justice　　430

Acknowledgments　　　　　　　　　　　　　439

Preface

We are called, one and all, called by the goodness of what there is, called by the goodness of what there is not but could be. Sometimes the call comes in words; sometimes the call is wordless.

> Day to day pours forth speech,
>   and night to night declares knowledge.
> There is no speech, nor are there words;
>   their voice is not heard;
> yet their voice goes out through all the earth,
>   and their words to the end of the world.
>
> (Psalm 19:2-4)

The psalmist often calls to worship: "Oh worship the Lord in the beauty of holiness." But God's majesty is itself a call to worship, as is God's grace a call to gratitude and God's will for our lives, a call to repentance. Liturgy is the answer to a heard call. So too the worth of my fellow human beings is a call, a call to treat them in a way that befits their worth, a call to treat them as they have a right to be treated. Justice is the answer to a heard call. Liturgy and justice are joined as answers to heard calls.

Some writers are driven by their own internal curiosity; some scholars are driven by the internal dynamics of their discipline. Sometimes that's been true for me; but often not. I have repeatedly found myself confronted by a call to give voice to a call. This collection of popular and semi-popular essays is a record of my attempt to answer those calls, composed in the hope that giving voice to those calls would make them more clearly heard.

The essays were written over the course of some fifty years. It was Mark Gornik and Greg Thompson who prodded me to put them together; they also made invaluable suggestions as to which essays from these past fifty years retained present-day relevance and how they could best be organized. Without their prodding, it would never have happened. I thank them warmly.

Those who read around in these essays will soon discern that the author is a member of the Reformed tradition of Christianity. They are an example of living within a religious tradition in the modern world, interpreting, supporting, criticizing. But a principle of selection that Mark, Greg, and I employed is that the essays would be of interest not only to those from the Reformed tradition but to those from other traditions as well, and further, that they would bear the promise of offering insights that others could appropriate in their own way. We hope, in short, that readers will discover universality in the particularity.

The essays have been lightly edited to remove stylistic infelicities and, in the early essays, to remove most gender-specific pronominal references to God and undo the exclusive use of grammatically masculine ways of referring to human beings. A few have also been edited to remove overlap with other essays when that did not destroy the flow of the argument. The concluding sections of "Contemporary Christian Views of the State" have been deleted because I no longer agree with what I said there. And in "Seeking Justice in Hope" I have drastically abbreviated my discussion of Aquinas on hope. Those who want a more extensive discussion of what Aquinas had to say about hope, along with those who think I am being unfair to the totality of what he had to say about hope, should consult the original.

Unless indicated otherwise, the translations of Scripture are generally from either the Revised Standard Version or the New Revised Standard Version.

The Grace That Shaped My Life

The grace that shaped my life came not in the form of episodes culminating in a private experience of conversion but, first of all, in the form of being inducted into a public tradition of the Christian church.

The reformation of the Christian church that occurred in the Swiss cities during the second quarter of the sixteenth century took two main forms. One eventuated in the movement known as Anabaptism. The other became embodied in the churches known throughout Continental Europe as Reformed, and in Scotland as Presbyterian. I was reared in the tradition of the Dutch Reformed Church transplanted to the United States. My parents had themselves in their youth emigrated from the Netherlands. The place was a tiny farming village on the prairies of southwest Minnesota — Bigelow.

Simplicity, Sobriety, and Measure

In his book on English dissenting movements, the poet and critic Donald Davie remarks that

> it was . . . John Calvin who first clothed Protestant worship with the sensuous grace, and necessarily the aesthetic ambiguity, of song. And who that has attended worship in a French Calvinist church can deny that — over and above whatever religious experience he may or may not have had — he has had an aesthetic experience, and

of a peculiarly intense kind? From the architecture, from church-furnishings, from the congregational music, from the Geneva gown of the pastor himself, everything breathes simplicity, sobriety, and measure.[1]

That's it exactly: simplicity, sobriety, and measure. We "dressed up" on the Lord's Day, dressed up *for* the Lord's Day, and entered church well in advance of the beginning of the service to collect ourselves in silence, silence so intense it could be touched. The interior was devoid of decoration, plaster painted white, ceiling pitched to follow the roof, peak high but not too high. The only "richness" was in the wooden furnishings. These were varnished, not painted; as a child I dwelt on the patterns in their unconcealed woodiness — perhaps because, coming from several generations of wood-workers, I was from infancy taught reverence for wood. We faced forward, looking at the Communion table front center, and behind that, the raised pulpit. Before I understood a word of what was said I was inducted by its architecture into the tradition.

Then the consistory entered, men dressed in black or blue suits, faces bronzed and furrowed from working in the fields, shining from scrubbing; this was the Lord's Day. Behind them came the minister. Before he ascended the pulpit one member of the consistory shook his hand; when he descended from the pulpit at the end of the service all the members of the consistory shook his hand, unless they disagreed. We sang hymns from here and there — nineteenth-century England, sixteenth-century Germany. But what remains in my ear are the psalms we sang. Every service included psalms, always sung, often to the Genevan tunes. Sometimes the services were in Dutch; then the older people sang the psalms from memory, always to the Genevan tunes. My image of the hymn tunes was that they jumped up and down. My image of the Genevan psalm tunes was that they marched up and down in stately, unhurried majesty — sometimes too unhurried for me as a child! The minister preached at length, often with passion, sometimes with tears, the content of the sermons usually doctrine followed by application. He led us in what was known as "the long prayer," during which the consistory stood, eyes closed, swaying back and forth. Four times a year we celebrated the Lord's Supper. In a long preliminary exhortation we were urged to contemplate the depth of our sins and the "unspeakable" grace of God in forgiving our sins through the

1. Donald Davie, *A Gathered Church* (New York: Oxford University Press, 1978), p. 25.

death and resurrection of Jesus Christ. Then, in silence alive, the bread and wine were distributed. The minister communicated last.

There was no fear of repetition. The view that only the fresh and innovative is meaningful had not invaded this transplant of the Dutch Reformed tradition in Bigelow, Minnesota. Through repetition, elements of the liturgy and of Scripture sank their roots so deep into consciousness that nothing thereafter, short of senility, could remove them. "Our help is in the name of the Lord, who has made heaven and earth," said the minister to open the service, unfailingly.

The cycle for one of the two sermons each Sunday was fixed by the Heidelberg Catechism. This catechism, coming from Heidelberg in Reformation times, had been divided up into fifty-two Lord's Days; the minister preached through the catechism in the course of the year, taking a Lord's Day per Sunday. It was doctrine, indeed, but doctrine peculiarly suffused with emotion — perhaps because, as I now know, it had been formulated for a city filled with exiles. The first question and answer set the tone; decades later they continue to echo in the chambers of my heart:

Q: What is your only comfort in life and death?
A: That I am not my own but belong to my faithful savior
   Jesus Christ.

A Sacramental Theology

If the aesthetic of this liturgy was simplicity, sobriety, and measure, what was its religious genius? The only word I have now to capture how it felt then is *sacramental;* it felt profoundly sacramental. One went to church to meet God; and in the meeting, God acted, especially spoke. The language of "presence" will not do. God was more than present; God spoke, and in the sacrament, "nourished and refreshed" us, here and now sealing his promise to unite us with Christ. Ulrich Zwingli had considerable influence on the liturgy of the Reformed churches; for example, it was he rather than Calvin who set the pattern of quadrennial rather than weekly Eucharist. In part that was because he insisted that the climax of the Eucharist was Communion, and he could not get his parishioners to communicate weekly, accustomed as they were to communicating just once a year; in part it was because he interpreted the Lord's Supper as entirely our action, not God's. But in word and tone, the liturgy I experienced was a liturgy of

3

God's action; it was "Calvinistic." During the liturgy as a whole, but especially in the sermon, and most of all during the Lord's Supper, I was confronted by the speech and actions of an awesome, majestic God. Of course, liturgy was our action as well, not just God's. We gave voice, always in song, never in speech, to praise and thanksgiving and penitence. The religious genius of the liturgy was interaction between us and God.

And throughout there was a passionate concern that we appropriate what God had done and was doing. We were exhorted to prepare ourselves so as to discern and receive the actions of God; it didn't happen automatically. It was as if the "secret" prayers of the Orthodox liturgy had been changed into exhortations and spoken aloud; the concern with right doing was the same. And we were exhorted, as we went forth, to live thankfully and gratefully. Max Weber argued, in his famous analysis of the origins of capitalism, that the energetic activism of the Calvinists was designed to secure the success that was taken as a sign of membership among the elect. I can understand how it would look that way to someone on the outside; and possibly there were some on the inside, English Puritans, for example, who did think and speak thus. But it has always seemed to me a ludicrous caricature of the tradition as I experienced it. The activism was rather the activism congruent to gratitude. Sin, salvation, gratitude: that was the scheme of the "Heidelberger." Conspicuous material success was more readily taken as a sign of shady dealing than of divine favor.

My induction into the tradition, through words and silences, ritual and architecture, implanted in me an interpretation of reality — a fundamental hermeneutic. Nobody offered "evidences" for the truth of the Christian gospel; nobody offered "proofs" for the inspiration of the Scriptures; nobody suggested that Christianity was the best explanation of one thing and another. Evidentialists were nowhere in sight! The gospel was report, not explanation. And nobody reflected on what we as "modern men" can and should believe in all this. The scheme of sin, salvation, and gratitude was set before us, the details were explained, and we were exhorted to live this truth. The modern world was not ignored, but was interpreted in the light of this truth rather than this truth being interpreted in the light of that world.

The picture is incomplete without mention of the liturgy of the family. Every family meal — and every meal was a family meal — was begun and concluded with prayer, mainly prayers of thanksgiving principally, though not only, for sustenance. We did not take means of sustenance for granted; my family was poor. Food, housing, clothes — all were interpreted as gifts from God — again the sacramentalism, and again, a sacramentalism of divine action rather than divine presence. Before the prayer following the meal there was a reading, usually from Scripture chosen on a *lectio continua* scheme, but sometimes from devotional literature, and often from a Bible-story book. Thus between church and home I was taught to read the Bible as doctrine, as Torah, and as narrative; that there might be tension among these never occurred to me.

The Center

The piety in which I was reared was a piety centered on the Bible, Old Testament and New Testament together. Centered not on experience, and not on the liturgy, but on the Bible; for those themselves were seen as shaped by the Bible. Christian experience was the experience of appropriating the Bible, the experience of allowing the Bible to shape one's imagination and emotion and perception and interpretation and action. And the liturgy was grounded and focused on the Bible: in the sermon the minister spoke the Word of God to us on the basis of the Bible; in the sacraments, celebrated on the authority of the Bible, the very God revealed in the Bible united us to Christ. So this was the Holy Book. Here one learned what God had done and said, in creation and for our salvation. In meditating on it and in hearing it expounded one heard God speak to one today. The practice of the tradition taught without telling me that the Bible had to be interpreted; one could not just read it and let the meaning sink in. I was aware that I was being inducted into one among other patterns of interpretation, the pattern encapsulated in the Heidelberg Catechism; sometimes polemics were mounted against the other interpretations.

The center from which all lines of interpretation radiated outward was Jesus — Jesus Christ. Of course I knew he was human; but the humanity of Jesus Christ did not function much in my imagination or anyone's interpretation. Jesus Christ was the incarnated second person of the Trinity. I must say in all candor (and with some embarrassment) that not until about five years ago, when I read some books on Jesus by Marcus Borg, E. P. Sanders, Ben Meyer, Tom Wright, and Gerd Theissen, books that set Jesus within the context of first-century Palestinian Judaism, did Jesus' polemic with the Pharisees finally make sense to me and did Jesus become a genuinely human figure.

Describing precritical modes of biblical interpretation in *The Eclipse*

5

of Biblical Narrative, Hans Frei remarks that "biblical interpretation [was] an imperative need, but its direction was that of incorporating extra-biblical thought, experience, and reality into the one real world detailed and made accessible by the biblical story — not the reverse." Then Frei quotes a passage from Erich Auerbach, in which Auerbach is contrasting Homer with Old Testament narrative:

> Far from seeking, like Homer, merely to make us forget our own reality for a few hours, it seeks to overcome our reality: we are to fit our own life into its world, feel ourselves to be elements in its structure of universal history. . . . Everything else that happens in the world can only be conceived as an element in this sequence; into it everything that is known about the world . . . must be fitted as an ingredient of the divine plan.

Frei then continues with the comment, "In the process of interpretation the story itself, constantly adapted to new situations and ways of thinking, underwent ceaseless revision; but in steadily revised form it still remained the adequate depiction of the common and inclusive world until the coming of modernity."[2] If Frei is right, the mentality in which I was reared was premodern; one of the ironies of history is that it now looks postmodern as well.

The Full Pattern

I remember my father sitting at the dining-room table during the long winter evenings in our house in the village on the Minnesota prairies, making pen and ink drawings. All his life long, I now believe, he wanted to be an artist; but he grew up in the Depression, child of displaced Dutch city dwellers consigned to farming in the New World, and it was never a possibility. There was in him accordingly a pervasive tone of disappointment. He was on intimate terms with wood; but wood was not yet art for him. I have since learned of Christians who see art as a device of "the enemy," something to be avoided at all costs. I have learned of other Christians who are torn in pieces by art, unable to leave it alone, yet told by

2. Hans Frei, *The Eclipse of Biblical Narrative* (New Haven, Conn.: Yale University Press, 1974), pp. 3-4.

6

those around them that art is "from the other side." My father-in-law was one of those troubled lovers of art. But not my father.

I have also learned of Christians for whom the life of the mind is "enemy." That too was not my experience. I take you now on our move from Bigelow to Edgerton, forty-five miles distant, in my early teens. My mother died when I was three. Of her I have only two memories: being held in her lap on a rocking chair when my arms were full of slivers, and seeing her lying still and pale in a coffin in our living room while I ate strawberries. After a few years of loneliness my father remarried and we moved to Edgerton, the village from which my stepmother, Jennie Hanenburg, came. The Hanenburgs were and are a remarkable family: feisty, passionate, bright, loyal. Though our family lived in the village, most of the others were farmers. So after morning church they all came to our house — aunts and uncles, cousins, everybody, boisterous dozens of them. Sweets were eaten in abundance, coffee drunk; and the most dazzling intellectual experience possible for a young teenager took place. Enormous discussions and arguments erupted, no predicting about what: about the sermon, about theology, about politics, about farming practices, about music, about why there weren't as many fish in the lakes, about what building the dam in South Dakota would do to the Indians, about the local schools, about the mayor, about the village police officer, about the Dutch Festival, about Hubert Humphrey. Everyone took part who was capable of taking part — men, women, teenagers, grandparents. I can hear it now: one aunt saying at the top of her voice, "Chuck, how can you say a thing like that?" And Chuck laughing and saying, "Well, Clara, here's how I see it." Then when it was time to go, everyone embracing.

I must mention especially my Aunt Trena, one of the most wonderful women I have known; she also died young. One Saturday afternoon I walked into her house and heard the Metropolitan Opera playing on her radio; to me as a young teenager it was caterwauling. So I asked her why she was listening to that. Her answer remains for me a marvel and a parable: "Nick, that's my window onto the world; sit down and let me explain it to you." She had never gone to school beyond the fifth grade; she was then trying to finish high school by correspondence.

Reverence for wood and for art in my father; reverence for the land and the animals in my uncles, sometimes even for machinery; longing reverence for music in my aunt; reverence for the life of the intellect in everybody. In the tenth book of his *Confessions* Augustine imagines the things of the world speaking, saying to him: Do not attend to us, turn away, attend to God. I was taught instead to hear the things of the world saying: Reverence us; for God made us as a gift for you. Accept us in gratitude.

It has taken me a long time to see the full pattern of the tradition. I think it was something like this: the tradition operated with a unique dialectic of affirmation, negation, and redemptive activity. On the reality within which we find ourselves and which we ourselves are and have made, I was taught to pronounce a differentiated yes and no: a firm yes to God's creation as such, but a differentiated yes and no to the way in which the potentials of creation have been realized in culture, society, and self. And I was taught, in response to this discriminating judgment, to proceed to act redemptively, out of the conviction that we are called by God to promote what is good and oppose what is bad, and to do so as well as we can; as an old Puritan saying has it, "God loveth adverbs." The affirmation of what is good in creation, society, culture, and self was undergirded by a deep sacramental consciousness: the goodness surrounding us is God's favor to us, God's blessing, God's grace. Culture is the result of the Spirit of God brooding over humanity's endeavors.

The tradition operated also with a holistic understanding of sin and its effects, of faith and of redemption. By no means was everything in society, culture, and personal existence seen as evil; much, as I have just remarked, was apprehended as good. The holistic view of sin and its effects instead took the form of resisting all attempts to draw lines between some area of human existence where sin has an effect and some area where it does not. The intuitive impulse of the person reared in the Reformed tradition is to see sin and its effects as leaping over all such boundaries. To the medievals who suggested that sin affects our will but not our reason, the Reformed person says that it affects our reason as well. To the Romantics who assume that it affects our technology but not our art, the Reformed person says it affects art too.

Corresponding to this holistic view of sin and its effect is then a holistic view as to the scope of genuine faith. Faith is not an addendum to our existence, a theological virtue, one among others. The faith to which we are called is the fundamental energizer of our lives. Authentic faith transforms us; it leads us to sell all and follow the Lord. The idea is not, once again, that everything in the life of the believer is different. The idea is rather that no dimension of life is closed off to the transforming power of the Spirit — since no dimension of life is closed off to the ravages of sin. But faith, in turn, is only one component in God's program of redemption. The scope of divine redemption is not just the saving of lost souls but the renewal of life — and more even than that: the renewal of all creation. Redemption is for flourishing.

Third, the tradition operated with the conviction that the Scriptures are a guide not just to salvation but to our walk in the world — to the fundamental character of our walk. They are a comprehensive guide. They provide us with "a world and life view." This theme of the comprehensiveness of the biblical message for our walk in this world matches, of course, the holistic view of sin and of faith.

The grace of God that shapes one's life came to me in the form of induction into this tradition. That induction into tradition should be an instrument of grace is a claim deeply alien to modernity. Tradition is usually seen as burden, not grace. But so it was in my case. If you ask me who I am, I reply: I am one who was bequeathed the Reformed tradition of Christianity.

Calvin College

And bequeathed the benefits of a remarkable institution in this tradition, Calvin College. Institutions are also not customarily seen as instruments of the grace that shapes one's life with God. But so it was in my case.

I had entered what seemed to me a world of dazzling brightness. In part it was a journey into self-understanding. For here, in this college of the tradition, I began to understand the tradition and thus myself. I learned how to live with integrity within this tradition, within any tradition — how to discern and embrace its fundamental contours while treating its details as adiaphora, how to discern and appropriate what is capable of nourishing life in one's own day and how to let the rest lie, how to empathize with the anxiety and suffering embodied in one's tradition and how to celebrate its accomplishments.

More important than coming to understand the tradition, I saw the tradition at work in some remarkably intelligent, imaginative, and devoted teachers. I came with the conviction that I was called to make my thoughts captive to Jesus Christ. But now I was plunged deep into the culture of the West — its literature, its philosophy, its theology, its science; everything; nothing was off-limits. The challenge constantly placed before us was to struggle to understand this massive inheritance "in Christian perspective." And more than that: ourselves to embody Christ in culture — ourselves to compose poetry and write philosophy and paint paintings that would breathe the Spirit of Christ. There are two cities, said one of our teachers, Harry Jellema, with gripping charisma, using the language of Augustine, there are two cities — then he would switch to the Latin — the *civitas Dei* and the *civitas mundi.* Your calling is to build the *civitas Dei.*

Here too nobody was offering evidences for the truth of Christianity, arguments for the inspiration of Scripture, proofs for the resurrection of Jesus, best explanation accounts of Christian faith. The challenge set before us was to interpret the world, culture, and society in the light of Scripture — to describe how things look when seen in Christian perspective, to say how they appear when the light of the gospel is shed on them.

It was heady stuff; and we students were as energized and instructed by each other as by our teachers. In my sophomore year I met Alvin Plantinga; we became at once dear friends and have remained that ever since. More important, from that time on we have engaged together in the project of Christian philosophy, parceling out the work, learning from each other — but let me be candid, I learning more from Al than Al from me. There was one college class in which Al and I were the only students, a course in Kant's *Critique of Pure Reason* taught by Harry Jellema. A few years back, Al gave the Gifford Lectures; a few years hence, I am slated to give them. Harry Jellema would have chuckled with delight at learning that all the students in one of his classes had become Gifford Lecturers. Too bad he's no longer alive — though perhaps he knows without my telling him. He was the pioneer, breaking up the sod for the second and third generations, for people like O. K. Bouwsma and William Frankena and Henry Stob and Al and myself, and lots of others; I continue to think that he was maybe the most profound of us all. Certainly the most charismatic.

No doubt some students were bored stiff with all this heady stuff. And some were there for reasons quite different from ours: they too had grown up in the tradition, but were angry with it, infuriated by all its rough edges. Their interest was not Nietzsche interpreted in the light of the tradition but Nietzsche for use as ammunition against the tradition. The arguments we had were wonderful!

I must say a word about Abraham Kuyper, who was in many ways the spiritual eminence behind the college. Kuyper was a turn-of-the-century Dutchman whose creativity came to expression in many areas — church, politics, academia, journalism. For our purposes, what was important was Kuyper's model of theory-construction. Since Aristotle, everybody in the West had regarded proper theorizing as a generically human activity. To enter the chambers of theory one must lay aside all one's particularities and enter purely as a human being. Our religions, our nationalities, our genders, our political convictions — we are to take them off and line them up in the entry. Of course we are never successful at this; always there are some peculiarities that we have failed to strip off. Part of what our peers in the room must do, whenever they notice that, is call it to our attention. It follows that proper theorizing does not eventuate in Muslim sociology or feminist philosophy or Marxist literary criticism or Christian literary criticism, but simply in human sociology, human philosophy and so forth.

Kuyper didn't believe it — didn't believe it was possible. He didn't think one could shed one's nationality or one's social class; but he especially insisted that one could not shed one's religion. A person's religion, on Kuyper's view, was not an inference or a hypothesis but a fundamental determinant of that person's hermeneutic of reality. Of course the hermeneutics of reality shaped by two different religions do not, by any means, yield differences of interpretation on everything; but unless the religions in question are very close, they yield enough differences to have consequences within the field of theorizing. Thus Kuyper thought that the goal of constructing a generically human philosophy was vain; philosophy, and academia generally, is unavoidably pluralistic. The only circumstance under which that would not be true would be that in which Christians, say, would practice amnesia about their religion while doing philosophy, and then remember it when arriving home or at church. Such amnesia Kuyper could not tolerate.

I believed this when first I learned of it in college days; I believe it still. It is a fascinatingly "postmodern" perspective; when I first read Thomas Kuhn's *The Structure of Scientific Revolutions* my main reaction was "Well, of course." I should add that sometimes Kuyper articulated his view in a much more "expressivist" form than I have given it above. That is to say, sometimes he talked as if the development of philosophy occurred, or should occur, just by expressing in philosophical form one's religious convictions. That seems to me mistaken. To become a philosopher is to enter the ongoing practice of philosophy. That practice is a malleable practice; though one is shaped, one also shapes. But no philosopher ever just gives expression to his inner self. And the Christian who engages in philosophy will seek to learn from the practice and its tradition as well as to contribute to the shaping of that practice.

Later I spent thirty years of my life as a teacher at Calvin College. Or better put, as a member of that community of Christian learning. That community has been for me an instrument of grace, supporting me in my

Christian reflections — challenging, correcting, supplementing, encouraging, chastising, disciplining. To know who I am, you must know that I was bequeathed the opportunity of being a member of that community. It was an instrument of grace. I miss it deeply. But a call is a call.

Cries of the Oppressed

A notice appeared in my mailbox at the college in the spring of 1978, inviting me to attend a conference in Chicago on Palestinian rights at the end of May, sponsored by Christians. To this day I do not know who sent it. I had celebrated with everyone else I knew the astounding victory of Israel in 1967; over the years, though, I had become more and more uneasy with Israel's treatment of the Palestinians. But I did nothing about this unease, did not even, as I recall, express it to anyone other than my wife. Now this invitation. The semester was over, I didn't feel like starting summer work yet, Chicago was only about a three and a half hour's drive away; so I went.

I had not knowingly met a Palestinian before; and my image of Palestinians was that they were all Muslims. Here in one place there were about 150 Palestinians; and obviously a good many of them, I have no idea how many, were Christians. They poured out their guts in rhetoric of incredible passion and eloquence. They spoke of how their land was being wrenched away from them, and how no one cared. They said that the land in which Jesus walked would soon have no more Christians in it, squeezed out by a Zionism supported by the West and Muslim fundamentalism in reaction. They asked why we in the West refuse to hear their cry. The U.N. representative of the PLO was given permission to come, but was forbidden by the State Department to speak to all of us at once; he might speak only to groups of five people or fewer. A person who had worked for the U.S. State Department in Israel and, while there, had been commissioned to prepare a report on the torture of Palestinians in Israeli jails, rehearsed the central parts of her report; she had been fired by the State Department a few days before.

I felt cornered, confronted — confronted by the word of the Lord telling me that I must defend the cause of this suffering people. My tradition yielded me the category: it was a call. Not to answer the call would be desecrating disobedience.

I have not changed my profession. But I have gone to the Middle East several times. I have bought and read yards of books. I subscribe to out-of-the-way journals. I became chair of the board of the Palestine Human Rights Campaign. I have written; I have spoken. It hasn't always been pleasant; the Palestinians are both immensely lovable and difficult to defend. But it is a sacred call. And I do all in my power, when answering the call, to remember the pain, the anxiety, and the rights of the Jewish people.

During the academic year 1980-81 Allan Boesak was at Calvin as our multicultural lecturer. He became, and remains, one of my dearest friends in all the world. I dedicated my book *Until Justice and Peace Embrace* to him; I cannot do better, to say what I found in him, than to quote what I said in my dedication:

> *for my dear friend Allan Boesak,*
> *black Reformed pastor and theologian from South Africa,*
> *in whose speech*
> *I have heard*
> *both*
> *the cries of the oppressed and the Word of the Lord*

I had been to South Africa in 1975 to attend a conference on behalf of Calvin College at the University of Potchefstroom. What I saw and heard there made me very angry; but it was almost exclusively whites that I talked with. Beginning with Allan, I have met the blacks.

Very little in my background had equipped me to deal with these experiences. Of course I believed that it was the calling of us who are Christian philosophers to develop a Christian theory of justice. But here I was confronted with injustice. Or rather — that's still too abstract — I was confronted with the faces and voices of people suffering injustice.

These experiences have evoked in me a great deal of reflection and reorientation. Justice has become for me one of the fundamental categories through which I view the world. I think of justice not so much as a virtue but as a condition of society: a society is just insofar as people enjoy what is due them — enjoy what they have a legitimate claim to. Previously the fundamental moral category for me was responsibility. Now I have come to see that the moral domain is an interplay between rights and responsibilities. To the Other in my presence I have responsibilities; but also the Other in my presence comes bearing rights. The violation of moral responsibility yields guilt; the violation of moral rights yields injury. The proper response to guilt is repentance; the proper response to moral injury is lament and outrage.

Slowly I began to see that the Bible is a book about justice; but what a strange and haunting form of justice! Not our familiar modern Western justice, of no one invading one's right to determine one's life as one will. Rather the justice of the widow, the orphan, and the alien. A society is just when all the little ones, all the defenseless ones, all the unprotected ones have been brought back into community, to enjoy a fair share in the community's goods, and a standing and voice in the affairs of the community. Biblical justice is the shepherd leaving the corral to look for the hundredth one and then throwing a feast when the one is found.

I hadn't seen their faces before, I hadn't heard their voices; that's what changed me. I have come to think that there is little passion for justice if the faces of suffering are hidden from view and the voices muffled. But horrible to know and say: in the presence of some of those faces and some of those voices, I have discovered in myself not empathy but loathing, fear, and resentment. Who shall deliver us from this bondage?

Lament for a Son

This was all before. I now live after, after the death of our son, Eric. My life has been divided into before and after.

To love is to run the risk of suffering. Or rather, in our world, to love is to suffer; there's no escaping it. Augustine knew it well; so Augustine recommended playing it safe, loving only what could neither die nor change on one — God and the soul. My whole tradition had taught me to love the world, to love the world as a gift, to love God through and in the world — wife, children, art, plants, learning. It had set me up for suffering. But it didn't tell me this: it didn't tell me that the invitation to love is the invitation to suffering. It let me find that out for myself, when it happened. Possibly it's best that way.

I haven't anything to say beyond what I've already said in *Lament for a Son*. There's a lot of silence in the book; no word too much, I hope. In the face of death we must not chatter. And when I spoke, I found myself moving often on the edges of language, trying to find images for what only images could say. The book is extremely particular; I do not speak about death, only about Eric's death. That's all I could do. But I have discovered, from what readers have told me, that in its particularity lies universality.

I see now, looking back, that in writing it I was struggling to own my grief. The modern Western practice is to disown one's grief: to get over it, to put it behind one, to get on with life, to put it out of mind, to insure that it not become part of one's identity. My struggle was to own it, to make it part of my identity: if you want to know who I am, you must know that I am one whose son died. But then, to own it redemptively. It takes a long time to learn how to own one's suffering redemptively; one never finishes learning.

Though there are strands in the Reformed tradition for which sovereignty is God's principal attribute, I don't think I ever thought of God much in terms of sovereignty. God was majesty for me, indescribable majesty. And graciousness, goodness; God is the one who blesses, blessing calling for gratitude. To be human is to be that point in the cosmos where God's goodness is meant to find its answer in gratitude: John Calvin told me that.

Now everything was different. Who is this God, looming over me? Majesty? I see no majesty. Grace? Can this be grace? I see nothing at all; dark clouds hide the face of God. Slowly the clouds lift. What I saw then was tears, a weeping God, suffering over my suffering. I had not realized that if God loves this world, God suffers; I had thoughtlessly supposed that God loved without suffering. I knew that divine love was the key. But I had not realized that the love that is the key is suffering love.

I do not know what to make of this; it is for me a mystery. But I find I can live with that. The gospel had never been presented to me as best explanation, most complete account; the tradition had always encouraged me to live with unanswered questions. Life eternal doesn't depend on getting all the questions answered; God is often as much behind the questions as behind the answers. But never had the unanswered question been so painful. Can I live this question with integrity, and without stumbling?

It moved me deeply to discover one day that John Calvin alone among the classical theologians had written of the suffering of God. Whenever he wrote of it, it was, so far as I could discover, in the same context: that of a discussion of injustice. To wreak injustice on one of one's fellow human beings, said Calvin, is to wound and injure God; he said that the cry of those who suffer injustice is the cry of God.[3]

---

3. When I mentioned these passages to one of the theologians of the tradition, he reacted sharply and said that of course Calvin did not intend such language to be taken seriously!

To Be Human

There's been a grace that's shaped my life. It came to me in the form of being inducted into a tradition of the Christian church, and in the form of participating in an institution, and in other ways as well which I haven't mentioned: in the form of persons such as my wife, my children, my friends.

But was it grace I experienced when I heard God saying to me, in the voice of the Palestinians and the South African blacks, you must speak up for these people? When God confronted the reluctant Jeremiah with his prophetic call, was that grace? And was it grace I experienced when my son was killed?

God is more mysterious than I had thought — the world too. There's more to God than grace; or if it's grace to one, it's not grace to the other — grace to Israel but not grace to Jeremiah. And there's more to being human than being that point in the cosmos where God's goodness is meant to find its answer in gratitude. To be human is also this: to be that point in the cosmos where the yield of God's love is suffering.

Part One

LITURGY

Trumpets, Ashes, and Tears

Every Sunday morning for almost 2,000 years now we Christians have left our beds, our tables, our fireplaces, and gone out onto the paths and roads and streets of our world, by foot, by horse, by bicycle, by car, from the dispersion of our daily existence to our liturgical assemblies. Then, after our divine service is finished, we go back again over the paths and roads and streets to our homes and places of work and recreation. Christian existence has from its beginnings followed this pattern of gathering and dispersing, this systolic-diastolic beat of contracting and expanding, assembling and scattering. The pattern is familiar to all. But what does it mean?

Also from the very beginnings of Christian existence this heartbeat of gathering and dispersing has followed the temporal one-plus-six rhythm of Sunday plus Monday-through-Saturday. Into the otherwise uniform flow of time has been introduced a septuple cadence, rather as the train traveller finds herself introducing into the uniform meter of the click of the wheels rolling over the joints in the track a rhythm of strong and weak. A systolic-diastolic heartbeat in a septuple cadence of one plus six — this from age to age has characterized the Christian way of being in the world. In my book *Until Justice and Peace Embrace* I inquired into the meaning of the septuple rhythm. Here I want to look into the meaning of the heartbeat. Specifically, what do the parts of the beat — the gathering and the dispersing — have to do with each other?

ONE CAN READILY DISCERN standard patterns of Christian thought on the matter. Some regard these two phases as not having anything at all to do with each other. They see them as jointly essential to the full Christian life but functioning side by side, not serving or conditioning or fulfilling or interpenetrating each other. The point has been made in various ways. Some say that the active life is jointly indispensable with the contemplative life for the full Christian existence. Others prefer to say that worship and work, liturgy and labor, must complement each other.

Most people who have reflected seriously on the matter have not been content with this side-by-side picture. They have tried to discern some inner connection between our life as gathered and our life as dispersed. Traditional Catholicism, for example, has thought along the following lines: Most of us throughout our daily lives are immersed in the sphere of the secular. But on Sundays, by our participation in the Eucharistic liturgy, we enter the sphere of the holy. In the liturgy we adore and bless God, and God's grace is sacramentally infused into us and Christ made bodily present before us. The contemplative adoration of God is the highest action we can perform in this our earthly existence; nonetheless, it is incomplete. We look forward to the beatific vision of God vouchsafed to the saints in heaven. To this end, the sacramental infusion of grace is indispensable. Our participation in the liturgy represents, then, both the beginning of our life of contemplation and the means of its completion. The fundamental significance of our life in the *secular* is that it preserves this present material and social existence of ours, which in turn enables us to participate in the liturgy. The active life *enables* the contemplative life; our lives as dispersed *make possible* our lives as assembled.

Traditional Reformed thought has often turned this model from traditional Catholicism on its head. Where the traditional Catholic saw Monday through Saturday as being for the sake of Sunday, the Reformed have seen Sunday as being for the sake of Monday through Saturday. Where the Catholic saw the significance of work as lying in its enabling of worship, the Reformed have seen the significance of worship as lying in its enabling of authentic work. Liturgy is for the sake of labor. Authentic earthly life does not consist in ordering our existence so as to catch as much as we now can of the Vision of God and receive the sacraments so that in heaven we shall experience the whole; it consists of struggling to serve God in the establishment of God's Kingdom here on earth. It consists, if you will, of the struggle to make our lives and our world holy. The assemblies are the place where the King's directives for the week are heard and where nourishment for the task is received. Our lives as assembled are instrumental to our lives as dispersed.

Tacit in both of these one-directional instrumentalisms is of course a priority as between the church gathered and the church dispersed, as between liturgy and labor, worship and work. In traditional Catholicism, the reception of grace and the adoration of the bodily-present Christ that together constitute the core of the liturgy are what is of supreme importance in life: our work in the world is in service of that. In the traditional Reformed view, our work in the world whereby we serve God in the obedience of faith is the supremely important thing: the liturgy is in service of that. But it is also possible to think in these hierarchical terms — that is, to think of worship as superior to work or of work as superior to worship — without viewing the relationship in an instrumental way. It is possible to think in terms of lower and higher without thinking of the significance of the lower as simply that of serving or enabling the higher.

Certainly Vatican II and the thought inspired by it does not limit the significance of our work in the world to its enabling of the liturgy. It grants to such work its own intrinsic significance. Yet quite clearly a priority remains. The formula toward which Vatican II gravitates is that the liturgy is *source and summit* of the Christian life. The liturgy nourishes our daily lives while being also the summit of the Christian life. That is clear, for example, in these passages from the *Constitution on the Sacred Liturgy* of Vatican II:

> Every liturgical celebration, because it is an action of Christ the Priest and of his Body, which is the Church, is a sacred action surpassing all others. No other action of the Church can equal its efficacy by the same title and to the same degree. . . .
>
> The sacred liturgy does not exhaust the entire activity of the Church. Before men can come to the liturgy they must be called to faith and to conversion. . . . To believers also the Church must ever preach faith and penance; she must prepare them for the sacraments, teach them to observe all that Christ has commanded, and encourage them to engage in all the works of charity, piety and the apostolate, thus making it clear that Christ's faithful, though not of this world, are to be the lights of the world and are to glorify the Father before men.
>
> Nevertheless the liturgy is the summit toward which the activity of the Church is directed; it is also the fount from which all her power flows. For the goal of apostolic endeavor is that all who are made sons of God by faith and baptism should come together to

praise God in the midst of his Church, to take part in the Sacrifice and to eat the Lord's Supper.

Though I know of no corresponding passage on the Protestant side that is quite so crisp as this from Vatican II, a great many Protestants in our century have indeed reversed this Catholic model of priorities. They would not reduce the significance of the liturgy to its service of our life in the world any more than contemporary Catholics would reduce the significance of our life in the world to its service of the liturgy. Yet they would say that the church is most fully realized as the body of Christ in the world, or performs the actions of supreme importance, at those points where a cup of cold water is given in the name of Christ — at those points where the poor hear good news, where the captives are sprung free, where the blind recover their sight, where the oppressed are liberated, and where all the dwellers on earth experience something of the shalom of the Year of Jubilee.

UP TO THIS POINT I have been sketching out models — ways of thinking, patterns of thought. Let me now begin to engage the issues by suggesting that we must resist choosing between these two positions. The body of Christ on earth is realized just as much in its struggle for justice and peace in the world as in its worship of the God of justice and peace. Its calling is fulfilled just as much in its adoration of the Holy One as in its struggle to make the world holy.

Jesus performed the works of healing and preaching, but also the works of praying and worshiping. And his Sonship was manifested no more in the one than in the other. It is true that when asked whether he was the long-expected one of Israel, Jesus pointed to his deeds of healing and preaching. But one of the decisive occasions on which he pointed to these messianic signs was during his attendance at the synagogue. Every faithful Jew was faithful in prayer and blessing, and every faithful Jew expected the Messiah to be faithful in these as well. These, though characteristic of the Messiah, would not be a distinguishing mark of him. Doing the works of shalom would be that. But if our Lord's Sonship is brought to realization both in his healing and in his praying, in the one no more than in the other, can we as his body be realized in any other way?

Yet surely we must go beyond this recognition of equal ultimacy. The relation of assembly to dispersal, worship to work, liturgy to labor, is not that of merely being side by side. The traditional Catholic who argued that the dispersion is in the service of the assembly and the traditional Reformed who argued that the assembly is in service of the dispersion both discerned something important. Both discerned that in some way these two phases of the heartbeat of the church, the systolic and the diastolic, are interrelated.

One way in which they are interrelated — and here I plant my feet firmly in the Reformed tradition — is that the liturgy does indeed serve our life in the world. It both directs and nourishes it. The liturgy is not just an instrument of the grace that gets us to heaven; it is also an instrument of the grace that guides and empowers us for our work as covenant partners with God in the coming of God's Kingdom. In Scripture and sermon we are confronted with God speaking; only someone who has heard almost nothing of the speech of God can doubt that that speech guides and directs our lives as dispersed. In the Lord's Supper we are, as the Reformed confessions put it, nourished and refreshed; only someone who has never experienced such nourishment and refreshment can doubt that this empowers us for our lives in dispersion.

But though this direction of the relationship of assembly and dispersal is profoundly important, I do not wish here to develop it further. The reality of liturgy pointing to life needs to be enriched, and our thought about it deepened; yet few today, at least in the Reformed camp, doubt that liturgy must point to life. A good many people, however — so it seems to me — are oblivious of the fact that life must also point to liturgy. Without denying the importance of liturgy pointing to life, I wish here then to reflect on life's pointing to liturgy.

WE LEAVE OUR HOMES, our offices, our playgrounds, and assemble for the liturgy. But we do not leave behind our *experience* in our lives of dispersion. We carry that experience along with us. A fundamental dimension of the liturgy is that in it we give expression, in concentrated and condensed ritualized form, to our experience in the world and our response to that experience. Let me point out three fundamental ways in which that is true.

We can begin with a fundamental theme in the thought of John Calvin. As Brian Gerrish, church historian at the University of Chicago, remarks in one of his essays on the thought of Calvin, to be human is for Calvin to be one of those points in the cosmos where God's goodness finds its response in gratitude. Thousands of passages could be cited as illustrations of this pervasive Calvinian theme. Here is just one, from near the opening of the *Institutes*: "Although our mind cannot apprehend God without rendering some honor to him, it will not suffice simply to hold that there is One whom all ought to honor and adore, unless we are also persuaded that he is the fountain of every good . . ." (I, ii, 1). The thought is clear. Considering God's mighty attributes may fill us with the conviction that this being *ought* to be honored and adored, and this in turn may induce us to render some honor to this mighty being. But this will not suffice for full-hearted honoring and adoring. We also need to be persuaded that this mighty being is *good* to us. In other passages Calvin makes clear that being persuaded of God's goodness is as much a matter of perception and experience as of intellectual conviction. If our devotion is to be full and authentic, we must not only be intellectually convicted of God's goodness and might but must *apprehend* the goods of the world *as gifts of God.* Whereas the secularist sees in the food that comes our way nothing other than something good, the Christian apprehends those goods as gift — rather in the way in which, when we are guests at a dinner, we experience the dinner not only as delicious but as a gift.

Though this theme of experiencing the goods of the world as a gift of God is indeed fundamental in Calvin, we should not allow our focus on it to make us lose sight of the other, neighboring, theme at which he hinted in the passage quoted and which he develops at length in other places. We honor God also because we experience the world as God's *glorious work.* The heavens declare the glory of God and the firmament shows his handiwork. Just as we, in looking at the work of an artist, do not apprehend it merely as a beautiful object but as the admirable work of an artist, so too the believer, in walking through the world, apprehends its wondrousness as the *glorious work* of God.

In short, for Calvin, to be a believer is to experience this world as a manifestation, a revelation, an epiphany of God. It is to experience it as a "sacrament" of God — not in some indefinite way but in the quite specific way of experiencing it as a gift to us and as God's glorious work. To such experiences, says Calvin, the only appropriate response is gratitude and adoration.

This same theme was eloquently developed in his own way by the late Russian Orthodox theologian, Alexander Schmemann. At creation, says Schmemann, "God blessed the world, blessed man, blessed the seventh day (that is, time), and this means that He filled all that exists with His love and goodness, made all this 'very good.'" To this act of God, Schmemann continues, "the only *natural* (and not 'supernatural') reaction of man, to whom God gave this blessed and sanctified world, is to bless God in return, to thank Him, to *see* the world as God sees it and — in this act of gratitude

24

and adoration — to know, name and possess the world." Schmemann goes on to say that

> all rational, spiritual and other qualities of man, distinguishing him from other creatures, have their focus and ultimate fulfillment in this capacity to bless God. . . . "*Homo sapiens*," "*homo faber*" . . . yes, but, first of all, "*homo adorans*." The first, the basic definition of man is that he is *the priest*. He stands in the center of the world and unifies it in his act of blessing God, of both receiving the world from God and offering it to God — and by filling the world with this eucharist, he transforms his life, the one that he receives from the world, into life in God, into communion with Him. The world was created as the "matter," the material of one all-embracing eucharist, and man was created as the priest of this cosmic sacrament.[1]

If we do indeed gratefully and adoringly experience our world as an epiphany of God, in the specific mode of gift and glorious work, then we do not leave these experiences behind but carry them with us as we leave our places of dispersion and come together into our assemblies. We come into our assemblies carrying trumpets of joy. We express our gratitude and adoration in word and song and gesture and color. We worship and adore God, we bless and praise God. And we do so not for something other than we have experienced in the world but precisely for what we have experienced. The celebration of the liturgy does not represent our turning away from a so-called profane or secular world to a so-called sacred world. It is our response to our apprehension of *this* world as gift and glorious work of God. As Schmemann puts it, "It is *this world* (and not any 'other world'), it is *this life* (and not some 'other life') that were given to man to be a sacrament of the divine presence, given as communion with God, and it is only through this world, this life by 'transforming' them into communion with God that man *was to be*."

BUT THERE IS MORE of our experience in the world that we come bearing to our assemblies than what I have discussed so far. To grasp this, we must leave Schmemann behind, for he scarcely takes note of this other part of our experience, at least not when speaking of the liturgy. But Calvin can still be our guide; for of this added dimension he was vividly aware.

---

1. Alexander Schmemann, *For the Life of the World* (Crestwood, N.Y.: St. Vladimir's Seminary Press, 1973), p. 15.

What every human being experiences as she makes her way through life is the presence of evil — evil in bewildering abundance, evil in personal forms and evil in social forms. It makes no difference whether we are believers or unbelievers, we find ourselves in the presence of moral evil. We are a fallen humanity. The experience of the believer, however, has an additional quality. The believer experiences the moral evil of humanity as waywardness, as sin, as alienation from God, as falling short of God, as rebellion against the holy law of God. Where the secularist sees only evil when beholding Auschwitz, of a depth that recedes beyond every attempt to grasp it, the believer sees sin against God of a depth that defies all grasping. Where the secularist sees only evil in looking at the arms race, the believer sees defiant idolatry. Just as one sees a child's resistance to its parent's just command not only as wrong but as disobedience, so too the believer experiences humanity's moral evil as something more than evil. She experiences it as disobedience to God. And sometimes, at least, she also sees God's judgment on this defiance. To these apprehensions she responds with sorrow and repentance, and with a plea for deliverance and mercy. As we leave our places of dispersion and travel to our assemblies, this experience of our world and our response to it we also carry with us. This, too, we cannot leave behind. We come bearing the ashes of repentance. And this experience also finds condensed ritualized expression in our liturgy. In word and song, gesture and color, we confess our sins and the sins of our world, pleading for deliverance and forgiveness. It was the Swiss Reformers who first introduced an explicit act of confession into the public liturgy of the Western church. For that innovation they had several reasons. But one, I think, was their vivid experience of the evil of the world as disobedience.

I SUGGEST THAT THERE IS yet one more thing that the believer experiences in his life of dispersion and which he brings with him to the liturgy. For this third, we must leave both Schmemann and Calvin behind, and almost every other theologian. Only a few contemporary theologians, Jürgen Moltmann foremost among them, have had the courage and insight to single out this third experience.

As we human beings travel through life we experience pain and suffering — in part our own, in part that of others. Some of this pain and suffering is non-innocent suffering; it is punishment for, or the consequence of, moral evil. But not all of it is that. The suffering of the Israelites in the brickyards of Egypt was not the consequence of their sin, nor was the suffering of the Jews in the camps of Auschwitz. Some of the suffering of our world even resists our seeing it as the counterpart of *anyone's* sin — the accidental death of a child, for example.

My question now is this: How does the believer experience such suffering? We saw that the believer apprehends the goods of the world as a gift, the wondrousness of the world as a glorious work, and the moral evil of the world as disobedience. Is there any counterpart in the believer's experience of the suffering of the world? Is the suffering of the world also some sort of epiphany of God? Or is our experience of suffering just separate from our experience of God?

Some believers experience some of humanity's suffering, perhaps some experience all of it, as the anger of God. The Old Testament *Book of Laments* closes with this cry of total desolation before the Almighty:

> Restore us to thyself, O LORD, that we may be restored!
>   Renew our days as of old!
> Or hast thou utterly rejected us?
>   Art thou exceedingly angry with us?

Other believers — I think mainly those who have not themselves suffered much — say that suffering is to be apprehended as one of the gifts of God. And yet others testify that what they experience in suffering is the absence of God, the abandonment of God. What the secularist sees just as unmerited suffering, they experience as God's mysterious and painful abandonment.

There is yet another possibility, a possibility rarely grasped in the Christian tradition and seldom grasped in the tradition of rabbinic Judaism, but present in the Bible. Nowhere has it been better expressed than in Isaiah 63, verse 9. Speaking of Israel and of God the writer says: "In all their affliction, he was afflicted." In our afflictions, God is afflicted. Over our suffering, God suffers. Over our mourning, God mourns. Over our weeping, God weeps. I suggest that what the believer sees in beholding the suffering of the world — the thought makes us tremble, I admit — is no less than the suffering of God. What the believer sees when beholding the rabbi from Nazareth on the cross is not only human blood from sword and thorn and nail, but the tears of God over the wounds of the world.

So the suffering of the world is also an epiphany of God — sometimes of the anger of God, sometimes of the gift of God, but always, I suggest, of the suffering of God. The God who has covenanted himself to humanity suffers over our suffering. The suffering of the world is not to be experienced as just other than God but as the suffering of God. To this epiphany, how else can *we* respond than with lament and intercession, crying out "How long, O Lord, how long? Deliver yourself, and us your children."

As you and I leave our places of dispersion and travel to our assemblies, we carry with us our experiences of the suffering of ourselves and of the world. But most of us do not experience God in this suffering. Most of us do not see it as an epiphany of God. And so, though we bring our experience of suffering to our assemblies, we do not know what to do with it there. Though praise and confession play large roles in our liturgies, lament plays only a minor role. We skip over those desperate psalms and songs of lament from ancient Israel. And our intercessions, which ought to be grounded in sorrow over the sorrow of the world, give voice at best to muffled cries of pain. The lament, "How long, O Lord?" is scarcely heard. Though we bring our tears of pain with us to our worship, we don't know how to cry them there. Tears in the assembly are regarded as liturgical failure. I suggest that a liturgy without tears is a failure. We must find a place for lament.

Of course, if the liturgy is to be authentic we must genuinely experience the world as gift and glorious work of God and feel the joy of gratitude; otherwise the songs of praise are mere sounds. We must genuinely experience the world as disobedient to God and feel the regret of repentance; otherwise the gestures of repentance are mere gestures. And we must genuinely experience the world as the suffering of God and feel the agony of lament; otherwise the words of intercession are mere words. Authentic experience and life in the world is a condition of authentic liturgy. If the condition is not satisfied, God finds our words, songs, and gestures deficient, sometimes even nauseous.

THE LITURGY of the Christian church, then, is for blowing the trumpets of joy over our experience of the world as gift and glorious work of God. It is for rubbing on the ashes of repentance over our experience of the world as disobedient to God. And the liturgy is for crying the tears of lament and intercession over our experience of the world as the suffering of God over the suffering of the world. We do each of these in its own place in the liturgy. In Holy Communion, mysteriously, we do them all together.

Praise, confession, lament; adoration, repentance, intercession. In entering the assembly we do not obliterate the world from our mind but carry along with us our experience of the world as a three-fold epiphany of God and our response to that experience. In the liturgy, while "holding in remembrance" what we have experienced of God, we give voice to our response. For that we need trumpets, ashes, and tears — all three.

The Tragedy of Liturgy in Protestantism

M any Christians have acknowledged anew in our day the call of the
gospel to struggle for the reform of a fallen world. With our ears we
have heard the cries of the people. And with our eyes we have read the call
of the prophets, and of Jesus whom we acknowledge as Lord, to struggle
for healing in the world. We have read that startling declaration of Jesus
that in him the age of shalom foretold by Isaiah is beginning to break in.
And we have read his call to us to carry on his work. We all acknowledge
that this implies coming to the aid of the victims in our world. Many of us
have come to see that it implies also opposition to those social structures
that victimize. But this latter insight brings anxiety in its train. A peculiar
worry often begins to haunt Christians when they come to see that discipleship incorporates commitment to struggle for reform of the social order rather than merely waiting patiently for God to inaugurate the
eschaton. Has not the Christian way of being-in-the-world now lost all
distinctiveness? Has not the church now become just one among other social reform agencies in the modern world? The worry becomes even more
acute whenever a program of action is laid out, since almost invariably
there will be others who agree with large parts of the program, others who
are concerned about mass poverty, the effects of nationalism, urban blight.
So not only is there no distinctiveness in the fact that the Christian's way of
being-in-the-world incorporates the struggle for the reform of a corrupt
social order; sometimes it seems that there isn't even any distinctiveness in
the particular goals of our struggle. So wherein lies the distinctiveness of
Christian existence?

Is it that Christians, though their goals are similar to those of others, have different motivations and a different framework of beliefs undergirding those motivations? Is it that they use Bible and church to energize and direct them whereas the secular reformists seem to do nicely without those? In short, is it just that they accompany their actions with a different *inwardness?*

It is my own conviction that the church, and humanity at large, neglects inwardness at its own peril. By "inwardness" I do not just mean motivation for social action along with the beliefs that undergird it. I mean contemplation: the cultivation of what in some traditions is called spirituality and in others, piety. It seems to me that amidst its intense activism, the Western world is starved for contemplation. Likewise it seems to me that the unmistakable witness of the Scriptures is that where genuine piety or spirituality is missing, there life as a whole is deeply wounded. Contemplation, spirituality, piety — these belong to authentic shalom, with influences radiating throughout the whole of our existence. So one way to deal with our concerns about the source of our distinctiveness is to confront them forthrightly and say: the inward life is important. Not all-important, but important.

Others have attempted another answer. They have insisted on backing up a bit and raising seriously the question of whether the social program of the Christian really is substantially like that of anyone else. Is it not as a whole fundamentally different, with different goals and different strategies? The Anabaptists believe that their rejection of violence makes their program significantly different from others; the Dutch neo-Calvinists believe that their embrace of "sphere sovereignty" and institutional pluralism does the same for them.

I think that this response also deserves serious consideration. Perhaps we leap too quickly to the conclusion that there is nothing distinctive in the comprehensive social program of the Christian. But on this occasion I invite my readers to consider a different answer. I want to explore *worship,* worship by way of participation in the liturgy of the church. More precisely, I want to explore the possibility that a rhythmic alternation of work and worship, labor and liturgy, is one of the significant distinguishing features of the Christian's way of being-in-the-world.

No doubt some readers will already be feeling disappointed and uneasy. You were hoping that I would mention something important, something significant, something that you could point to without embarrassment when engaged in discussion with a Marxist, for example, and say:

"Here, on this important part of practice we differ." But you would feel embarrassed mentioning participation in the liturgy as an important distinctive because you think that the Marxist would dismiss it with a wave of the hand as unworthy of adult consideration.

But let me ask: Why should you let the Marxists (or anyone else) determine *your* scale of importance? Why say to them, "You tell me what you think is important and then I'll see if I can find a difference between us that fits *your* standard of importance." Perhaps one significant difference between you and them lies in different standards of importance. But let that point pass. For in all likelihood, the disappointment that you feel when I bring the liturgy into the discussion is the result of your own feeling that it is not really important.

Deeply embedded in the thought framework of the modern church as a whole, and especially in that of the churches of my own tradition, the Reformed/Presbyterian, is the conviction that the liturgy has no importance of its own, that its importance lies entirely in the benefit it renders to our life in the world — so that if one has the inner strength to live that life without benefit of liturgy, then liturgy can be nicely passed by. The language will vary, but the idea remains, that the only point of Sunday is its benefit for Monday through Saturday; that the liturgy is fundamentally nothing more than a refueling stop; that the church *is mission,* this being understood in such a way that ideally the church would never be gathered for worship but always dispersed for work.

But is it true that the whole point of the liturgy is to benefit our life in the social world? Does liturgy have no importance of its own? I want to explore that question, along with another yet more fundamental: could it be that when participation in the Sunday liturgy of the church is missing, then life as a whole is altered in a certain way? Is it not possible that the liturgy *authenticates* our action in the world?

We tend to think of our responsible work in the world as a solid, complete reality in itself, but we do not typically think of liturgy this way. It would be difficult to find a book on liturgy written since the Second World War that did not discuss the relation of the liturgy to the Christian's life in the world. On the other hand, it is easy to find books on Christian social action that say nothing at all about the relation of such action to the Christian liturgy.

That fine theologian of the Orthodox Church, the late Alexander Schmemann, defines *secularism* in one of his writings as "a negation of worship." "It is," he says, "the negation of man as a worshiping being, as *homo adorans*. Perhaps you would wish to define the term differently. But the suggestion that the human being is meant to be a worshiping being — might there be some profound truth in that? And might it be that a certain inauthentic secularity begins to characterize our work in the world when that truth is denied in practice?"

Let us follow the thought of Schmemann a bit farther. At creation, he writes, "God blessed the world, blessed man, blessed the seventh day (that is, time), and this means that He filled all that exists with His love and goodness, made all this 'very good.'" To this act of God, he continues, "the only *natural* (and not 'supernatural') reaction of man, to whom God gave this blessed and sanctified world, is to bless God in return, to thank Him, to *see* the world as God sees it and — in this act of gratitude and adoration — to know, name and possess the world." He goes on to say that "all rational, spiritual and other qualities of man, distinguishing him from other creatures, have their focus and ultimate fulfillment in this capacity to bless God. . . . 'Homo sapiens,' 'homo faber', . . . yes, but, first of all, 'homo adorans.'"[1]

Thus, says Schmemann, the world is a *sacrament* of God. Both in its totality as cosmos and in its becoming as history, it "is an *epiphany* of God, a means of His revelation, presence, and power." Correspondingly, "worship is truly an essential act, and man an essentially worshiping being" (p. 120).

Even from these few brief passages one can see why Schmemann will have nothing to do with the suggestion that worship involves a turn away from this so-called profane world to a so-called sacred world. Worship is the response to one's apprehension of the ultimate meaning and nature of this world, not of some other world. Furthermore, worship has nothing to do with the denigration of this world. It is for one's enjoyment of *this* world that one blesses God. "It is *this world* (*and not* any 'other world'), it is *this life* (and not some 'other life') that were given to man to be a sacrament of the divine presence. . . ." (p. 100).

I want to express my hesitation about one point in Schmemann's thought. It seems to me that he tends to run together our activity of worshiping God with our awed and grateful acceptance of the world as a sacrament of God. I myself would say that worshiping God is but one expression of that acceptance. Another is our responsible development of the potentials of the world, and yet another is love of neighbor. The human person is indeed *homo adorans*, but also *homo laborans* and *homo amans*.

1. *For the Life of the World* (Crestwood, N.Y.: St. Vladimir's Seminary Press, 1973), p. 15.

But that just brings me back to Schmemann's main point: worship is grounded in one's apprehension of the world as a sacrament of God. It consists, in awed and grateful response to that apprehension, of blessing God, of praising God. And this is not to be regarded as something pleasant to do if one just happens to have a taste for it, if one just happens to be "religious." Such apprehension is the recognition of the reality of things; it belongs to our true nature to respond to that apprehension by worship. Worship is ontologically grounded.

It is now easy to see that for the individual who apprehends the world as a sacrament of God, work and worship are fundamentally connected. Both are expressions of gratitude; together they constitute the two phases of the manifestation of devotion.

Nothing that I have said so far speaks to the uniqueness of Christian worship. The worship of the Christian has continuities with the worship of humanity generally. Yet Christian worship is also significantly different.

"I am the Alpha and Omega," says God in the book of Revelation, the one "who is and who was and who is coming." The doctrine of God constructed by the classical theologians was that of a God outside of time, dwelling in eternity, ever-present, with no past and no future, impassive, immutable. The presentation of the biblical writers is profoundly different: God is past and future as well as present because God's *actions* are past and future as well as present. Central to the character of Christian worship is the fact that the God worshiped is apprehended as engaged in a history that is both God's and ours but of which God is Lord and we are not. In this fundamental respect, Christian worship is a descendant of the worship of old Israel.

Recall the farewell speech of Moses to the tribes of Israel as we find it in the book of Deuteronomy. Like mighty gongs struck over and over, three themes interweave throughout the speech: *remember, expect,* and *take heed.* Israel is forever to remember that the God who created the heavens and the earth has liberated it from the bondage of toiling in the brickyards of Egypt. It is forever to live in the confident expectation that God will be faithful to the covenant, bringing them into the promised land and blessing them. And in the open space between faithful remembrance and confident expectation, the people are to take heed of God's commandments, commandments that are not the imposition of some alien duty but which have been given for the good of the people (10:13), so that they might have life (4:1). What was unique in the life of Israel was that its work and worship were to be its way of keeping faith with the God whose actions of liberation and blessing in the course of history it was forever to re-member and expect. The overarching background of Christian work and worship, though different in its content, is identical in its structure.

From this all-embracing context of the God worshiped being a God who acts in history, we can move inward to notice that in Israel, work and worship were to be done in rhythmic alternation — or rather, work and *rest* were to alternate; with worship occurring in the context of rest. Wor-ship is to take place in the context of a rhythmic temporal structure in our daily (and yearly) existence. "The seventh day is a sabbath of solemn rest, a holy convocation," one of "the appointed feasts of the LORD" (Lev. 23:2-3).

What is the meaning of this instruction to introduce the rhythm of six-plus-one into our daily existence? We can divide the question, asking first the meaning of that *rest* with which labor is to alternate and asking, second, the meaning of that alternating rhythm itself.

Once we notice that the rest was to echo the completion of creation and the deliverance from Egypt, we see the fundamental meaning of this component of rest in the rhythmic alternation of six-plus-one in daily ex-istence: Human life is meant to include something more than labor, some-thing more than the industrious struggle for the mastery of the world and the reform of society. It is to include delight in creation. And once we grasp how deeply the Jewish concept of "doing as a memorial" entered into Jew-ish liturgical theology, I think we must conclude that this rhythmic alter-nation was itself a liturgical act, a life-long recapitulation, a life-long do-ing-in-memorial, of God's great acts of creation and delighting in creation and of liberating God's people from the "iron furnace" of Egypt (Deut. 4:20). Each seven-day cycle served as a memorial, an enacted re-presenta-tion, of the great cycles of God's creative activity and rest and of Israel's en-forced toil in Egypt and subsequent deliverance to freedom.

Not only was Israel's recognition of God as Alpha and Omega in cre-ation and liberation the *context* within which it conducted its work and worship. And not only was that recognition embodied in its life by way of its memorial liturgical practice of work alternating with rest. The *specific activities of worship* prescribed for those celebrative days of feast were themselves understood by the people — in good part, anyway — as do-ings-in-memorial of God's great actions. As Max Thurian suggests in *The Eucharistic Memorial,* Israel understood and practiced virtually all aspects of its worship as doing-in-memorial.

There is no need to show in detail how. Christian worship represents a continuity of structure but an alteration of content when compared to the worship of Israel. The church also conducts its worship within the context of remembering and expecting; but the event at the center of its remembering is the resurrection of Jesus and the great event at the center of expecting is the full arrival of God's Kingdom. The day of the week on which it rests is now the first day, that is, the day of the resurrection, the day that early Christians already called "the Lord's Day." Thus the rhythm becomes a one-plus-six rhythm rather than a six-plus-one rhythm. And at the pivotal center of its worship on that day is its celebration of the Lord's Supper as a memorial of its Lord.

After this rapid excursion through a theology of liturgy, we can now return to our inquiry into the interrelation of work with worship, of labor with liturgy, in Christian existence. Earlier we saw that for one who sees the world and history as a sacrament of God, work and worship have a common basis: gratitude. Now we can go deeper. The Christian's way of being-in-society is embraced, along with his manner of worship, within his way of being-in-history. Work and rest are locked together in that one-plus-six rhythm that is the celebration of God's new creation and our liberation. Thus when the day of rest is dropped out of life, the memorializing rhythm of life as a whole is destroyed.

In turn, on that day of rest we celebrate in memorial the remembered and expected acts of God at the center of which are Christ's resurrection and the arrival of the Kingdom of shalom. Whereas our remembering and expecting are the abiding context within which we do our daily work, in worship we celebrate in memorial the very actions remembered and expected. We bring context into foreground. When we drop worship out of the day of rest, we destroy this practice of bringing to the fore (in memorializing celebration) the actions that constitute the abiding context of our existence.

Yet one more connection can be discerned. If the worship is performed but the works of mercy and justice are missing, a shadow is cast over the worship and its authenticity is brought into question. For this very same God whom we are to worship by celebrating God's deeds in memorial also requires of us that, in grateful response to those deeds, we take heed of God by doing the works of mercy and justice. But can we not also say that if the works of mercy and justice are performed but the worship is missing, then a shadow is cast over those works and *their* authenticity is brought into question? For this very same God, whom we are to heed by doing works of mercy and justice in gratitude for those deeds of God's that we remember and expect, also requires of us that we celebrate in memorial those deeds. Work and worship are mutually authenticating.

Bonhoeffer was profoundly right when he said that only the one who helps the Jews may sing the Gregorian chant. But will not the one who helps the Jews in the spirit of taking heed to the God whose deeds he remembers and expects also sing the Gregorian chant?

And now at last I come to "the tragedy of liturgy in Protestantism" of which the title of my article speaks. I submit that there is a tragedy of liturgy in Protestantism, specially, though by no means exclusively, within the Reformed/Presbyterian tradition. The tragedy consists in there being so little within this tradition of the very thing we have been discussing: *worship.* The tragedy consists in the fact that within this tradition, and in Protestantism more generally, there is a suppression of the central Christian actions of celebrating in memorial.

When one looks at the actions that constitute the liturgy of the church, one sees that they comprise two different directions, two different orientations. Some are actions directed toward us: God addresses us and we are the recipients. These are the actions of *proclamation,* central to which are the reading of Scripture and the preaching of the sermon. But there are also actions directed toward God: We address God and God is the recipient. These are the actions of *worship* in the true sense. The Christian liturgy is an interchange between actions of proclamation and actions of worship.

Even a brief glance at the history of the Christian liturgy makes clear how difficult it has been for the church to hold these two directions in balance. The Roman and Orthodox traditions have historically found it difficult to give due weight to the dimension of God's addressing us in judgment and grace — in short, to proclamation. The Protestant tradition has historically found it difficult to give due weight to the dimension of our addressing God in love and devotion — in short, to worship. No liturgy has ever been wholly one or the other. Yet liturgies differ profoundly in their emphases; and the tragedy of liturgy in Protestantism — particularly in the Reformed tradition — is that the worship dimension is suppressed, sometimes radically so. The liturgy is no longer "eucharistic"; and a fundamental dimension of the life of the church and of the existence of the Christian is thereby stunted.

I have no wish to play down the proclamation dimension of the liturgy, nor to suggest that everything in that dimension of Protestant liturgy is in good health. When the liturgy is in good health, the people gather as a community around the Word of God and receive from it inspiration, guidance, and consolation for their work in the world. It is hard for me to imagine Christian action in the world retaining its vitality and its direction without such gathering and listening. What so often happens instead is that in countless ingenious and lazy ways, the sharp sound of the Word of God is muffled so as to protect the status quo. These points are all worth developing further. But here our discussion has led us to focus on that other dimension of liturgy: worship.

What naturally results from the diminution of the worship dimension in liturgy is the starkness that is so characteristic of much of Protestant liturgy and its setting. So little of the multifaceted richness of our humanity is here manifested! So many renunciations! Here words rule all. What also results from the suppression of the worship dimension of liturgy is a seriousness, a sobriety, an absence of joy, that is contrary to the spirit of the divine rest and the people's liberation that we are to remember in memorial. When proclamation overwhelms worship in the liturgy, we must expect joy to be diminished.

The diminution of the worship dimension in Protestant liturgy occurred already in the first and second generations of the Swiss Reform, during which the most radical liturgical reform that the Christian church has ever known took place. It is not difficult to understand why the shift away from worship to proclamation occurred there. The Swiss reformers found the people of their parishes profoundly ignorant of the Christian gospel and desperately in need of teaching; so they gave renewed significance to reading and preaching. That by itself, though, would not have led to the tragedy I have in mind. The fateful step occurred when Zwingli, and then others after him, made the Lord's Supper no longer a regular part of the Christian liturgy. From its very beginnings the Lord's Supper was the church's great doing-in-memorial and its great expression of thanksgiving. Now that became only occasional. It is not difficult to understand why Zwingli took the step he did. But the consequences have been tragic.

One of the major results of Vatican II has been that the Catholic Church has taken a giant step in its liturgy in the direction of Protestantism. Next to the Swiss Reform, the liturgical reform of Vatican II is the greatest in the history of the church. I am profoundly convinced that we Protestants must how take an equally large step in the direction of Catholicism — or rather, in the direction of our common ancient tradition — by reinstituting the Lord's Supper as a regular part of the church's liturgy. This, in my judgment, is the decisive step that must be taken if we wish once again to have a balance of worship and proclamation. For this is the great feast in which we hold in remembrance Jesus Christ and look forward to the coming of his Kingdom of shalom. This is the great thanks-giving (eucharist) for creation and for the liberations of exodus and resur-rection. This is the great circle in which we declare our unity as "a holy people" across all nations.

If worship is balanced with proclamation in the Christian liturgy, and if, in turn, liturgy is set within the rest-of-delight whereby Christians de-clare, with that one-plus six rhythm of their daily existence, that the strug-gle for the embodiment of justice and shalom in the world does not exhaust the true life, then the distinctiveness of the Christian's way of being-in-the-world will not be confined to inwardness. It will be there for all to see.

Justice as a Condition of Authentic Liturgy

I myself . . . say that prayers and thanksgiving made by worthy persons are the only sacrifices that are perfect and well-pleasing to God.

Justin Martyr,
Dialogue with Trypho the Jew, 117.2

Because of all your wonderful dispensation towards us, with open mouths and uncovered faces we give you thanks and glorify you without ceasing in your Church, which has been redeemed by the precious blood of your Christ, offering up praise, honor, thanksgiving and adoration to your living and life-giving name, now and at all times forever and ever.

The Liturgy of Saints Addai and Mari

Part of what identifies the Christian church as a distinct people in history is that it engages in the Christian liturgy. Sunday after Sunday the members of this people gather together from their places of dispersion to celebrate the divine service. A second aspect of the church's identity is that it embraces the writings of the Old and New Testament as canonical Scriptures. Christianity is a religion of the book, though not in the way that Judaism and Islam are. For the center of its religion is not the book but the one on whom the book is focused: Jesus of Nazareth. The book centers on a presentation and interpretation of Jesus, and the church is "the Jesus party" in history.

This Jesus of Nazareth practiced and spoke of justice. "Blessed are those who hunger and thirst for justice, for they shall be satisfied," he said in his Sermon on the Mount. And he added, "Blessed are those who are persecuted for the sake of justice, for theirs is the kingdom of heaven" (Matt. 5:6, 10). In calling humanity to practice and struggle for justice, and in blessing those who do, Jesus was standing in continuity with the great prophetic tradition of the Old Testament, and he used that tradition to interpret himself. The God of the Old Testament loves justice and calls people to love as God loves. Thus the canonical Scriptures, which we of the church who assemble for the divine liturgy embrace, is a book that calls us to practice justice and to share in the struggle against injustice, doing so in the name of God and in the course of its witness to the prophets and to the one whom we follow, Jesus.

THE ISSUE I WISH TO DISCUSS is now before us. Liturgy and justice — what do these two have to do with each other? Our intuitions tell us that they are not meant to sit side-by-side in our Christian existence but are meant somehow to interact with each other, authenticating each other, expressing and nourishing each other.

Often they don't do this. Often those concerned with issues of social justice say or suggest that the essence of the church is to be found in how it embodies itself in the world. Its essence will be revealed if it lives justly and charitably when dispersed. Such persons regularly treat liturgy as a more or less dispensable practice and regard concern with liturgy as a distraction and a danger. On the other side, those concerned with liturgy often say or suggest that the essence of the church is revealed in its gathering for the celebration of the liturgy. Such persons regularly treat the practice of justice as more or less dispensable and regard concern with issues of social justice as a distraction and a danger. Often they call this danger "horizontalism." And then there are those who see the essence of the church in evangelism; they regard *both* liturgy and justice as more or less dispensable and view concern with them as distracting at best and dangerous at worst.

My thesis is that all such attitudes are aberrations. The church is to gather for the celebration of the liturgy, and when it is dispersed it is to practice and struggle for justice and to spread the word about its Lord. When one of these is thought to be closer to the essence of the church than the other, aberration has set in; and that aberration always shows itself in distortion of that very activity that was thought to reveal the essence.

Here I will have to be content with explaining just one of the many connections between the doing of justice and the celebration of the liturgy. Before I set out, however, let me briefly explain how I understand liturgy, and how I understand justice. Liturgy I view fundamentally as action. As the great contemporary Catholic liturgical scholar J. A. Jungmann puts it, "Liturgy is not simply ceremonial — the ceremonies are simply the outward signs of a more profound action. Nor is liturgy merely a set of rules and regulations or an established procedure — rather it is itself the act."[1] It may be added that on this understanding of liturgy, all sub-communities of the Christian church participate in liturgy. Not all of them have printed instructions, prayers, and the like. Not all of them have ceremonial. But all of them assemble and in their assemblies engage in liturgical actions. Furthermore, if we look closely we will see that always those actions exhibit two distinct orientations. Some are actions by the people oriented toward God — actions of praise, of confession, of worship, of thanksgiving, and so on. Others are actions oriented toward the people — actions of Scripture reading, of preaching, of absolving, of greeting, of blessing. I myself would say that some, at least, of these latter actions are actions done by *God*. The liturgical agent is not just the assembled people but God. In any case, those who say that liturgy is worship (typically these being persons with a Catholic or Orthodox mentality) and those who say that liturgy is proclamation (typically these being persons with a Protestant mentality) are both speaking too simplistically. From the earliest days of the church, and always since, liturgy has been both. Actions of both orientations belong to liturgy — the word "liturgy" etymologically meaning public service, or more precisely, service performed by someone for the benefit of the public.

As for justice, we will not go wrong if we think of the essence of justice along the lines suggested already by the ancient Roman lawyers, namely, justice consists in a person's being treated in a way that is due him or her — to which we may add that justice is also manifested in *a group's* being treated in a way that is due *it*. Justice consists in being treated as one has a right to be treated, as one has a legitimate claim to be treated. Our fundamental disagreements over justice are not disagreements over the bare concept of justice but disagreements over which ways of being treated we have a right to. They are not disputes over the concept of justice but over the contours of justice. In this article I will be guided in my understanding of the contours of justice by the prophetic words of the Old and New Tes-

1. J. A. Jungmann, *The Liturgy of the Word* (Collegeville: Liturgical Press, 1966), pp. 1-2.

tament. Important things can and should be said about the contours of justice that are not said in the Scriptures. Nothing is said in Scripture about freedom of speech and of religion, for example. Nonetheless, what the Scriptures do say about the contours of justice will be for us authoritatively formative.

Let me mention two clues as to how the biblical writers think of the contours of justice. First, over and over they say that God *loves* justice. In the current political climate in the United States the justice in view is seldom anything other than retributive justice. It's a reliable rule of thumb that when present-day politicians speak of justice, they have in mind punishing criminals. But nowhere do the biblical writers suggest that God loves punishing people. So when they say that God loves justice, they must have something in mind other than retributive justice. When God, speaking through Amos, said, "Let justice roll down like a mighty river," the meaning is not, "May prisons multiply and police forces expand." God did not mean, "May criminals writhe as they receive their just deserts."

A second provocative clue to the prophetic understanding of the contours of justice is the repeated reference in the Old Testament to widows, orphans, aliens, and the poor. Over and over when justice is spoken of it is these four groups that are brought to the fore. Reflecting on the significance of this frequent four-fold citation leads one deep into the biblical understanding of the contours of justice. By contrast, when Plato spoke of the just society, widows, orphans, aliens, and the poor were nowhere in view. The fundamental contour of justice is identified by Plato with a certain kind of "law and order." A society is just when authority is exercised by wise persons and pervasively obeyed. Evidently for the biblical writers, the fundamental contour of justice is something different. The just society is the society in which all the weak and voiceless ones have been brought into the community so as to enjoy its goods.

ALMOST EVERYONE in the Christian community operates with some view as to what would deprive liturgical actions of their authenticity. Recently, I attended a service in which the minister said that, though reared in Methodism, he had left it because, in his experience, Methodists too often just mouth their liturgical forms without putting their hearts into them. In his view, liturgy loses its authenticity when the words are not said with full conviction and attention. Others would say that liturgy loses its authenticity when those who engage in it do not hold the right doctrines, or when the liturgy departs from the apostolic tradition, or when it is led by someone who is not validly ordained or who performs it in ways not authorized. For some, liturgy is inauthentic when women do not occupy a significant role in the liturgy; for others, liturgy loses its validity when women *do* occupy a significant role. Though we differ in our views as to the conditions that must be satisfied if liturgical actions are to be authentically performed, almost everyone in the church has some view on the matter.

In the biblical writers one also finds such views. A prominent theme in them is that liturgical actions lose their authenticity when those who participate in the liturgy do not practice and struggle for justice. More generally, one finds in the biblical writers the theme that the authenticity of the liturgy is conditioned by the quality of the ethical life of those who participate. Before we begin our reflections on this theme, let us pause for a moment to let ourselves find this biblical connection between liturgy and justice remarkable. Let us allow ourselves to be surprised, astonished, taken aback by it. In the liturgy we sing hymns of praise to God. Why isn't it enough that we do this with awareness and intensity? Why isn't it enough that we mean the words we sing? Of course it is important that we also act ethically. But why does our failure to act ethically cast a shadow over our liturgical praise? Why aren't these two just separate? Again, in the liturgy we participate in the intercessory prayers. Perhaps we pray for God to give bread to those who lack it. Can't we mean that when the words are said? And if we mean it, isn't that enough? Hasn't the genuineness of our prayer been secured by our meaning what we say? What does our ethical practice have to do with the authenticity of our intercessory prayers?

Cultic liturgical actions have often been understood as devices for currying favor with God. Clearly, the Old Testament prophets regarded that as a common understanding of the cult in their own day; and J. A. Jungmann contends that in Western Europe on the eve of the Reformation, "Hearing Mass was reduced to a matter of securing favors from God."[2] The idea is that God likes the things we do in the liturgy. They give God pleasure and make God feel well-disposed to us who do them. We can expect that God will express this feeling by acting graciously toward us. Indeed, enough of such pleasing liturgical actions may compensate, in God's eyes, for a rather poor ethical life. They will atone for our sins; they will propitiate God.

On this understanding of liturgy, the suggestion that injustice would bleed liturgy of its authenticity is just nonsensical. Yet we all know the judgment of the Old Testament prophets on the matter. Liturgy in the ab-

---

2. J. A. Jungmann, "Liturgy on the Eve of the Reformation," *Worship* 33 (1959): 511.

sence of justice does not please God; it nauseates God. Gregorian chants, Genevan psalms, Lutheran chorales, Anglican anthems, Orthodox troparions — they disgust God when sung in the presence of injustice.

> I hate, I despise your feasts,
>> and I take no delight in your solemn assemblies.
> Even though you offer me your burnt offerings and cereal offerings,
>> I will not accept them,
> and the peace offerings of your fatted beasts
>> I will not look upon.
> Take away from me the noise of your songs;
>> to the melody of your harps I will not listen.
> But let justice roll down like waters,
>> and righteousness like an everflowing stream.
>
> (Amos 5:21-24)

Perhaps not many of us in the modern Western world think of liturgy as a strategy for currying favor with God. We see ourselves as having advanced beyond such primitive views. We are inclined to think of it rather as an occasion to escape from the ambiguity, boredom, pressure, and corruption of ordinary life and to center ourselves on God. We see it as an occasion to be alone with God, to draw near to God, to focus on the transcendent. Liturgy for us is flight to God rather than propitiation of God.

On this understanding of liturgy it is also hard to see why injustice would bleed it of its authenticity. The authenticity of liturgy is interior to the cultic actions themselves and to the present mentality of the participants. Yet to us who hold this escapist view, the biblical writers say the same thing that they say to those who hold the wheedling view:

> Behold, in the day of your fast you seek your own pleasure,
>> and oppress all your workers.
> Behold, you fast only to quarrel and to fight
>> and to hit with wicked fist.
> Fasting like yours this day
>> will not make your voice to be heard on high.
> Is such the fast that I choose,
>> a day for a man to humble himself?
> Is it to bow down his head like a rush,
>> and to spread sackcloth and ashes under him?

Will you call this a fast,
   and a day acceptable to the LORD?
Is not this the fast that I choose:
   to loose the bonds of wickedness,
   to undo the thongs of the yoke,
to let the oppressed go free,
   and to break every yoke?
Is it not to share your bread with the hungry,
   and bring the homeless poor into your house;
when you see the naked, to cover him,
   and not to hide yourself from your own flesh?

                                         (Isaiah 58:3b-7)

And here is yet another passage in which the point is the same:

What to me is the multitude of your sacrifices?
   says the LORD;
I have had enough of burnt offerings of rams
   and the fat of fed beasts;
I do not delight in the blood of bulls,
   or of lambs, or of he-goats.
When you come to appear before me,
   who requires of you this trampling of my courts?
Bring no more vain offerings;
   incense is an abomination to me.
New moon and sabbath and the calling of assemblies —
   I cannot endure iniquity and solemn assembly.
Your new moons and your appointed feasts
   my soul hates;
they have become a burden to me,
   I am weary of bearing them.
When you spread forth your hands,
   I will hide my eyes from you;
even though you make many prayers,
   I will not listen;
   your hands are full of blood.
Wash yourselves; make yourselves clean;
   remove the evil of your doings from before my eyes;
cease to do evil,

>   learn to do good;
> seek justice,
>   correct oppression;
> defend the fatherless,
>   plead for the widow.
> Zion shall be redeemed by justice,
>   and those in her who repent, by righteousness.
>
> (Isaiah 1:11-17, 27; cf. Jeremiah 7:1-11)

Let me halt the course of our questions for just a moment to consider a certain hesitation about what I have been saying. I have cited these well-known passages from Amos and Isaiah as examples of the prophetic insistence that the authenticity of a community's liturgy is conditioned by whether or not it practices and struggles for justice. It might well be asked, however, whether the passages cited do not make a different, and even more radical, point: that justice is to *displace* liturgy.

If these passages were all we had to go on, that would be a compelling interpretation. But they are not all we have to go on. And to me at least it seems clear that if we set these passages within the context of the totality of the prophetic literature, then the prophetic insistence is not that liturgy be abolished, nor even that sacrifice be abolished, but that liturgy practiced in the absence of justice is so seriously malformed that God finds it disgusting.

On the other side, however, let me emphasize once more that these passages are not saying merely that God wants justice *as well as* prayer, mercy *as well as* praise, love *as well as* Eucharist. The call for justice *as well as* liturgy has often and eloquently been made in recent years — for example in this passage in which Jürgen Moltmann is speaking of Dietrich Bonhoeffer:

> He fought passionately against the withdrawn piety of those who put up with every injustice on earth because they have long since resigned themselves to it and only live life here in a half-hearted way. But he opposed with equal passion the flat and trivial this-worldliness of those who consider themselves enlightened, who want to enjoy the present, resign themselves in the face of the future, and therefore only live half-heartedly and without fervour. An other-worldly piety, which wants God without his kingdom and the blessedness of the soul without the new earth, is really just as atheistic as the this-worldliness which wants its kingdom without God, and the earth without the horizon of salvation. God without the

world and the world without God, faith without hope and hope without faith are merely a mutual corroboration of one another.[3]

The point that Moltmann here attributes to Bonhoeffer, and with which he allies himself, is profoundly correct. It will underly all that I say in what follows. Yet it remains a *both/and* point: *both* liturgy *and* justice. The *not/ unless* point on which I wish to reflect is different and more radical: *not* authentic liturgy *unless* justice.

Let us begin our attempt to extract the underlying pattern of thought in what has sometimes been called "the prophetic critique of the cult" by looking at another well-known biblical passage: Micah 6. The passage as a whole is structured as a sort of trial scene. God presents a grievance against the people: They no longer remember what has been done for them (one finds similar trial scenes in which God expresses grievance against the people in Deuteronomy 32 and Psalm 50). The people then reply to the grievance: They *are* remembering. They have faithfully been bringing offerings to atone for their sins. What more does God want?

In reply, God explains what true remembering would be.[4] God's opening trial speech begins with a moving cry of lament, "O my people," and then moves on to a brief recital of God's salvific acts. God does not have to be wheedled and cajoled into acting graciously toward Israel. God has freely initiated Israel's deliverance and redemption from slavery. But Israel has forgotten, not perhaps in the sense that it has put God's acts out of mind but in the sense that it is living a life of forgetfulness. The grievance as a whole is a pained call for remembering:

> O my people, what have I done to you?
>   In what have I wearied you?
>   Answer me!
> For I brought you up from the land of Egypt,
>   and redeemed you from the house of bondage;
> and I sent before you Moses, Aaron, and Miriam.
> O my people, remember what Balak king of Moab devised,
>   and what Balaam the son of Beor answered him,

3. Jürgen Moltmann, *The Church in the Power of the Spirit* (New York: Harper and Row, 1977), p. 283.

4. I have found the discussion of Leslie C. Allen particularly helpful in *The Books of Joel, Obadiah, Jonah and Micah*, The New International Commentary on the Old Testament (Grand Rapids: Eerdmans Publishing Co., 1976), pp. 362-75.

and what happened from Shittim to Gilgal,
    that you may know the saving acts of the LORD.

God's interlocutor in the polemic is represented as baffled by this lament, be the bafflement real or feigned. Israel offers sacrifices. Why isn't God satisfied with those? Are the sacrifices perhaps too cheap? Does God want more expensive sacrifices? Year-old calves entirely consumed in the offerings? Thousands of rams? Instead of a bit of oil, rivers of it? Human bloodletting? Is it sacrificial murder that God wants? Some commentators have argued that the form of this answer imitates a cultic entrance liturgy in which a worshiper asks the priest concerning the conditions for admittance to the sanctuary and receives an official answer (for other examples, see Psalms 15 and 24, and Isaiah 33:14-16):

With what shall I come before the LORD,
    and bow myself before God on high?
Shall I come before him with burnt offerings,
    with calves a year old?
Will the LORD be pleased with thousands of rams,
    with ten thousands of rivers of oil?
Shall I give my first-born for my transgression,
    the fruit of my body for the sin of my soul?"
                        (cf. Hosea 12:6; 1 Samuel 15:22)

We all know the prophet's response to this cry of bafflement:

He has showed you, O man, what is good;
    and what does the LORD require of you
but to do justice, and to love kindness,
    and to walk humbly with your God?

What is the connection here between the divine lament over Israel's forgetfulness of God's salvific acts and the divine plea for justice? Why is *Israel's* doing of justice the response God wants to *God's* acts of deliverance? Commentators are agreed that the connection is to be found in the idea of covenant. Lying in the background of the prophetic critique of the cult, making that critique intelligible, is the conviction that there is a covenant in effect between God and Israel. Indeed, one finds a similar covenant formulation differentiated into the two parts of a recital of God's saving acts and a call to ethical obedience in Exodus 10:3-6, Joshua 24:1-28, and 1 Samuel 12:6ff.

The Lord our God, says Moses in Deuteronomy, has made a covenant with us, the people Israel. In keeping with God's promise to our forefathers, God has delivered us out of the brickyards of Egypt and is bringing us into a fair and pleasant land. Now God asks of us that we in response love God above all and express our love by keeping God's commandments:

> Hear, O Israel: The LORD our God is one LORD; and you shall love the LORD your God with all your heart, and with all your soul, and with all your might. And these words which I command you this day shall be upon your heart; and you shall teach them diligently to your children. . . . (Deut. 6:4-7a)

In turn, if we do keep God's commandments, God will love us, bless us, and multiply us (Deut. 7:13).

The pattern is clear: deliverance, obedience, blessing. And once we see that the obedience includes justice, then it's obvious that the pattern of thought in Micah is just an expression of the conviction that there is a covenant between God and Israel. "Justice, and only justice, you shall follow," says Moses, "that you may live and inherit the land which the LORD your God gives you." (Deut. 16:20)

A NEW QUESTION now arises, however. If one loves someone, then, other things being equal, one will do what the person asks. If we love God, we will do what God commands. But why does God command Israel to live this particular kind of life, including a life of justice? What is the connection between God's redemptive activity and the particular commands that God issues? Or is there none? Does God just arbitrarily pick out of the blue a certain way of life and then ask Israel to live it, as a test perhaps, a trial, rather like the arbitrary trials imposed in some of the Greek myths and in some of the classic fairy tales? Is the covenant to be understood as an arrangement in which God saves Israel and then bargains with them that if they will undertake some arbitrary trials, God will bless them?

Let me suggest that there is nothing at all arbitrary about the connection. Why did God save Israel? Did God just want Israel free, liberated? Was that the whole of God's purpose? Once Israel had crossed the Red Sea did God say, in effect, "My purpose has been achieved. You are out of Pharaoh's grasp. You are liberated"? Not at all. Liberation was not an end in itself. Liberation was on the way to a certain mode of life, on the way to Israel's flourishing. God's deliverance of Israel was no more, though also no less, than a step on the way to that mode-of-being that God had promised to the patriarchs (Deut. 6:10ff.). What God wanted for the people Israel was not just liberation but that mode of flourishing that is called shalom in the Old Testament. Wanting shalom for them lord the expression of God's love.

How do the commandments fit into this purpose? How does the keeping of the commandments fit into shalom? "The Lord," said Moses, "commanded us to do all these statutes *for our good always*" (Deut. 6:24). There is the clue. The keeping of the commandments is a component in shalom. Keeping the commandments is not something that God has arbitrarily stipulated as a condition for blessing Israel — the thought being that God might just as well have commanded other things. Justice is not something on which, by arbitrary divine fiat, the blessings of shalom will ensue. Justice is itself a component in shalom. The blessings do not and cannot by themselves constitute shalom. In the project of struggling for shalom, God and Israel are engaged together; neither party can achieve the goal without the contribution of the other. Without our justice there is no shalom. And without God's blessing there is also no shalom.

The point is made in various ways in Deuteronomy. In one passage Moses says to the people that the keeping of the commandments "will be your wisdom and your understanding in the sight of the people, who, when they hear all these statutes, will say, 'Surely this great nation is a wise and understanding people'" (Deut. 4:6). He also says that Israel is to keep the commandments so that "it may go well with you" (Deut. 4:40; 5:29, 33; 6:3). And in yet others, as we have already seen, he says to the people that the keeping of the commandments is "for your good" (cf. Deut. 6:24). The pattern of thought comes to its clearest and fullest expression in the closing paragraph of Deuteronomy 6:

> When your son asks you in time to come, "What is the meaning of the testimonies and the statutes and the ordinances which the Lord our God has commanded you?" then you shall say to your son, "We were Pharaoh's slaves in Egypt; and the Lord brought us out of Egypt with a mighty hand; and the Lord showed signs and wonders, great and grievous, against Egypt and against Pharaoh and all his household, before our eyes; and he brought us out from there, that he might bring us in and give us the land which he swore to give to our fathers. And the Lord commanded us to do all these

statutes, to fear the LORD our God, for our good always, that he might preserve us alive, as at this day. And it will be righteousness for us, if we are careful to do all this commandment before the LORD our God, as he has commanded us."

It is, then, no mystery why Micah represented God as calling for justice in response to God's saving acts instead of calling for something quite different. God saves for shalom, for life abundant. And there is no life abundant without the people's justice. The significance of the covenant is that God and the people have jointly pledged to travel together on the road to human flourishing — God blessing, the people exhibiting wisdom, righteousness, justice, love, and mercy. The biblical critique of humankind is that we live with the illusion that we can get the blessing without the ethic and that the blessing will be enough for the flourishing — believing, in turn, that the way to secure the blessing without the ethic is to engage in the actions of the cult. Walter J. Burghardt is speaking of his own Catholic community, but what he says applies to all:

> Does the Church have a role to play in the social, political, and economic orders? Many Christians, many Catholics, shout a resounding no. As they see it, the Church, as Church, has *no* commission to right human injustice. The Church is a spiritual institution, and its mission is sheerly spiritual: it is a channel that links the human person with God. The Church's charge is to help us know, love, and serve God in this life and to be happy with him forever in the next. Oh yes, poverty and politics, injustice and inhumanity, may stand as barriers to God's grace. If they do, then the Church must struggle against them — but not as a direct facet of its mission, only as obstacles at the outer edge of its vocation. The Church's commission is to gather a band of true believers who will prepare themselves by faith and hope for the redemptive action by which God establishes his Kingdom at the end of history.[5]

We now understand the connection, in Micah, between the divine lament over Israel's forgetfulness of God's salvific actions and the divine plea for justice. And we understand the dismissal of cultic actions as a substi-

---

5. Walter J. Burghardt, S.J., "Preaching the Just Word," in *Liturgy and Social Justice,* ed. Mark Searle (Collegeville: The Liturgical Press, 1980), p. 38.

tute for justice. Yet there is no reason to suppose that Micah or any of the other prophets was in favor of the abolition of the cult. Their conviction was rather that the authenticity of the cult depends on the ethical existence of those who practice the cult. Why is that? Why is the cult not a self-contained phenomenon which God wants *in addition to* justice and mercy? Are not the actions of the cult to be seen as also making their contribution to that mode of flourishing which is shalom? Justice is not a means to shalom but a component of it. Is the liturgical praise of God not also a component? Not coveting is a component of shalom. Is intercessory prayer not another component? Why this strange biblical *not/unless?* Why are we first to practice justice and then bring our sacrifices? Why are we first to show mercy and then do our fasting? The inclination of most of us religious people is first to do our singing and then, if time, energy, and persistence are left, to tend to justice. Why the biblical reversal?

It must be that the prophets are operating with a certain understanding of the meaning, the significance, the import of liturgical actions. Their understanding of the proper role of liturgical actions in our lives is an understanding that refuses to see those actions as an addendum to the other things we are called to do but instead sees their import as consisting in a certain relation they have to those other things. An attentive reading of the prophets makes clear that it is not just sin-offerings — sacrifices meant to atone for sin — that are the subject of their critique.

The prophetic critique of the cult is grounded in the conviction that the point of the liturgy is to give symbolic expression to the commitment of our lives to God. The point of liturgy is not the performance of certain self-contained actions such as confession and praise, no matter how sincere and appropriate those actions. Liturgy is for giving voice to life, to lives of faith. In our lives we seek to obey God; in the liturgy we praise the one whom we seek to obey and confess our failings. In our lives we demonstrate our love of God; in the liturgy we bless and praise the God we love. In our lives we strive to be like God: holy, merciful, just. In the liturgy we intercede with God to be our guide and support. It follows that if our lives are not in fact committed to God, then going through the motions of the liturgy constitutes a malformation so serious as to anger God. If in our lives we do not struggle for the feeding of the hungry, then interceding with God for the hungry constitutes a disgusting malformation. If in our lives we do not actively imitate the divine longing for justice, then professing devotion to God in the liturgy is a disgusting malformation. Liturgy is for giving voice to life oriented toward God. This we learn from the prophetic insistence that the words and gestures without the life disgust God.[6]

In my reflections on the biblical *not/unless* theme I have thus far focused entirely on the Old Testament; but the very same theme carries over into the New.

Twice in Matthew, Jesus is recorded as referring to Hosea's prophecy:

> For I desire steadfast love and not sacrifice,
>> the knowledge of God, rather than burnt offerings.
>>
>> (Hosea 6:6)

The situation in one case is that Jesus has once again violated the Pharisaic rules for holiness by having a meal with tax collectors and those pursuing unsavory professions. The Pharisees, in reaction, once again level their accusations. Jesus responds, "Go and learn what this means, 'I desire mercy, and not sacrifice.' For I came not to call the righteous, but sinners" (Matt. 9:13). The situation in the other case is that the disciples of Jesus have violated the rules for ritual cleanness by their behavior on the sabbath. When this is accusingly remarked upon, Jesus responds, "If you had known what this means, 'I desire mercy and not sacrifice,' you would not have condemned the guiltless" (Matt. 12:7).

The *not/unless* theme also comes to the surface in the "woes" passage of Matthew 23, where Jesus unfavorably contrasts the cultic act of tithing with the doing of justice:

> Woe to you, scribes and Pharisees, hypocrites, for you tithe mint
> and dill and cummin, and have neglected the weightier matters of
> the law, justice and mercy and faith; these you ought to have done,
> without neglecting the others. (Matt. 23:23)

---

6. Compare the following passage from Irenaeus, *Against Heresies* IV, xviii, 3: "For if anyone shall endeavour to offer a sacrifice merely to outward appearance, unexceptionably, in due order, and according to appointment, while in his soul he does not assign to his neighbour that fellowship with him which is right and proper, nor is under the fear of God — he who thus cherishes secret sin does not deceive God by that sacrifice which is offered correctly as to outward appearance; nor will such an obligation profit him anything, but (only) the giving up of that evil which has been conceived within him, so that sin may not the more, by means of the hypocritical action, render him the destroyer of himself. . . . Sacrifices, therefore, do not sanctify a man, for God stands in no need of sacrifice; but it is the conscience of the offerer that sanctifies the sacrifice when it is pure, and thus moves God to accept (the offering) as from a friend."

It comes to the surface again in the argumentative episode recorded in Matthew 15, which Jesus concludes with these words:

> Well did Isaiah prophesy of you when he said: "This people honors me with their lips, but their heart is far from me; in vain do they worship me, teaching as doctrines the precepts of men."

And it comes to the surface once again when, in Matthew 5:23-24, Jesus says:

> So if you are offering your gift at the altar, and there remember that your brother has something against you, leave your gift there before the altar and go; first be reconciled to your brother, and then come and offer your gift.

In all these passages one finds the prophetic theme continued: the authenticity of our cultic and liturgical acts is conditioned by the quality of our ethical existence. The theme is even more awesomely expressed in Mark 11:25, where Jesus says that forgiveness in heaven is conditioned by forgiveness on earth: "And whenever you stand praying, forgive, if you have anything against any one; so that your Father also who is in heaven may forgive you your trespasses." It is this thought that underlies the petition in the Lord's Prayer, "Forgive us our trespasses, as we forgive those who trespass against us."

I suggest that it is also along these same lines that we must understand what Paul says about the celebration of the Lord's Supper at Corinth (1 Cor. 11:27-29). There has been a great deal of discussion about Paul's injunction to his readers to "discern the body." Does he mean that they are to discern Christ's body in the eucharistic bread or that they are to discern the body of believers in those who are present at the assembly (which, of course, Paul also describes as "Christ's body")? Though the latter interpretation seems to me the better, given the context, the arguments on the matter strike me as indecisive. And for our purposes it makes no difference, since Paul makes clear his conviction that the person who eats the bread and drinks the cup of the Lord "in an unworthy manner" is not merely doing so inauthentically but, worse, is "profaning the body and blood of the Lord." The question, then, is how one eats the bread and drinks the cup in an unworthy manner? One can do so, no doubt, in many ways, but the way that Paul actually has in mind is clear from the context. If one participates in the eucharist while there are divisions and factions in the church (for example, divisions whereby those who are well-to-do "humiliate those who have nothing" [1 Cor. 11:22]), then one has done so in an unworthy manner.

Very early in its history, the church took these words with utmost seriousness. In *Didache* 14, probably written sometime in the first century, we find the instruction that before one participates in the eucharist one must confess one's transgressions "that your sacrifice may be pure." And then the writer adds, "Let none who has a quarrel with his companion join with you until they have been reconciled, that your sacrifice may not be defiled." Confession and reconciliation were a condition for the celebration of the eucharist. It did not take long for the kiss of peace to enter the liturgy as the liturgical expression of reconciliation. And eventually the Roman church instituted a whole system of private confession and stipulated that one must confess and be absolved before receiving the elements of the eucharist.

We all know, in general outline at least, what happened to this liturgical element and this liturgical prescription. Though the kiss of peace remained in both the Eastern and Western liturgies, it became a dead letter. No longer did the people pass the peace to each other as the sign that they were reconciled; and confession and absolution became, in the late Middle Ages, one more addition to all the practices by which people tried to buy favors from God without altering their ethical existence.

Confronted with this corruption the Reformers, as part of their radical reform of the cult, rejected the private confessional entirely and put two substitutes in its place: They "fenced" the table with both stern admonitions and rigorous discipline, and they made confession and absolution regular components of the public liturgy. The thought underlying these attempts to be faithful to the biblical *not/unless* theme was nowhere more eloquently expressed than in a passage from Calvin's *Institutes:*

> Paul enjoins that a man examine himself before eating of this bread or drinking from this cup. By this (as I interpret it), he meant that each man descend into himself, and ponder with himself whether he rests with inward assurance of heart upon the salvation purchased by Christ; whether he acknowledges it by confession of mouth; then, whether he aspires to the imitation of Christ with the zeal of innocence and holiness; whether, after Christ's example, he is prepared to give himself for his brethren and to communicate himself to those with whom he shares Christ in common; whether, as he is counted a member by Christ, he in turn so holds all his brethren as members of

his body; whether he desires to cherish, protect, and help them as his own members. Not that these duties both of faith and of love can now be made perfect in us, but that we should endeavor and aspire with all our heart toward this end in order that we may day by day increase our faith once begun. (IV, xvii, 40)

Eventually, of course, the reforms of which these eloquent words were an explanation suffered their own corruption and degradation. Rather than looking at those, however, let me conclude this brief historical sketch with what seems to me the finest liturgical expression of the prophetic theme that comes to us from the early Reformation. It occurs in the eucharistic prayer composed by Cranmer for the 1549 *Book of Common Prayer*:

And here we offer and present unto thee, O Lord, our self, our souls and bodies, to be a reasonable, holy, and lively sacrifice unto thee; humbly beseeching thee, that whosoever shall be partakers of this holy communion may worthily receive the most precious body and blood of thy Son Jesus Christ, and be fulfilled with thy grace and heavenly benediction, and made one body with thy Son Jesus Christ, that he may dwell in them, and they in him.

The declaration in this prayer that we "offer and present" our selves, our souls, and our bodies as "a reasonable, holy, and lively sacrifice" is, of course, an echo of Paul's appeal in Romans 12:1 "to present your bodies as a living sacrifice, holy and acceptable to God." It should be regarded as a third way — a way in addition to confession and the sign of unity — in which the prophetic *not/unless* theme finds recognition in the liturgy. We do not just offer to God this and that. We offer ourselves, our lives.

The language of offering and sacrifice in the liturgy has been the subject of reams of controversy. The notion of an atoning, propitiatory sacrifice must be rejected. But the offering of our lives is exactly what the prophets called for; and the liturgical declaration and expression of such offering is profoundly appropriate. To the objection that any sacrifice we may make is unworthy, I find the words of Rowan Williams in his little book *Eucharistic Sacrifice: The Roots of a Metaphor* eminently appropriate:

The effect of Christ's sacrifice is precisely to make us 'liturgical' beings, capable of offering ourselves, our praises, and our symbolic gifts to a God who we know will receive us in Christ. . . . We are always in danger . . . of *regression* in the Christian life: the basic fact of our unqualified dependence on grace can become an alibi, a refusal to assume the authority we in fact have as baptized Christians. . . . We have been given our selves, our Christian selves, as a free gift: to trust God means also to trust ourselves and our worth in his eyes. The haunting image of *Addai and Mari,* of praise offered "with uncovered faces," speaks volumes about proper Christian self-love. We need to acknowledge that God's gift in making us his children is a *real* gift, and we may do this by trusting his will to receive what we are and what we offer. Our liturgy should celebrate sanctification as well as justification.[7]

Worship acceptable to God, authentic worship, is the worship of a pure heart. And the only pure heart is the heart of a person who has genuinely struggled to embody God's justice and righteousness in the world and genuinely repented of ever again doing so only halfheartedly. The worship of such a person consists, then, of giving voice and symbolic expression to the concerns and commitments of the heart. This, I have suggested, is the biblical vision.

Once we catch the vision, the question we began with fades away to be replaced with its near opposite. We asked why liturgy could not have its own independent, self-contained authenticity quite apart from the mode of life of those who engage in it. The answer we have gained leads us now to ask: Why isn't the expression in life of the concerns and commitments of the heart sufficient? Why is it important also to give voice and symbolic expression to those concerns and commitments in the liturgy? I have throughout assumed that it is important. I cannot on this occasion, however, defend that assumption.

I close by considering a question that these reflections will have suggested to some: Does not the line of argument that I have developed imply a sort of "works-righteousness"? I think not. Consider some authentic liturgical expression of gratitude or praise or penitence — that is, some liturgical expression of one or the other of these that satisfies whatever you regard as a condition of its authenticity. I have suggested that everybody does believe that there are such conditions. Should such an act be regarded as somehow making the doer righteous before God, as undoing or com-

---

7. Rowan Williams, *Eucharistic Sacrifice: The Roots of a Metaphor* (Branicote: Grove Books, 1982), p. 27.

pensating for his or her sin? Everybody in the Christian tradition would answer "No" to this question. My argument, that a commitment to justice is one condition of the authenticity of liturgy, does nothing at all to change the correctness of the "No" answer.

Liturgy, Justice, and Holiness

B ack and forth in the Christian liturgy echoes the language of holiness. Already by the fourth century the *Sanctus* had been introduced into the eucharistic prayer. The people, in response to the recalling of God's nature and the narrative of God's actions, are invited to join their voices with those of the hosts of heaven in the words:

> Holy, holy, holy is the Lord of Sabaoth;
> heaven and earth are full of thy glory.

The acclamation derives, of course, from the ecstatic song of the hosts of heaven that Isaiah heard when standing in the temple (Isa. 6:3):

> Holy, holy, holy is the Lord of hosts;
> the whole earth is full of his glory.

The song was heard again by John of Patmos in one of his visions:

> Holy, holy, holy, is the Lord God Almighty,
> who was and is and is to come.

In the Orthodox liturgy of John Chrysostom, the priest responds to the people's acclamation of the *Sanctus* with the words: "Holy and most holy art thou, and excellent is thy glory, who so loved thy world that thou didst give thine only-begotten Son, that whosoever believeth in him should not perish, but have everlasting life." In the liturgy of Basil the Great, the liturgy used in the Orthodox church on those few occasions in the year when the liturgy of John Chrysostom is not used, the response of the priest to the *Sanctus* similarly picks up the theme of holiness: "Holy indeed and most holy art thou, and no bounds are there to the majesty of thy holiness; and just art thou in all thy works, for in righteousness and true judgment hast thou ordered all things for us."

The theme of God's holiness is struck much earlier in the Orthodox liturgy, however, than at the singing of the *Sanctus*. Indeed, the theme pervades the Orthodox liturgy, more so than it does any other liturgy of Christendom. Before the reading of Scripture the priest says:

> For thou art holy, our God,
> and to thee we ascribe glory,
> to the Father, and to the Son,
> and to the Holy Spirit,
> now and for ever and for evermore.

To this the people respond with the so-called *Trisagion Hymn*, that is, the "thrice-holy" hymn. Three times they sing:

> Holy God,
> Holy and mighty,
> Holy and immortal one,
> have mercy on us.

This is followed with the words:

> Glory to the Father, and to the Son,
> and to the Holy Spirit;
> now and ever and for evermore. Amen.
> Holy immortal one, have mercy on us.
> Holy God,
> Holy and mighty,
> Holy and immortal one,
> have mercy on us.

The theme of holiness does not only surface in liturgies in the form of acclamations and ascriptions addressed to God. For example, in the liturgies of both John Chrysostom and Basil the Great we find the following dialogue between priest and people, occurring just before communion as the priest lifts up the sanctified bread:

> Holy things unto the holy.
> One only is holy, One only is Lord, Jesus Christ, to the glory of God the Father. Amen.

There is a variety of earlier versions of this same dialogue. For example, in the Liturgy of Saints Addai and Mari, coming to us from Syria, the dialogue takes this form:

> The holy thing to the holies is fitting in perfection.
> One holy Father, one holy Son, one holy Spirit. Glory be to the Father and to the Son and to the Holy Spirit to the ages of ages. Amen.

"Holy God," "holy people," "holy things" — back and forth these phrases echo in the classic liturgies. The acknowledgment and hymning of holiness is a preoccupation of the Christian liturgy. It's true that those who come from some free-church tradition will find a good deal of this liturgical language strange. But in those traditions the Reginald Heber hymn, "Holy, Holy, Holy, Lord God Almighty," set to the familiar tune of John B. Dykes, occupies a prominent and much-loved place.

I would guess many of us feel that when it comes to holiness, we have left behind such earthly, horizontal concerns as justice and entered a higher realm, the realm of the transcendent, of the divine. To cite the words of the Orthodox liturgy one more time,

> We, who mystically represent the cherubim
> and sing the thrice-holy hymn to the
> life-giving Trinity,
> let us lay aside the cares of life,
> that we may receive the King of all.

My project in this article is to argue that there is no such dichotomy between holiness and justice — not if we understand holiness aright. God's justice is a manifestation of God's holiness; our justice is a reflection of God's holiness. When we deal with justice, we are dealing with the sacred.

61

Injustice is desecration. The preoccupation of the liturgy with holiness does not separate liturgy from justice. To the contrary, holiness binds liturgy and justice together.

WE CAN BEGIN by noticing that the acknowledgment of *God's* holiness is inseparable from recognition of the imperative for *us* to be holy. This is suggested by the refrain, occurring several times in the Old Testament and picked up in the New, "You shall be holy, for I, the LORD your God, am holy" (Lev. 11:44-45; 19:2, 26; 1 Pet. 1:16). It is likewise suggested by the *epiclesis* in the eucharistic prayer of the classic Christian liturgies. Let me this time cite a contemporary example, from the Presbyterian Church USA:

> Merciful God,
> by your Holy Spirit bless and make holy
> both us and these your gifts of bread and wine,
> that the bread we break
> may be the communion of the body of Christ,
> and the cup we bless
> may be the communion of the blood of Christ.
> Here we offer ourselves to be a living sacrifice,
> holy and acceptable to you.
>
> (Great Prayer of Thanksgiving C)

In its *Constitution on the Sacred Liturgy*, Vatican II goes a step farther and says that the liturgy as *a whole* is for our sanctification, as well as for the glorification of God:

> From the liturgy, and especially from the Eucharist, grace is poured forth upon us as from a fountain, and the sanctification of men in Christ and the glorification of God to which all other activities of the Church are directed, as toward their end, are achieved with maximum effectiveness. (Para. 10)

Members of other traditions of Christendom than the Catholic might disagree with, or hesitate over, one or another part of this sentence. What almost no one will dispute is that the liturgy is for making us holy.

However, to recognize that there is an imperative to holiness, and that the liturgy is not only for acknowledging God's holiness but also, in response to recognizing the imperative, for making us holy and for interceding with God that he make us holy, is not yet to see any particular connection between holiness and justice. That connection is what we must explore. We shall begin by asking what holiness is. For nothing in the language of liturgy and devotion is more alien to our contemporary secular mentality than speech about holiness. Once upon a time the concept of holiness was fundamental to the way in which human beings thought about reality and experience. That time — for us at least — is past.

A GOOD WAY to set out is to consider what Jonathan Edwards, that great theologian of holiness, says on the matter. In his well-known *Religious Affections*, Edwards distinguishes between what he calls the *natural* attributes of God and the *moral* attributes. By "God's natural attributes" Edwards has in mind those attributes "of strength, knowledge, etc. that constitute the greatness of God. . . ."[1] Edwards then goes on to say that the

> moral excellency of an intelligent being, when it is true and real . . . , is holiness. Therefore holiness comprehends all the true moral excellency of intelligent beings: there is no other true virtue, but real holiness. Holiness comprehends all the true virtue of a good man; his love to God, his gracious love to men, his justice, his charity, and bowels of mercies, his gracious meekness and gentleness, and all other true Christian virtues that he has, belong to his holiness. So the holiness of God in the more extensive sense of the word, and the sense in which the word is commonly, if not universally used concerning God in Scripture, is the same with the moral excellency of the divine nature, or his purity and beauty as a moral agent, comprehending all his moral perfections, his righteousness, faithfulness and goodness. (pp. 255-56)

Edwards goes on to say that it is the holiness of God that first, and above all, draws us to God. Again I cannot do better than quote Edwards's own lucid prose:

> that kind of excellency of the nature of divine things, which is the first objective ground of all holy affections, is their moral excel-

---

1. Jonathan Edwards, *Religious Affections* (New Haven: Yale University Press, 1959), p. 256.

lency, or their holiness. Holy persons, in the exercise of holy affections, do love divine things primarily for their holiness: they love
God, in the first place, for the beauty of his holiness or moral perfection, as being supremely amiable in itself. Not that the saints, in
the exercise of gracious affections, do love God only for his holiness; all his attributes are amiable and glorious in their eyes; they
delight in every divine perfection; the contemplation of the infinite
greatness, power, and knowledge, and terrible majesty of God, is
pleasant to them. But their love to God for his holiness is what is
most fundamental and essential in their love. (p. 256)

In support of his claim that God's holiness is what fundamentally grounds
our love of God, Edwards remarks that

Natural qualifications are either excellent or otherwise, according
as they are joined with moral excellency or not. Strength and
knowledge don't render any being lovely, without holiness; but
more hateful: though they render them more lovely, when joined
with holiness. . . . And so it is in God, according to our way of conceiving of the divine Being: holiness is in a peculiar manner the
beauty of the divine nature. Hence we often read of the beauty of
holiness. (p. 257)

Thus it is, says Edwards, that

A true love to God must begin with a delight in his holiness, and
not with a delight in any other attribute; for no other attribute is
truly lovely without this, and no otherwise than as (according to
our way of conceiving of God) it derives its loveliness from this; and
therefore it is impossible that other attributes should appear lovely,
in their true loveliness, till this is seen; and it is impossible that any
perfection of the divine nature should be loved with true love, till
this is loved. If the true loveliness of all God's perfections, arises
from the loveliness of his holiness; then the true love of all his
perfections, arises from the love of his holiness. (pp. 257-58)

On Edwards' account there is a very straightforward link between holiness and justice — or more precisely, between holiness and the virtue of
justice. In both God and human beings, the virtue of justice is one of the

manifestations of holiness. For justice is one of those "moral excellencies" that go to make up the holiness of an "intelligent creature." To use Edwards's language, justice is a "holy affection." We may add that, on Edwards's view, "Gracious and holy affections have their exercise and fruit in Christian practice. I mean, they have that influence and power upon him who is the subject of them, that they cause that a practice, which is universally conformed to, and directed by Christian rules, should be the practice and business of his life" (p. 383). The practice of the virtue of justice yields justice.

EDWARDS'S ACCOUNT captures some, at least, of what goes into our concept of holiness. But it does not, I suggest, capture the whole of it. For on Edwards' account, we human beings find the holiness of God, once we recognize it, altogether attractive. Edwards speaks repeatedly of the beauty and the sweetness of holiness. But recall once again the visionary experience of Isaiah in the temple. Isaiah's response upon hearing the *Sanctus* hymn of the host of heaven was to recoil and burst out with the well-known words, "Woe is me! For I am lost; for I am a man of unclean lips, and I dwell in the midst of a people of unclean lips; for my eyes have seen the King, the LORD of hosts!" (Isa. 6:5). We need not deny that Isaiah felt something of the attraction of which Edwards speaks; but predominantly he felt fright, terror, awe. It is of course this peculiar paradoxical experience of *sweet terror,* of attraction to what frightens one, that Rudolf Otto placed at the center of his phenomenology of the holy in his famous book *The Idea of the Holy.* Edwards grants, of course, that we may be struck with terrifying awe before the face of God. But he suggests that it is our awareness of God's *natural* excellencies that produces this experience, when those natural excellencies are perceived without a similar perception of God's moral excellencies — that is, God's holiness. Holiness, on Edwards's account, is all beauty — no terror.

Karl Barth, in his discussion of God's holiness, enables us to take a necessary step beyond Edwards. Rather than seeing God's holiness as the totality of God's moral excellencies, Barth sees God's holiness as a facet of God's grace; and God's grace he sees, in turn, as one of the perfections of the divine love. One of Barth's concerns is to avoid the picture, with which Edwards operates, of holiness as one-among-other excellencies of God. On Barth's view grace is, as it were, an adverbial qualification of God's love — God loves in a gracious manner. And holiness is in turn an adjectival qualification of God's grace — the graciousness of God's love has a holy quality to it. "When God loves," says Barth, revealing His inmost being in the fact that He loves and therefore seeks and creates fellowship, this being and doing is divine and distinct from all other loving to the extent that the love of God is grace. Grace is the distinctive mode of God's being in so far as it seeks and creates fellowship by its own free inclination and favour, unconditioned by any merit or claim in the beloved, but also unhindered by any unworthiness or opposition in the latter — able, on the contrary, to overcome all unworthiness and opposition. (CD, II/1, p. 353)

Wherein, then, lies the *holiness* of God's gracious loving? In this, says Barth:

As holy, it is characterised by the fact that God as He seeks and creates fellowship, is always the Lord. He therefore distinguishes and maintains His own will as against every other will. He condemns, excludes and annihilates all contradiction and resistance to it. (p. 359)

Though this is Barth's official explanation of holiness, the thought behind the words remains for us somewhat inarticulate. Better, I think, are these words:

The bond between the concepts of grace and holiness consists . . . in the fact that both point to God's transcendence over the resistance which His being and action encounter from the opposite side. When we speak of grace, we think of the fact that His favourable inclination towards the creature does not allow itself to be soured and frustrated by the resistance of the latter. When we speak of holiness, we think, on the other hand, of the fact that His favourable inclination overcomes and destroys this resistance. To say grace is to say the forgiveness of sins; to say holiness, judgment upon sins. But since both reflect the love of God, how can there be the one without the other, forgiveness without judgment or judgment without forgiveness? (p. 360)

Barth's first step, in comparison with Edwards, is to sharpen Edwards's reference to the moral excellencies of God. Those moral excellencies are all seen by Barth as located in God's love; they are the perfections of the divine love. Barth's next step is to say that this loving has the quality of grace — that is, of forgiveness. But there cannot be forgiveness, he argues, without judgment. And it is this *judging* character of God's love, implicit in its forgiving character, that grounds God's holiness.

It is, then, only as God affirms His victorious good will, as the concept of grace implies, that what holiness specially denotes is true and actual — the aloofness with which God stands over against the resistance He encounters, His judgment upon sin. He exercises this judgment, His judgment, in such a way that it can be manifest and truly appreciated and experienced as divine judgment only in this way, the way of grace. But of course it must also be said that this way leads necessarily and unavoidably to the truth and reality of judgment, and therefore to the holiness of divine grace. (p. 361)

The holiness of God consists in the unity of His judgment with His grace. God is holy because His grace judges and His judgment is gracious. (p. 363)

As Barth himself goes on to remark, this account explains at once the intimate connection in the Scriptures between the recognition of God's holiness and our feelings of awe — a connection that we found missing in Edwards's account.

For our purposes, however, the gain we made in proceeding from Edwards to Barth comes with a certain loss. Though we seem now to have a surer grasp on the concept of holiness, the connection of holiness to justice seems to have slipped away. So let us take yet a further step in our exploration of the nature of holiness. What Isaiah says, remember, upon hearing the *Sanctus* sung in heaven, is that "I am a man of unclean lips, and I dwell in the midst of a people of unclean lips." You and I are inclined to interpret this as Isaiah's confession that he has violated the moral law of God — that he has, in that way, sinned against God. That is how Barth interprets it. Almost certainly that is not what Isaiah had in mind, however — or at least, not the whole of what he had in mind. A pursuit of what he might have meant by "uncleanness" will take us deeper into an understanding of holiness.

My guide here will be the remarkable discussion by the British anthropologist Mary Douglas in her book *Purity and Danger*. Her chapter on "The Abominations of Leviticus" succeeds in illuminating the cleanliness regulations of Leviticus and Deuteronomy to an extent that no one before her, to the best of my knowledge, had ever managed.

Every society, so Douglas argues, operates with certain distinctions between the clean and the unclean — though in our modern Western society these are less prominent than they are in most societies and have been blurred, and obscured from view, by an overlay of hygienic distinctions. Fundamental to Douglas's argument is her contention that to understand the clean/unclean distinctions of any society one must understand "the principles of patterning on which they constructed their universe," including their social universe (p. 7). Roughly speaking, a society judges as unclean those things that blur and threaten its patterning of society and reality. The challenge for an anthropologist, when confronted with a given society's regulations concerning defilement, is to discern the sense of cosmic and social pattern that lies behind these regulations.

Within this general framework, Douglas offers a fascinating proposal concerning the clean/unclean distinctions to be found in Leviticus and Deuteronomy — this after she has first briefly canvassed the attempts at explaining these regulations that are to be found in the literature. Some have argued that hygienic intuitions lay behind these regulations. Douglas notes that there is no evidence for this hypothesis. Others have suggested that they are purely arbitrary regulations instituted by God to discipline Israel. Douglas remarks that this explanation is the renunciation of any attempt at explanation. Yet others have argued that the clean and unclean animals were allegories of virtues and vices. For this hypothesis there is also no evidence. Last, some have argued that the point of the regulations was to protect Israel from foreign influence. Douglas acknowledges that although some of the regulations probably did have this effect, there was nonetheless a great deal of foreign influence in Israel's life against which no regulations were instituted. Thus we are left wondering why these particular influences merited prohibition. As Douglas rather drily remarks,

> it is no explanation to represent Israel as a sponge at one moment and as a repellent the next, without explaining why it soaked up this foreign element but repelled that one. . . . The Israelites absorbed freely from their neighbours, but not quite freely. Some elements of foreign culture were incompatible with the principles of patterning on which they were constructing their universe; others were compatible. (p. 43)

It is, then, the pattern of cosmic and social order reflected in Israel's regulations concerning defilement that Douglas tries to discern. Before she does so, however, she notes a remarkable feature of the way in which these regulations are presented in both Leviticus and Deuteronomy. In both cases they are the elements of a holiness code. God declares himself to be holy, this holiness connected with God's deliverance of Israel from Egypt — a confirmation, apparently, of Barth's understanding of holiness. And God then calls Israel to be holy as God is holy. It is to reflect God's holiness that Israel is called to observe, among other things, the cleanliness regulations. In Leviticus 11:44-45, we read:

> For I am the LORD your God; consecrate yourselves therefore and be holy, for I am holy. You shall not defile yourselves with any swarming thing that crawls upon the earth. For I am the LORD who brought you up out of the land of Egypt, to be your God; you shall therefore be holy, for I am holy.

Israel is called to an *imitatio dei* throughout its daily existence: be holy as I am holy. And to be holy, she must avoid defilement. This remarkable connection between holiness and cleanness suggests that if we can discern the pattern of the cleanness regulations of old Israel, we will also have discerned the lineaments of its understanding of holiness.

Before we set out on the attempt to discern this pattern, one more point must be introduced. Over and over it is said that blessing will come to Israel if it keeps itself clean whereas Israel will be cursed if it defiles itself. This prompts Douglas to say about the regulations that

> observing them draws down prosperity, infringing them brings danger. We are thus entitled to treat them in the same way as we treat primitive ritual avoidances whose breach unleashes danger to men. The precepts and ceremonies alike are focussed on the idea of the holiness of God which men must create in their lives. So this is a universe in which men prosper by conforming to holiness and perish when they deviate from it. (p. 50)

There can no be doubt, says Douglas, that "holiness" means, for one thing, *set apart*. In fact this seems to be its root sense. But this doesn't tell us much. Set apart with respect to what? "Granted," says Douglas, "that its root means separateness, the next idea that emerges is of the Holy as wholeness and completeness" (p. 51). The clue to the holiness code is its concern with wholeness and completeness, these understood in both a physical and a social sense.

We can begin uncovering the pattern by taking note of some of those holiness regulations that do not, strictly speaking, involve defilement. "The culture of the Israelites," remarks Douglas, "was brought to the pitch of greatest intensity when they prayed and when they fought. The army could not win without the blessing; and to keep the blessing in the camp, the camp was to be preserved from defilement like the Temple" (p. 53). Consider, then, these instructions that the officers were to issue to the men in camp:

> Then the officers shall speak to the people saying, "What man is there that has built a new house and has not dedicated it? Let him go back to his house, lest he die in the battle and another man dedicate it. And what man is there that has planted a vineyard and has not enjoyed its fruit? Let him go back to his house, lest he die in the battle and another man enjoy its fruit. And what man is there that has betrothed a wife and has not taken her? Let him go back to his house, lest he die in the battle and another man take her." (Deut. 20:5-7)

The pattern seems clear. Those with significant projects that are incomplete, unfinished, are not to fight Israel's battles.

We can move next to the regulations concerning blemished and unblemished individuals. The animals offered in sacrifice must be unblemished specimens, and the priests offering the sacrifices must likewise be unblemished. We read that "no man of the descendants of Aaron the priest who has a blemish shall come near to offer the LORD's offerings by fire . . ." (Lev. 21:21). So also lepers were unclean; and priests might come into contact with corpses only if they were those of their close relatives.

Next, if we think of the human body as a sort of container, we can understand why bodily issues were regarded as making one unclean. "When any man has a discharge from his body his discharge is unclean," we read in Leviticus (15:2). And likewise, "When a woman has a discharge of blood which is her regular discharge from her body, she shall be in her impurity for seven days, and whoever touches her shall be unclean until the evening" (15:19). The special importance of temple and army camp made it especially important that the regulations concerning bodily issues be honored in these precincts. In Deuteronomy we read that

> When you go forth against your enemies and are in camp, then you shall keep yourself from every evil thing. If there is among you any man who is not clean by reason of what chances to him by night, then he shall go outside the camp; but when evening comes on, he

shall bathe himself in water, and when the sun is down, he may come within the camp. (23:9-11)

The pattern Douglas suggests — of wholeness, completeness, perfection, unity, integrity — does indeed seem clear in all these particulars. But what, finally, about the distinction between clean and unclean animals? Douglas's suggestion is that the Israelites saw a certain right and proper order as embedded in creation. Clean animals are those that exhibit this order; unclean ones, those that in some way violate the order, mix it up. Though they may be perfect specimens of their kind, their very *kind* has a certain imperfection about it. Their very kind represents a violation of the proper boundaries; their very kind is malformed. Specifically, Israel worked with the distinction between the sky, the earth, and the water; and it had notions as to the proper form of locomotion in these. Those animals that violated the right form of locomotion for animals of their element were unclean. Thus worms and snakes are unclean because, instead of walking or hopping on earth, they crawl; eels are unclean because they move in water without fins; and birds with no wings, or inadequate wings, are unclean because they cannot fly.

Along the same lines we can now interpret the distinction between those animals that are clean to eat and those that, if eaten, will defile one. Douglas reminds us that the Israelites, as an agricultural people, would have given pride of place in their thought about animals fit to eat to their own domesticated animals. When they asked what it was that differentiated these from others, they noticed that these animals both chewed their cud and had cloven hooves. This then defined for them the boundary between those animals fit for eating and those that would defile one. We can conclude, once again, "that holiness is exemplified by completeness. Holiness requires that different classes of things shall not be confused" (p. 53). And so, says Douglas,

> If the proposed interpretation of the forbidden animals is correct, the dietary laws would have been like signs which at every turn inspired meditation on the oneness, purity, and completeness of God. By rules of avoidance holiness was given a physical expression in every encounter with the animal kingdom and at every meal. Observance of the dietary rules would thus have been a meaningful part of the great liturgical act of recognition and worship which culminated in the sacrifice in the Temple. (p. 57)

But where is justice in all this? Right at hand. Thrown right into the middle of the regulations concerning the clean and the unclean, the complete and the incomplete, the blemished and the unblemished, are regulations concerning justice. Where you and I would see a sharp distinction, no distinction is drawn. Near the beginning of Deuteronomy 7, for example, we read, "For you are a people holy to the Lord your God, and the Lord has chosen you to be a people for his own possession, out of all the peoples that are on the face of the earth." This is followed immediately by the instruction, "You shall not eat any abominable thing." What follows is a list of unclean animals. But shortly the list is broken off and some of the Jubilee regulations are introduced. For example, "At the end of every seven years you shall grant a release. And this is the manner of the release: every creditor shall release what he has lent to his neighbor; he shall not exact it of his neighbor, his brother, because the Lord's release has been proclaimed" (15:1-2). Then certain regulations are introduced concerning what we would regard as the cult proper. And those, in turn, are followed by an injunction to pursue justice concluding thus: "Justice, and only justice, you shall follow, that you may live and inherit the land which the Lord your God gives you" (16:20). In short, the pursuit of justice is treated as part of the pursuit of holiness. If we are to be holy as God is holy, we must pursue justice. Injustice is desecration.

What's the connection? It's not explicitly said. But then not much here is explicit. We have to try to *spy* the pattern. Part of the connection seems to be that a just judgment rendered in cases of conflict requires rectitude (Deut. 16:18-19); and as Douglas remarks about the list of actions found in Leviticus 19,

> Developing the idea of holiness as order, not confusion, this list upholds rectitude and straight-dealing as holy and contradiction and double-dealing as against holiness. Theft, lying, false witness, cheating in weights and measures, all kinds of dissembling such as speaking ill of the deaf (and presumably smiling to their face), hating your brother in your heart (while presumably speaking kindly to him), these are clearly contradictions between what seems and what is. (pp. 53-58)

I think it is plausible, however, to see justice and holiness as connected by more than rectitude. An important clue to the contour of justice as understood in the Bible is the repetitious reference to the four social classes of

72

widows, orphans, aliens, and the impoverished. If society is to be just, such people must be rightly treated. The refrain is to be found not only in the prophets and Psalms but in Deuteronomy. The Lord God, says Moses in his great farewell speech to his people, "executes justice for the fatherless and the widow, and loves the sojourner, giving him food and clothing" (Deut. 10:28).

What, in particular, does the repetitious reference to widows, orphans, aliens, and the impoverished suggest as to the biblical understanding of the contours of justice? It seems quite clear: the widows, the orphans, the aliens, and the impoverished were the marginal ones in old Israelite society. They were the ones who had little or no voice in the society and whose claim on the goods of society was, accordingly, fragile and precarious. If the society is to be a *just community,* there must be social arrangements and practices that assure to such people a voice in society and a fair share in its goods. At the most fundamental level, those goods are the goods of sustenance. But as we learn from the Sabbath regulations, all the members of society also have a claim to a fair share in the Sabbath rest of the community — in its refreshment. We could cite other goods as well.

In short, what we find in Deuteronomy is that haunting biblical theme of God searching for the hundredth one, of God leaving the ninety-and-nine to search for the one who is not yet incorporated into God's shalom and asking us to accompany God on that search. A dimension of this is what nowadays is called "the preferential option for the poor."

With this understanding in mind of the contours of justice, it is not at all difficult to see why justice is treated as a manifestation of holiness. The unjust society is a society in which wholeness and integrity are lacking. It is a society in which people exist on the margins, on the periphery, hanging on rather than being incorporated into the life and flourishing of the community. Such a society fails to mirror the wholeness of God. And when we as Christians recall that this God whose holiness we are called to reflect in our lives and societies is himself a trinitarian community, then it is obvious that the unjust society is an unholy society. It does not mirror God's communitarian wholeness.

ONE MORE ISSUE must be considered before we can close our discussion. But before we explore that issue, let us stand back for a moment to reflect on what we have learned. Fundamental to the Old Testament understanding of holiness is the contrast between God's wholeness on the one hand and, on the other, the brokenness of self, society, and creation as a whole. The Torah throws up before us a tremendous variety of modes of brokenness. And what the Torah asked of old Israel is that it reflect the holiness of God by avoiding the broken things of our creaturely existence and pursuing wholeness. The conclusion is compelling that God's holiness is God's wholeness. Barth saw God's holiness as confronting us in our sin. Our own reflections lead to the conclusion that that is not the whole of the picture. God's holiness confronts us in the totality of our brokenness; and that confrontation will not always be in the form of judgment; sometimes it will be in the form of lament. Of course it's true that sin is also a form of brokenness. So the right way to make the point is this: God confronts us not only in our ethical brokenness but in our brokenness as a whole. It is in that confrontation that we discern God's holiness, God's wholeness. What Isaiah heard hymned by the hosts of heaven as he stood in the temple was the awesome wholeness of God. And what he so powerfully felt, by contrast with that holiness, was his own brokenness and the brokenness of the world with which he came into contact.

You and I, as modern Western men and women, have different notions of brokenness from those found in Leviticus and Deuteronomy. Though injustice is still for us a mode of brokenness, we do not see worms as examples of brokenness. For us it is quite all right if some of earth's animals crawl rather than walk or hop. The assumptions concerning defilement that underlay old Israel's holiness code have become alien to us. But for us who are Christians there is a second way in which we find ourselves distanced from the holiness code of old Israel. The words and actions of Jesus mean for us that instead of avoiding, in one way or another, the broken people of this world, we are to embrace them.

LET ME DEVELOP this final theme by calling attention to the central argument in Marcus J. Borg's *Conflict, Holiness & Politics in the Teaching of Jesus*.[2] (Borg, I might add, is a participant in what some have begun to call the third quest for the historical Jesus.) To read the New Testament after the Old is to be struck by the fact that the New Testament, and in particular the Gospels, speaks very little of holiness. In principle that might be an insignificant silence. Borg contends that it is significant. Earlier I quoted the passage from Deuteronomy in which the leader of the army is told to dismiss from the camp all those who have significant incomplete projects. With that passage in mind, consider Jesus' parable of the Great Feast,

---

2. Marcus J. Borg, *Conflict, Holiness & Politics in the Teaching of Jesus* (New York: E. Mellen Press, 1984).

found both in Matthew 22:1ff. and Luke 14:16ff. Let me quote the passage as it occurs in Luke:

> A man once gave a great banquet, and invited many; and at the time for the banquet he sent his servant to say to those who had been invited, "Come; for all is now ready." But they all alike began to make excuses. The first said to him, "I have bought a field, and I must go out and see it; I pray you, have me excused." And another said, "I have bought five yoke of oxen, and I go to examine them; I pray you, have me excused." And another said, "I have married a wife, and therefore I cannot come." So the servant came and reported this to his master. Then the householder in anger said to his servant, "Go out quickly to the streets and lanes of the city, and bring in the poor and maimed and blind and lame. . . . For I tell you, none of those men who were invited shall taste my banquet."

Though the allusion to the Deuteronomy passage seems unmistakable, the point of Deuteronomy has been inverted. Where in Deuteronomy the officer orders those with incomplete projects to leave the camp, here in Luke the host erupts in anger when those with incomplete projects beg off attending his dinner. And yet more remarkable, the host expresses his anger by inviting to the banquet those very ones whose blemishes would have been seen by the writers of Deuteronomy as making them unsatisfactory for reflecting the holiness of God: the maimed, the blind, and the lame.

Borg's thesis helps us to understand these astonishing reversals. The thesis goes like this: When Rome occupied Jerusalem and the temple in 63 B.C. and made Palestine part of the Roman empire, "Religious Jews were faced with the question, 'What did it mean in these circumstances to be loyal to Yahweh?' The answer provided by the postexilic development was clear: be holy." What arose in Israel was a cluster of movements dedicated to the pursuit of holiness. These movements were at one and the same time movements of renewal within Israel and movements of resistance to Rome.

As to how to be holy, different movements had different views. But common to all was the conviction that holiness entailed separation from those who were unclean and the careful observance of Torah, especially its Sabbath regulations, its cultic regulations, and its regulations concerning defilement. The Essenes, so as to pursue a separated, Torah-faithful holiness, withdrew to the desert and set up a separated community. The Pharisees tried to practice holiness within general society — and the holiness they practiced was not just the holiness Torah prescribed for Israelites in general but that which it prescribed for priests. "For the Pharisees, Israel was to be a Kingdom of priests and a holy nation, following the same laws of purity that normally applied only to priests in the Temple" (p. 58). The project of the Pharisees was to make the home a little temple with its paterfamilias a little priest.

The effect of those various holiness movements, dedicated both to internal renewal and resistance to Rome, was sharp internal divisions within the Jewish people. Not only were the various movements in conflict with each other; division was heightened between those within such movements and those on the outside. From their desert fastness the Essenes launched sharp attacks on the temple priesthood. And the Pharisees sharply separated themselves not only from Gentiles but from those called "sinners" in the New Testament — those engaged in unsavory and unacceptable occupations. These were counted by the Pharisees as Gentiles, no longer members of the holy people. To a greater or lesser extent the Pharisees also separated themselves from those of the common people who did not follow their own stringent purity regulations.

Within this maelstrom of holiness movements aimed at renewal and resistance, Jesus initiated another renewal movement. But the essence of the Jesus movement, on Borg's interpretation, was a new and different vision of what Israel was to be — a new paradigm and not just a new strategy for attaining the old paradigm. Jesus, says Borg, "challenged the quest for holiness and replaced it with an alternative vision" (p. 75). We are indeed to reflect God. But instead of trying to be holy as God is holy, we are to be merciful as our Father in heaven is merciful (Luke 6:36). "Where Judaism spoke of holiness as the paradigm for the community's life Jesus spoke of mercy," says Borg, And he adds that "This conclusion is supported by the near silence of the synoptic tradition in applying the term 'holy' to God or the community" (p. 128). Whereas those engaged in the pursuit of holiness were concerned to separate themselves from external sources of defilement, Jesus says by contrast, "There is nothing outside of a man which by going into him can defile him" (p. 98).

What is it that Jesus meant by mercy? One of many clues is to be found in the passage immediately preceding Luke's report of Jesus' injunction, "Be merciful even as your Father is merciful." There we read that "God makes his sun rise on the evil and on the good, and sends rain on the just and the unjust." The thought is clear: The mercy of God is an *inclusive* mercy embracing the evil and unjust along with the good and the just (p. 128).

Borg proceeds, within this general perspective, to interpret a good many of the incidents in Jesus' life and to exegete a good many of the parables. It is my own experience that over and over his approach proves illuminating. We come to understand why Jesus had dinner with tax collectors and sinners. And we come to understand the extreme annoyance of the Pharisees over this practice. These people were the very paradigm of the unclean, contact with whom defiled one. The angry accusations of the Pharisees evoked many responses from Jesus. His response, as recorded in Luke, included three great parables — the parable of searching for the lost sheep, the parable of searching for the lost coin, and the parable of receiving back the lost son who had defiled himself to the extent of herding swine for a Gentile. In each case the point was the same: rejoice over the one brought in.

Borg summarizes his argument as follows:

> Jesus' understanding of God as merciful and of the norm for Israel's development as mercifulness account for his opposition to the quest for holiness. The shift in paradigm was directly responsible for . . . two highly specific yet centrally important applications . . . : table-fellowship with the outcasts, and love of enemies. The first was possible because God was merciful — that is, forgiving, accepting, nourishing of righteous and sinner alike; because God accepted such as these, God's children — Israel — were to do so as well. For Israel's internal life, this understanding pointed toward greater inclusiveness, toward an overcoming of the "intra-cultural segregation" which increasingly marked her life. The second was possible and necessary for the same reason, but with primary implications for Israel's "external" life, her relationship to Rome. To be merciful meant to eschew the path of violence. (p. 137)

But is it true that we find in Jesus "opposition to the quest for holiness"? Granted that Jesus was opposed to the *Pharisees'* search for holiness. And granted that he speaks hardly at all of God's holiness, speaking instead of God's mercy, love, and compassion. Nonetheless, it would be extraordinary if he who taught us to pray, "Our Father who art in heaven, hallowed be thy name," meant to repudiate all concern with holiness. Furthermore, what Jesus over and over insists on in his polemics with the Pharisees is not that we repudiate the Torah but that we rightly appropriate it. A right appropriation requires penetrating to its essence. It would be remarkable if Jesus thought that the Torah, in its essence, had nothing to do with the holiness of God. "Woe to you, scribes and Pharisees, hypocrites!" Jesus is re-corded in Matthew (23:23) as saying, "for you tithe mint and dill and cummin, and have neglected the weightier matters of the law, justice and mercy and faith . . ." (cf. Luke 11:42). Borg's comment on this passage seems to me correct:

> To the extent that the imitation of God as holy led to this meticu-lous concern to the neglect of the weightier matters of Torah, holi-ness was inappropriate as the dominant model for Israel's self-understanding and understanding of God. Instead such emphasis was subordinated to a concern pointing to the different dominant paradigms designated by the terms justice, mercy, and faithfulness. These, like holiness, were all characteristics of God and should on an imitatio dei model be characteristic of the community which would be faithful to Yahweh. (p. 102)

What we find in Jesus, so it seems to me, is not the repudiation of holi-ness but a radically new understanding of how we are to reflect God's holi-ness. In Jesus we find, if you will, a new hermeneutic of Torah's concern with holiness. The holiness of the community is not to be located in which animals it eats and avoids eating, in whether it does or does not tolerate in-complete projects in its army camps, in how it handles those who have bodily issues, in how it classifies the plant and animal kingdoms. The holi-ness of a community resides centrally in how it treats human beings, both those who are members of the community and those outside, even those outside who are "enemies." Specifically, the holiness of a community does not consist in its whole members avoiding contact with those who are blemished and diseased, broken and wayward. There is none who is truly whole. It consists in the members of the community embracing the broken ones, working and praying for their healing. It consists in having dinner with prostitutes, traitors, and paupers. It consists in healing the blind, the lame, and the leprous. We learn from Jesus that the community that shuns the broken ones can never be a whole community — that is, can never be a *holy* community. The holy community is the merciful community, the just community.

The Pharisees regarded their table fellowship as a little temple. Per-haps Jesus understood his own table fellowship in the same way. Of course it was a radically different kind of fellowship that he instituted — a radi-cally inclusive one, an accepting fellowship instead of a rejecting one, a fellowship of justice and mercy. For Jesus understood differently how we are to become a holy community. At this table/temple fellowship of Jesus, "the poor and maimed, the blind and lame" are present. In any case, Paul understood the new community that Jesus instituted as a new sort of temple — Paul of course being the former Saul the Pharisee. Twice over he uses the temple metaphor in speaking to his readers of the church — in 1 Corinthians 3:16-17 and in Ephesians 2:19-22. Especially the latter passage sounds the theme of inclusiveness:

> So then you are no longer strangers and sojourners, but you are fellow citizens with the saints and members of the houschold of God, built upon the foundation of the apostles and prophets, Christ Jesus himself being the cornerstone, in whom the whole structure is joined together and grows into a holy temple in the Lord.

"Holy things for the holy," says the Orthodox priest as he raises the bread before the people. And the people answer, "One only is holy, one only is Lord, Jesus Christ, to the glory of God the Father." Jesus does not repudiate such language. Instead he offers us a new understanding of how we are to respond to God's holiness and how we are to reflect it.

God's holiness is God's wholeness — God's awesome wholeness. Face to face with that wholeness, we feel acutely our own sinfulness and brokenness. "Woe is me! For I am lost; for I am a person of unclean lips, and I dwell in the midst of a people of unclean lips; for my eyes have seen the King, the Lord of hosts!" In the tension of the contrast between God's awesome wholeness and our own tragic brokenness, we discern God's forgiving judgment and God's lament. And so, instead of cringing in terror, we in thankful confidence join in the heavenly hymn, "Holy, holy, holy, is the Lord God of hosts."

But God asks us for more than liturgical acknowledgment of God's holiness. God asks that we, in our communities, reflect God's holiness, God's wholeness. Jesus, the Son of the Father, showed us what it is to do that. It is to befriend the broken ones and work for their healing. It is to struggle for justice — for the day when all those on the margins have been given place and voice in the community and when the enemy has been befriended.

Holiness joins liturgy and justice. In the liturgy we hymn God's holiness. In lives of justice and mercy we reflect God's holiness. In the liturgy we voice our acknowledgment of God's holiness. In the struggle for justice we embody that acknowledgment.

If God Is Good and Sovereign, Why Lament?

Praise and lament — two components of the Christian life. There are more, of course, many more. Repentance, for example. But at least these two: praise and lament.

Or is that true? Are both of these *really* parts of the Christian life? No one doubts that praise of God is part of the Christian life. There may be times in our lives when we find it difficult to praise God, yet no believer doubts that praise is a component within the well-formed Christian life. But what about lament?

No doubt most Christians, if asked, would *say* that lament is part of the well-formed Christian life. We all know that there are laments in the Psalms; we all sing them, or participate in their reading. So it would not feel right to say, flat out, that lament has no place in the Christian life. But it's open to question whether we all really believe it. The "victorious living" mentality currently sweeping through American Christianity has no place for lament. Likewise the megachurches have no place for it. Lament does not market well. If one goes beyond the words and looks at contemporary American Christianity as it actually exists — looks at how it lives its life and expresses its faith — one comes to the conclusion that most of it does not believe that lament is part of the Christian life. This is in spite of what it may think is the catechetically correct answer to give if directly asked whether it is.

What Is Lament?

We must start by considering what lament is. I shall take the biblical laments, particularly the laments of the Psalms, as my paradigms. Psalm 22 is a particularly good example, since all the basic elements are present there; some of the other lament psalms are truncated.

The lament, at its heart, *is giving voice to the suffering* that accompanies deep loss, whatever that loss may be. Lament is not *about* suffering. Lament is not *concerning* suffering. Lament does not count the stages and try to identify the stage in which one finds oneself. Lament is the *bringing to speech* of suffering, the *languaging* of suffering, the *voicing* of suffering. Behind lament are tears over loss. Lament goes beyond the tears to voicing the suffering.

To voice suffering, one must name it — identify it. Sometimes that is difficult, even impossible. The memories are repressed so that the suffering is screened from view. Or one is aware of it, in a way; but naming it, identifying it for what it is, would be too painful, too embarrassing. So, one resists. Then one cannot lament. One suffers without being able to lament. Lament is an achievement.

One must not only name one's suffering if one is to voice it; one must also *own* it. Instead of *disowning* it one has to admit it as part of who one is — a part of one's narrative identity. If someone asks, "Tell me who you are," one says, maybe not immediately but eventually, "I am someone who went through a painful divorce," "I am someone who suffered the loss of a child," "I am someone who was fired after twenty years of faithful work." To disown one's suffering is to try to delete it from one's narrative or prevent it from ever becoming a part — to try to forget it, put it behind one, get on with things. Lament, in requiring that one voice one's suffering, requires that one not only name it but own it. Owning one's suffering is often difficult: it is painful or embarrassing to incorporate one's suffering into one's life story.

Listen now to the psalmist:

> But I am a worm, and no man;
>   scorned by men, and despised by the people.
> All who see me mock at me,
>   they make mouths at me, they wag their heads;
> "He committed his cause to the Lord; let him deliver him,
>   let him rescue him, for he delights in him!"

(Ps. 22:6-8, RSV)

I am poured out like water,
  and all my bones are out of joint;
my heart is like wax,
  it is melted within my breast;
my strength is dried up like a potsherd,
  and my tongue cleaves to my jaws;
  thou dost lay me in the dust of death.

Yea, dogs are round about me;
  a company of evildoers encircle me;
  they have pierced my hands and feet —
I can count all my bones —
  they stare and gloat over me;
they divide my garments among them,
  and for my raiment they cast lots.

(Ps. 22:14-18, RSV)

Lament is more, though, than the voicing of suffering. The mere voicing of one's suffering is complaint, not lament. Lament is a cry to *God*. This presupposes, of course, that lament is the action of a believer. This cry to God has two main components, interconnected, with sometimes the one more prominent, sometimes the other. First, lament is the cry to God for deliverance: "Deliver me, O God, from this suffering." Listen again to the psalmist:

But thou, O LORD, be not far off!
  O my help, hasten to my aid!
Deliver my soul from the sword,
  my life from the power of the dog!
Save me from the mouth of the lion.

(Ps. 22:19-21a, RSV)

Second, lament is the cry to God of "Why?" "Why, O God, is this happening? I don't understand it. Where are you, O God? I cannot discern your hand in this darkness."

My God, my God, why have you forsaken me?
  Why are you so far from helping me, from the words
    of my groaning?

O my God, I cry by day, but you do not answer;
   and by night, but find no rest.

(Ps. 22:1-2, NRSV)

Rouse yourself! Why do you sleep, O LORD?
   Awake! Do not cast us off forever!
Why do you hide your face?
   Why do you forget our affliction and oppression?
For we sink down to the dust;
   our bodies cling to the ground.
Rise up, come to our help.
   Redeem us for the sake of your steadfast love.

(Ps. 44:23-26, NRSV)

Loss, deep loss, is the shattering of meaning. The shattering of meaning at one point in one's life has rippling consequences throughout one's life; one's life as a whole threatens to lose its sense. For the believer, the meaning of life is tied up with her experience and understanding of God. Now, suddenly, there is a rip in her whole fabric of meaning. So the believer cries to God — who else to cry to? — not only for deliverance from suffering but also for deliverance from the threat of meaninglessness. "Why, O God? Why is this happening? What sense does this make? We thought you were good, powerful, and knowledgeable. We thought we understood your ways. But of this, we can make no sense. Why is this happening? Where are you, O God? Why are you absent?"

In the full-fledged lament there is one more component: a *yet*. The *yet* is an expression of the endurance of faith. Or, somewhat more precisely, the *yet* is a praise-full accounting of God's gracious actions in the past — an accounting, thus, of the *grounds of faith*. Yet will I praise you. Sometimes the *yet is* not only retrospective but prospective. Not only *have* I praised you for what *have been* the signs of your goodness; I *will again* praise you for the goodness you *will again* show.

Yet you are holy,
   enthroned on the praises of Israel.
In you our ancestors trusted;
   they trusted, and you delivered them.
To you they cried, and were saved;
   in you they trusted, and were not put to shame.

83

Yet it was you who took me from the womb;
    you kept me safe on my mother's breast.
On you was I cast from my birth,
    and since my mother bore me you have been my God.
Do not be far from me,
    for trouble is near
    and there is no one to help.

(Ps. 22:3-5, 9-11, NRSV)

Calvin's Argument for the Stifling of Lament

If one thinks that any of these components is irrelevant or improper — the voicing of suffering, the cry to God for understanding and deliverance, the expression of the endurance of faith and praise — if one thinks that any of these elements is irrelevant or improper, then one will not lament. One may do something rather like lament. One may pick and choose among the components of lament; but one will not engage in fully formed lament.

I submit that the mainline theology of the Christian church has stifled the lament in just this way; it has told us that one or the other of these components is irrelevant or improper. There are other causes of the stifling of lament. As I indicated earlier, one may be unable or unwilling to voice one's suffering, or the marketplace mentality may invade Christianity and forbid it. However, on this occasion, I will concentrate on the stifling of lament by our theologians.

Some have said that the component of lament that is the cry for deliverance is misguided. Few have been so forthright about this as Rabbi Harold S. Kushner in his popular book, *When Bad Things Happen to Good People.*[1] God couldn't do anything about our suffering even if God wanted to, says Kushner; so crying to God for deliverance makes no sense. One finds the same thesis concerning the impotence of God defended in a great deal of contemporary theology, though never with such panache. God — so it is said — cannot intervene in the causal order. God set our entire cosmos going; and God is capable of undoing the whole thing. But God and the causal order are not of such a sort that God could intervene *within* the causal order.[2]

---

1. Harold S. Kushner, *When Bad Things Happen to Good People* (New York: Schocken Books, 1981).

2. Two examples of this line of thought are the following: John Macquarrie, *Principles*

Before contemporary theology came on the scene, it was much more customary for theologians to question the propriety of one of the other components within lament, or to offer a different ground for questioning the propriety of the cry for deliverance. Augustine, for example, questioned the propriety of giving voice to suffering. In his *Confessions* he recollects the time, before his conversion, when he wept without restraint over the death of his best friend and the time, after his conversion, when, in spite of his attempts at restraint, he wept over the death of his mother. In both cases he says that he is telling us, his readers, about these episodes so as to confess his sin. His grief, he says, was the sign that he had been guilty of too much worldly affection. The things of this world are to be used, not enjoyed. We are to find our enjoyment in God and God alone — and in the prospect of ourselves and our friends and relatives dwelling forever in the presence of God. Grief, though not itself precisely sinful, is the mark, the sign, of a sinful orientation of life. In Augustinian piety, lament is displaced by confession of sin.

More — much more — could be said about Augustine's thought on these matters. But since I have already done that in another place,[3] let me on this occasion develop, in some detail, Calvin's thought, for Calvin was interestingly different from Augustine. Calvin also questions the propriety of one of the components of lament, with the consequence that lament is also stifled in Calvinist piety. But Calvin focuses his objections on a different component of lament from that on which Augustine focused, with the consequence that lament is not displaced in Calvinist piety by confession of sin but by patience. Let's see how his thought goes.

Calvin took sharp exception to the denigration of God's work as creator that he discerned in Augustine—though, no doubt because of his admiration for Augustine, he attributes the view in question not to Augustine but to those he calls "new Stoics." "Among the Christians," he says, "there are also new Stoics, who count it depraved not only to groan and weep but also to be sad and care ridden."[4] On this, they are quite wrong, says Calvin. We are

---

of Christian Theology (New York: Charles Scribner's, 1977); and Langdon Gilkey, "Cosmology, Ontology, and the Travail of Biblical Language," reprinted in *God's Activity in the World: The Contemporary Problem*, ed. Owen C. Thomas (Chico: Scholars Press, 1983).

3. See my essay "Suffering Love," in *Philosophy and the Christian Faith*, ed. Thomas V. Morris (Notre Dame: University of Notre Dame Press, 1988), 196-237.

4. John Calvin, *Institutes of the Christian Religion*, ed. John T. McNeill, trans. Ford Lewis Battles, Library of Christian Classics, vol. 20 (Philadelphia: Westminster, 1960), III, viii, 9.

not to be utterly stupefied and to be deprived of all feeling of pain. [Our ideal] is not [that of what] the Stoics of old foolishly described [as] "the great-souled man"; who, having cast off all human qualities, was affected equally by adversity and prosperity, by sad times and happy ones — nay, who like a stone was not affected at all.[5]

The Stoic ideal paints "a likeness of forbearance that has never been found among men, and can never be realized."[6] For it is contrary to our created nature.

Thus afflicted by disease, we shall both groan and be uneasy and pant after health; thus pressed by poverty, we shall be pricked by the arrows of care and sorrow; thus we shall be smitten by the pain of disgrace, contempt, injustice; thus at the funerals of our dear ones we shall weep the tears that are owed to our nature.[7]

And if there be any doubt that it is indeed our created rather than our fallen nature that comes to expression in our grief, then the example of Jesus is confirmation.

Our Lord and Master has condemned ["this iron philosophy"] not only by his word, but also by his example. For he groaned and wept both over his own and others' misfortunes. And he taught his disciples in the same way: "The world," he says, "will rejoice; but you will be sorrowful and will weep." And that no one might turn it into a vice, he openly proclaimed, "Blessed are those who mourn." No wonder! For if all weeping is condemned, what shall we judge concerning the Lord himself, from whose body tears of blood trickled down? If all fear is branded as unbelief, how shall we account for that dread with which, we read, he was heavily stricken? If all sadness displeases us, how will it please us that he confesses his soul "sorrowful even to death"?[8]

Upon his mother's death, after his conversion, Augustine stifled his sobs,

5. Ibid.
6. Ibid.
7. Ibid., III, viii, 10.
8. Ibid., III, viii, 9.

dissembled to his friends, lost control, chastised himself, confessed to God. That is definitely not the mode of piety that Calvin affirms.

As one would expect, Calvin's attitude toward grief is intertwined with, and supported by, his attitude toward enjoyment of the things of this world. In a remarkable passage[9] he argues that we should appreciate grasses, trees, and fruits not just for their utility in keeping us nourished and warm but for their "comeliness"; and that we should appreciate wine and oil not only because they are useful but because wine gladdens the heart and oil makes the face shine. As if he had his eye on Augustine's use/enjoyment distinction, Calvin asks rhetorically whether God did "not, in short, render many things attractive to us, apart from their necessary use?" So let this "be our principle; that the use of God's gifts is not wrongly directed when it is referred to that end to which the Author himself created and destined them for us, since he created them for our good, not for our ruin."

The underlying point is this. Augustine saw the things of the world primarily as the *works of* God; he urges us to look away from them to their maker. They are to be regarded and received as useful only for our continued existence and for our approach to God. Pervasive in Calvin, by contrast, is the insistence that we are to see the things of this world not only as the *works* of *God* but also as the *gifts* of God, gifts not only for utility but for delight. "This life, however crammed with infinite miseries it may be, is still rightly to be counted among those blessings of God which are not to be spurned. Therefore, if we recognize in it no divine benefit, we are already guilty of grave ingratitude toward God himself."[10]

One cannot overemphasize the pervasiveness in Calvin of this theme of the world as God's gift to us for our use and delight and the counterpart theme of the propriety of gratitude. Never has there been a theologian more imbued with the sense that in cosmos, history, society, and self we meet God — more specifically, God's goodness. "Away, then, with that inhuman philosophy which, while conceding only a necessary use of creatures, not only malignantly deprives us of the lawful fruit of God's beneficence but cannot be practiced unless it robs a man of all his senses and degrades him to a block."[11]

So far, so good. But let us dig deeper. We must bear our grief and suf-

---

9. Ibid., III, x, 2.
10. Ibid., III, ix, 3.
11. Ibid., III, x, 3.

fering with patience, says Calvin. Immediately after the passage quoted above about weeping at funerals, Calvin says that he

> decided to say this in order to recall godly minds from despair, lest, because they cannot cast off the natural feeling of sorrow, they forthwith renounce the pursuit of patience. This must necessarily happen to those who make patience into insensibility, and a valiant and constant man into a stock. For Scripture praises the saints for their forbearance when, so afflicted with harsh misfortune, they do not break or fall; so stabbed with bitterness, they are at the same time flooded with spiritual joy; so pressed by apprehension, they recover their breath, revived by God's consolation. In the meantime, their hearts still harbor a contradiction between their natural sense, which flees and dreads what it feels adverse to itself, and their disposition to godliness, which even through these difficulties presses toward obedience to the divine will.[12]

What did Calvin mean by *patience* and why did he recommend it? The clue is contained in the following passage. This "general axiom is to be maintained, that all the sufferings to which human life is subject and liable are necessary exercises by which God partly invites us to repentance, partly instructs us in humility, and partly renders us more cautious and more attentive in guarding against the allurements of sin for the future."[13] God is the ultimate agent of our suffering and grief. It is for our good that God causes us to suffer; suffering in general, and grief in particular, are to be interpreted as manifestations of the goodness of God. The world is, as it were, a vast reformatory. That is why we are not to follow the "new Stoics," trying to violate our nature by becoming numb. If the prisoner is allowed opium, incarceration loses its unpleasantness and reformation does not result.

God's attempt to reform us by sending us suffering presupposes the presence in us of a nature that finds certain things painful. When we first heard Calvin speak, it sounded as if he was saying that grief over the death of someone one loves is the response of our created nature to the death of those we love. That note is not entirely missing from Calvin. But it is not

---

12. Ibid., III, viii, 10.

13. John Calvin, *Commentaries on the First Book of Moses Called Genesis,* vol. 1, trans. John King (Grand Rapids: Baker, 1979), p. 179.

the dominant note. The dominant note is that grief and suffering are manifestations of God's gracious attempt to reform us.

The appropriate attitude then is patience, forbearance, even gratitude. "But, if it be clear that our afflictions are for our benefit, why should we not undergo them with a thankful and quiet mind?"[14]

> Yet such a cheerfulness is not required of us as to remove all feeling of bitterness and pain. If there were no hardness in poverty, no torment in diseases, no sting in disgrace, no dread in death — what fortitude or moderation would there be in bearing them with indifference? But since each of these, with an inborn bitterness, by its very nature bites the hearts of us all, the fortitude of the believing man is brought to light if, tried by the feeling of such bitterness, however grievously he is troubled with it, yet valiantly resisting, he surmounts it.[15]

> Therefore in patiently suffering these tribulations, we do not yield to necessity but we consent for our own good. These thoughts, I say, bring it to pass that, however much in bearing the cross our minds are constrained by the natural feeling of bitterness, they are as much diffused with spiritual joy.[16]

We are to interpret our sufferings as God's instrument for reforming our souls until they are fit for fellowship with God. Accordingly, we are to discipline ourselves to endure those sufferings with patience, even with gratitude.

Calvin's piety of suffering is now clear. We are indeed to voice our suffering, to speak it — thus, to name it and own it. But are we to cry out for deliverance? That's not clear; if something is for my good but unpleasant, do I ask to be delivered from it? What is abundantly clear is that one does not cry out *Why?* Because we know why. Suffering is sent by God for our good. There is no mystery. God is neither absent nor are God's ways in these matters mysterious.

14. Calvin, *Institutes*, III, viii, 11.
15. Ibid., III, viii, 8.
16. Ibid., III, viii, 11.

A Theology for Lament

I suggested that lament does not market well and that, given the marketplace character of American religion, one must expect that its place in American religion will be at best peripheral. I also suggested that the voicing of suffering that lament incorporates is sometimes impossible and often painful. Nevertheless, we would be most imperceptive if we thought that those factors are alone in accounting for the near absence of lament among us. As we have seen, the theologians of the Christian tradition have called lament into question. Some, like Augustine, thought it wrong to voice suffering — unless one does so in the context of confession of sin. Others, such as Langdon Gilkey and John Macquarrie, argue that it is misguided to cry to God for deliverance since God cannot intervene in the causal order. Yet others, like Calvin, argue that it is misguided to cry out *Why?* since we know why. These are, of course, just a small handful of theologians; but they are representative.

We must choose, then, between the massive weight of our theological traditions, on the one hand, and following the psalmist and permitting ourselves to lament, on the other. Should we decide to choose against the tradition, our doing so must not be quick or glib. Augustine, Aquinas, Calvin, and Schleiermacher were genius theologians. We must realize what we are doing when we make the choice; we must be aware of the consequences. But as for me, I choose for lament.

In so doing I have on my side the biblical examples. But it would be a mistake to take the biblical examples of lament as a brute feature of the biblical literature — inexplicable but there. Behind and beneath the lament, giving intelligibility to the lament, is a principle that runs throughout the biblical witness. I shall call it, the *each and every principle.* God desires that each and every human being flourish as an animalic person until full of years, and God desires of you and me that we desire that end for ourselves and for our fellow human beings as well. It is because almost all of our theologians and philosophers, in one way or another, reject this principle, that they have stifled the lament.

Each and every. When the writer of the opening chapter of Genesis speaks of God as pronouncing benediction over the animals, it is appropriate to understand this as a generic benediction. May you, the lions, flourish. May you, the robins, flourish. And so forth. If all we had to go on was that opening chapter of Genesis, then it would be plausible to understand the benediction that God pronounces over humanity in the same way. But as Scripture proceeds it becomes abundantly clear that that is not the way God's benediction over humanity is to be understood. Of course there is a generic dimension to the benediction, "Be fruitful and multiply." But God's desire is also that each and every one of us should flourish. God is not satisfied when ninety-nine of the one hundred are safely in the corral; God goes out to look for the hundredth one. That, surely, is the point of the prophetic focus on the widows, the orphans, the aliens, and the poor, and on Jesus' healing of cripples and his enjoying the sanctity of meals with the unsavory and ritually unclean members of his society. May each and every one of you flourish — that is the divine benediction of which you and I are recipients.

Flourish as animalic persons. At creation, God performed that strange work, that experiment, as it were, of blending into one being the animalic and the angelic so that we human beings are both persons and animals, both animals and persons — animalic persons, personic animals. God did it intentionally of course. And God beheld what God had made, and saw that it was very good. The shalom that God desires for us is shalom within our creaturely condition and circumstance.

Flourish until full of years. We human beings have a design plan. According to that plan, we slowly age; then, when full of years at around threescore years and ten, or by virtue of strength, four score years, we die. That is built into our design plan as personic *animals*. God does not desire, and takes no delight in, early death; God desires that we shall live until full of years.

To put it all together once again: God desires that each and every one of us should flourish until full of years as animalic persons — personic animals. God desires that you and I should desire the same end. Thus it is that from the seedbed of Christianity have emerged medical science, technology, advanced learning, and art. It would be strange indeed if God asked of you and me that we promote medical science so as to extend life, and promote technology, art, and learning so as to enhance human flourishing, while God remains indifferent to whether or not we flourish until full of years.

But something has gone terribly awry with respect to this desire of God. We do not know why. What we know is only that God, out of love for the creature, has committed Godself to undo the ravages and calls on you and me to join in that struggle. Some philosophers and theologians, including Christian philosophers and theologians, have argued that nothing at all has gone awry; everything is going just exactly as God wants it to go.

Others have offered explanations for why it is that not everything is going as God desires it should go. Though I cannot argue the case here, I regard all strategies of both sorts as failures — at bottom because each, so far as I can tell, violates that *each and every principle* that I take to legitimate the psalmic laments and to be a deep strand in biblical teaching.

Consider Augustine. Augustine does not agree that God desires that we flourish in this animal existence of ours, finding delight and fulfillment therein. He enjoins us to turn away from this earthly existence toward the eternal. Thus lament is stifled. Consider Calvin. Calvin concedes the propriety of finding delight and fulfillment in this earthly existence of ours. But he says that the suffering that comes our way is for our good and that we must, accordingly, endure it with grateful patience. Thus lament is stifled anew. Speaking personally, it is Calvin's view that I am to endure with grateful patience the suffering that I experience on account of the early death of my son. My reply to Calvin is a question: "What about my son? Perhaps my suffering over his death does make me a better person. But what about the benediction God pronounced over my son that he would flourish until full of years?" Should Calvin reply, "But he's better off now," I answer, "It was over our earthly existence as animalic persons that God pronounced the benediction. The shalom that God desires for us is embodied shalom."

So I join the psalmist in lament. I voice my suffering, naming it and owning it. I cry out. I cry out for deliverance: "Deliver me, O God, from this suffering. Restore me, and make me whole." I cry out for explanation, for I no more know in general why things have gone awry with respect to God's desire than did the psalmist. "Why, O God, is this happening? Why is your desire, that each and every one of us should flourish here on earth until full of years, being frustrated? It makes no sense." To lament is to risk living with one's deepest questions unanswered.

The cry occurs within the context of the *yet* of enduring faith and ongoing praise, for in raising Christ from the dead, we have God's word and deed that God will be victorious in the struggle against all that frustrates God's desire. Thus divine sovereignty is not sacrificed but reconceived. If lament is indeed a legitimate component of the Christian life, then divine sovereignty is not to be understood as everything happening just as God wants it to happen — or happening in such a way that God regards what God does not like as an acceptable trade-off for the good thereby achieved. Divine sovereignty consists in God's winning the battle against all that has gone awry with respect to God's will.

Part Two

JUSTICE

Why Care about Justice?

D o the doing of justice and the struggle to undo injustice belong to Christian piety? Are they components of Christian spirituality? I am not asking here whether the Christian shares in some general human obligation to act justly and to work for the alleviation of injustice. I mean to ask whether the failure to act justly and the failure to support the struggle to undo injustice are marks of defective *Christian* piety. I mean to ask whether doing justice and struggling to undo injustice are motivated and required by the wellsprings of *Christian* life and action.

To almost all of us who ally ourselves with the Christian church, this is a most unfamiliar question. If we were reared in the Orthodox or Catholic traditions, we will have been taught to think that the specially pious person is the one who participates in the liturgy with regularity and fidelity. If we were reared in the Anglo-American evangelical tradition, we will have been taught to think that the specially pious person is the one who reads her Bible faithfully, engages much in personal prayer, and openly and freely speaks of Jesus Christ and what he means to her. If we were reared in the Reformed tradition, we will have been taught to think that the specially pious person is the one who regularly attends church and faithfully seeks to serve the Lord in his daily work and life. If we were reared in certain branches of the Anabaptist tradition, we will have been taught to think that the specially pious person is the one who in charity ministers to the poor of the world. None of us will have been taught to think that piety calls for justice. Perhaps something else does, but not spirituality.

Now I firmly believe that authentic Christian piety includes participation in the liturgy, includes drinking from the wells of Scripture, includes personal prayer, includes giving the testimony of a witness, includes endeavoring to transmute one's daily work into obedient service, includes extending the hand of charity. But does it also include doing justice and struggling to undo injustice? To answer this question it would be relevant to consider the witness of the Christian tradition. In this article, however, I shall limit myself to reflecting on the witness of Scripture.

Over and over the Old Testament confronts us with the declaration that God loves justice. To read Isaiah 61 is to hear God saying, "I the LORD love justice" (v. 8). To join Israel and the church in taking on one's own lips the words of Psalm 37 is to find oneself saying that "the LORD loves justice" (v. 28). And these are but two examples from a multitude.

Furthermore, God's love for justice is declared to be an active love: God *does* justice. "The LORD works vindication and justice for all who are oppressed" we sing when we bless the Lord with the words of Psalm 103 (v. 6). And when we cry for deliverance with the words of Psalm 140 we say,

> I know that the LORD maintains the cause of the afflicted,
>> and executes justice for the needy.
>
> (v. 12)

But why does God love justice? Into what larger pattern does God's love of justice fit? An ancient, enduring, and prominent strand of Christian theology sees God's love of justice as grounded in God's anger with those who disobey God's commands. God's love and practice of justice are God's love and practice of *retributive* justice. But I think it starkly clear that the passages which speak of God's love of justice are not pointing to God's delight over the writhings of those who are justly punished; God has no such delight. God's love for justice is grounded in God's love for the victims of injustice. And God's love for the victims of injustice belongs to God's love for the little ones of the world: for the weak, defenseless ones, the ones at the bottom, the excluded ones, the miscasts, the outcasts, the outsiders. It is true, indeed, that God is angry and disgusted over what happens in human affairs; but in good measure God's anger and disgust are with those who violate and frustrate God's love for the little ones of the world by victimizing rather than protecting them. God is the one

> who executes justice for the oppressed;
>> who gives food to the hungry.

The LORD sets the prisoners free;
   the LORD opens the eyes of the blind.
The LORD lifts up those who are bowed down;
   the LORD loves the righteous.
The LORD watches over the sojourners,
   he upholds the widow and the fatherless;
but the way of the wicked he brings to ruin.

(Psalm 146)

God's love for justice, I suggest, is grounded in God's special concern for the hundredth one.

The LORD maintains the cause of the afflicted,
   and executes justice for the needy.

(Psalm 140:12)

Why is that? What is the connection between love for justice and love for the little ones of the world? What is the connection between hatred of injustice and disgust with those who violate one's love for the weak ones? Well, justice is present in society when people receive or enjoy the goods that are due them. Or to put it from the other side, focusing more on distributive than on retributive justice: Justice is present in society when people enjoy those goods to which they have a rightful claim: protection against assault, freedom to worship as they see fit, sufficient food to live and work, etc. Now the strong and powerful ones in a society will generally be able to secure such goods on their own. Hence to find out whether a society is just, one must look not at the powerful but at the weak: Do the practices, laws, and institutions of the society secure *to them* the enjoyment of the relevant goods? The test is not whether the economically powerful have enough to eat — they almost always do; but whether the economically *powerless* have enough. Justice is society's charter of protection of its little ones. That is why the biblical writers, when speaking about justice and injustice, always point to the aliens and the widows and the orphans. The Lord God, says Moses in his farewell speech to his people, "executes justice for the fatherless and the widow, and loves the sojourner, giving him food and clothing" (Deut. 10:18).

A long tradition of Christian reflection grounds the claims of justice in respect for the image of God which is present in every human being. I heartily agree that such respect requires doing justice. But that line of thought is at best implicit in the biblical writers. For the most part they see God's love of justice as part and parcel of God's special concern for the weak ones.

Father of the fatherless and protector of widows
    is God in his holy habitation.
God gives the desolate a home to dwell in;
    he leads out the prisoners to prosperity.

(Psalm 68:5-6)

Who is like the LORD our God,
    who is seated on high,
who looks far down
    upon the heavens and the earth?
He raises the poor from the dust,
    and lifts the needy from the ash heap,
to make them sit with princes,
    with the princes of his people.
He gives the barren woman a home,
    making her the joyous mother of children.

(Psalm 113:5-9)

Recent discussions in various North American periodicals make it abundantly clear that we who are well-to-do members of the core of our present world-system do not like this message. We are offended by this declaration of God's special concern for the hundredth one. We are disgusted by this picture of God as searching the highways and byways of our world for the ones who are still outside. Does God not love the rich ones, the believing ones, the athletic ones, the ones with 20/20 vision, as much as God loves the poor, the unbelieving, the lame, the blind? Does God not love the ninety and nine as much as the hundredth? Or if we do not seem to be getting anywhere with that line, we try the opposite tack: Are *we* not all poor, all unbelieving, all lame, all blind? Are not all one hundred of us outsiders, hence all equally the subjects of God's love?

Of course it is true that God loves every human being. God loved the whole wide world so much and in such a way as to deliver up his own Son to suffering and to disgusting execution. And of course it is true that God delights in the righteous. But whoever affirms the teaching of the Scriptures will have to interpret God's universal love and God's delight in righteousness in such a way as to be compatible with God's special love for the outsider.

How can that be done? Perhaps along the following lines. God's love includes God's universal beneficence: God's desire for the flourishing of each of God's human creatures. But God's love also includes God's suffering over the suffering and waywardness of God's children. God is pained by the sight of those who suffer malnutrition and starvation. God is pained by the suffering of those whose neck is under the oppressor's boot. God is pained by the suffering of aliens and orphans and widows deprived of protection by law. God is pained by the suffering of the psalmist surrounded by backbiting critics. When these suffering people address their lament to God, they strike in God a responsive chord. God's love for the victims of our world is God's suffering love. It is in that love that God's love of justice is grounded. The tears of God are the soil in which God's love of justice is rooted.

What the secularist sees merely as good things coming his way, the believer sees as gifts from God. What the secularist sees merely as a stupendously intricate world, the believer sees as a glorious work of God. What the secularist sees merely as wrongdoing, the believer sees as sin. So too, what the secularist sees merely as justice, the believer sees as giving God joy. And what the secularist sees merely as injustice, the believer sees as making God suffer. For the believer, justice and injustice are sacramental realities. God loves the ninety and nine along with the one; but God suffers over the plight of that one.

Yet it is also true that God's suffering love for the one is the other side of God's longing for the flourishing of all one hundred. It is the other side of God's longing for the shalom of all God's human creatures. An ever-beckoning temptation for the Anglo-American evangelical is to assume that all God really cares about for God's human creatures here on earth is that they are born again and thus destined for salvation — to assume that the only kind of lostness God cares about is religious lost-ness. On this view, God leaves the ninety and nine and goes out in search of that one who is not a believer; but God does not go out in search of the one who is poor, does not go looking for the one who is oppressed. But if we understand the shalom for which God longs in this narrow, pinched way, then all those biblical passages about God's love for justice must remain closed books to us.

What God desires for God's human creatures is that comprehensive mode of flourishing that is shalom. Shalom includes religious reconciliation; but it includes vastly more as well. Insofar as someone is suffering injustice, just insofar one of the goods to which that person has title, a good essential to her flourishing, is not being enjoyed by her. God's love of justice is grounded in God's longing for the shalom of God's creatures and in God's sorrow over its absence. The contours of shalom can be discerned from the contours of the laments to which God gives ear.

I HAVE SPOKEN thus far of God's love of justice and of the grounding of that love in God's suffering love for the little ones of the earth who are deprived of shalom. But of course the biblical writers do not only picture God as lover and practitioner of justice. They also present God as *commanding us* to do justice and as pronouncing judgment on those who do not. "Justice, and only justice, you shall follow," says Moses in that farewell speech to which I have already referred, "that you may live, and inherit the land which the LORD your God gives you" (Deut. 16:20). The command is intensified in the prophets. In a passage from Amos which by now has entered deep into the consciousness of humanity (5:21-24) God says,

> I hate, I despise your feasts,
>> and I take no delight in your solemn assemblies.
> Even though you offer me your burnt offerings and cereal offerings,
>> I will not accept them,
> and the peace offerings of your fatted beasts
>> I will not look upon.
> Take away from me the noise of your songs;
>> to the melody of your harps I will not listen.
> But let justice roll down like waters,
>> and righteousness like an ever-flowing stream.

The same command to do justice occurs in an equally well-known passage from Micah. The passage opens with intense poignancy as God expresses pained lament to Israel — not now humanity lamenting to God but God lamenting to humanity:

> O my people, what have I done to you?
>> In what have I wearied you?
>> Answer me.
> For I brought you up from the land of Egypt,
>> and redeemed you from the house of bondage.

The prophet then imagines someone, stung by this divine lament, asking what would please God and ease God's sorrow:

With what shall I come before the LORD,
   and bow myself before God on high?
Shall I come before him with burnt offerings,
   with calves a year old?
Will the LORD be pleased with thousands of rams,
   with ten thousands of rivers of oil?

We all know the prophet's answer:

He has showed you, O man, what is good;
   and what does the LORD require of you
but to do justice, and to love kindness,
   and to walk humbly with your God?

(Micah 6:1-8)

Given our discussion of God's love of justice and the place of that love in God's character, it is now no mystery why God commands us to practice justice and to struggle against injustice. Only if we purge our societies of injustice will God's suffering love for the victims of the world be relieved. The believer's doing of justice is grounded in her desire to answer the lament of God and relieve the divine suffering. It is grounded in her own suffering love of God.

But perhaps we should see more behind the command than this. The command to do and struggle for justice is also the command to imitate God, to image God. As God is just, so are we to be just. We are to be icons of God, imaging God's justice in our justice. Again the farewell speech of Moses makes the point: God "executes justice for the fatherless and the widow, and loves the sojourner, giving him food and clothing. Love the sojourner therefore; for you were sojourners in the land of Egypt" (Deut. 10:18-19). "You shall not pervert the justice due to the sojourner or to the fatherless, or take a widow's garment in pledge; but you shall remember that you were a slave in Egypt and the LORD your God redeemed you from there; therefore I command you to do this" (Deut. 24:17-18). As God has heard our laments and satisfied our longings, so we are to hear the laments of the poor among us, the weak and oppressed.

Perhaps this theme of the doing of justice as grounded in the imitation of God — of the doing of justice as *constituting our imaging* rather than just *manifesting our respect* for the image — opens up yet another dimension of our topic. Several times over in his farewell address Moses says to his people that they are a people holy to the Lord their God, for God has chosen them to be a people for his own possession (7:6; 14:2, 21; 26:19). It is in this context that all the regulations of Deuteronomy are set: the regulations concerning clean and unclean animals, the regulations concerning the cleanness and uncleanness of persons, the regulations concerning the dismissal of those soldiers from battle who have large unfinished projects back home, the proscriptions against idolatry and various forms of immorality, the regulations insuring that the sacrificial animals will be unblemished, the regulations whereby the community is to purge itself — and the regulations concerning justice. Holiness was not only set-apartness; holiness was also unity, purity, completeness, perfection. And the idea behind the Mosaic legislation seems to have been that Israel's being holy to God is as much task as status. Israel is to *become* holy and to *institute* in its life memorial remembrances of God's holiness. Its life is to become unified, pure, complete, and perfect like unto God's; and it is to incorporate quasi-liturgical memorials of God's holiness. In its life it is to imitate and celebrate the holiness of God. And for that, it must do justice.

The implications relevant to our concerns here are clear: there is something of the unholy about injustice. Injustice is a form of desecration. The call to justice is grounded in the call to be holy even as God is holy. Justice is sacral. It is no wonder, then, that Deuteronomy and the prophets move so fluidly back and forth between condemnations of idolatry, of immorality, and of injustice. All are desecrations.

> Thus says the LORD:
> "For three transgressions of Israel,
>   and for four, I will not revoke the punishment;
> because they sell the righteous for silver,
>   and the needy for a pair of shoes —
> they that trample the head of the poor into the dust of the earth,
>   and turn aside the way of the afflicted;
> a man and his father go in to the same maiden,
>   so that my holy name is profaned;
> they lay themselves down beside every altar,
>   upon garments taken in pledge;
> and in the house of God they drink
>   the wine of those who have been fined.
>   (Amos 2:6-8)

In summary of what we have seen thus far: The believer's doing of justice and struggling for the undoing of injustice is motivated by his desire to imitate God and obey God's command. In turn, God's command to do justice is grounded in God's suffering love for the little ones of the world and in God's longing to have a people which reflects and celebrates his own holiness. Hence the believer's doing of justice and struggling for the undoing of injustice is also motivated by his sharing in God's suffering love for the little ones of the world and by the desire to be holy even as God is holy.

ALL THAT I HAVE SAID so far has been based exclusively on the Old Testament. I have delineated the place of justice in Old Testament piety. I have avoided mingling New with Old Testament evidence; and I have done so in order to be able to address myself to that large group in the evangelical community who insist that the propriety of such piety has passed away. New Testament piety, they say, in contrast to Old, does not include to any significant degree the doing of justice and the struggle for the undoing of injustice here in this present age. It's true that God's heart goes out to the weak ones of the world; it's true that God longs for shalom; it's true that God longs for a community to reflect and celebrate God's holiness. But God does not command you and me to fulfill these divine longings by struggling for justice. Justice and injustice pertain to social structures and practices. The New Testament does not tell us to go out and try to reform society. It tells us, to the contrary, that the struggle for such reform is always futile. It tells us that this present evil world is hopeless, that it must and will pass away. We are to fasten our hearts in hope and prayer on the coming of the New Jerusalem. In the New Jerusalem there will be justice, there will be shalom, there will be holiness. But for that city we do not work. We wait. God and God alone will bring it about. The fundamental posture of the Christian in the world is hopeful, patient, suffering waiting, coupled with witnessing to the worth of such waiting.

> The creation waits with eager longing for the revealing of the sons of God; for the creation was subjected to futility, not of its own will but by the will of him who subjected it in hope; because the creation itself will be set free from its bondage to decay and obtain the glorious liberty of the children of God. We know that the whole creation has been groaning in travail together until now; and not only the creation, but we ourselves, who have the first fruits of the Spirit, groan inwardly as we wait for adoption as sons, the redemp-

tion of our bodies. For in this hope we were saved. Now hope that is seen is not hope. For who hopes for what he sees? But if we hope for what we do not see, we wait for it with patience. (Romans 8:19-25)

There can be no doubt that expectant waiting is indeed a fundamental component of New Testament spirituality. But that scarcely settles the issue before us. The issue is rather of the *form* that our waiting is to take. Are we to resign ourselves to the injustice of the world while patiently waiting for the coming of God's Reign to sweep it all away; or are we to struggle for its alleviation while patiently waiting for the coming of God's Reign to bring our efforts to fruition? Are we to tolerate our human injustice while waiting for God's justice, or are we to await God's justice as the fruition of our struggle against human injustice? Are we to await the fulfillment of our social endeavors as well as of our social hopes; or are we to await only the fulfillment of our social hopes?

The issues here are so deep that I cannot possibly discuss them in adequate detail. Let me confine myself to what usually proves to be the central issue: Did Jesus teach that the holy, just, and peaceful Reign of God which the prophets foretold and for which Israel was commanded to work is to remain unseen until the coming of the New Jerusalem, or did he teach that already in his work that holy, just, and peaceful Reign was breaking in? No Christian denies that God will bring about that prophetic vision of the just and holy shalom. But do we await its implementation while enduring its absence, or do we await its completion while discerning its coming?

After John the Baptist was arrested, says Mark in his Gospel, "Jesus came into Galilee, preaching the gospel of God, and saying, "The time is fulfilled, and the kingdom of God is at hand; repent, and believe in the gospel."" Matthew records the same events: Jesus, after hearing that John had been arrested, "began to preach, saying, 'Repent, for the kingdom of heaven is at hand.'" But Matthew adds an important detail to his narration. After hearing of John's arrest, and before beginning to preach, Jesus withdrew to Capernaum in the region of Zebulun and Naphtali, so as to fulfill Isaiah's prophecy that:

The land of Zebulun and the land of Naphtali,
toward the sea, across the Jordan,
Galilee of the Gentiles —
the people who sat in darkness
have seen a great light,

and for those who sat in the region and shadow of death
light has dawned.

(Matt. 4:15-16)

Luke's report of the beginning of Jesus' ministry adds yet other details. In the course of his tour through Galilee, Jesus maintained his practice of going to synagogue on the sabbath. One sabbath, upon being handed the book of Isaiah in the synagogue, he read the opening of chapter 61:

The Spirit of the Lord is upon me,
because he has anointed me to preach good news to the poor.
He has sent me to proclaim release to the captives
and recovering of sight to the blind,
to set at liberty those who are oppressed,
to proclaim the acceptable year of the Lord.

(Luke 4:18-19)

He then sat down; and with the gaze of all the worshipers fixed on him, he said, "Today this scripture has been fulfilled in your hearing."

One more specimen of Jesus' self-interpretation of his ministry is important. John, while sitting in prison, began to hear news of the doings of Jesus, the one whom he himself had baptized. These reports led him to turn over in his mind the question whether Jesus was or was not the expected one. So he sent some of his followers to ask Jesus himself the question, "Are you he who is to come, or shall we look for another?" Jesus' answer came in two stages. First, "in that hour he cured many of diseases and plagues and evil spirits, and on many who were blind he bestowed sight." Then, with a clear allusion to Isaiah, he said to John's followers,

Go and tell John what you have seen and heard: the blind receive their sight, the lame walk, lepers are cleansed, and the deaf hear, the dead are raised up, the poor have good news preached to them. And blessed is he who takes no offense at me. (Luke 7:19-23; see also Matt. 11:2-6)

In short, Jesus interpreted his ministry in terms of the messianic expectations of Isaiah; the long-expected Reign of God was, in his person and work, decisively breaking in. Those expectations were expectations for the coming of full-orbed shalom, for the arrival of holiness upon earth. Jesus' ministry was not the ministry of telling us patiently to await the sight of God's shalom; it was the ministry of displaying that shalom by healing those blemishes incompatible with shalom: blindness, lameness, leprosy, hopelessness, onerous religious obligations, social exclusion.

Of course we all know painfully well that the coming of God's Reign was not completed by Jesus and is not yet completed. Jesus did not produce that Reign in its fullness. We have to interpret his work in the light of that fact. The category that John regularly uses in his Gospel is that of *sign;* Jesus performed signs. Traditionally these signs have been interpreted as proofs or evidence: Jesus produced miracles as evidence of his divine authority. But surely if we take seriously those passages to which I have pointed, in which the shalom envisaged in the Old Testament is said to be breaking into our existence in the work of Jesus, then we have to interpret the signs as more than this. What Jesus produced were not in the first place proofs of his divinity but *signs of the Kingdom.* And these signs are *samples.* A sample indicates qualities of the whole cloth from which it is cut. The works of Jesus were cut from the cloth of the Kingdom to which they pointed. In them, shalom was signified by being manifested.

Those who say that we must wait rather than work for justice regularly observe that Jesus did not struggle to change social structures nor explicitly command us to do so. But surely that fact can now be seen to be of no significance. With little imagination we can all think of other aspects of shalom that Jesus did not effect. What matters is that Jesus embraced that entire vision of shalom. He did not exclude from it the references to justice. On the contrary, he said that he had come to proclaim release for the captives and to set at liberty those who are oppressed. What I find painful is that so often those very people who do not work but only wait for justice, on the ground that Jesus neither changed social structures nor explicitly told us to do so, happily send their sons into the armies of the world to defend their own nations. One must ask where Jesus did or commanded any such thing.

What remains to consider is how you and I are to participate in this coming of the Kingdom that Jesus both announced and signified by manifesting. The answer can be approached from many different angles. One of the most important, it seems to me, is from the angle of the New Testament declaration that the church is the body of Christ on earth. Jesus is no longer physically present among us. Yet we are not to think of him as simply absent from earth. The church on earth is to be seen as his body; and in that body his Spirit is present. The conclusion seems unavoidable, that we are to carry on, with such means as are given to us, Jesus' work of proclaiming the coming of the Kingdom and producing samples of its shalom. We are to live with the outcasts, we are to console the brokenhearted, we are to heal the lepers, we are to lift the burdens of legalistic religion, we are to release the captives, we are to liberate the oppressed. And we are to do all these as signs — as *sampling* signs — in lives that are lives of discipleship. Obeying and imitating God now acquires the new quality of following Jesus. While enjoying such bits of health and justice as there are in our world, and struggling for their increase, we are to say to ourselves and to all humanity: Remember, there is more.

I HAVE SAID THAT God's longing for justice and God's practice of justice are grounded in God's love for the little ones of the world; and I have suggested that Christian piety will incorporate the struggle to imitate God and follow Jesus in these respects. Let me close, then, by referring to the picture sketched out in Psalm 72 of the good ruler who imitates God in his justice:

> Give the king thy justice, O God,
>   and thy righteousness to the royal son!
> May he judge thy people with righteousness
>   and thy poor with justice!
>
> Let the mountains bear prosperity for the people,
>   and the hills, in righteousness!
> May he defend the cause of the poor of the people,
>   give deliverance to the needy,
>   and crush the oppressor!
>
> May he live while the sun endures,
>   and as long as the moon,
>   throughout all generations! . . .
> May all kings fall down before him,
>   all nations serve him!
>
> For he delivers the needy when he calls,
>   the poor and him who has no helper.
> He has pity on the weak and the needy,
>   and saves the lives of the needy.
> From oppression and violence he redeems their life;
>   and precious is their blood in his sight.

How painfully different are the present rulers of our world — including those of our own country — from this ruler, whose goodness resides in his justice and whose justice is grounded in suffering love for the weak, the needy, and the oppressed.

For Justice in Shalom

In Chapter II of *Until Justice and Peace Embrace,* I argued that there are two fundamental dynamics shaping the modern world: freedom by mastery and freedom of self-determination. In the light of this, we may perhaps summarize the discussion in the chapters that followed in this way: liberation theology, with its emphasis on salvation, affirms the importance of freedom of self-determination, but never succeeds in incorporating into its vision, in any satisfactory way, freedom by mastery. The Amsterdam school, with its emphasis on creation, affirms the importance of freedom by mastery, but never succeeds in incorporating into its vision, in any satisfactory way, freedom of self-determination. To guide our thoughts, we need some vision yet more comprehensive than either of these. Of course there is no substitute for careful, informed, and specific reflection; but is there some comprehensive vision that can serve to orient those reflections and thereby keep us from losing our way? When architects design buildings, they begin with an image of forms and lights and shadows to which they gradually give increasing articulation. Is there any such image for us here?

I think there is. It is the vision *of* shalom — *peace* — first articulated in the Old Testament poetic and prophetic literature but then coming to expression in the New Testament as well. We shall see that shalom is intertwined with justice. In shalom, each person enjoys justice, enjoys his or her rights. There is no shalom without justice. But shalom goes beyond justice.

Shalom is the human being dwelling at peace in all his or her relationships: with God, with self, with fellows, with nature. It is shalom when

The wolf shall dwell with the lamb,
    and the leopard shall lie down with the kid,
and the calf and the lion and the fatling together,
    and a little child shall lead them.
The cow and the bear shall feed;
    their young shall lie down together;
    and the lion shall eat straw like the ox.
The sucking child shall play over the hole of the asp,
    and the weaned child shall put his hand on the adder's den.

(Isa. 11:6-8)

But the peace that is shalom is not merely the absence of hostility, not merely being in right relationship. Shalom at its highest is *enjoyment* in one's relationships. A nation may be at peace with all its neighbors and yet be miserable in its poverty. To dwell in shalom is to *enjoy* living before God, to *enjoy* living in one's physical surroundings, to *enjoy* living with one's fellows, to *enjoy* life with oneself.

Shalom in the first place incorporates right, harmonious relationships to *God* and delight in God's service. When the prophets speak of shalom, they speak of a day when human beings will no longer flee God down the corridors of time, a day when they will no longer turn in those corridors to defy their divine pursuer. Shalom is perfected when humanity acknowledges that in its service of God is true delight. "The mountain of the house of the LORD," says the prophet,

shall be established as the highest of the mountains,
    and shall be raised above the hills;
and all the nations shall flow to it,
    and many peoples shall come, and say:
"Come, let us go up to the mountain of the LORD,
    to the house of the God of Jacob;
that he may teach us his ways
    and that we may walk in his paths."

(Isa. 2:2-3)

Second, shalom incorporates right harmonious relationships to other *human beings* and delight in human community. Shalom is absent when a society is a collection of individuals all out to make their own way in the world. And of course there can be delight in community only when justice

110

reigns, only when human beings no longer oppress one another. When "justice shall make its home in the wilderness, / and righteousness dwell in the grassland" — only then will it be true that "rightousness shall yield shalom, / and its fruit be quietness and confidence for ever" (Isa. 32:16-17). In shalom,

> Love and Fidelity now meet,
>   Justice and Peace now embrace;
> Fidelity reaches up from earth
>   and Justice leans down from heaven.
>
> (Psalm 85:10-11)

Third, shalom incorporates right, harmonious relationships to *nature* and delight in our physical surroundings. Shalom comes when we, bodily creatures and not disembodied souls, shape the world with our labor and find fulfillment in so doing and delight in its results. In speaking of shalom the prophet spoke of a day when the Lord would prepare

> a banquet of rich fare for all the people,
> a banquet of wines well matured and richest fare,
> well matured wines strained clear.
>
> (Isa. 25:6)

He spoke of a day when the people "shall live in a tranquil country, / dwelling in shalom, in houses full of ease" (Isa. 32:18).

I said that justice, the enjoyment of one's rights, is indispensable to shalom. That is because shalom is an *ethical* community. If individuals are not granted what is due them, if their claim on others is not acknowledged by those others, if others do not carry out their obligations to them, then shalom is wounded. That is so even if there are *no feelings* of hostility between them and the others. Shalom cannot be secured in an unjust situation by managing to get all concerned to feel content with their lot in life. Shalom would not have been present *even if* all the blacks in the United States had been content in their state of slavery; it would not be present in South Africa *even if* all the blacks there felt happy. It is because shalom is an ethical community that it is wounded when justice is absent.

But the right relationships that lie at the basis of shalom involve more than right relationships to other human beings. They involve right relationships to God, to nature, and to oneself as well. Hence, shalom is more than an ethical community. Shalom is the *responsible* community in which God's laws for the multifaceted existence of God's creatures are obeyed.

Shalom goes beyond even the responsible community. We may all have acted responsibly and yet shalom may be wounded, for delight may be missing. Always there are sorrows in our human existence that we are at a loss to heal. It is in this context that we must ultimately see the significance of technology. Technology makes possible advance toward shalom; progress in mastery of the world can bring shalom nearer. But the limits of technology must also be acknowledged: technology is entirely incapable of bringing about shalom between ourselves and God, and it is only scarcely capable of bringing about love of self and neighbor.

I have already cited that best known of all shalom passages, the one in which Isaiah describes the anticipated shalom with a flourish of images of harmony — harmony among the animals, harmony between human beings and animals: "Then the wolf shall live with the sheep. . . ." That passage, though, is introduced with these words:

> Then a shoot shall grow from the stock of Jesse,
> and a branch shall spring from his roots.
> The spirit of the LORD shall rest upon him,
> a spirit of wisdom and understanding,
> a spirit of counsel and power,
> a spirit of knowledge and the fear of the LORD.
>
> (Isa. 11:1-2)

That shoot of which Isaiah spoke is he of whom the angels sang in celebration of his birth: "Glory to God in highest heaven, and on earth his *peace* for men on whom his favor rests" (Luke 2:14). He is the one of whom the priest Zechariah said that he "will guide our feet into the way of *peace*" (Luke 1:79). He is the one of whom Simeon said, "This day, Master, thou givest thy servant his discharge in *peace;* now thy promise is fulfilled" (Luke 2:29). He is the one of whom Peter said that it was by him that God preached "good news of *peace*" to Israel (Acts 10:36). He is the one of whom Paul, speaking as a Jew to the Gentiles, said that "he came and preached *peace* to you who were far off and *peace* to those who were near" (Eph. 2:17). He is in fact Jesus Christ, whom Isaiah called the "prince of peace" (Isa. 9:6).

It was this same Jesus who said to the apostles in his Farewell Discourse, "The words that I say to you I do not speak on my own authority;

but the Father who dwells in me does his works. Believe me that I am in the Father and the Father in me; or else believe me for the sake of the works themselves" (John 14:10-11). And then he added, "I say to you, he who believes in me will also do the works that I do; and greater works than these will he do" (John 14:12).

Can the conclusion be avoided that not only is shalom God's cause in the world but that all who believe in Jesus will, along with him, engage in the works of shalom? Shalom is both God's cause in the world and our human calling. Even though the full incursion of shalom into our history will be divine gift and not merely human achievement, even though its episodic incursion into our lives now also has a dimension of divine gift, nonetheless it is shalom that we are to work and struggle for. We are not to stand around, hands folded, waiting for shalom to arrive. We are workers in God's cause, God's peace-workers. The *missio Dei* is *our* mission.

An implication of this is that our work will always have the two dimensions of a struggle for justice and the pursuit of increased mastery of the world so as to enrich human life. Both together are necessary if shalom is to be brought nearer. Development and liberation must go hand in hand. Ours is both a cultural mandate and a liberation mandate — the mandate to master the world for the benefit of humankind, but also the mandate

> to loose the chains of injustice
>> and untie the cords of the yoke,
> to set the oppressed free
>> and break every yoke . . .
> to share your food with the hungry
>> and to provide the poor wanderer with shelter —
> when you see the naked, to clothe him,
>> and not to turn away from your own flesh and blood.
>
> (Isa. 58:6-7)

The shalom perspective incorporates but goes beyond the creation perspective of the Amsterdam school. At the same time, it incorporates but goes beyond the salvation perspective of the liberation theologians.

The Wounds of God:
Calvin's Theology of Social Injustice

M any attempts have been made to show that one or another feature of the modern Western world can be traced back to the thought and practice of the early Calvinists. Though the evidence on these matters proves surprisingly elusive and ambiguous, I am inclined to think that there is substantial truth in many of these claims. But whatever that truth, the modern world has been made. And the world made, in spite of high hopes during its adolescence, has proved to be pervaded by social injustice and thick with social misery. On these there is, in Calvin himself, a pattern of theological reflection that is rich, creative, provocative, and extraordinarily bold. I wish to lay out that pattern: Calvin's theology is a theology of the tears of the social victim. It's a theology that, to my knowledge, all the Calvin scholars miss. But it is a theology that, in my judgment, we in our privileged corner of the world would be well advised to take seriously. Perhaps doing so will help us to hear — genuinely to *hear* — the cries of the victims.

To understand the boldness of Calvin's thought on these matters, we must glance briefly at the dominant pattern of medieval thought on the place of suffering in human and divine life. This is not the place to survey, even in glancing fashion, the thousand years or so of medieval thought on these matters. I shall confine myself to looking at Augustine, on the ground that Augustine was both the most powerful shaper of the medieval mentality on these matters and was already thoroughly typical of that mentality.

In a passage from Book IV of the *Confessions,* Augustine exposes to full view the grief that overwhelmed him upon the death of a school friend from his home village of Tagaste in North Africa:

> My heart grew sombre with grief, and wherever I looked I saw only death. My own country became a torment and my own home a grotesque abode of misery. All that we had done together was now a grim ordeal without him. My eyes searched everywhere for him, but he was not there to be seen. I hated all the places we had known together, because he was not in them and they could no longer whisper to me, "Here he comes!" as they would have done had he been alive but absent for a while. . . . My soul was a burden, bruised and bleeding. It was tired of the man who carried it, but I found no place to set it down to rest.

It comes as a jolt to us to discover that at the time of writing this moving and eloquent passage, Augustine regarded the behavior here described as thoroughly disgusting. Between the grief and the writing, Augustine had embraced the Christian faith. His reason for exposing his bygone grief was to share with his readers his confession to God of the senselessness and sinfulness of a love so intense for a being so fragile that its destruction could cause such grief. "Why do I talk of these things?" he asks. And he answers, "It is time to confess, not to question."

The death of his friend occurred before Augustine's embrace of the Christian faith; the death of his mother, after. That embrace made his response to his mother's death profoundly different. "I closed her eyes," he says in Book IV,

> and a great wave of sorrow surged into my heart. It would have overflowed in tears if I had not made a strong effort of will and stemmed the flow, so that the tears dried in my eyes. What a terrible struggle it was to hold them back! As she breathed her last, the boy Adeodatus [Augustine's son] began to wail aloud and only ceased his cries when we all checked him. I, too, felt that I wanted to cry like a child, but a more mature voice within me, the voice of my heart, bade me keep my sobs in check, and I remained silent.

His struggle for self-control was not successful. Augustine reports that after the burial, as he lay in bed thinking of his devoted mother, "the tears which I had been holding back streamed down, and I let them flow as freely as they would, making of them a pillow for my heart. On them it rested. . . ." So now, he says to God, "I make you my confession. . . . Let any man read it who will. . . . And if he finds that I sinned by weeping for my mother, even if only for a fraction of an hour, let him not mock at me . . . but weep himself, if his charity is great. Let him weep for my sins to you. . . ." The sin for which Augustine wants the person of charity to weep is not so much the sin of weeping over the death of his mother as the sin of which that weeping was a sign. He was, says Augustine, "guilty of too much worldly affection."

How are we to understand the mentality here coming to expression? Along the following lines, I suggest. Augustine, with all the ancients, held that to be human is to be in search of happiness — *eudaemonia* in Greek, *beatitudo* in Latin. Furthermore, Augustine aligned himself with the Platonic tradition in his conviction that one's love, one's *eros,* is the fundamental determinant of one's happiness. Augustine never imagined that a human being could root out *eros* from his or her existence. Incomplete beings that we are, we inescapably long for fulfillment. The challenge, accordingly, is to choose objects for our love such that happiness is attained.

Now it was as obvious to Augustine as it is to all of us that grief ensues when that which we love is destroyed or dies, or is altered in such a way that we no longer find it lovable. In reflecting on his grief upon the death of his friend he says,

> I lived in misery like every man whose soul is tethered by the love of things that cannot last and then is agonized to lose them. . . . The grief I felt for the loss of my friend had struck so easily into my inmost heart simply because I had poured out my soul upon him, like water upon sand, loving a man who was mortal as though he were never to die.

The cure is to detach one's love from such objects and to attach it to something immutable and indestructible. For Augustine, the only candidate was God. "Blessed are those who love you, O God. . . . No one can lose you . . . unless he forsake you."

I see no reason to interpret Augustine as opposed to all enjoyment of earthly things: of food, of drink, of conversation, of art. Suspicious and wary, yes; opposed, no. What he says is only that we should root out the *love* of such things — by which I understand him to mean all attachment to things such that their destruction would cause us grief. To enjoy the taste of kiwi fruit is acceptable provided one's enjoyment is not such that if it proves unattainable, one grieves. Though we must not love the world, we may enjoy the world. Yet it must be admitted that Augustine says little or nothing by way of grounding the legitimacy of such enjoyment. In the famous passage in Book X of the *Confessions* where the things of creation "speak," what they say is not, "Receive us with enjoyment as God's blessing" but "Turn away from us to our maker." Further, Augustine was fond of saying that things of this world are to be used *(uti),* whereas only God is to be enjoyed *(frui).*

Augustine thought that one's struggle to eliminate love for earthly things is never complete in this life; the newly oriented self never wholly wins out over the old. That introduces a new mode of grief into our lives — a legitimate mode of grief, if you will. We are to grieve over the repetitious reappearance of the old self — and correspondingly, to rejoice over the extent of its disappearance. And also — most extraordinary — we are to grieve over the sins of others and to rejoice over their repentance. Each of us is to be joined in a solidarity of rejoicing and grieving with all humanity — rejoicing and grieving, however, over the *right* things, namely, over the religious condition of our souls. I am to rejoice and grieve over the religious condition of my soul and, in the very same way, to rejoice and grieve over the religious condition of your soul.

This exception is important. Yet the general rule is that we are to struggle to eliminate grief from our lives by struggling to concentrate our love on God alone.

All this has been about us human beings. What Augustine says about God is the more or less obvious counterpart. God's life is through and through blissful. God is free of all emotional disturbance. Of sympathy, *Mitleiden,* with those who are suffering, God feels nothing, as also God feels no pain over the shortfall of godliness in God's errant creatures. God's state is what the Greeks called *apatheia,* apathy. God dwells eternally in blissful nonsuffering *apatheia.* Nothing that happens in the world alters God's blissful, unperturbed serenity. God is not oblivious to the world; there is in God a steady disposition of benevolence toward God's human creatures. But this disposition to act benevolently proceeds on its uninterrupted successful course whatever transpires in the world.

For this picture of God, Augustine and the other ancients had fundamentally two reasons. They were persuaded that God's existence is perfect existence; and they could not imagine perfect existence as anything other than through-and-through blissful. And since they thought that God was changeless, they did not think that God's perfected existence was something God had to await; that would itself have been a mark of imperfection.

Second, they held that if God were to suffer and grieve, something outside God would have to bring that about in God — humanity's evildoing, perhaps. But God's changeless character and existence is not affected by anything outside Godself. God is the unconditioned condition of everything not identical with Godself. It was these two lines of thought that led to the classical doctrine of the blissful apathy of God.

Now LET US TURN to Calvin. I shall present at once the most vivid points of contrast, and then trace the path that led Calvin to his conclusions. In the course of carrying out his project of commenting on the books of the Bible, Calvin was confronted with verses 5 and 6 of Genesis 9. The passage is this:

> I will demand an account of every man's life from his fellow man.
>   He who sheds man's blood,
>   shall have his blood shed by man,
>   for in the image of God
>   man was made.

Calvin's commentary on this passage runs, in part, as follows:

> Men are indeed unworthy of God's care, if respect be had only to themselves; but since they bear the image of God engraven on them, he deems himself violated in their person. Thus, although they have nothing of their own by which they obtain the favour of God, he looks upon his own gifts in them, and is thereby excited to love and to care for them. This doctrine, however, is to be carefully observed, that no one can be injurious to his brother without wounding God himself. Were this doctrine deeply fixed in our minds, we should be much more reluctant than we are to inflict injuries.

The thought is striking: God "deems himself violated in their person"; "no one can be injurious to his brother without wounding God himself." And, as if to make clear that his speaking thus is not some fancy rhetorical flourish on his part, to be taken with less than full seriousness, Calvin adds that this doctrine "is to be carefully observed." It is to be "deeply fixed in our minds." To inflict injury on a fellow human being is to wound God; it is to cause God to suffer. Behind and beneath the social misery of our world is the suffering of God. If we truly believed that, says Calvin, we would be much more reluctant than we are to participate in victimizing the poor, the oppressed, and the assaulted of the world. To pursue justice is to relieve God's suffering.

A second passage worth having in hand before we trace out the path that led Calvin to these striking conclusions is his commentary on Habakkuk 2:5-6. The text on which he is commenting is this:

> "[T]he arrogant man shall not abide.
> His greed is as wide as Sheol;
>   like death he has never enough.
> He gathers for himself all nations,
>   and collects as his own all peoples."
> Shall not all these take up their taunt against him, in scoffing derision of him, and say,
> "Woe to him who heaps up what is not his own —
>   for how long? —
>   and loads himself with pledges!"

Commenting especially on the cry, "How long?" Calvin says:

This also is a dictate of nature. . . . When any one disturbs the whole world by his ambition and avarice, or everywhere commits plunder, or oppresses miserable nations — when he distresses the innocent, all cry out, How long? And this cry, proceeding as it does from the feeling of nature and the dictate of justice, is at length heard by the Lord. For how comes it that all, being touched with weariness, cry out, How long? except that they know that this confusion of order and equity is not to be endured? And this feeling, is it not implanted in us by the Lord? It is then the same as though God heard himself, when he hears the cries and groanings of those who cannot bear injustice.

Again, the thought is striking. Not only is the perpetration of injustice against one's fellow human beings the infliction of suffering upon God. The cries of the victims are the very cry of God. The lament of the victims as they cry out "How long?" is God giving voice to God's own lament.

119

WHAT, THEN, IS THE LINE of thought that led Calvin to such an extraordinarily bold theology of social injustice? We may begin, perhaps, with his opposition to the Augustinian position on the place of grief in human life — to that modified Stoicism according to which we are to pursue the elimination of all grief by struggling to love God and God alone, in the meanwhile grieving over nothing else than our own failure and that of our fellows to accomplish this project. "Among the Christians," says Calvin, "there are also new Stoics, who count it depraved not only to groan and weep but also to be sad and care ridden" *(Institutes,* III, viii, 9). On this they are quite wrong, says Calvin. Our goal

> is not to be utterly stupefied and to be deprived of all feeling of pain. [Our ideal] is not [that of what] the Stoics of old foolishly described [as] "the great-souled man": one who, having cast off all human qualities, was affected equally by adversity and prosperity, by sad times and happy ones — nay, who like a stone was not affected at all. (Ibid.)

One reason for repudiating the Stoic ideal is that it paints "a likeness of forbearance that has never been found among men, and can never be realized" (ibid.). In setting before us this impossible ideal, it distracts us from the attitude toward suffering that we ought in fact to cultivate.

> Thus afflicted by disease, we shall both groan and be uneasy and pant after health; thus pressed by poverty, we shall be pricked by the arrows of care and sorrow; thus we shall be smitten by the pain of disgrace, contempt, injustice; thus at the funerals of our dear ones we shall weep the tears that are owed to our nature. *(Institutes,* III, viii, 10)[1]

---

1. "I decided to say this," says Calvin, "in order to recall godly minds from despair, lest, because they cannot cast off the natural feeling of sorrow, they forthwith renounce the pursuit of patience. This must necessarily happen to those who make patience into insensibility, and a valiant and constant man into a stock. For Scripture praises the saints for their forbearance when, so afflicted with harsh misfortune, they do not break or fall; so stabbed with bitterness, they are at the same time flooded with spiritual joy; so pressed by apprehension, they recover their breath, revived by God's consolation. In the meantime, their hearts still harbor a contradiction between their natural sense, which flees and dreads what it feels adverse to itself, and their disposition to godliness, which even through these difficulties presses toward obedience to the divine will" *(Institutes,* III, viii, 10).

Calvin has a second reason for rejecting the Stoic ideal. "Our Lord and Master," he says,

> has condemned [it] not only by his word, but also by his example. For he groaned and wept both over his own and others' misfortunes. And he taught his disciples in the same way: "The world," he says, "will rejoice; but you will be sorrowful and will weep" (John 16:20). And that no one might turn it into a vice he openly proclaimed, "Blessed are those who mourn" (Matt. 5:4). No wonder! For if all weeping is condemned, what shall we judge concerning the Lord himself, from whose body tears of blood trickled down (Luke 22:44)? If all fear is branded as unbelief, how shall we account for that dread with which, we read, he was heavily stricken (Matt. 26:37; Mark 14:33)? If all sadness displeases us, how will it please us that he confesses his soul "sorrowful even to death" (Matt. 26:38)? *(Institutes, III, viii, 9)*

The discipline that we are to undertake in the face of sickness, death, poverty, disgrace, indignity, and injustice is not the discipline of no longer grieving over these, of becoming indifferent to them. Following the example of Christ, we are to let our God-given nature take its course, paying to justice the honor of grieving upon being treated unjustly, paying to life the honor of grieving upon the death of those we love. We are to let our wounds bleed, our eyes tear. The discipline we are to undertake is the discipline of becoming patient in our suffering. I shall have something to say shortly about the nature of Calvinistic patience and why Calvin thinks it appropriate.

Calvin's opposition to Stoicism and Augustinianism, then, was grounded in his conviction that they set for us an impossible and inappropriate ideal, contrary to our created nature, thus distracting us from the achievable and appropriate ideal of patience in suffering. But it is easy to see that Calvin's attitude toward grief also fits in with, and is supported by, his attitude toward enjoyment of the things of this world.

In a quite remarkable passage *(Institutes, III, x, 2)*, Calvin argues that of grasses, trees, and fruits we should appreciate not only their utility as nourishment but their beauty of appearance and pleasantness of odor and taste; of clothes we should appreciate not only their utility for keeping us warm but their comeliness; and of wine and oil we should appreciate not only that they are useful but that wine gladdens our hearts and that oil makes our faces shine. As if with his eye on Augustine's use/enjoyment distinction, Calvin asks rhetorically whether God did "not, in short, render many things attractive to us, apart from their necessary use?" He answers that God did. And let this, he says, "be our principle; that the use of God's gifts is not wrongly directed when it is referred to that end to which the Author himself created and destined them for us, since he created them for our good, not for our ruin."

The point is clear. Augustine saw the things of the world almost exclusively as the *works* of God; hence he urges us to look away from them to their maker. They are to be seen as benefit only so far as they are useful for our continued existence and for our approach to God. Pervasive in Calvin, by contrast, is the insistence that we are to see the things of the world not only as God's works but as God's *gifts* to us. And they are to be seen as God's gifts not only so far as they are useful but also so far as they are enjoyable. "This life," says Calvin, "however crammed with infinite miseries it may be, is still rightly to be counted among those blessings of God which are not to be spurned. Therefore, if we recognize in it no divine benefit, we are already guilty of grave ingratitude toward God himself" *(Institutes* III, ix, 3).

One cannot overemphasize the pervasiveness of this theme in Calvin — the theme of world as gift for use and enjoyment, and the counterpart theme of the propriety of gratitude. Never, in this regard, was there a more sacramental theologian than Calvin, one more imbued with the sense that in world, history, and self, we meet God. "Away, then, with that inhuman philosophy which, while conceding only a necessary use of creatures, not only malignantly deprives us of the lawful fruit of God's beneficence but cannot be practiced unless it robs a man of all his senses and degrades him to a block" *(Institutes,* III, x, 3).

I SAID THAT to understand Calvin's theology of the tears of the social victim and to appreciate its boldness, we must discern his anti-Stoical and anti-Augustinian view of the place of grief in human existence — and correlatively, his view of the place of enjoyment. On Calvin's view, one does not say to the person suffering poverty or the indignity of injustice that she should not care about those things enough to grieve over their deprivation — that she should love only God. To the contrary, one encourages grief. But there is a second thing we have to see if we are to trace out the path that led Calvin to his radical conclusions — namely, his thoughts on the image of God in the human being.

"'So man was created in the image of God'; in him the Creator himself willed that his own glory be seen as in a mirror" *(Institutes,* II, xii, 6). What Calvin means, of course — and what he says in his Latin — is that *human beings* were created in the image of God. "God looks upon Himself, as one might say, and beholds Himself in men as in a mirror" (sermon on John 10:7; quoted in T. F. Torrance, *Calvin's Doctrine of Man)*. "God's children are pleasing and lovable to him, since he sees in them the marks and features of his own countenance. . . . [W]henever God contemplates his own face, he both rightly loves it and holds it in honor . . ." *(Institutes,* III, xvii, 5).

The thought is clear: God beholds what God has made. God observes that human beings are icons of Godself. God observes that they mirror God, that they image God, that they are likenesses of God. In this God delights. This grounds God's love for them. God delights, of course, in all God's works. But human beings are singled out from other earthlings in that in them God finds God's own perfections mirrored back to Godself.

A consequence of the fact that each human being mirrors God is that we as human beings exist in profound unity with each other: to see another human being is to see another creature who delights God by mirroring God. No more profound kinship among God's creatures can exist than this. Furthermore, each of us mirrors God in the same respects — though, as we shall shortly see, some do so more, some less. Thereby we also, in a derivative way, resemble each other. One could say that we mirror each other. In looking at you and me, God finds Godself mirrored. Accordingly, in my looking at you I too discern, once my eyes have been opened, that you mirror God — and more, I discern that you mirror me. I discern myself as in a mirror. I discern a family likeness. As Calvin puts it,

> We cannot but behold our own face as it were in a glass in the person that is poor and despised . . . though he were the furthest stranger in the world. Let a Moor or a Barbarian come among us, and yet inasmuch as he is a man, he brings with him a looking glass wherein we may see that he is our brother and neighbor. (Sermon on Galatians 6:9-11; quoted in R. S. Wallace, *Calvin's Doctrine of the Christian Life*, p. 150)

There were those who argued that this image of God in us can be, and in some cases has been, obliterated. Calvin firmly disagreed:

> Should anyone object, that this divine image has been obliterated, the solution is easy; first, there yet exists some remnant of it, so that man is possessed of no small dignity; and, secondly, the Celestial Creator himself, however corrupted man may be, still keeps in view

the end of his original creation; and according to his example, we ought to consider for what end he created men, and what excellence he has bestowed upon them above the rest of living beings. (Commentary on Genesis 9:6)

There is nothing that can happen to a human being, and nothing a human being can do, to bring it about that the image of God in that person is obliterated. Though a person's mirroring of God can be painfully distorted, blurred, and diminished, it cannot be eliminated.

Naturally we want to know wherein lies our iconicity. In what respects do we mirror God back to Godself and then to each other? Calvin offers two rules of thumb for answering this question. In the first place, our iconicity is to be discerned in what differentiates us from the other earthlings: "the likeness of God extends to the whole excellence by which man's nature towers over all the kinds of living creatures" *(Institutes,* I, xv, 4). Second, keeping in mind that our likeness to God can be increased and diminished, we must follow the rule that the fundamental goal of our human existence is to become as like unto God as possible — or, to use the language of the Orthodox tradition, to become as "divinized" as possible. And what would a human being's full likeness to God be like? The answer to that question we apprehend in Jesus Christ, who is "the express image of the Father."

When we follow these two rules of thumb, looking at our uniqueness and looking at Jesus Christ, one thing we learn is that we are like God in being capable of understanding; and the more our understanding expands — especially our understanding of God — the more we become like God. We learn also that we are like God in being capable of governing our affections and thereby our actions; and the more our heart is upright, the more like God we become. For Calvin, these two are the principal resemblances. But there are others as well. Our (mandated) governance of creation is a mirroring of God's governance, and our formation of communities is a mirroring of that perfect community which is the Trinity. No doubt some of us today would wish to add yet other themes — for example, that our creativity is a mirroring of God's creativity.

Back, though, to understanding of mind and uprightness of heart. In no human being, says Calvin, are the capacity and the realization of these entirely absent. No human being fails to mirror God in these respects; in all there is some capacity for understanding and goodness and some realization of those capacities. Accordingly, whenever we come across a human being, we are to act in accord with our coming across an icon of the Holy One in whom the Holy One finds delight.

Calvin grounds the claims of love and justice in this phenomenon of our mirroring God. The standard picture of Calvin is that obligation, duty, responsibility, and the call to obedience loom large in his thought, and indeed they do. Yet for Calvin there is something deeper than these. All of us in our daily lives are confronted with other human beings. We find ourselves in the presence of an Other who, by virtue of being an icon of God, makes claims on us. Moral reflection can begin either from responsibility or from rights — from the responsibilities of the Agent or from the claims of the Other. The degree to which Calvin begins from the claims of the Other is striking. The pattern is displayed with great insistence in this passage from the *Institutes* (I have altered the translation slightly):

> The Lord commands all men without exception "to do good." Yet the great part of them are most unworthy if they be judged by their own merit. But here Scripture helps in the best way when it teaches that we are not to consider what men merit of themselves but to look upon the image of God in all men, to which we owe all honor and love. . . . Therefore, whatever man you meet who needs your aid, you have no reason to refuse to help him. You say, "He is a stranger"; but the Lord has given him a mark that ought to be familiar to you, by virtue of the fact that he forbids you to despise your own flesh. You say, "He is contemptible and worthless"; but the Lord shows him to be one to whom he has deigned to give the beauty of his image. You say that you owe nothing for any service of his; but God, as it were, has put him in his own place in order that you may recognize toward him the many and great benefits with which God has bound you to him. You say that he does not deserve even your least effort for his sake; but the image of God, which recommends him to you, is worthy of your giving yourself and all your possessions. Now if he has not only deserved no good at your hand, but has also provoked you by unjust acts and curses, not even this is just reason why you should cease to embrace him in love and to perform the duties of love on his behalf. You say, "He has deserved something far different of me." Yet what has the Lord deserved? . . . It is that we remember not to consider men's evil intention but to look upon the image of God in them, which cancels and effaces their transgressions, and with its beauty and dignity allures us to love and embrace them. *(Institutes, III, vii, 6)*

Several things in this passage are striking, in addition to the insistent grounding of the claims of charity and justice in our ineradicable iconicity. One is Calvin's adamant insistence that, given that it is our iconicity that grounds these claims, the virtuousness of the Other is irrelevant. Always the perpetrators of injustice want it otherwise: If the blacks in South Africa just behave, they will be given a voice in their governance. If the Palestinians just behave, they will be allowed to engage in discussions about their future.

But how exactly does the fact that each of us is an icon of God ground our claim to justice and love? One would expect Calvin to say at this point that it is the *great dignity* inherent in being an icon of God that grounds the claim of the Other on me: this dignity calls for respect, and there is no other way of showing the appropriate respect than by justice and love. Calvin does speak this way now and then. But his emphasis falls elsewhere. For one thing, he insists that the claim of the Other on my love and justice is grounded in the fact that she and I are kinsfolk, in the deepest possible way, by virtue of jointly imaging God. Perhaps this comes out most vividly in Calvin's commentary on Isaiah 58:6-7. The text on which he is commenting is this:

> Is not this the fast that I choose:
> > to loose the bonds of wickedness,
> > to undo the thongs of the yoke,
> to let the oppressed go free,
> > and to break every yoke?
> Is it not to share your bread with the hungry?
> > and bring the homeless poor into your house;
> when you see the naked, to cover him,
> > and not to hide yourself from your own flesh?

Calvin's commentary on this passage runs (in part) as follows:

> It is not enough to *abstain* from acts of injustice, if you refuse your assistance to the needy. . . . By commanding them to "break bread to the hungry," God intended to take away every excuse from covetous and greedy men, who allege that they have a right to keep possession of that which is their own. . . . And indeed, this is the dictate of common sense, that the hungry are deprived of their just right, if their hunger is not relieved. . . . At length he concludes — *And that you hide not yourself from your own flesh.* Here we ought to observe the term *flesh,*

by which he means all men universally, not a single one of whom we can behold, without seeing, as in a mirror, "our own flesh." It is therefore a proof of the greatest inhumanity, to despise those in whom we are constrained to recognize our own likeness.

In short, to fail to practice the requirements of justice and charity toward one's fellow human beings is to fail in the duties of kinship, and thereby to act with "the greatest inhumanity."

But there is another way in which the iconicity of the Other who is in my midst grounds her claim to love and justice on my part. It is this other way that brings us finally to the place where we began. "God Himself, looking on human beings as formed in His own image, regards them with such love and honour that He Himself feels wounded and outraged in the persons of those who are the victims of human cruelty and wickedness" (R. S. Wallace, *Calvin's Doctrine of the Christian Life,* p. 149, summarizing passages from various of Calvin's sermons).

For Calvin, the demands of love and justice lie not first of all in the *will* of God, which is what much of the Christian tradition would have said; nor do they lie first of all in the *reason* of God, which is what most of the rest of the tradition would have said. They lie in the sorrow and in the joy of God, in God's suffering and in God's delight. If I abuse something that you love, then at its deepest what has gone wrong is not that I have violated your command not to abuse that object of your affection — though you may indeed have issued such a command and I will accordingly have violated it. It lies first of all in the fact that I cause you sorrow. The demands of love and justice are rooted, so Calvin suggests, in what Abraham Heschel in his book on the prophets has called the *pathos* of God. To treat unjustly one of these human earthlings in whom God delights is to bring sorrow to God. To wound God's beloved is to wound God. The demands of justice are grounded in the fact that to commit injustice is to inflict suffering on God. They are grounded in the vulnerability of God's love for us, God's icons. God is not *apathe.*

Though I do not propose to develop it here, it is worth noting that this theme of the wounding of God is also given a specifically christological and sacramental development in Calvin. At one point in his discussion of the Eucharist he says:

We shall benefit very much from the Sacrament if this thought is impressed and engraved upon our minds: that none of the brethren can be injured, despised, rejected, abused, or in any way offended by us, without at the same time, injuring, despising, and abusing Christ by the wrongs we do; . . . that we cannot love Christ without loving him in the brethren. . . . *(Institutes, IV, xvii, 38)*

BEFORE CONCLUDING, we must return to Calvin's doctrine of *patience*. Augustine, it will be remembered, said that we should struggle to eliminate all attachments to things such that the disappearance or alteration of these things would cause us grief. Calvin's position was profoundly different. We should not try to alter our created nature; we should honor it. To indignity, death, injustice, and a multitude of other evils in this life, grief is not only the normal but the appropriate response. The discipline to be undertaken is not that of loving only God but that of being patient in our suffering. Patient grief is to be our stance.

When confronted with the prospect of the occurrence of some event likely to cause one grief, one can pursue the Augustinian course of struggling to alter one's nature so that, when the event occurs, one feels no grief. But one can also pursue the opposite course of trying to avert the occurrence of that event. Did Calvin, in recommending patience, mean to recommend that we should also renounce this latter course? Did he mean to say that we should no more seek to change the world than ourselves — that we should let the threatening episodes just flow over us? Is Calvinist patience passive acceptance?

The suggestion lacks even initial plausibility. What characterized the Calvinist movement as a whole was its dynamic restlessness; much of that can be traced to Calvin himself — to his actions in Geneva, but also to his words. It is true that, when it came to the political realm, Calvin insisted that those not in positions of political authority were not to revolt. But not revolting is very different from passively accepting — as we all know, and as the members of the city council in Geneva experienced to their dismay in their struggles with Calvin.

The truth is that Calvin vigorously and unflinchingly denounced corruption in the church, tyranny in the polity, and inequitable wealth in the economy. And though it would not be inconsistent to denounce bishops, tyrants, and bosses while yet counseling passive acceptance of their orders and actions, Calvin regularly took the next steps of urging resistance to evil and struggle for reform, and of himself practicing what he preached. In a famous passage from his commentary on Daniel (6:22), Calvin, while not recommending revolt even as a last resort, unmistakably recommends defiant disobedience:

. . . Earthly princes lay aside all their power when they rise against God and are unworthy of being reckoned in the number of mankind. We ought rather utterly to defy them than to obey them whenever they are so restive and wish to spoil God of his rights and, as it were, to seize upon his throne and draw him down from heaven.

Given the situation depicted in the book of Daniel, it might with some justice be wondered whether Calvin here has his eye merely on freedom of worship. When that is denied us, we must disobey. But in his discussion of patience in the *Institutes,* Calvin puts the struggle for justice and the struggle for the freedom of the gospel on the same footing: We are called to both, and both may yield suffering and the honor of the martyr:

. . . To suffer persecution for righteousness' sake is a singular comfort. For it ought to occur to us how much honor God bestows upon us in thus furnishing us with the special badge of his soldiery. I say that not only they who labor for the defense of the gospel but they who in any way maintain the cause of righteousness suffer persecution for righteousness. *(Institutes,* III, viii, 7)

In short, Calvinist patience is not the patience of passive acceptance but the patience of one who suffers as she struggles against the world's evils.

In his discussions on patience, there seem to be two things especially that Calvin emphasizes, the presupposition of his whole discussion being that we must preserve our vulnerability to suffering and not stifle the cry of grief when such suffering comes. First, we must seek to discern God's goodness in our suffering and respond accordingly. Given Calvin's conviction that nothing happens without God's permission, all suffering was regarded by him as ultimately either God's chastisement or God's blessing.[2] But chastisement is itself for our good, not merely retributive. Thus, although that over which one legitimately grieves is truly evil, the suffering underlying the grief is beneficial for shaping us to the life of God's King-

---

2. "Whether poverty or exile, or prison, or insult, or disease, or bereavement, or anything like them torture us, we must think that none of these things happens except by the will and providence of God, that he does nothing except with a well-ordered justice" *(Institutes,* III, viii, 11).

dom. Suffering is indispensable to the "making" of souls. Only the wounded heart can be whole. This "general axiom is to be maintained," says Calvin, "that all the suffering to which human life is subject and liable is a necessary exercise by which God partly invites us to repentance, partly instructs us in humility, and partly renders us more cautious and more attentive in guarding against the allurements of sin for the future" (Commentary on Gen. 3:19). "But if it be clear that our afflictions are for our benefit, why should we not undergo them with a thankful and quiet mind?" (*Institutes*, III, viii, 11). Second, the suffering we experience as the result of struggling for God's cause in the world embeds us more firmly in the life of God's Kingdom. We find joy and comfort in the fact that "we share Christ's sufferings in order that as he has passed from a labyrinth of all evils into heavenly glory, we may in like manner be led through various tribulations to the same glory" (*Institutes*, III, viii, 1).

Calvinist patience, then, is the paradoxical, unstable combination of grieving over the pain and deprivation that come one's way as one lives a life incorporating struggle for the gospel and for justice, of thankfully allowing one's suffering to contribute to the "making" of one's soul, and of taking joy from being united through one's suffering more firmly with the Christ who cried out upon the cross and the God who is wounded by the world's wounds. Especially the first and last of these points comes out in these remarkable passages from the *Institutes:*

> Therefore, whether in declaring God's truth against Satan's falsehoods or in taking up the protection of the good and the innocent against the wrongs of the wicked, we must undergo the offenses and hatred of the world, which may imperil either our life, our fortunes, or our honor. Let us not grieve or be troubled in thus far devoting our efforts to God, or count ourselves miserable in those matters in which he has with his own lips declared us blessed. Even poverty, if it be judged in itself, is misery; likewise exile, contempt, prison, disgrace; finally, death itself is the ultimate of all calamities. But when the favor of our God breathes upon us, every one of these things turns into happiness for us. . . . What then? If, being innocent and of good conscience, we are stripped of our possessions by the wickedness of impious folk, we are indeed reduced to penury among men. But in God's presence in heaven our true riches are thus increased. If we are cast out of our own house, then we will be the more intimately received into God's family. If we are vexed and de-

spised, we but take all the firmer root in Christ. If we are branded with disgrace and ignominy, we but have a fuller place in the Kingdom of God. If we are slain, entrance into the blessed life will thus be open to us. *(Institutes,* III, vii, 7)

Scripture, then, by these and like warnings gives us abundant comfort in either the disgrace or the calamity we bear for the sake of defending righteousness. Consequently, we are too ungrateful if we do not willingly and cheerfully undergo these things at the Lord's hand. . . . Yet such a cheerfulness is not required of us as to remove all feeling of bitterness and pain. . . . If there were no harshness in poverty, no torment in diseases, no sting in disgrace, no dread in death — what fortitude or moderation would there be in bearing them with indifference? But since each of these, with an inborn bitterness, by its very nature bites the hearts of us all, the fortitude of the believing man is brought to light if — tried by the feeling of such bitterness — however grievously he is troubled with it, yet valiantly resisting, he surmounts it. *(Institutes,* III, viii, 8)

Therefore, in patiently suffering these tribulations, we do not yield to necessity but we consent for our own good. These thoughts, I say, bring it to pass that, however much in bearing the cross our minds are constrained by the natural feeling of bitterness, they are as much diffused with spiritual joy. *(Institutes,* III, viii, 11)

These imposing words, the words of one who himself was an exile and himself suffered a good many indignities, words so different in tenor from Augustine's, find striking parallels today in the words of some of the liberation theologians from Latin America, South Africa, and black North America. Perhaps, indeed, only those who suffer the pain of injustice, poverty, indignity, and exile far more intensely than most of us do, can adequately interpret them for us.

Let me close by stating once more the main themes in Calvin's theology of social injustice: To perpetrate injustice on a fellow human being is to wound God; the cries of the victims are the expression of divine suffering. Thus the call to justice is rooted ultimately in the pathos of God, in God's vulnerable love. The call to justice is the call to avoid wounding God; the call to eliminate injustice is the call to alleviate divine suffering. If we believed that, and believed it firmly, we would be far more reluctant than we are to participate in the acts and the structures of injustice. If we believed that and believed it firmly, we would ceaselessly struggle for justice and against injustice, bearing with thankful, joyful patience the suffering which that struggle will bring upon us.

Lest Your Brother Be Degraded in Your Sight

Prison reform, spurred on by the incidents at Attica and San Quentin, has become the social action cause of the year. Poverty, segregation, the war — without being ended, these have dropped below the horizon of public consciousness. Now every periodical crossing my desk has articles about prison reform. Everybody is trying to "get with it." But we all know from past experience that, after remaining in the forefront for a year or so, prison reform will be replaced by some new social action cause. We also know what it is that will in all likelihood bring the next cause to our attention. Violence.

This whole pattern, these waves of fashion in social reform, is thoroughly repulsive. There is something wrong about reform movements that are so lacking in steadfast seriousness. There is something wrong about a society in which people must resort to violence and threats of violence in order to receive consideration of their just complaints. And yes, there is something wrong in our liberal establishment when in its sympathy for the anti-war demonstrator it becomes hostile towards the hard-hat worker, when in its sympathy for the inner-city black person it sneers at the white suburbanite, when in its sympathy for the prison inmate it ignores the guard. In this whole emerging pattern there is more than a little that calls for the incisive and healing Word of God.

But though Christians may heartily despise these waves of fashion in social reform, they cannot avoid saying something about Attica and San Quentin. What must be said?

Well, before we pronounce the Word of the Lord we had better confess guilt. Among the prayers of the Christian tradition are to be found prayers for prisoners: "For those in prison, condemned or exiled, we call upon thee." "Show thy compassion to all prisoners and captives." And so forth. Yet I cannot remember the last time I heard a prayer for prisoners offered in my church. Can you? Many conservative churches demonstrate concern for the "souls" of prisoners. But the Christian church cares little about the physical and psychological condition of prisoners. It tends to think that they, whatever their conditions, are getting their just deserts. Yet at the same time we profess to be disciples of a man who, at the close of his life, was unjustly condemned, imprisoned, and executed as a common criminal.

There is a passage in the Old Testament that penetrates to the heart of the Attica situation and to the situation of our prisoners in general. It provides a clear criterion for deciding what it is that God is saying to us today. It is found in Deuteronomy 25:2-3, and it runs thus: "If the guilty man deserves to be beaten, the judge shall cause him to lie down and be beaten in his presence with a number of stripes in proportion to his offence. Forty stripes may be given him but not more; lest, if one should go on to beat him with more stripes than these, your brother be degraded in your sight."

The root evil, I submit, is that we have allowed our brothers in prison to be degraded in our sight. Worse, we *aim* to degrade them. One of the prisoners at Attica was quoted as saying, "We no longer wish to be treated as statistics, as numbers. We want to be treated as human beings. We will be treated as human beings." Yet when the bodies of the dead inmates were shipped to the morgue they had only numbers attached whereas the bodies of the dead hostages were honored with their names. After the slaughter had ceased, Gov. Rockefeller said, "Our hearts go out to the families of the hostages who died at Attica"; no word of sympathy was forthcoming for the families of the dead inmates.

One can easily go on. When order had been restored at Attica the prisoners were forced to run naked through a gauntlet of guards who beat them with their rifle stocks. And after order had been restored at San Quentin the prisoners were forced to lie naked in the prison courtyard for the better part of a day. George Jackson at San Quentin pleaded for an end to the humiliating procedure whereby the parole board tantalized him with the prospect of release if he would just change his attitude while at the same time it was they, in secret session, who decided whether he had sufficiently changed his attitude. One of the prisoners' demands at Attica was for the right to worship as their conscience demanded; apparently not even the elemental right of freedom to worship is to be given to our prisoners. And at Attica and elsewhere prisoners are forced to work in prison shops for financial rewards so small that one would be embarrassed to give them to one's children as allowance.

To go on would be tedious. You have read the same things I have. We have degraded our brothers. We call our prisons "houses of correction." They are in fact stables of degradation. Degradation brutalizes. Degradation enrages. Degradation does not correct.

Why this degradation in the midst of our "enlightened" society? Is it perhaps the case that once a society has lost the conviction that all human beings are created by God and objects of God's loving concern, that then it no longer has sufficient resources for resisting the treatment of human beings as animals? Is it perhaps the case that Christians have also lost this conviction?

You remember the stories from Attica about prisoners throwing themselves over the bodies of their hostages in order to prevent the hostages from being killed. That a human being should give his life for the one who has flogged him — in that too God speaks.

An Evening in Amman

Father Eliya Khoury is a Palestinian Arab. Born and reared in the West Bank, he is now in his 60s, I would judge, the Assistant Bishop in the Jerusalem diocese of the Anglican Church. My wife and I met him in Amman, however, not in Jerusalem. Some years ago the Israeli authorities imprisoned Fr. Khoury for eight months (two of them in solitary confinement) and then, without granting him a hearing, expelled him from Israel. He had been too outspoken in condemning the injustices being wreaked on his people. Now, in exile, he is serving a small congregation of Palestinians in Amman.

No doubt many North Americans think of all Palestinians as Muslim — and fanatical. Indeed, we tend to think of the entire Middle East, apart from some outposts in Jerusalem and Bethlehem, as empty of Christians except for a few struggling groups established by Protestant missionaries some time in this century. The truth is that this is where the Christian church began and where it has never died out. Here are to be found the most ancient churches in all of Christendom. There has always been a Christian presence in the Middle East, and not just in the places of pilgrimage. What makes us overlook these our brothers and sisters?

My wife and I were part of a group of Americans who visited the Middle East this spring, not vacationing but attempting as Christians to understand the situation of the church there and the conflict of peoples and religions. In Lebanon we talked to the head of the Maronite church, the head of the Armenian church, a bishop of the Melkite church, and representatives of the Middle East Council of Churches; we also spoke with Muslims, with representatives of the Lebanese government, of the PLO, of the rightist Falangist Party, and of the Syrian Nationalist Party. During a stay of a few days in Jordan, en route to Israel, a friend of ours said to us, "You must meet Fr. Khoury." Although a meeting with the entire group could not be arranged, my wife and I did have the chance to talk to Fr. Khoury in a small room on the bottom floor of what appeared to be a sort of home and parish house combined.

Let me present to you Fr. Khoury's witness. The blend of sorrow, hope, and passion with which he spoke I cannot convey. I can only give his words. I did not take notes while he was speaking. But as soon as we got back to our hotel I jotted some things down. That was hardly necessary. His words were indelible.

Why, he asked, has the church abandoned us Christians here in the Middle East? We are deserted, forgotten by the church of the whole world. Why? Why do the Christians in America support the Zionists instead of supporting us, their brothers and sisters in Christ? I do not understand. They do not even notice us. We are abandoned. Perhaps the Palestinian has not known how to cry out.

We are caught between the Israelis and the Muslims. The Muslims see Western Christendom as behind Israel. They see Israel as an outpost of the West — of the *Christian* West. They want no part of it. I tell you, they are becoming fanatic, worse than any time in my memory. And if things continue as they are, they will make martyrs of us. We are willing to become martyrs if that is demanded of us. We shall remain faithful. But you are forcing us to become unworthy martyrs, martyrs in an unworthy cause.

My people, my Christian people, are being destroyed, squeezed between Israel and the Muslims. A few years back 12½ percent of the Palestinians were Christians. Now only 6 percent are. We are constantly shrinking, constantly getting smaller. What has happened? Have the people abandoned Christ? Have they converted to Islam or Judaism? No, they have not. They are being forced out of Israel by its Zionist policies. Israel is destroying the church in Palestine. Soon, in the land of our Lord, there will be no Christians left. The old ones have their homes taken from them by the Israelis, confiscated. The young ones, seeing no future, leave — for the United States, for South America, anywhere. Why do you Christians in America support the Zionists, when the Zionists are destroying the church in Palestine? Why do you not support your brothers and sisters in Christ?

And now I am told that conservative Christian groups in the United

States are planning to start a radio station aimed at the Muslims. Why do you not speak to us first about such things? Why do you ignore us? Why do you act as if there are no Christians here? We have lived with the Muslims for a thousand years. Why do you not first ask our advice? You say that we have not been successful in evangelizing the Muslims. What do all your Western missionaries have to show for their efforts? I tell you, this will only make the Muslims more nervous, more suspicious, more fanatic. Our oppression will become worse. It would be easier to convert the devil himself at this point than to convert a Muslim. Today he is not receptive. You will cause Christianity to disappear from the Middle East unless you stop this "American evangelism" — and unless your government settles the Palestinian problem.

I run a small school here in Amman. To this school come both Christians and Muslims. I do not try to convert the Muslim children. I try to show them that Christians and Muslims can live together in peace. Unless the Muslims believe that, and unless the Zionists cease their oppression, the church here in the Middle East will disappear.

What I need for my own congregation is a small place where we can meet during the week. My people must meet, so that they can support each other in these difficult days. But we have no money. So I went to Europe, to ask the Christians there for money. Do you know what they told me? They told me that *they* had decided that it was unwise for the church to spend money on buildings. Why do the churches in the rest of the world not trust us? Instead of piping in their Western evangelism, why do they not support us — in building meeting places for our people, and schools, and in holding discussions between Christians and Muslims so that we can learn to live together? Believe me. I love Jesus Christ. I love the gospel. I speak from the standpoint of that love. I say: Trust us. Do not compete with us. Support us. We know the Muslim. We live with him.

Eventually Israel will see that the Palestinians are its only doorway into the Arab world. It will see that its only hope is to form a society in which Jews, Muslims, and Christians live together. The first step to that will be a Palestinian state on the West Bank and in Gaza, with East Jerusalem as its capital. But that won't happen until you Americans help to settle the Palestinian issue — until you see the justice of our cause. You are driving us into the arms of the Russians, where we do not want to be. And you are destroying the church.

God will not desert us. And we will not desert God. Perhaps I sound despairing. But I am not. I live in the hope that our Lord will come. But how much must we suffer? Help us, before it is too late. Unless the baby in its crib cries out, it is not heard. Perhaps we haven't known how to cry out.

Please convey this to my Christian brothers and sisters in America. You may use my name.

Death in Gaza

As I write these words, rioting has been going on in Gaza and the West Bank for five weeks. More than thirty Palestinians have been shot and killed. This is the Israeli government's count; one can be sure that it is not too high. No figures have been released of late on how many have been hospitalized with wounds. More than two thousand Palestinians have been arrested, again by the government's count. All of these, so Israel has announced to the world, will be given fair trials in military court. Defense lawyers in Gaza and the West Bank have boycotted the trials as pure sham; they discovered that they were not permitted to consult with their clients, nor even to see the charges, before the trials actually took place. A Spanish jurist who visited some trials said that they each took between just six and nineteen minutes. Typically those condemned for stone-throwing are fined about a year's worth of wages and given six months in jail. Yesterday it was announced that thirty Palestinians have been incarcerated under "administrative detention," and that others will join these. To be held under administrative detention means that one can be held in jail for six months without any charges being filed, and that at the end of the six months a new order for administrative detention can be issued — and so on until one has rotted in prison.

Over the years there have been recurrent reports of torture of Palestinians in Israeli prisons. These have always been denied by the Israeli government. Recently, however, the Landau Commission of the Israeli Supreme Court conceded that Israel's internal security service (Shin Bet) had "routinely" employed violence in extracting confessions from Palestinians, and had routinely resorted to lies by its officers to conceal this. The Commission did not find this all bad, however, and recommended that no one be prosecuted. It disapproved of the "untrammelled violence" of the past two decades, but declared legitimate a blend of "tricks" and "psychological pressure." Should these fail to get the results desired, interrogators were free to resort to "moderate physical pressure."

Just today the Israeli government announced that it had deported four Palestinians and planned to deport more. These will then join the more than twenty-five hundred who have been deported since 1967. Egypt, Jordan, and Lebanon have all announced that they will refuse to accept any further deportees. Syria's intentions have been clear enough without public announcement. These four were put on a helicopter, dropped off during the night in the Israeli "security district" of Southern Lebanon, and told to walk north. No civilized country in the world deports people born on its own land — and I include, under "civilized country," South Africa. The practice clearly contravenes international law; if Nicaragua did it, there would be an uproar in this country. Nonetheless, Israel has regularly used the practice and has made clear that it intends to continue doing so. Deportation orders can be appealed to the Israeli Supreme Court. But no deportation appeal has ever succeeded. Defense lawyers are not permitted to see or hear the evidence against the accused. In addition to all the above, homes are being blown up, individuals placed under house and town arrest, collective punishment is being imposed, and entire villages have been placed under strict curfew.

From American politicians there has been, with extremely rare exceptions, only stony silence. Of all the presidential candidates, only Jesse Jackson, so far as I have been able to tell, has said anything on behalf of the Palestinians. Jack Kemp complained that the United Nations was "picking on Israel" when it deplored Israel's tactics. As Congress wound up its session in December, no Congressman stood up to express sympathy for the Palestinians — this in spite of the fact that the riots and shootings were going on while Congress was meeting. Time and courage were found, however, for vigorous speeches about the violations of rights in Nicaragua, in Russia, in Afghanistan. Mary McGrory, in one of her columns, reports that she asked a Congressman at a holiday party why no one had spoken out. The answer she got was revealing: "Of course nobody spoke out. We are too intimidated. We are afraid of the Israeli lobby. We are afraid of our Jewish constituency." I doubt that that is the whole of the matter. Indifference toward the Palestinians, edging toward hatred of them, is also a factor.

One would, of course, not expect any sympathy for the Palestinians from such shining defenders of American democratic capitalism as Jeanne Kirkpatrick, Jesse Helms, and Elliott Abrams. They are not only unwavering defenders of Israel but also of South Africa and Chile. Consistency is their virtue. However, on the basis of firebreathing speeches against South Africa, one might have expected a word from Ted Kennedy, Alan Cranston, and Daniel Inouye to remind us that justice and liberty are undivided. All but the blind can see the similarities between Israel and South Africa. Not a word was said.

It would not be true, though, to say that Congress was entirely unresponsive to the killings. Its response was to hand over yet more of your and my money to Israel — all the while wringing its hands over the budget deficit. Three billion dollars of nonrepayable economic and military aid was given to Israel — over none of which the U.S. exercises any sort of supervision whatsoever. It is true that, by law, Israel is to use its U.S.-provided armaments only for defensive purposes. But when Israel dropped antipersonnel bombs on the citizens of Beirut, that was judged defensive in nature, as was its flying thousands of miles to drop bombs on the PLO offices in Tunis. It is not easy to imagine a scenario in which Israel used its U.S.-provided weapons in a way that the U.S. government would judge nondefensive. So to all intents and purposes, the $3 billion is an unrestricted gift.

Congress also passed a provision to refinance Israel's old $9 billion debt to the U.S., so as to reduce its interest rates. This is expected to be worth about $2 billion. And — to cut the narrative short — Congress provided Israel with up to $180 million to develop a defensive system against short-range tactical missiles — this being part of Reagan's Star Wars system. It is no mystery why the Palestinians angrily regard you and me as paying for the army and providing the bullets that gun them down. It is no mystery why they resentfully regard you and me as financing the Jewish settlements on land confiscated from them without compensation. The only mystery in the matter is why you and I should find it inexplicable that they have these attitudes, and that we should be baffled as to why, now and then, they strike against American citizens.

It is worth taking note of an oddity in Congress's actions. As a result of Sen. Inouye's intervention, you and I have also contributed $8 million to Ozar Hatorah, a New York–based Jewish organization, to subsidize schools for North African Jews settled in Paris. Apparently the French government was somewhat taken aback by this burst of American generosity. Our State Department's proposal to Congress, to appropriate $23 million to "improve the quality of life" of the Palestinians, was on the other hand, soundly rejected by Congress.

In fairness one must add that the U.S. ambassador to Israel, Thomas Pickering, used some rather strong language in criticism of Israel's tactics; and that the U.S. abstained from voting against the Security Council resolution deploring Israel's tactics — this after first managing to get "censure" replaced with "deplore" in the resolution. The other fourteen members of the Security Council all voted for the resolution. Lest anyone be confused by these diplomatic thrusts, however, Secretary of State George Shultz said last week that the relations of the United States to Israel remained as strong as ever. Any rational Israeli politician would conclude from all this that when it comes to the Americans, go by what they do, not by what they say.

Another provision in the omnibus bill passed by Congress in late December orders the administration to close all Palestinian information offices in the U.S. sponsored by the PLO within ninety days, and makes it illegal for any U.S. citizen to receive PLO funds to advocate its views. This gag on free speech is rather nicely called "The Anti-Terrorism Act of 1987." Nobody claimed that the PLO offices had done anything other than what all information offices in the U.S. are allowed to do. Up to last September, the PLO sponsored two information offices — one at the UN and one in Washington, D.C. They gave Palestinian views to Americans in speeches and publications; the one in Washington was operated by an American citizen, Hasan Abd al-Rahman. But in 1986, the Prime Minister of Israel, Yitzak Shamir, remarked that he would like to see them both closed down. The powerful Jewish lobby, AIPAC (American Israel Public Affairs Committee) took up the cause. Congress was poised last summer to pass a bill initiated by Senators Dole and Kemp demanding the closings. The administration, foreseeing that closing the UN office would violate international agreements, tried to assuage Congress by closing the Washington office on its own. It did so in a most creative way. First it used the power of the Secretary of State, under the Foreign Missions Act, to redesignate the Washington office as a "foreign mission," this in spite of the fact that the PLO had not requested such an upgrading; and then on the very same day, September 15, it ordered this "foreign mission" closed within thirty days. The Justice Department had rendered the judgment that an information office could not be legally closed down if it had not broken the law, whereas a foreign mission could be. The reason, according to a spokesman for Shultz, for closing the office was to "demonstrate U.S. concern over terrorism committed and supported by organizations and individuals affiliated with the PLO." As it turned out, however, AIPAC was not satisfied. It went back to Congress; and Congress obligingly passed the law ordering the administration to close *all* PLO offices located within the United States. The fact that this almost certainly violates the U.S. Bill of Rights, and that closing the UN office certainly violates international law, did not deter Congress from its passion to follow the wishes of the Israeli government and the Jewish lobby and get rid of this source of information about the Palestinians.

It must be, one says, that the U.S. is deeply indebted to Israel and wishes to show its gratitude. Well, consider only the events of this past year. Jonathan Pollard, a U.S. citizen, was caught engaged in massive spying on the U.S. for Israel, and was sentenced to life imprisonment by a U.S. federal judge. The Israeli response was to promote the two generals who had supervised him. Again: In the fall of 1986, Congress passed its sanctions bill against South Africa. A provision in the bill stipulated that any nation trading with South Africa could no longer receive aid from the U.S. The administration was required to issue a report to Congress by May, 1987. In May the administration notified Congress that Israel was trading with South Africa. Congress suppressed the report. And again: All through the year we have heard tales about Israel's role in the Iran-Contra caper, and about its resistance to cooperating with the U.S. investigating committees. Of this, however, the Senate committee run by Daniel Inouye wished to know nothing. What it wanted to know was what the President of the U.S. knew and when he knew it — about Iran and the Contras.

I think all this should be called what it is. On the part of the Israelis, it is appalling brutality and self-righteous cynicism. On the part of American politicians, it is appalling moral depravity and hypocrisy.

Over and over it is said that terrorism is the issue. Terrorism is not the issue. It is not the issue for us. The Contras in Nicaragua are, by any reasonable definition, a terrorist group. They terrorize civilian populations for the purpose of achieving political ends. Not only do we allow them to spread their information freely in this country; we pay them to do so and to conduct their terrorism. The Contras have killed many more civilians than has the PLO, in spite of their much shorter existence.

Neither is terrorism the issue for Israel. Mubarak Awad is a Palestinian who advocates non-violent means of opposition to Israeli policies. He has established, in Jerusalem, the Palestinian Centre for the Study of Non-Violence. Israel was on the verge of deporting him last spring when the U.S. ambassador expressed strong disapproval; he remains in Israel up to this time, though without his deportation order having been cancelled.

Israel's stated reason for its action is that Awad stirs up unrest; and that, though he is a native Palestinian, he took out a U.S. citizenship while living in the United States as a student. Thousands and thousands of Israelis are American Jews who, while now living in Israel, have kept their U.S. citizenship; rather than being deported, they are placed in subsidized housing. Or again: Hanna Siniora, editor of the Arab newspaper *Al-Fajr* in Jerusalem, has also consistently opposed force, to the loss of his reputation among many Palestinians. Recently he proposed that rioting be replaced by a gradually escalating boycott of Israeli products, beginning with cigarettes. He was notified that if he held a press conference to call for the beginning of the boycott, he would be arrested. So the issue is not terrorism, or even violence. Israel wishes to snuff out all Palestinian resistance, be it violent or peaceful; it wishes even to snuff out all expressions of Palestinian identity. American politicians support them in this. It is the *leaders* among the Palestinians that Israel has calculatingly deported over the years — not rock-throwing young hoodlums but university presidents, mayors, bishops, and scholars. (That seems also to be true of the four who have just been deported.)

Israel has fundamentally five options with respect to the Palestinians. It can preserve the status quo, in which it tries to keep 1.5 million Palestinians in subjection while depriving them of their civil rights. It can try to drive the Palestinians into Jordan and then declare that Jordan *is* the Palestinian state. It can annex the occupied territories and make those who dwell there Israeli citizens, albeit second-class ones, like the Arabs who are presently citizens of Israel. It can try to work out some arrangement with Jordan whereby some sort of joint rule over the Palestinians is established. Or it can accede to a separate Palestinian state, thereby granting the Palestinians the same right it has claimed so fiercely for itself over the years. The two solutions which the great bulk of Israelis have always rejected are the third and the fifth; there is no consensus on which of the others to pursue. The Palestinians are under no circumstances to have their own independent state; and the Palestinians are under no circumstances to be made citizens of Israel — this last because the Palestinians will outnumber the Jews in the region by around the year 2000, and the "Jewish character" of the state of Israel will then be threatened. Though the U.S. talks about trading land for peace, it has always, in the last resort, supported Israel in whatever form of rejectionism it chose, and has for more than ten years now refused to talk to the only group recognized by the Palestinians themselves as their representative, the PLO. Thus for the U.S. and Israel to pin the label of "rejectionism" on the PLO in particular and the Palestinians in general is a classic case of projection. Everyone knows that the PLO has been willing for some time now to settle for a separate state — and to recognize Israel as part of the bargain. Recently the courageous Jewish Israeli journalist Israel Shahak wrote that "Shortly after June 1967 I formed the opinion, based on the mood of Israeli Jews and the facts created by the Israeli government, that the occupation of all the territories conquered in the war, including Sinai, would last for a long time and that nothing short of war or *real* pressure by the U.S. would reverse the situation."

I think it not unlikely that we will eventually see the deep significance of the 1987-88 riots to be that Israel's opportunity of settling for a separate Palestinian state has been lost, and that the Palestinians will now settle for nothing less than what Israel has always most feared, a binational state. Israeli officials have accused the PLO of inciting the riots. But the Palestinians hardly need anybody to incite them. The riots took the PLO by surprise; it took Arafat several days to make his first public statement about them, pretty clearly because he didn't know what was going on. The riots were, by everyone's report, the spontaneous outburst of resentment against an occupying power by people who have nothing to lose. They will continue, and increase. Apparently they are now as much inspired by the radical religious sentiments of certain Islamic groups as by the nationalist sentiments of the PLO. In that mixture lies a fateful new potential. The PLO has always argued for what it called a "secular state" — by which it meant a state in which people of all religions and races are treated in nondiscriminatory fashion. Radical Islam is opposed to secular states; what it wants for itself is Islamic states. It appears to me that in the current mixture of ideologies among the Palestinians, radical Islam is on the rise and nationalist Palestinianism is on the decline. After all, what has nationalism achieved, other than rejection and oppression? That means that it is becoming more and more likely that if the Palestinians do secure their own state, it will be a discriminatory Islamic state, to match the discriminatory Jewish state. Or perhaps, as I suggested above, radical Islam will no longer settle for its own Palestinian state alongside Israel, as the PLO was willing to settle for, but will settle only for all of Palestine. Either way, I think the hope for a nondiscriminatory Palestinian state alongside Israel faded away sometime during this past decade into fantasy and illusion. The chance has been lost.

Whichever of the two scenarios proves correct, binational state or separate Islamic state, the hopes of the Arab *Christians* within Palestine have also been crushed into illusion sometime during this past decade. Christians are discriminated against in the present Jewish state; they will be even more discriminated against in a discriminatory Islamic state. For Islam sees the miseries of the Palestinians as due to the *Christian* West. All the fidelity of Arab Christians to the gospel, all their rich contributions to the cause of Arab nationalism, will have been washed into the sands of the Middle East. As Islam takes over from Palestinian nationalism, Arab Christians can only stand by and watch — and fear. I fully expect that when the crunch comes, American fundamentalist and liberal Christians will skip off and try to wash their hands of all responsibility; but the tribunal of history will judge that the blood did not wash away.

And what of the Jewish people, whose cup of suffering, whether through their own folly or the brutality of others, seems never to end? It was of course folly in the first place to think that the security of the Jewish person in the world would lie in the formation of a tiny Levantine state whose land had been seized by force from its native inhabitants. Zionism is among the great illusory failures of the 20th century. The security of Jewish people lies in countries like the U.S. But one knows for a surety that there will also come a time when U.S. politicians will dance away from the issue — just as the Reagan administration danced away from Lebanon, pleading no responsibility whatsoever for the murderous anarchy of that now-sad country. What will happen then to the Jews in the Middle East? I do not know. They will be in danger.

When will American Christians, and American politicians — and the American Jewish lobby — wake up to the enormous tragedy unfolding before our eyes?

The Troubled Relationship
between Christians and Human Rights

An obvious aspect of the troubled relationship between Christians and human rights is that Christians have participated in some of the most egregious violations of human rights. Sometimes this happened because they sold their soul to one and another nationalism or patriotism: in serving what they judged to be the interests of their people or country, they wronged those who were not of their people or country. Sometimes this happened because they sold their soul to mammon; in pursuit of their own wealth, they wronged the neighbor. But sometimes they have used explicitly Christian reasons for wronging the other; sometimes they have gone so far as to claim that they were acting out of Christian love.

On this occasion, I want to focus my comments not on the ways in which Christians have participated in violating human rights but on the discomfort of many American Christians with the conceptuality of natural and human rights, and even with the conceptuality of justice. My evidence for the claim that many American Christians do experience this discomfort is necessarily in large part anecdotal; I know of no social scientific research on the matter. Let me mention just one of the many anecdotes in my bag of evidence. It was reliably reported to me that at the last national assembly of my own denomination, a speaker got up and declared, in objecting to one of the documents before the assembly, that the word "rights" should never appear in any document of the church. I am told that no one arose to disagree with him; the document was rejected.

To anecdotes can be added, as evidence, the sizable number of writers who have urged Christians to repudiate the idea of natural rights, promi-

148

nent among these being Alasdair MacIntyre, and Joan and Oliver O'Donovan. Some have gone farther and urged that Christians avoid rights-talk in general, and even that they avoid talk of justice; Stanley Hauerwas is an example.

I must insert a qualification. When their own perceived interests and convictions are at stake, often those same Christians who express discomfort with rights-talk happily employ such talk: they defend the rights of parents, they defend religious rights, they argue for the right to prayer in the public schools, they discuss abortion in terms of the right to life. I assume that what is going on here is that they have observed that the great reform movements of the twentieth century were all conducted in terms of rights and have decided to borrow the rhetoric of those movements for the purpose of advancing their own interests and convictions — apparently without noticing the irony of what they were doing.

I think I understand why many of my fellow Christians are uncomfortable with rights-talk. Though they have several reasons for discomfort, the dominant reason is that they hear such talk as expressing and promoting an attitude of possessive individualism. Rights-talk, so they believe, is for insisting on getting what one thinks one is entitled to. They find such insistence incompatible with the call of the Christian gospel to extend oneself in loving service to the neighbor.

The more intellectual among them support this aversive reaction to rights-talk in general by subscribing to a popular narrative concerning the origin of the idea of natural rights. The idea of natural rights, so it is commonly said, arose out of the individualistic political thought of the Enlightenment — the word "secular" usually prefacing the word "Enlightenment." A variant on this narrative is that though the political philosophers of the secular Enlightenment certainly employed the concept of natural rights, they did not originate it; it first made its appearance centuries earlier when the nominalist William of Ockham introduced and employed the idea in the course of defending his fellow Franciscans against attacks from the pope.

As I suggested earlier, a good many Christians are uncomfortable not only with the conceptuality of rights but with the conceptuality of justice, whether or not justice is thought of in terms of rights. It is commonly assumed, by Christians and non-Christians alike, that justice has been supplanted in the New Testament by agapic love, this being understood as gratuitous benevolence. The love that Jesus attributed to God and enjoined on us with respect to our neighbors is said to be a love that promotes the well-being of the neighbor whether or not justice requires it. Agapic love is justice-blind and justice-indifferent. The exemplary and paradigmatic example of such love is said to be God's forgiveness of the sinner; forgiveness does not render to the wrongdoer what justice requires, since justice does not require forgiveness.

Given this widespread understanding of Christian love, it is no accident that Christian social agencies and international aid organizations almost always formulate their mission in terms of charity rather than justice; they see themselves as charitable organizations. Jesus' Parable of the Great Assize, as it was traditionally called, has long been the grand charter of Christian social work; "as you do it unto one of the least of these, so also you do it unto me," says Jesus. That which Jesus cites as done unto the least of these is understood not as rendering to her what justice requires but as extending to her the hand of charity.

It is my conviction that until these roots of discomfort with the conceptuality of justice, with the conceptuality of rights, and with, in particular, the conceptuality of natural rights, are rooted out, a great many Christians will be indifferent if not hostile to the struggle for human rights — except when it comes to their own interests. In a world where a billion or more people are Christians, that constitutes a serious impediment to the cause of human rights. And rooted out they must be. For in my judgment, they are seriously misguided. Let me explain.

It is of course true that one can use the language of rights to insist that one get what one sees oneself as entitled to. But if that is the extent of one's employment of rights-language, one is abusing the language. All moral language can be abused. When the authoritarian gets hold of duty-language, he abuses it by highlighting the duties of others while downplaying his own. When the possessive individualist gets hold of rights-language, he abuses it by insisting on his own entitlements to the ignoring of those of others. When some part of moral language is abused, the appropriate response is to resist the abuse, not to throw out the language.

When you come into my presence, you come bearing morally legitimate claims on me as to how I treat you; if I fail to honor those claims, I wrong you. Likewise when I come into your presence I come bearing morally legitimate claims on you as to how you treat me; if you fail to honor those claims, you wrong me. The situation is completely symmetrical. The language of rights is for bringing these normative social facts to speech. And *social* facts they are; rights, like duties, require at least two. The difference is that when I think of your and my normative social relationship in terms of my duties, I focus on myself and my agency; when I think of it in terms of your rights, I focus on you and on the actions that respect for your worth require of me.

What then about the narrative which says that the idea of natural rights was born of either the individualism of the Enlightenment or the nominalism of Ockham, and that possessive individualism is in its DNA? As the result of the work of such eminent legal historians as Brian Tierney and Charles Reid, we now know that both of these narratives are flatly false. Tierney, Reid, and others have shown beyond the shadow of a doubt that the canon lawyers of the twelfth century had already articulated and were employing the concepts of natural and human rights. No one has yet suggested that these canon lawyers were infected by possessive individualism.

That raises the question: where did the twelfth-century canon lawyers get these concepts from, or were they original with them? My own answer is that though the canon lawyers may have been the first to articulate these concepts with clarity, one finds a recognition of what have come to be called "natural human rights" in the church fathers — for example, in the claim made by many of the fathers that the excess goods of the wealthy "belong to" the impoverished.

And where did the recognition by the church fathers of the phenomenon of natural human rights come from, or was it original with them? My view is that it comes from the New Testament, and back beyond that, from the Hebrew Bible. I realize that this is a highly controversial claim. On this occasion I cannot defend the claim; in my book, *Justice: Rights and Wrongs*, I do so at length. Here I can only give a glimpse of how part of my defense goes.

One clue to the fact that rights are recognized in some piece of discourse, even though the concept itself may not be employed, is that persons are understood as susceptible to being wronged; to be wronged is to be deprived of that to which one has a right. In turn, one of many clues to the fact that persons are understood as susceptible to being wronged is that someone is said to have forgiven someone. One can only forgive someone if he has wronged one, and only *for* the wrong he did one. The declaration that God forgives runs throughout the Hebrew Bible. God forgives us for wronging God — for depriving God of the worship and obedience to which God has a right.

Another clue to the fact that rights are recognized in some piece of discourse, even though the concept itself may not be employed, is that persons are understood as having a worth that requires of us that we treat them in certain ways. Obviously God is understood in the Hebrew Bible as having such worth. But so too are human beings. The writer of Psalm 8 exclaims over the elevated status of human beings in the cosmic scale of beings; they bear the image of God. In Genesis 9, murder is declared to be a deed worthy of corporal punishment because "in his own image God made humankind."

I said earlier that many of my fellow Christians have embraced the common narrative which says that the concept of natural human rights was an invention of the secular Enlightenment or of the nominalist Ockham and carries possessive individualism in its DNA. Having accepted the narrative, they have handed over the concept of natural human rights to the secularists among us and announced that henceforth they will confine themselves to talking in terms of benevolence, charity, freedom, and the like. I find this painful. The recognition of natural human rights is a gift of the Hebrew and Christian Scriptures to the world. Once one has affirmed that each human being has the worth that ensues upon being created in the image of God and being redemptively loved of God, the recognition that each and every human being has natural human rights is right there in front of one.

"Half right," many of my fellow Christians will reply. "Right about the Hebrew Bible, wrong about the New Testament. In the New Testament, justice and rights have been supplanted by agapic love — by gratuitous, justice-blind, benevolence." Here I can give just one of several reasons for concluding that this interpretation is mistaken. I hold that justice is at the core of the New Testament; pull justice out and everything unravels.

Jesus declares in Matthew 22 that the two greatest commandments in the Torah are that you shall love the Lord your God with all your heart, with all your soul, and with all your mind, and that you shall love your neighbor as yourself. What Jesus cites here as the second of the two greatest commandments in the Torah is taken from Leviticus 19. Let me quote the passage that leads up to the command. The situation is that Moses is delivering to his fellow Israelites God's instructions on how they are to treat their fellow Israelites and the resident aliens among them:

> You shall not render an unjust judgment; you shall not be partial to the poor or defer to the great; with justice you shall judge your neighbor. You shall not go around as a slanderer among your people, and you shall not profit by the blood of your neighbor.

You shall not hate in your heart anyone of your kin; you shall reprove your neighbor, or you will incur guilt yourself. You shall not take vengeance or bear a grudge against any of your people, but you shall love your neighbor as yourself: I am the LORD.

The injunctions Moses delivers fall into two groups. Some are injunctions to practice primary justice toward the neighbor; some are injunctions on how to treat the neighbor who has violated primary justice. Israelites are not to render unjust judgments, neither against the poor nor against the powerful. They are not to slander their neighbors. When a neighbor is in trouble, they are not to stand idly by. They are to reprove those who do wrong; but they are not to bear grudges against them, hate them, or take vengeance on them. In short, each is to love his neighbor as himself.

Love and justice are not pitted against each other; rendering justice is a manifestation of love. To be faithful to our own scriptures, we who are Christians must articulate and employ an understanding of love which incorporates the pursuit of justice rather than being blind and indifferent to what justice requires. New Testament love, I submit, is not gratuitous benevolence, blind to justice.

Had I conducted this discussion in the usual way, I would have conceded that the UN documents on human rights are a glorious legacy of the secular Enlightenment and gone on to ask whether there are nonetheless Christian reasons for getting on board with human rights. I hold that the assumptions behind this way of conducting the discussion are all wrong. The right question to ask, the question I have asked, is why so many Christians are reluctant to embrace human rights as a precious part of their own heritage, and whether the grounds of their reluctance are tenable.

Christians apparently constitute a majority of the American populace. If large numbers of those of us who are Christians are uneasy about human rights claims, we had better expect that our country will continue to treat human rights in the politicized, self-serving way that it so often does. We had better expect that our president, be that the current holder of the office or another, will lecture those countries who are not our allies on their violations of human rights while at the same time conducting the affairs of our own country as if our enemies were creatures of little or no worth. We had better expect that he and his administration will engage in legalistic arguments as to whether or not certain detainees have habeas corpus rights and whether certain forms of hard treatment constitute torture, ignoring the fact that even these hostile detainees are human beings who possess the precious worth of bearing God's image and being objects of God's love. We had better expect that he and his administration will refuse to join the ancient church fathers in acknowledging that impoverishment amidst wealth is not a shortfall of optional charity but a violation of justice.

Six Days in South Africa

The call from Allan Boesak came early on the morning of Tuesday, October 15: would I come to Capetown as soon as possible to testify on his behalf in the hearing to get his bail conditions lifted?

I had come to know Allan in the academic year 1980-81, when he was the first of the multi-cultural lecturers at Calvin College. He and I, his family and mine, became close friends. To the call for help from a brother one does not say No. But could I really be of help — I, a philosophy professor from a college in mid-western America?

Saturday night I was on the plane in New York, visa in hand, and on Sunday night I stepped out to be greeted by Allan, his wife, and one of their friends, Henry Bredekamp. We had to cut short our catching up around their kitchen table because the next day Allan and I had to go early into downtown Capetown to prepare the case with his attorneys.

As we were driving into the city the next day there once again flooded over me the feeling I had so strongly experienced here before, of the enormous antiquity of this land. Is it these huddling hills, ground down but not away by ages of wind and washing rain? Is it these trees and flowers designed in the exuberance of earth's spring but now lined and toughened with years? I do not know. But it feels as if creation began here, the Ancient of Days here first trying his hand at separating land from water, calling forth life, working out from here to my own land of sharp peaks and frail columbines. A land at rest, youth's striving past, wise with years, ripe. On the road before us I saw a strange khaki-colored vehicle — rather like a bus but open at the top so that if people stood up in it their heads would poke out. The glass at the sides was obviously bulletproof, and everything else was plated with armor. "What's that?" I asked. "A casspir," said Allan. I didn't ask what casspirs were for.

During my stay I saw a casspir in action only on videotape. Police were standing up in the casspir, pointing guns at school children, while other police were standing on the ground firing tear gas cannisters into a high school. The police force was integrated — mostly white, but some black. The school was not integrated: only black children came pouring out, sneezing, coughing, crying hysterically, tumbling over the fence, faces mingling fear and hate. Apparently their crime was that they had been active in protest rallies in preceding days.

Henceforth there will be no such videotapes. The South African government has forbidden the photographing of disturbances, on the ground that photographers have been paying people to conduct the disturbances. I do not know who might have been paid in the disturbance I saw photographed.

For twenty-six days during September Allan had been held in solitary confinement. With one exception, the only person he saw during that time was his interrogator, Major Nel. His wife was allowed to see him just once, for one hour, with Major Nel standing by watching and listening. She was not allowed to talk about happenings in South Africa and the world, only about their family. The third week of solitary detention had been for Allan a period of spiritual crisis. He described the experience for his congregation in the first sermon he preached after being released from detention. His captors allowed him no book other than his Bible, neither did they allow him any paper.

Upon releasing him from jail, the government filed charges against him — though even now the bill of charges is not final. The charge, currently, is that of sedition, as specified in the security legislation. The acts Boesak is alleged to have committed, which the government contends are acts of sedition, are recommending a consumers' boycott, recommending a school boycott, recommending disinvestment, and helping to plan an illegal march on Pollsmoor prison. Allan denies that he ever recommended a school boycott. He freely admits having done the other things — though whether these are acts of sedition, as defined in the security legislation, are matters never yet tested in court.

Some years ago various people in the United States advocated a boycott of California lettuce. In South Africa that would be an act of sedition, punishable with twenty years in prison.

THE BAIL CONDITIONS on which Boesak was released included such normal conditions as the payment of 20,000 Rand, the stipulation that he not communicate with state witnesses, and the stipulation that while out on bail he not recommit the acts for which he was being charged. But the other conditions had the effect of placing him under house arrest; they made it impossible for him to do the work to which he has been called.

Accordingly, the hearing was to ask the court to order the government to lift the "house arrest" conditions. His attorney would argue that if the government wanted to ban him, then they had better do so straightforwardly and live with the consequences. What they could not do is ban him under the guise of setting bail conditions.

The bail conditions Boesak was protesting were that he sign in at the Bellville police station every day before 9:00 a.m.; that he be in his house every night between 9:00 p.m. and 6:00 a.m.; that he not leave his suburb of Bellville without the written permission of the police; that he surrender his passport; that he attend no meeting of more than ten people, except for regular services at his own church, without written permission of the police; that he not visit any educational institution except to pay house calls on student members of his congregation; that he not submit to any media interviews; and that he not attend any funerals except with police permission.

In the lawyers' offices I learned that the legal profession in South Africa is like that of England in that it is divided up into solicitors and barristers. Solicitors do the ordinary run of legal work which does not require argument in court, in addition to preparing material for court cases; barristers argue the cases in court. Boesak's solicitor, Essa Musa, in cooperation with the junior counsel with whom he works closely, Seraj Desai, had decided to secure as senior counsel for this case an Afrikaner, Henrik Viljoen, head of the South African lawyers' association. Viljoen had never before defended in a political case. Over the course of the week I came to admire his skill, his integrity, and his courage. He remarked at the end that it had been the most instructive week of his life!

I also learned, that first day, that South Africa has two court systems: that of the magistrates and that of the judges. Judges are appointed in approximately the same way as in the United States. Criminal cases and cases on appeal are heard by the judges. Other cases are heard by magistrates. Magistrates are civil servants. Subject to certain conditions, their promotion, demotion, and release are at the pleasure of the government. Boesak's case would be heard in magistrate's court.

To prevent crowds, the case had been moved from Capetown to the small village of Malmesbury about 45 minutes away. We learned that the proceedings would begin on Wednesday and then resume again on Friday. I would be the first witness, since I could not stay into the next week and senior counsel was unable to predict how long the testimony would take.

What was it that they wanted from me? To testify that it was indeed indispensable for Boesak to have his passport back if he was to do the work that the Reformed churches of the world had asked him to do in appointing him as head of the World Alliance of Reformed Churches. To testify, also, that Boesak, of all people, would not flee the country and fail to stand trial. Third, if it became relevant, to testify that I had always known him to recommend nonviolent resistance. And finally, if the government contended that ministers of the gospel, such as Boesak, should stick to purely "spiritual" matters and stay out of politics, to testify that an important strand in the Reformed tradition has always refused to accept any dichotomy between the "spiritual" and the political.

AFTER A LONG DAY of preparation we returned to the Boesak home in Bellville — which now in daylight I could see to be a simple, somewhat dull suburb reserved for "colored" people. I learned that the section of Bellville in which Boesak lives has just one road going in and out, being entirely surrounded by a large industrial park and by freeways. The environment of the Boesak home is enlivened by the lights and noise of a large plastics factory right across the fence.

We stepped into a house full of people milling about: the four Boesak children running in and out with their school friends, and adults popping in to hear how the case was going, to give Allan one and another piece of information, to solicit his advice, to cheer him on. That is how it would be every evening while I was there; every evening would be open house.

The next morning I was introduced to another daily routine. About 7:15 a call came informing Allan about the people who had been taken into detention the night before — many of them friends and acquaintances. For the rest of the week the same call would come each morning a bit after 7:00. On Friday morning the caller reported that more than 80 people in the Cape area had been arrested, including the entire executive of the regional council of churches, the entire local executive of the United Democratic Front, student leaders, academic leaders, and others. One of those detained was Charles Villa-Vicenzio, theologian from the University of Capetown. Charles is an acquaintance of mine who had been scheduled to come over to the Boesaks that evening.

"Where is Charles being held?"

"They won't tell us."

"Why is he being held?"

"No charges are filed."

"Can any of us find out where he is and go to see him?"

"The security legislation allows only his attorney to see him."

Then, as if the security legislation did not already give the police all the powers they could use, on Saturday morning a state of emergency was declared in the Cape area. Under the state of emergency, not even an attorney may see the detainee, nor are police obligated to publish a list of those detained. I heard on the Monday following that Charles's office at the university had been ransacked by the police, as had the offices of the regional council of churches and those of the UDF. It was also on that Monday that the government forbade the news media from photographing or tape-recording any disturbances.

SHORTLY AFTER the phone call on that Tuesday morning, Allan and I set out again for Capetown. On the way we stopped at the Bellville police station. A policeman gave Allan a salute of sorts as we entered; I watched as Allan signed his name in a book which had lots of names in it. Upon our leaving, a black man ran from across the street to whisper how much he supported Allan in what he was doing. As we got back on the highway, a new, bright yellow casspir rumbled along ahead of us.

We arrived in central Capetown a bit early for our meeting; so we strolled for a while through those magnificent old gardens in the center of the city. As we entered the gardens some black people sitting on a bench recognized Allan and jumped up and warmly shook his hand, some calling him Busakwe. So it went continuously as we walked along: perhaps eight out of every ten blacks recognized Boesak and jumped up to greet him.

After walking through the gardens, we entered the professional building to go up to the law offices. Here almost everyone was white. No one uttered a word of recognition in the elevators or the corridors; instead, most of them carefully pointed their faces away and then glanced at us out of the corners of their eyes in that sly way all of us adopt when we want to look at someone without appearing to look.

WEDNESDAY MORNING we drove out to Malmesbury. Malmesbury, I would judge, is a village of some 2500 people. Police were everywhere in the center of the village. I asked someone how many he thought there were. Maybe 200, he said. I had not seen such a concentration of firepower since early 1982 in Beirut. These police were older, though, and more professional, than the militia in Beirut. The courtroom held about 60 people, kept in order by three police. Almost all in the audience were black. The main language of the hearing was English, but when a witness felt more comfortable with Afrikaans, the language shifted over to that for his testimony.

In South African law there are three standard considerations for setting bail. The State wants to be assured that the accused will stand trial, that he (or she) will not interfere with State witnesses, and that while out on bail he will not again commit the acts with which he is charged. The State had stipulated in its bail conditions that Boesak not do either of the latter two; these stipulations he was not contesting. Hence the only issue left — so it seemed — was whether he would likely flee the country if his "house arrest" were lifted.

I stepped into the witness box and was sworn in. I testified that if ever anyone deserved to be released on his own recognizance, it was Boesak. All he stood for, and all he had been struggling for, would come crashing down if he did not stand trial. And I testified that Boesak had to be present on the international scene if he was to do the work that the worldwide church had asked him to do.

In his cross-examination of me the State attorney revealed his strategy — though not to me at the time. He never questioned my testimony that Boesak would stand trial. Nor did he question my testimony that Boesak was needed on the international scene. Thus it would seem that all the "house-arrest" conditions should be lifted. What purpose in law did they serve other than assuring the State that Boesak would be available for trial? Instead the State attorney pressed me on Boesak's commitment to nonviolence. I testified, as firmly as I knew how, that he was indeed committed to nonviolent protest. Then the questioning shifted course.

"You know, do you not, that there is good deal of unrest and violence in South Africa at present?"

"Yes, I have read about that."

"And you are aware that a good deal of this unrest and violence has followed speeches by Boesak?"

"About that I do not know. But I have read that violence followed the speech of the State President in August. Yet your government does not seem to regard that as a reason for silencing the State President."

"No further questions."

To Boesak's attorneys the strategy of the State was now clear. South African law contains a provision which says that beyond the standard considerations, bail conditions may also be set by reference to State security. It appears that considerations of State security have never in fact been decisive in setting bail. What the State would argue was that in this case, for the first time, State security should be the decisive consideration. But how exactly did they think that Boesak endangered the security of the State of South Africa? That would become clear in due course.

Boesak himself was to be the next witness, but before he took the stand, a recess was declared. Most of us went out into the courtyard — we few whites amidst the blacks, all surrounded by white policemen. There was a great deal of laughter and joking. Suddenly I remembered what I had also noticed in the Middle East: the oppressors are grim while the oppressed laugh. The policemen keeping their eye on us were all grim. Even grimmer was Major Nel, who was to testify against Boesak for the State on Friday. He had found a chair in the courtroom separated from the rest of us; there he remained sitting in catatonic sobriety, legs crossed, staring fixedly across the room while we were outside in the courtyard.

Back inside, Boesak was put in the witness box. In cross-examining him, the State attorney, quite incredibly, gave him wide-open opportunities to make eloquent speeches, never cutting him off.

"How can we be assured that if your passport is returned, you would not simply leave the country and not stand trial?"

"I would never abandon my people. To the contrary, I would relish standing trial to speak the truth about this country."

"Is it not true that you think it appropriate to engage in political activities in addition to your work as minister?"

"I do not regard my political activities as something in addition to my call as minister of the gospel. I come from a tradition, the Reformed tradition, in which we refuse to separate the political from the spiritual. As Abraham Kuyper said, there is not one square inch of this world which does not belong to the Lordship of Jesus Christ." (Allan says that here he saw a smile cross the face of the magistrate; later we learned that he is an elder in the Dutch Reformed Church.)

"But is it not true that you have condoned violence?"

"I have consistently preached against violence. I have said that violence destroys the soul of those who commit violence. It is destroying the soul of the Afrikaner. Do you think I want it to destroy the soul of my own people as well? Besides, I have always said to the young people, You throw stones, they shoot bullets."

"But do you not agree that your speeches are very emotional, and that they may well provoke violence, whether you intend that or not?"

"Show me a single case in which that has been true."

"We shall produce evidence on Friday."

The court adjourned for lunch. We emerged from the courthouse to a crowd of a thousand people, mostly black, neatly lined up along the street. They let forth a mighty cheer when they saw Boesak; and when he walked across the street to shake hands with some, they broke their policed ranks and swirled around. For lunch we drove out of the white village to a restaurant in the adjoining black township. After perhaps a half hour inside we came out to find ourselves again in the midst of a cheering crowd, this time of about twelve hundred students chanting "Boesak, Boesak, Boesak," each one trying to shake Boesak's hand.

FRIDAY IT WAS the State's opportunity to present its case. Major Nel was one of the two witnesses, the other being Captain van Schalkwijk, head of the riot police in Bellville. The strategy was now perfectly clear: to argue that Boesak's speeches provoked violence, that this violence endangered State security, and that accordingly his bail conditions should remain approximately as they were. The State cited some four or five episodes which it regarded as decisive evidence that Boesak's speaking produced violence. Viljoen's cross-examination of the witnesses was elegant drama. It was alleged that Boesak had spoken at the University of the Western Cape on July 25 and that, as the result of his speech, the students had rioted on July 26.

Viljoen: "Major Nel, are you quite certain that the speech occurred on July 25?"

Nel: "Yes, I am."

"And that the riot occurred on the 26th?"

"Yes."

"And that it was Dr. Boesak who spoke on the 25th?"

"That is correct."

"No one else?"

"No, just Dr. Boesak."

"And that he spoke at the University of the Western Cape?"

"Yes."

"And that the riot occurred at the same university?"

"Yes."

"The next day?"

"Yes."

"Well, I do not wish to embarrass you, Major. But Dr. Boesak could not have spoken at the University of the Western Cape on July 25. He was in the United States on that day. He has plane tickets to prove it."

"Then my information must have been mistaken."

What was happening, I asked myself. Whatever else was to be said about the Afrikaners, I had always thought that they were competent. But this was incompetence beyond belief.

Another key episode in the State's case was a riot of the students at the University of the Western Cape on July 29. Van Schalkwijk had a photo of Boesak among the uproarious students.

Viljoen: "Did you hear what Boesak said to the students?"

Van Schalkwijk: "No, I did not."

"So you don't directly know that he was stirring them up to violence?"

"No."

"Might he not instead have been trying to calm them down?"

"That is possible."

At this point Viljoen presented as witness an official from the university who testified that, on the day in question, a riot was already taking place at the university when the Rector called Boesak at his home and asked him to come to the university as soon as possible to calm the students down.

So it went, for all the other alleged episodes of Boesak's provoking violence. What we were seeing, I concluded, was the incompetence which flows from the arrogance of power. When political clout wins all your cases, then competence is a dispensable commodity. I remembered the incompetence of the State's testimony at the inquest into Steve Biko's death. But in spite of the incompetence, the magistrate in that case decided in favor of the State.

Apparently chastened by the repeated, "Then my information must have been mistaken" of his witnesses, the State attorney in his closing argument never tried to connect Boesak to violence. He just said that South Africa was experiencing a great deal of unrest and that there was ample ground in the law for setting bail by reference to State security. No doubt he was hoping that the magistrate's mind would draw connections that his own argument did not. Viljoen was eloquent in showing that the State's case was entirely void of merit. We emerged from the courthouse into a yet larger crowd of yet more loudly cheering admirers than on the Wednesday before.

The hearing had gone in Boesak's favor beyond anything we had dared hope. On the evidence, and on the law, the magistrate simply could not decide anything other than to lift all the contested provisions. Insofar as one could read his face, he was sympathetic. Yet we were apprehensive. Magistrates are, after all, human beings, with a natural desire to please their superiors. What we expected was a compromise which, while giving Allan some of what he asked for, would not seriously embarrass the State.

The Boesak house that late afternoon was filled with laughter and excited talk. Over late supper we talked. Together we watched a videotape of one of the UDF rallies at which Allan had spoken. Clearly these rallies were not only very moving occasions but also great fun, with singing, chanting, and riming. Here is part of one of the rimes:

> Die oumas, die oupas,
> die mammas, die pappas,
> die boeties, die sussies,
> die hondjies, die katjies,
> is saam in die struggle.

> The grandmas, the grandpas,
> the mamas, the papas,
> the brothers, the sisters,
> the dogs, the cats,
> are together in the struggle.

Each time Allan would shout out the first words — for example, "die oumas" — and the people in rhythm would shout out the response — "die oupas." They would also intersperse the lines with the Xhosa sentence, *Amandla ngawethu* — "The power is ours." The effect was hypnotic.

Saturday evening the Boesaks drove me to the airport. After a warm farewell at the ticket counter, I walked straight ahead to the passport checker. "Was that Dr. Boesak you were with there?" he asked. "Yes, I replied." He wrote something down. "I see from this that you stayed at 6 Hoekstraat in Bellville; isn't that Dr. Boesak's address?" "Yes," I said. He wrote again, much more lengthily this time. Then he sent me on my way with the hope that I would have a good trip back.

Monday a week later the magistrate was to deliver his opinion. So around 6:00 p.m. Capetown time I called to find out the news. The background noise in the Boesak house told me. The magistrate had ordered lifted all the contested provisions, with the exception of the 20,000 Rand payment, and had gone out of his way to scold the State for the incompetence of its case. A man of courage and integrity! Allan added something ominous: "I think the government is going to play tricks with me and not give my passport back." Next day his suspicion was confirmed: the government refused to obey the magistrate's order to return the passport. Thus do those who so loudly trumpet the supreme value of law and order disobey their own laws when that seems good in their eyes. They prize order — their order — more than law.

It is now almost three weeks since I returned; for two weeks now my mail has daily brought me a sheaf of letters, most of them anonymous, trying to correct my views about South Africa and about Allan Boesak. Most of the letter writers include clippings of newspaper editorials from around the U.S. which I may not have noticed, and pamphlets which may not have come my way.

Boesak supports communism, the letters say.

I asked Allan about the photograph of him with the communist flag behind him which Jerry Falwell's organization and others have been circulating. That picture, he told me, was taken at the big funeral in Cradock. Some eight or ten other clergymen were also present. During his speech he noticed a photographer with a big zoom lens moving around on the floor in front of him; he wondered why the photographer wanted to take a picture of him from below up. He learned later that the photographer was trying to get him lined up with the flag, and that he was using a zoom lens to reduce the apparent distance between Boesak and the flag. Boesak did not see the flag, and has never, he insists, seen a communist flag at a funeral or a UDF rally or any other meeting he has attended. His own guess is that the police planted the flag and hired the photographer. He publicly accused the police of having done so and received no reply. On the other hand, he added, if it was planted by communists, it probably did them good to attend a good Christian burial service.

The trouble in South Africa, say the letters, is being stirred up by outside agitators, specifically by communists.

We Americans revolted against the British to throw off an oppression mild by twentieth-century standards. Was our revolt due to outside agitators? The Afrikaners revolted against the British to throw off an oppression mild by comparison with that which they are wreaking on the blacks. Was their revolt due to outside agitators? May it not be that blacks like oppression no more than whites? May it not be that at some point they too say, "Enough"? May it not be that they too have a sense of dignity and do not want it trampled on? Why this racist assumption that were it not for outside agitators, blacks would be content with oppression?

South Africa, the letters say, is the last bastion of the free world and of Western values in southern Africa. If the government there falls, the communists will take over.

What is one supposed to say to Allan Boesak? That he preach contentment-in-suffering to his people? That he keep them away from the prophetic literature of the Bible on the chance that their reading of that might prove inflammatory? That he distort the biblical witness lest his people hear the biblical call for justice and start asking for their rights, with the result that the government will fall and the communists take over and Western values disappear? That he tell them that apartheid is an example of Western values and that they should prize those values? Is communism to be held at bay throughout the world by propping up repressive regimes and concealing the liberating message of Scripture? Are we endlessly to dun the Soviets for their oppression and be silent about other oppression, lest if we say anything we weaken our oppressor friends and let the Soviets come flooding in? Is that how communism is to be fought? On the contrary, communism feeds precisely on situations of oppression; in desperation people turn to the East for liberation when from the West they get only a brushoff. If the white government of South Africa would tomorrow start talking seriously to representative members of the black community, communism would have no more chance in South Africa than it does in the United States. But if the South African government resists such talks, and if the United States is seen as acquiescing in such resistance, communism will indeed gain a foothold in South Africa. Communism's greatest promoter in southern Africa is the South African government and its policies.

We should "lay off" the Afrikaners, the letters say. They are changing. They must be allowed to change at their own speed lest chaos result.

Suppose there were no pressure on the Afrikaners to change — what reason is there to think that they would change? Instead we would hear that apartheid is working and that the blacks are happy, for one hears no complaints. That's what we heard in the United States before the civil rights movement took hold — "our blacks in the South are happy, so why change?" Let the insultingly racist suggestion be repudiated that the choice is between oppressive white rule and black chaos. The black leaders in South Africa no more favor chaos than do the whites. They too recognize that change will have to be gradual. They too realize that politics is the art of the possible. But give us a sign, they say — give us a real sign. If you could put this whole vast system of apartheid into effect with such wrenching rapidity, why is it that you cannot dismantle it? asked Bishop Tutu in a recent speech. "We have told the South African government we know that fundamental change of the sort we demand, political power sharing, cannot come about overnight. After all, politics is the art of the possible and this we know too."

But, say the letters, though the black leaders in South Africa may think they are engaging in peaceful protest, look at all the violence they are provoking.

It ill becomes Americans and Afrikaners suddenly to recommend pacifism as everywhere the road to reform except when dealing with communists. Those who praise the American Revolution and those who sing of the Boer War lack moral standing to urge pacifism on the oppressed people of the world. But apart from that, of the more than 800 people killed on the streets of South Africa over the past year, at least 600 have been unarmed blacks killed by the police. Who is the perpetrator of violence? Why do we never notice state violence — except of course when perpetrated by communist states?

But, say the letters, we agree that apartheid must go; we only disagree with the methods that Boesak and his cohorts are using.

What methods do you want them to use? They are committed to peaceful protest. During the planning of the Pollsmoor march Boesak cabled Louis le Grange, Minister of Justice, saying "Please give peaceful protest a chance." The only alternatives to peaceful protest are no protest and violent protest.

But, say the letters, we are not against peaceful protest; it's the breaking of laws that we oppose.

There comes a time when one must obey God rather than human beings. And the State is not god, nor even the South African state. Suppose that to quiet the unrest produced by anti-abortion rallies and marches in the United States, our government passed a law forbidding any such rallies and marches. Would those who regard abortion on demand as a murderous business — I count myself among them — then think it their Christian duty to melt quietly away? Then why is it different for the blacks in South Africa opposing the murder of their already born children?

But, say the letters, the blacks are better off in South Africa than any other place in Africa; they have no ground for protest.

Many contest that claim. But suppose it is true. Why do we suddenly assume that people, if they are black, should live by bread alone? Why do we insist that blacks trade in their rights for a mess of pottage? The American revolutionaries fought not because they wanted to be better off but because they wanted their rights. The Afrikaners fought not because they wanted to be better off but because they wanted their rights. Why are blacks supposed to be different? Talk to Afrikaners for a while and they will give you long narrations of acts of charity extended to the blacks by them and their relatives and friends. I am not sceptical of those narrations — though one has to balance them with narrations at least as long of acts of brutality. But what the blacks are saying is not, Stop your brutality and give us your charity. They are saying: Stop your brutality and give us our rights.

But, say the letters, Boesak is not willing to talk to Botha.

That is not true. Boesak and Bishop Tutu and the rest are indeed willing to talk to President Botha. But they want to be assured that the talk will be serious talk, not just a ploy. Tutu in the speech I referred to pointed to what he would regard as signs of seriousness: a common citizenship for all South Africans, abolition of the pass laws, cessation of population removals, and a uniform educational system. You and I as white Americans must resist our indigenous temptation to devise a solution for South Africa. We must urge the whites in South Africa to resist the same temptation. We must insist on just one thing: that the whites in South Africa talk seriously with those blacks acknowledged by the blacks as their leaders, as to how they can all live together in their common land with justice and peace and prosperity. Until the white government talks to Mandela, Boesak, Tutu, and Tambo, we can be sure that it is not yet serious.

But, say the letters, Boesak has prayed for the downfall of his government. How can a Christian do that?

Yes, he has. And shouldn't we all? What else does one pray for when confronted with a tyrannical regime hard of heart?

THROUGH A HAZE of blood and tears I saw the ripe sere brooding hills of that beautiful land. When will the haze lift? When, in that land where it seems creation itself began, will re-creation begin? When will the serene peace of those ancient hills embrace justice among the people?

Seeking Justice in Hope

Every human endeavor that is not coerced requires, as a minimum, the hope that its goal will be achieved. Optimism is not required — optimism being understood as the expectation that one will achieve what one endeavors. The ambulance attendant who endeavors to resuscitate the person pulled down by waves at the beach may not expect to succeed in his endeavor; he may not be at all optimistic. Yet as long as he sees some hope, he tries. If he thinks there is no hope, he gives up and stops trying.

Maybe there are one or two sorts of exceptions. Imagine a person who has just suffered considerable paralysis as the result of an accident. The doctors are now trying to determine the extent of the paralysis. One of them says to the patient, "See if you can wiggle your right thumb." So the patient tries. In this case, the person does not know whether there's a chance of his wiggling his right thumb. He does not know one way or the other as to whether it is hopeless. He tries to wiggle his right thumb so as to find out. But apart from cases in which one tries to do something so as to find out whether it's hopeless, or alternatively, to prove that it is hopeless, endeavor presupposes hope — not optimism necessarily, but hope. Though let it be said that often we give up on an endeavor if we are not optimistic about its success; it's just not worth trying.

I

In this essay I want to reflect on the sort of hope that working for justice requires. Working for justice does not require optimism; sometimes one works for justice in situations like that of the ambulance attendant who tries to resuscitate his patient without expecting to succeed. What working for justice does require is hope — hope of a peculiar sort, as we shall see. I should state here at the beginning that these will be *Christian* reflections on the sort of hope that the struggle for justice requires.

Thomas Aquinas, in the first Part of the second Part of his *Summa theologiae*, Question 40, Article 1 *(resp.)*, offers a characteristically lucid analysis of hope. Hope, at bottom, is a special form of desire, says Aquinas. It is unlike fear in that its object is a *good* of some sort — or at least, something that the agent regards as good. It is unlike joy in that its object is a future rather than a present good. It is unlike the desire for small things in that, in Aquinas's words, its object is "something arduous and difficult to obtain." We do not, he says, "speak of anyone hoping for trifles which are in one's power to have at any time." And it is unlike despair in that "this difficult thing is something possible to obtain: for one does not hope for that which one cannot get at all." An admirable analysis, I say!

Later, in Question 62 of the same Part of his *Summa*, Aquinas asks whether hope, along with faith and charity, is appropriately regarded as one of the theological virtues or whether it is an intellectual or moral virtue. First he explains the difference.

> The object of the theological virtues is God Himself, Who is the last end of all, as surpassing the knowledge of our reason. On the other hand, the object of the intellectual and moral virtues is something comprehensible to human reason. Wherefore the theological virtues are specifically distinct from the moral and intellectual virtues. (Art. 2, *resp.*)

Aquinas then argues that faith, hope, and charity are theological virtues. His argument goes like this. For human beings, there is the possibility of a "supernatural happiness," this consisting in a delighted knowledge of God that goes beyond what can be achieved by the use of our ordinary human capacities. If we human beings are to achieve supernatural happiness, we need some sort of supplement to our creaturely capacities — some sort of "supernatural" addition. Aquinas takes faith, hope, and charity to be the result of such an "addition." He explains the relationship among the three as follows:

> First, as regards the intellect, man receives certain supernatural principles, which are held by means of a Divine light: these are the articles of faith. . . . Second, the will is directed to this end . . . as something attainable; this pertains to hope. . . . [And] the will is, so to speak, transformed into that end; this belongs to charity. (Art. 3, *resp.*)

What I want to take from this quick dip into the deep waters of Aquinas's *Summa theologiae* is his claim that Christian hope is hope for consummation — consummation here being understood as a supernatural mode of union with God. Christian hope, as Aquinas understands it, is not hope for what might transpire in history. Hence it has nothing in particular to do with the struggle and longing for justice in this present world of ours. Christian hope is not hope that our struggle for justice will bear fruit, nor is it hope that our longing for justice will be satisfied; it is hope for a state of happiness that transcends history. I judge that in understanding Christian hope in this way, Aquinas is representative of a long and prominent strand of Christian thought.

II

I hold that it is a theological mistake to confine Christian hope to hope for consummation. Recall the numinous episode of the burning bush reported in Exodus 3. The curiosity of Moses, the fugitive shepherd, was piqued one day by a flaming bush that was not consumed. He went to investigate. As he approached he heard, from the region of the bush, the sound of a voice calling him by name but telling him to keep his distance and take off his shoes, for this is holy ground. The speaker then identified himself — what Moses heard was indeed the speech of a speaker, not just sounds in the air or voices haunting a disturbed mind. "I am the God of your father, the God of Abraham, the God of Isaac, and the God of Jacob," said the speaker. Having thus identified himself, God went on to say that "I have seen the affliction of my people who are in Egypt, and have heard their cry because of their taskmasters; I know their sufferings, and I have come down to deliver them out of the hand of the Egyptians, and to bring them up out of that land to a good and broad land, a land flowing with milk and honey."

Now jump to the song (in Luke 1) that the elderly Zechariah was moved by the Spirit to sing upon the birth of his son, John, the one known to us as John the Baptist:

Blessed be the Lord God of Israel,
for he has visited and redeemed his people,
and has raised up a horn of salvation for us
in the house of his servant David,
as he spoke by the mouth of his holy prophets from of old,
that we should be saved from our enemies,
and from the hand of all who hate us;
to perform the mercy promised to our fathers,
and to remember his holy covenant,
the oath which he swore to our father Abraham, to grant us
that we, being delivered from the hand of our enemies,
might serve him without fear,
in holiness and righteousness [justice] before him
all the days of our life.

The theme in both passages is not consummation but deliverance — and correspondingly, not the hope for consummation but the hope for deliverance. Let me elaborate this distinction a bit. In *Eccentric Existence: A Theological Anthropology,* my erstwhile colleague David Kelsey argues, with great imagination and cogency, that the story Christian scripture tells of how the triune God relates to what is other than God has three distinct story lines: the story line of how God relates as creator and sustainer to what is other than God, the story line of how God relates as deliverer or redeemer to what is other than God, and the story line of how God relates as consummator to what is other than God. Christian theology is unique among the theologies and philosophies of humankind in that it articulates this threefold narrative — that is, articulates the threefold way in which the three-person God relates to all that is other than God.

Kelsey argues that these three story lines, though mutually involving, are nonetheless independent; none is a mere component or implication of another. To a person who has heard of God only as creator and sustainer, the news of redemption and of consummation comes as *news* — *good* news. Redemption and consummation are not simply the outworking of the dynamics of creation. Likewise the story line of consummation does not imply that of redemption, nor vice versa. If God's creatures had acted as God wanted them to act, so that there was no need for the deliverance of which the One in the burning bush spoke nor for that which Zechariah expected, God might nonetheless have promised and effected consummation. Conversely, God might have redeemed us from the evils that haunt creation without offering us that consummation which is a *new* creation. The story lines of consummation and redemption do not even presuppose the story line of creation. They do, of course, presuppose that there are beings who can be redeemed and whose existence can be consummated by a mode of existence that goes beyond what "the flesh" is capable of. But they do not, as such, presuppose that the totality of what is other than God has been created by God, nor that the creating and sustaining God is also the God who consummates and redeems.

III

What is it that God delivers people from? From affliction, and from the suffering caused by affliction, says God to Moses. From our enemies, says Zechariah. Those whom God delivers are delivered from those who wrong them. I do not say that God's deliverance is *confined* to the deliverance of those who are wronged from those who wrong them; we must allow that God also delivers us from suffering that is not the consequence of wrongdoing — "natural evils," as they are called. But the deliverance of which God spoke in the burning bush and the deliverance that Zechariah expected was deliverance from being wronged.

What is it to be wronged? It is to fail to receive or enjoy what is *due* one. Each of us finds himself or herself in the situation of lacking all sorts of things that would be good to have. By itself, that is not a sign that we are being wronged. We are wronged just in case we are deprived of some good that is due us. Another way of making the same point is to say that one is wronged when one is deprived of some good to which one has a right. The concept of some good *being due one* is the same as that of *having a right to* that good. Yet a third way of making the same point is that one is wronged when one is treated unjustly. To put it positively rather than negatively: justice is present in some community insofar as its members enjoy those goods that are due them, those to which they have a right.

What we have then is this: the deliverance of which God spoke to Moses in the flaming unconsumed bush and of which Zechariah spoke over his newborn son is deliverance from injustice. And more generally: the story line in the biblical narrative that tells of God's deliverance speaks centrally of God's delivering people from injustice. There is, thus, no mystery as to why it is that in the redemptive story line of Scripture God is over and over characterized as *just,* as *doing justice,* and as *loving justice.* The story line of the Trinitarian God as deliverer and redeemer cannot even get going without the concepts of justice and injustice.

To fully understand the way in which justice and injustice figure in the scriptural story line of redemption we must take a further step and distinguish between, on the one hand, what I shall call *doing justice,* and on the other hand, what I shall call *seeking justice. Doing justice* to someone consists of not wronging that person, of not violating that person's rights, of not treating that person unjustly, of not being responsible for that person's not enjoying what is due him or her. By contrast, *seeking justice* presupposes a case of injustice and consists of trying to bring about justice in that situation. Sometimes seeking justice is a special case of doing justice. That would be the case, for example, if it is the *right* of a person who is being treated unjustly that I, a bystander, try to eliminate that injustice. Even though I am not the one who wronged the person, nonetheless I would not be doing justice if I did not try to get rid of the injustice.

We have to distinguish, in turn — things are getting a bit complicated now! — between two sorts of justice that one can seek to bring about when confronted with a case of injustice. One can seek *retributive* justice; that is to say, one can seek to bring it about that the wrongdoer suffers some kind of retribution, pays some sort of "price," for his wrongdoing. Or one can seek what I shall call *liberating* justice; that is to say, one can seek to bring it about that the victim is freed from the injustice being perpetrated upon him.

Sometimes retributive justice is relevant but liberating justice is not; that happens when the act of injustice has already ceased, perhaps because the victim is dead. Sometimes liberating justice is relevant but retributive justice is not; that happens when somebody is being wronged and, though it is appropriate to seek their liberation, the cause of their being wronged is so diffused across some social structure that it is impossible to pinpoint responsibility.

When Scripture speaks of God as just, sometimes what it has in mind is that God does justice to God's creatures, that God treats them justly; on other occasions what it has in mind is that God executes retributive justice. But what is intrinsic to the story line of redemption is God's *liberating* justice. God liberated Israel from the injustice of her slavery in Egypt. And much later, speaking in Nazareth on a Sabbath morning, Jesus announced to his hearers that the following words were being fulfilled as he spoke:

> The Spirit of the Lord is upon me,
> because he has anointed me to preach good news to the poor.
> He has sent me to proclaim release to captives
> and recovering of sight to the blind,
> to set at liberty those who are oppressed,
> to proclaim the acceptable year of the Lord.
>
> (Luke 4:18-19)

Return now to hope. The Christian hopes for two things: she hopes for redemption and she hopes for consummation. She hopes for deliverance within this created order, especially deliverance from injustice; and she hopes for a transformed mode of existence that goes beyond God's work as creator and sustainer — a new creation, a new age, not brought about by the dynamics of creation. Two distinct hopes, neither to be assimilated to the other: hope for the just reign of God within this present creation, and hope for a new creation.

IV

In the Gospel of Matthew we read that the last words spoken on earth by Jesus to his disciples began, "All authority in heaven and on earth has been given to me" (28:18). This theme, of all authority now belonging to Christ, is picked up at various points in the Pauline letters — most extensively in First Corinthians 15. Let me quote:

> Christ has been raised from the dead, the first fruits of those who have fallen asleep. For as by a man came death, by a man has come also the resurrection of the dead. For as in Adam all die, so also in Christ shall all be made alive. But each in his own order: Christ the first fruits, then at his coming those who belong to Christ. Then comes the end, when he delivers the kingdom to God the Father af-

ter destroying every rule and every authority and power. For he must reign until he has put all his enemies under his feet. . . . When all things are subjected to him, then the Son himself will also be subjected to him who put all things under him, that God may be everything to every one.

What does this mean — that upon his resurrection, all authority in heaven and earth has been given to Christ, to be retained by him until such time as he has defeated all competing rule, authority, and power, at which time he will deliver the kingship to the Father? What does it mean that Christ is now king and will remain king until he has fully pacified the realm?

A fully adequate answer to this question would require the careful elaboration of at least two lines of thought: an exegetical study of the line of thought in those New Testament passages where this proclamation of Christ as king comes to the surface, and a study of the Old Testament background to these passages so as to discern the connotations of "king" and "kingship." This is obviously not the place to develop adequately either of these approaches. I confine myself to a brief indication of the relevant Old Testament background.

The Old Testament writers were well acquainted with bad kings. What they had to say about bad kings is much less relevant to our purposes here, however, than what they had to say about good kings. The *locus classicus* is the opening of Psalm 72. Let me quote part of it:

> Give the king thy justice, O God,
>   and thy righteousness to the royal son!
> May he judge thy people with righteousness,
>   and thy poor with justice!
> Let the mountains bear prosperity for the people,
>   and the hills, in righteousness!
> May he defend the cause of the poor of the people,
>   give deliverance to the needy,
>   and crush the oppressor!
> . . . .
> May all kings fall down before him,
>   all nations serve him!
> . . . .
> For he delivers the needy when he calls,

the poor and him who has no helper.
He has pity on the weak and the needy,
    and saves the lives of the needy.
From oppression and violence he redeems their life;
    and precious is their blood in his sight.

What comes through emphatically in this passage is that the business of the good king is justice. Prosperity is also invoked. But it is not from the king that one expects prosperity; one expects it, or hopes for it, from the favorable operations of the natural order, here symbolized as "the mountains" and "the hills." Further, the king's concern with justice is not so much *doing justice* as *seeking justice* — struggling to relieve *in*justice. The good king delivers the needy, defends the cause of the poor, and saves the weak and needy from oppression and violence.

Let us now go back to what Paul might mean when he says that all authority belongs to Christ until such time as all competing power and rule have been conquered, at which time Christ will hand the kingship over to God the Father. Given this Old Testament background, what else could he mean but that Christ is now at work in the world seeking justice — that is, working for the abolition of injustice? Paul's implicit thought must be that there are two kinds of kingship, the kind that consists in the administration of a polity in which there is no injustice, and the kind that consists in struggling to overcome the injustice present in some polity. Christ's kingship is of the latter sort. When Christ's conquest of injustice has been completed, that kind of kingship will no longer be needed, whereupon the Father will exercise the former kind.

I do not suppose I have to argue here that those over whom Christ has authority are not confined to the members of the church; Christ's authority extends to all humankind. There has been a powerful tendency in Christian political theology of the latter part of the twentieth century to place the church at the center of reflections on social justice and governmental authority. That seems to me a mistake. It is indeed as a member of the church that the Christian, including then the Christian theologian, speaks and acts. That is the epistemological and ontological location of the Christian. Only when standing in that location can one hear the totality of the story of the threefold way in which the triune God relates to all that is other than God. But the story heard when standing in that location is far more than a story about the church. It is — to speak now only of the story line of redemption — a story that tells the good news of Christ working to undo the wrongs that we inflict on each other, working to undo injustice.

V

It is rather often said that whereas most of humanity has thought in terms of a cyclical view of history, Judaism introduced a linear view. I cannot speak to whether there are linear views of history to be found outside Judaism and its sphere of influence. What does seem to me indubitably true is the converse: Judaism introduced a linear view of history — though not in the way that this claim is generally understood. In the Wisdom literature of the Old Testament, where there is little if anything of the story lines of redemption and consummation, only that of creation, there is also little if anything of a linear view of history. The picture is that of nothing new under the sun. Everything comes around again: springtime and harvest, birth and death, dawn and dusk, poverty and wealth. It is in the story lines of redemption and consummation that one finds a linear view of history — not because the biblical writers narrating these story lines had an ontology of time but because the redemption and consummation story lines are inherently linear. They are stories of new things happening and yet to happen, not of the same old things happening yet again.

Fundamental to modernity are a blending and secularizing of the story lines of Scripture in such a way that there is thought to be good ground within the natural order for expecting that society will someday be liberated from injustice and each of us will flourish until we die. A few scientists have even speculated that eventually a technology will be discovered that halts aging, thereby eliminating death due to old age. Those who successfully dodge fatal accidents will be able to retain the vigor, the agility, the curiosity, the libido, of a twenty-five-year-old.

This is optimism, not hope, grounded in creation, not God. The claim or assumption is that there are grounds within the natural order for expecting this happy turnout. Hope in the power of Christ to establish his kingdom of justice is replaced by optimism grounded in the powers of nature and humankind to secure both justice and well-being.

Jean-Francois Lyotard's claim to fame is his announcement of the end of all grand meta-narratives of progress. The announcement seems to me premature. It's true that those narratives have died which located the ground for optimism in the potentials of central economic planning and non-democratic political regimes; a vivid telling of the dashing of those hopes can be found in Jonathan Glover's book, *Humanity: A Moral History of the Twentieth Century*.[1] But the lesson drawn in most quarters of the West is not that we should give up on optimism; the lesson drawn is rather that our optimism should be grounded on the potentials for justice and well-being borne by a market economy combined with a democratic polity. This particular meta-narrative, far from being dead, is flourishing as never before.

Christian writers and laypeople in the modern world have regularly succumbed to the temptation to jump on the bandwagon of one or another of the optimistic meta-narratives of modernity, justifying the jump by declaring that those particular dynamics of creation identified by the narrative in question are the *means* whereby Christ is bringing about his just rule. After all, God does use secondary causes, does he not? Some have thought that Marxism successfully identified those dynamics, others that Nazism successfully did so; some have thought that American nationalism contained the crucial dynamics. Many now think that market capitalism combined with political democracy does so.

These conflations of Christian hope with secular optimism are one and all heretical. Though they all propose keeping God in the picture as the principal cause of those secondary causes that they identify, they nonetheless all conflate the story line of redemption with the story line of creation. Rather than redemption being seen as God's unexpected good news for a creation mysteriously haunted by wrongdoing, redemption is seen as the playing out of the potentials of creation. Let it be added that the currently popular meta-narrative, mentioned above, is as implausible as all the others. Rather than expecting that market capitalism in combination with democracy will bring the end of injustice, should we not instead expect that the increasing integration of economies around the globe into one capitalist system will bring about a truly calamitous worldwide economic collapse?

VI

If the hope that Christ will bring about his just kingdom is not to take the form of optimism concerning the potentials of one and another dynamic

1. New Haven: Yale University Press, 2000.

within creation, what form is it then to take? Let me begin my answer with what will initially seem like a diversion. On 15 June 1985, a large number of Christians in South Africa participated in a "Prayer Service for the End to Unjust Rule." It was of course to God that they addressed their prayer — not to the African National Congress, not to the South African government, not to anything at all other than God. The "Prayer of Petition" that they together uttered on that day went as follows:

> This day O God of mercy
> We bring before you all those
> Who suffer in prison,
> Who are oppressed,
> Who mourn those who died in freedom struggles
>> in places like Soweto, Cross Roads, Uitenhage,
>> Sharpeville and many places not known to us.
> Deliver us from the chains of apartheid, bring us all
>> to the true liberty of the Sons and Daughters of God.
> Confound the ruthless, and grant us the power of your kingdom.

In an open letter from prison issued on 23 March 2001, and addressed to Kader Asmal, the Minister of Education in the South African government, Allan Boesak wrote as follows about the place of prayer within the struggle to overturn apartheid:

> . . . prayer is not doctrinal formulations or the mumbling of magical formulas. Neither is it an escape from our earthly responsibilities. Rather it is a call to take up those responsibilities, not on our own, but in total dependence on the grace of God and in the power of God.
>
> Yes, for this very reason our prayers are sometimes political. They must be, because all the world is the Lord's, and there is no area of life, not a single inch, that is not subject to the lordship of Jesus Christ. So politics and politicians cannot consider themselves outside the demands of the gospel or outside the circle of prayer. We pray for politics, not because we feel so much at home there, in that world of intrigue and compromise, of betrayal and awesome responsibility, but because even there we must assume our positions as believers. Even there we must dare to name God, to confess God within the womb of politics, and so challenge every idolatry

that seeks to displace God in the lives of God's people. And so we came together to pray for transformation, political and societal and economic; and we prayed for personal transformation, for conversion, so that people might be driven by inner conviction rather than by political expediency.

We pray also because we believe passionately in the power of prayer. Prayer changes things, Christians say, and that is true. It is that conviction, you will remember, that inspired us in 1985 to call for a day of prayer for the downfall of the apartheid regime. We prayed then in the midst of a storm too, and we were viciously condemned by all who felt themselves threatened by a God who listens to the prayers of the oppressed. We were vilified by those whose interests could not abide the changes we were praying for. But the thing is, God heard our prayers, things changed, and apartheid is no more.

And it is not as if this is something new. We have always believed this. God is a God of liberation and those deeds of liberation can be seen throughout history, beginning with the liberation of the people of Israel from slavery. And Christians have shared this faith with others in this country for so long as anyone can remember. My own participation in the struggle for liberation in this country was based on, and inspired by, my faith in Jesus Christ.

[Christians] come together to pray because they are deeply convinced that transformation that is only social, economic and political, however indispensable, is not enough. They believe that we need the power of God in our lives so that transformation can be fundamental. Let me be bold, Minister: South Africa would not be free today if there were not such people, and South Africa needs them today more than ever before. As you reflect on the history of South Africa as you did last Wednesday, please do not forget this. More than anything our struggle was sustained by prayer and faith. I know. I was there. Denying this historical truth will only exacerbate our already grave situation.

The occasion of Boesak's writing this letter was that two days before, on 21 March 2001, forty-five thousand Christians had gathered in the Newlands stadium in Cape Town to pray for peace, justice, and true reconciliation, while only about three hundred had shown up for an ANC rally at which Kader Asmal was the main speaker. In a fit of pique, Asmal attacked the assembly of Christians as exclusivist.

I submit that Christian hope for liberating justice will take the form, among other things, of prayer. It will take the form of petitionary prayer: it will pray in hope for the undoing of injustice, not only for the undoing of injustice in general but for the undoing of particular injustices. It will have the courage to name injustices and then to pray for the undoing of the injustices named. And if those named injustices are undone, Christian hope will then offer prayers of thanksgiving, not just for the undoing of injustice in general but for the undoing of the named injustices.

What this obviously presupposes is the courage to identify the hand of God in history. To name the injustices for whose undoing one thanks God in Christ is to identify the signs in history of Christ's liberating work.

In addition to taking the form of prayer, Christian hope for liberating justice takes the form of struggling for such justice. *Ora et labora* has always been the conviction of the Christian church. Not just praying and then, in addition, working — praying for one thing and working for another — but working for the very thing for which one prays. Which of course presupposes, once again, naming the injustice. One cannot struggle for the undoing of the injustice whose alleviation one has prayed for without naming it. The Christians of South Africa struggled for that for which they prayed; its name was, the overthrow of the apartheid regime.

You and I have been schooled to become extremely edgy when anyone proposes to identify the hand of God in history. With good reason: some of the things that have been identified as the doings of that hand are appalling. We don't have any particular trouble naming some case of injustice and struggling for its elimination. But we become nervous when we name that same injustice in our prayers and pray to Christ that he will crown with success our efforts at alleviating that injustice. And we become *extremely* nervous when, upon the success of our endeavors, we thank Christ for the alleviation of that named injustice. For how else is this to be interpreted but as identifying the hand of Christ in history? To thank Christ for some named case of liberating justice presupposes, like it or not, identifying that as a sign of Christ's liberating work in history. And that makes us nervous.

VII

Jacques Ellul concludes his book, *The Politics of God and the Politics of Man*, with a quite extraordinary chapter that he titles "Meditation on Inutility." "In spite of God's respect and love for man," says Ellul, in spite of God's extreme humility in entering into man's projects in order that man may finally enter into [God's] own design, in the long run one cannot but be seized by a profound sense of the inutility and vanity of human action. To what end is all this agitation, to what end these constant wars and states and empires, to what end the great march of the people of Israel, to what end the trivial daily round of the church, when in the long run the goal will inevitably be attained, when it is always ultimately God's will that is done, when the most basic thing of all is already achieved and already attained in Jesus Christ? One can understand the scandalized refusal of modern man who can neither accept the inutility of what he has done nor acquiesce in the overruling of his destiny.[2]

Ellul's point is clear. Christian hope for liberating justice is not an optimism grounded in the potentials of creation but hope grounded in the promise that Christ will bring about his just and holy kingdom. That hope is to take the form, in part, of our participation in Christ's cause by ourselves working for liberating justice. But then we learn that God moves in mysterious ways, sometimes bringing our best efforts to naught, sometimes wresting liberation out of appalling evil. And that leads us to ask, what's the point of working in God's cause when God will bring about that cause in whatever way God pleases? What's the point of faithfully seeking justice if our efforts are overruled while justice is wrested from the efforts of those who perpetrate injustice? Is the struggle for justice not futile?

Ellul's response — not so much an answer, I would say, as a response — is, "Just obey." No matter what, obey.

There is a divine law, which is a commandment, and which is addressed to us. Hence we have to fulfill it to the letter. We have to do all that is commanded. The sense or conviction of the utter futility of the work we do must not prevent us from doing it. The judgment of uselessness is no excuse for inaction. . . . Pronounced in advance, futility becomes justification of scorn of God and his word and work. It is after doing what is commanded, when everything has been done in the sphere of human decisions and means, when in terms of the relation to God every effort has been made to know the

2. Jacques Ellul, *The Politics of God and the Politics of Man,* trans. Geoffrey W. Bromiley (Grand Rapids: Eerdmans, 1972), p. 190.

will of God and to obey it, when in the arena of life there has been full acceptance of all responsibilities and interpretations and commitments and conflicts, it is then and only then that the judgment takes on meaning: all this (that we had to do) is useless; all this we cast from us to put it in thy hands, O Lord; all this belongs no more to the human order but to the order of thy kingdom. Thou mayest use this or that work to build up the kingdom thou art preparing. In thy liberty thou mayest make as barren as the fig-tree any of the works which we have undertaken to thy glory. This is no longer our concern. It is no longer in our hands. What belonged to our sphere we have done. Now, O Lord, we may set it aside, having done all that was commanded.[3]

There is something profoundly right about this. Christian hope for liberating justice takes the form of working to undo injustice in the confidence that, in ways mysterious to us, Christ will make use of what we have done, along with that which others have done, good and bad, for the coming of the rule of justice in his kingdom. What I find missing in Ellul, however, is the willingness to identify the signs of Christ's redemptive work. We do our work and then we say, "Make of it what you will, O Lord." That implies that our prayers of petition and thanksgiving for Christ's redemptive work of righting the wrongs of the world must always remain general; they can never name a particular injustice that we petition Christ to remove; they can never name a particular injustice for which we give thanks to Christ that it has been removed. To discern whether this refusal to identify the signs is acceptable I think we must look at what Christians under oppression who cried to God for deliverance have felt compelled to do. The black South African Christians found themselves compelled not only to name the injustice that they petitioned God to remove but compelled to name the righting of injustice that they thanked God for bringing about. To do that is to identify the signs of Christ's redemptive action.

The solution is not to refrain from identifying the signs of Christ's redemptive rule but to resist the arrogance of supposing that our identifications are indubitably correct and complete. Sometimes we miss the signs; sometimes what we took to be a sign proves not to be that. Likewise we must resist the arrogance of supposing that the signs of Christ's redemptive action coincide with the goals of our successful endeavors. Sometimes

---

3. Ellul, *Politics of God*, pp. 195-96.

what we achieved proves, to our deep disappointment, not to be very liberating at all; sometimes what seemed to us a failure proves to be surprisingly liberating. Christian hope for liberating justice is both confident as to its ground in Christ and humble as to our ability to discern the ways in which our endeavors contribute to the coming of Christ's rule of justice.

VIII

A good many of Rembrandt's paintings were initially painted by apprentices in his workshop; Rembrandt then applied the finishing touches. Sometimes what a gifted apprentice handed over to the master was already so much like a Rembrandt that little remained for the master to do; on other occasions, though the preliminary painting came from the hand of the same gifted apprentice and was again very close to being a Rembrandt, it nonetheless fell short in such a way that the master had to do a lot of re-painting in order to bring it up to his standards. On other occasions, the apprentice was so incompetent that Rembrandt had to do a major re-painting in order to make it a Rembrandt; on a few occasions, though the apprentice was again very incompetent, he nonetheless somehow produced a painting that required only a bit of tweaking by the master to bring it up to standard.

The apprentices hoped that they would produce paintings that would require very little re-painting by the master; some even dared hope that someday the master would say, "It's right just as it is." But the master so regularly surprised the apprentices with what he did to their productions that they became quite tentative in their expectations as to what he would do. They did not entirely give up expectations; but by and large they just stood back and expected once again to be surprised. However, they did become rather good at discerning when the master had completed a painting and when a painting still needed his touch. The ability to recognize when a painting was a true Rembrandt was, of course, important for them; how else could they aim at producing such paintings?

Some of the apprentices, observing that sometimes a quite bad production on their part required just a bit of tweaking while at other times a rather good production required massive repainting, asked Rembrandt about the point of their work: what's the point of our undergoing all this training and producing all these paintings if our best productions sometimes require a lot of reworking and our worst sometimes almost none?

Rembrandt would have none of this. Do your best to paint a Rembrandt, he insisted. I've been at this a long time; trust me. I would much rather have you try your best than have you just slack off. What you do is important for my work. Trust me, it is.

Hondurans Seek Justice

I touched down in Tegucigalpa, the capital of Honduras, around noon on Saturday, March 20 (2010). For several years Kurt Ver Beek had been urging me to come and witness first-hand the work of la Asociación para una Sociedad más Justa (Association for a More Just Society), abbreviated as ASJ. Now finally the opportunity to do so had opened up. I was joined by a few other visitors from the United States.

Over the course of my five-day visit I was moved and inspired by the dedication, tenacity, imagination, and courage displayed by the staff and leadership of ASJ. I was also fascinated by the way in which the association has crafted its struggle against injustice to the particularities of Honduran society — particularities very different from those of North American society. And I was intrigued by the distinct understanding of the task of the state that was implicit in the work of the association, and by what it was doing to get the state to carry out its task, particularly with respect to the poor.

ASJ is a Christian organization. Most of us are aware of North American Christian organizations doing relief and development work in various parts of the so-called Third World, World Vision being the largest and perhaps the best known of these. Some of us are also aware of North American Christian organizations dealing with one and another form of injustice in the Third World, International Justice Mission being the largest of these. ASJ is different from these in that it is a Honduran organization. It was founded in 2000 by Ver Beek and five others, four of them native Hondurans; its staff has always been almost entirely Honduran, and its leadership is now entirely Honduran. It was while working for a North American relief organization that Ver Beek, a Calvin College graduate, saw the need for an organization that was indigenous to Honduras and focused not on relief and development but on dealing with the most egregious of the injustices present in Honduran society. The association now has fifty-five people on its staff, about three-quarters of them women.

The association has three major projects: the Peace and Justice Project, which is a victims' rights program, the Labor Rights Project, and the Land Rights Project. (Be it noticed that ASJ is not shy of using the word "rights.") Each morning the person or persons in charge of one of the projects described the project to us; then in the afternoon we went out into the field.

Roberto (a pseudonym used for security reasons) heads up the Peace and Justice Project; before coming to ASJ he worked in military intelligence and as an investigator into corruption cases for the Honduran IRS. The Peace and Justice Project provides investigative, legal, and psychological aid to poor victims of violent crime, and assists under-equipped, overworked, and frightened government officials in carrying out their responsibilities toward these victims; when necessary, it prods officials to carry out their responsibilities. Roberto's description of his project set the stage for the descriptions of the other projects as well.

Roberto observed that it is commonly said that the failure of Honduran officials to deal with crime against the poor is due to corruption — graft and bribery. Both he and Kurt argued, however, that though there are indeed corrupt officials, the fundamental problem is not corruption but fear and a pervasive lack of trust. Poor people do not trust the police, the judicial system, or the bureaucracy. The police do not trust the prosecutors, the prosecutors do not trust the police. The result is that the poor are afraid to take action when they are the victims of crime or illegal treatment; they fear that if they file a report with the police or some government official, the person or organization that wronged them will retaliate. The police and prosecutors likewise fear that they will be the victims of retaliation if they take action. There is plenty of evidence that these fears are warranted. What I saw, more clearly than ever before, is that justice is impossible in the midst of pervasive fear and distrust.

A missionary that I talked to described the Hondurans as the most passive people he had ever encountered; he had previously worked in the Dominican Republic and Haiti. By the end of my visit I had concluded that describing the Hondurans as passive is not on target. Nor is it correct to describe them as simply accepting the wrongs done to them. Though they put up with them, they do not cease to say "This should not be." Better to describe them as believing that, because government cannot be trusted, there's nothing to be done in bringing to justice those who have wronged them. Thirty years of democracy have brought them nothing.

I leave it to historians to explain how this climate of distrust developed. Discussions later in the week made clear, however, that the theology dominant in the churches, both Protestant and Catholic, is intertwined with the ingrained habit of doing nothing when one is victimized. In the final judgment, God will punish those who perpetrate crimes and violate the law, and will reward those who patiently put up with the wrongs done to them; it is not for us to undertake God's work. Later in the week we were told that Paul's injunction in Romans 12, "never avenge yourselves, but leave room for the wrath of God; for it is written, 'Vengeance is mine, I will repay, says the Lord,'" is widely interpreted as meaning exactly this. It's not the business of Christians to bring those who perpetrate crimes and violate the law to the bar of earthly justice; meting out justice is God's business.

It's my view that this is a serious and fateful misinterpretation of Paul. Paul is not saying that Christians are to refrain from seeking that justice be done to wrongdoers. He is saying that Christians are not to engage in tit-for-tat retribution. They are not to think in terms of repaying, of getting even, of exercising vengeance. Seeking that justice be done is very different from trying to get even.

This other-worldly theology supports the habit of putting up with the wrongs done to one because government cannot be trusted; conversely, the social habit gives relevance to the theology. When I talk to North American Christians about the biblical imperative to seek justice, the objection I often get is that love supersedes justice in the New Testament. This response reflects a very different theology and biblical exegesis from that which is dominant in Honduras; but the outcome is very nearly the same. Either way, Christians do not seek justice.

The Peace and Justice Project has targeted two of the impoverished neighborhoods in Tegucigalpa, one of 30,000 and the other of 70,000 inhabitants, as places where it will stand alongside the victims of violent crime. When the police in these neighborhoods refuse or decline to investigate crime, whether because of lack of resources, because of fear of reprisal by criminals, or because, even if arrests are made, fearful witnesses will refuse to testify, ASJ has itself stepped in to conduct investigations (the police have to verify the information and make arrests). It has assisted prosecutors in preparing criminal cases. And, when witnesses refuse out of fear to testify in court, ASJ has employed a recourse allowed in Honduran law of "protected witnesses." Witnesses to a crime appear in court hooded from head to foot; as they testify, their voices are technologically altered. In the six years that the Project has been operating, it has played a significant, often decisive, role in the conviction of more than one hundred perpetrators of crime. Homicides in the targeted neighborhoods have been reduced from 42 in 2005 to 9 in 2009; over the same period, the number of homicides throughout Honduras has more than doubled, from 2,155 to 5,012.

In the afternoon we were driven up into one of the targeted neighborhoods, Villa Nueva, and invited into a neat, clean, small, and humble living room. Two women spoke of the rape of their daughters and told of how the police declined to do anything until ASJ intervened; the perpetrators were discovered, apprehended, and convicted. A young man spoke of being shot and wounded, and told of how, in his case too, the police declined to do anything until ASJ intervened; the perpetrators were discovered, apprehended, and convicted. There were no dry eyes in the crowded room.

The next day Claudia Mendoza described for us the Labor Rights Project. Since 1954 Honduras has had a progressive set of labor laws, this the outcome of a massive labor strike against two U.S. banana companies. When it comes to poor workers, however, the laws are often not enforced, partly because of woefully inadequate resources for government investigators, partly out of fear on the part of investigators and prosecutors, and partly because workers fear that if they file a complaint, they will either become the victim of reprisals or be arbitrarily fired. (The high rate of unemployment means that there are always others to take the place of those who are fired.) ASJ has concentrated its efforts on two of the most abused groups, namely, cleaning workers and security guards. The association has now educated more than seven thousand workers on their rights and has been instrumental in winning cases for 135.

A number of companies in Honduras offer security guards on contract to organizations and individuals. Among these, one of the most notorious for its treatment of employees is Setech. Setech employees are sometimes not paid for months at a time, they are forced to work 24-hour shifts, they are not paid overtime, they are arbitrarily fired, and so forth.

Dionisio Diaz Garcia was one of the ASJ lawyers assigned to investigate the practices of Setech and other security and cleaning companies; he managed to bring many systematic violations of the labor laws to the attention of the relevant authorities. On December 4, 2006, Dionisio was assassinated as he was headed for court to participate in a hearing involving security guards. Two men on a motorcycle pulled up alongside his car on a busy street in Tegucigalpa, one of them shot Dionisio at point blank range, and they sped off. Kurt told me that upon hearing the news he fully expected that most of the staff of ASJ would resign; the work was just too dangerous. Only one person left. This is part of what I had in mind when I spoke of the courage of the staff and leaders of ASJ.

Though the assassination of Dionisio occurred in broad daylight and was witnessed by a good many people, some in other cars, some sitting alongside the road selling things, it was only with great difficulty that ASJ was able to get any of these eye witnesses to talk. Eventually a few did, and the perpetrators were identified and apprehended. Both had worked for the Setech organization; the driver of the motorcycle was an active police officer at the time of the killing. Two of the witnesses testified as "protected witnesses" at the trial. The court found their testimony credible, and the two men were convicted of murder. Both are now in jail. ASJ is now working to help and prod Honduran justice authorities to identify and bring to justice those who planned and ordered the assassination.

Claudia concluded her discussion of the Labor Rights Project around 10:30 in the morning; we then went out into the field. First we visited a 1100-bed public hospital whose patients consist almost exclusively of the very poor; the care is free. We tried to engage some of the cleaning women in conversation, but they refused to say anything. ASJ learned recently that they have been told by the company that if they are caught talking to anybody about how they are treated or paid, they will be summarily fired. Shortly one of the top managers of the hospital appeared. He showed us around various areas of the hospital, and explained to us that one of his biggest problems was what he called "the attitude" of some of the workers.

The hospital is surrounded by a high security fence; the gates were tended by guards wearing Setech uniforms. As we were waiting for our van to arrive, we found two guards who were willing to talk. Both told us that they were regularly forced to work 24-hour shifts. One said that he had not been paid for more than a month, the other, that he had not been paid for three months. When we asked whether this happened often, they said it did. When we asked whether the company eventually gave them their back pay, they said that sometimes it did and sometimes it did not. Both were middle-aged men with families; the one who said he had not been paid for three months said he had seven children. Why had they lost their fear of talking to strangers? That never became clear. Perhaps they had decided that being without a job would not be much different from having this sort of job.

Our field trip in the afternoon was to the attorney general's office. Here we met with the head of the division dealing with human rights violations, with the head of the division dealing with crimes against children, and with the director of the prosecutors in the Dionisio case. They expressed their gratitude for the many ways in which ASJ had been of assistance to them: conducting investigations, finding witnesses, encouraging witnesses to testify, lending the prosecutors cars when they found themselves without transportation, and so forth. It became clear in the course of the discussion, however, that ASJ was by no means a lap-dog for the government. The ASJ representatives declared that they too appreciated the level of cooperation between their staff and that of the attorney general's office; but they made clear that they would continue to file complaints, both verbal and written, when they found officials negligent in carrying out their responsibilities. The people from the attorney general's office nodded to indicate that they were well aware of this! I was struck by the large number of women in the upper echelons of the attorney general's staff. Someone remarked that women tend to be more courageous than men.

It was in the course of these discussions in the attorney general's office that there came into focus for me the distinctive stance of ASJ toward government. The implicit assumption in everything ASJ does is that it is the task of government to establish justice in society by instituting a system of just laws, by enforcing those laws, and by securing justice when the laws are violated. Given this assumption, ASJ then does three things: it stands alongside the victims and defends their cause, it holds government officials responsible for enforcing the laws and finding and punishing violators, and it assists the officials in carrying out this task. On the last two of these points: the association does not try to execute an end-run around government, nor does it content itself with dispensing aid and charity to victims; it holds government officials responsible. But it also does not content itself with issuing denunciations; it assists officials in carrying out their task. These observations led me to recall what St. Paul says concerning the task of government in chapter 13 of his letter to the Romans. Government, says Paul, is the servant of God for our good; God has assigned to it the task of "executing wrath on the wrongdoer." We are to give it "due respect."

There in the attorney general's office I also found myself reflecting on how different is ASJ's stance toward government from that of the members of the so-called Tea Party movement presently sweeping across the United

States. The members of the Tea Party movement declare loudly that they want lower taxes, no deficits, less regulation of business, no bailouts, no regulation of firearms, no welfare — though it turns out that a good many of them are on Social Security and Medicare. The rhetoric is relentlessly negative; no suggestions are forthcoming as to which programs should be cut or eliminated if government is both to lower taxes and eliminate the deficit. Government is the enemy; government deserves no respect. That it is the task of government to secure justice never crosses the lips of the Tea Party people. The *New York Times* of March 27, 2010, reports (p. A 17) the results of a recent Quinnipiac University poll of Tea Party members: it turns out that they are "disproportionately white evangelical Christian." Apparently the evangelical Christians in the Tea Party movement have either not read Romans 13 or, if they have, don't take it seriously.

Let me jump ahead a bit. The last afternoon of my visit we attended a meeting of ASJ with the head of a large grocery chain and the head of the firm that does cleaning work on contract for the chain; Claudia, Kurt, and an ASJ lawyer represented ASJ. ASJ has been publicizing and protesting some of the abusive ways in which the cleaning firm treats its workers; a sixty-year-old cleaning woman who had been ordered to take a pregnancy test or be fired had come along with the ASJ team. The head of the cleaning firm was clearly very angry. I will quote exactly, without comment, some of the English translation of what he said: "People in Honduras are always playing the victim. You should have asked my permission before you talked to my workers. There are always people who complain. I've got rights too. Why don't you talk about my rights, why do you only talk about their rights? The Bible tells us to love our neighbors. I'm helping these people by giving them jobs. Let's talk about Christian principles. I'm using my talents. The Bible says that those who are given many talents must use them. I was given many talents. We all have the right to get more than we have. Let the state regulate what I do; you stay out of it. I'm not going to let anybody tell me how to run my company. Leave me alone. I can sue you for slander. I insist on the freedom to do what I want to do. I don't owe anybody any explanations."

On the third morning, Keila Garcia, Byron Zuniga, and Gilda Espinal described the Land Rights Project for us. Tegucigalpa is built on a series of steep ridges; over the past thirty years or so there has been a large influx of poor people who have built houses on outlying ridges. Ownership of the land on which they built was often obscure or contested. Though they always paid someone for their plot of land, it was often not clear that they were paying the right party. Sometimes they never received a title even though they paid the asking price; sometimes the title they received proved invalid. Five years ago the government passed a land reform act. The details of how the act works need not concern us. Suffice it to say that large landowners who can establish ownership wind up with a fair price, and that residents, after paying a fair price for their plots or establishing that they have already paid a fair price, are given clear title to their plot. ASJ has assisted some 60,000 poor families in the Tegucigalpa and San Pedro Sula areas in getting clear title to their plots.

Our field trip in the afternoon consisted of going up into one of the neighborhoods, Los Centenos, where ASJ has been instrumental in helping the people get their titles. The residents were immensely proud of these titles; they displayed them, asked to be photographed holding them, etc. But what I found just as impressive and moving was something Keila, Byron, and Gilda had taken for granted and neglected to mention. The area we visited contained four distinct communities. We learned that whereas the city installed water, sewer, and electrical systems in middle-class neighborhoods, each of these poor communities had to install these systems on its own. In order to do so and deal with other business, each had instituted an organizational structure with a president, a vice-president, a secretary, and a treasurer. Candidates were nominated for these offices, and the community held an election. Women were prominent among the officers. This was small-scale democracy at work. This was activity, not passivity. I asked two of the male vice-presidents leading us around what they did for a living. One said that he was a security guard, the other said that he was retired from being a security guard. I did not ask which firm they worked for. I wish I had.

My visit was all-too-short; I left Honduras on Thursday. But my impressions were vivid, and my memories are indelible. I had seen the faces and heard the voices of some of the wronged and vulnerable in Honduras. And I had witnessed first-hand the work of a thoroughly indigenous organization which, in the name of Christ, defends the cause of the "downtrodden" and, with great tenacity and courage, both insists that the government bring to justice those who have wronged them and assists government in doing so. We here in North America cannot copy what ASJ is doing. We can, however, be moved and inspired to seek justice with courage and tenacity in a way that fits our own situation.

Those who want to learn more about ASJ can do so by consulting the following website: www.asjhonduras.org.

Part Three

CHURCH

"When Did We See Thee?"

W e sent our missionaries into the Chicago ghetto of Lawndale — we of the Christian Reformed Church. Our efforts bore success. Success in the usual sense that a Christian Reformed congregation was formed. Success in the profound sense that some people accepted the good news and that others found the quality of their Christian lives enriched and deepened. Thus a wonderful new member was added to that part of the body of Christ which is the Christian Reformed Church. A congregation with its own precious qualities, capable of making a unique and essential contribution to the whole.

The members of the congregation were black. It's a *black* ghetto. And this black ghetto of Lawndale is cheek-by-jowl with the white ghetto of Cicero.

The members of the Lawndale congregation became convinced that, if their children were to live the Christian life, they needed Christian day school education. The secular, and educationally inferior, public schools of the city of Chicago could not serve as boot-camp for young black Christians.

The missionaries told them about a Christian day school right over the line in Cicero, a school whose supporters were chiefly members of Christian Reformed congregations in Cicero. The people, the black people, applied for admission of their children to the Christian day school in Cicero.

No black people live in Cicero. Lots of them work there. They cross the boundary into Cicero in the morning. They cross the boundary out of

Cicero in the evening. Cicero had a race riot in 1951 when a black man and his family moved in. The black man and his family quickly moved out. Cicero stoned Martin Luther King when he marched there.

The board of the Christian day school in Cicero refused admission of the black children in 1965. They refused their admission in 1966. And in 1967. In 1968. In 1969. The Board also operates a Christian high school in Elmhurst. It admitted black students there.

The Board spoke of two reasons for refusing to admit black students into its elementary school in Cicero. One was the racism in its own constituency. Some members of its constituency said that if black students were admitted, they would withdraw their own children. The other was fear. The Board said that if black students were admitted, there would be serious danger to the school property and to the welfare of the children. They're probably right on this last point. The Cicero police and fire departments would probably give very minimal protection. But the Board has vigorously rejected every proposal that other means of protection be sought — legal injunctions against the City of Cicero, state police, national guard.

Two reasons, racism and fear for the future. The Board at no point worked *with* the Lawndale people in trying to find a solution. The record shows that it has throughout humiliated them and treated them as adversaries.

The tragedy is profound. It has many facets. I speak of only one. God sent among us a people with wonderful Christian virtues. To our theological sophistication they brought a simple faith. To our solemnity they brought joy. To our racism they brought a longing for fellowship across the old walls of partition. To our fear for the future they brought the hearty confidence that God and God's angels would protect the children and the future of Christian education.

God sent among us a poor people, a suffering people. God sent them among us who, though rich, are suffering, suffering from lack of faith and joy and fellowship and confidence. God sent them among us not only that we could show mercy to them but that they could show mercy to us. Not only that they could humbly accept our gifts but that we could humbly accept theirs. Not only that they could see the face of Christ in our virtues but that we could see the face of Christ in theirs.

God sent them to teach us about the Christian life in the way God usually teaches people about the Christian life — by having it embodied and ensouled before our eyes. But we closed our eyes. God sent them among us for our good. But on them we wreaked our wrong. In doing so, we wronged ourselves.

The tragedy of Lawndale and Cicero is one more example of the tragedy of humankind. We don't hear God when God speaks. Once again God's Word was spoken by outcasts. We expected it to be spoken by the respectable and the powerful.

The Bible and Women:
Another Look at the "Conservative" Position

W hat I wish to discuss in this article is the *typical* use of Scripture by a group of people in my own denomination, the Christian Reformed Church, when the subject of the ordination of women is debated. Though I don't like labeling people, I do need some convenient tags; so in what follows I shall use the word "conservative" to refer to the person who opposes the ordination of women and the word "progressive" to refer to the one who favors ordination.

The situation in the CRC at the time of writing (1979) is that the 1978 Synod adopted the following recommendation: "that consistories be allowed to ordain qualified women to the office of deacon, provided that their work is distinguished from that of elders." A number of congregations have, in the intervening year, done just that; but the controversy, which has been under active synodical consideration since 1970, has not died down. The 1979 Synod will have to deal with several dozen overtures and appeals, some asking that the decision of 1978 be clarified (*how* is the work of women deacons to be "distinguished" from that of other consistory members?), others that it be overturned as contrary to the teaching of Scripture. It is on these latter protests that I shall concentrate.

Over and over the conservative in the CRC charges the progressive: "You are playing fast and loose with the Bible, throwing out passages which clearly say that God wants no woman ever to have any authority over any male or do any speaking in the church; and you do so because you have been infected by the secular Women's Lib Movement." Conservatives conclude that in "the women's issue" the CRC is engaged in a battle for the

Bible against the insidious inroads of secularism. They see this issue as a test of biblical fidelity.

The opposite is true. It is the conservatives who typically play fast and loose with the biblical text. Two strategies characterize their handling of the crucial passages. One might be called *pick-and-choose:* take what you like and ignore what you don't like. The other I shall call the *selectively-applied-principle* strategy: elicit from a text a general principle which, if it were true, would keep women out of church office; but then don't make other perfectly obvious applications of the principle just affirmed.

Decisive for the conservative position are just two, very brief, passages: 1 Corinthians 14:34-35, and 1 Timothy 2:11-12. From the entirety of the Old and New Testaments there are just two passages decisive for his case. Of course, it may nonetheless be a good case. But we must remember that we are not dealing with a pervasive biblical theme.

Sometimes, indeed, conservatives cite passages in addition to the two decisive ones. In 1 Timothy 3:2 we read that "a bishop must be above reproach, the husband of one wife"; some have inferred from this that since women are unable to meet the second qualification, they cannot be ordained. But why don't those who draw this inference agitate to keep unmarried and widowed *men* out of the clergy? That is what I mean by the selectively-applied-principle strategy.

In 1 Corinthians 10–14, Paul is speaking to the disorderly church in Corinth about good order in the assemblies. The fundamental principle, he says, is that in the gatherings each member's gifts must, out of love, be used for building up the body. There must be the kind of order in the assemblies which allows that to happen. Then toward the end of the passage, in verses 33-35 of chapter 13, he says this:

> As in all the churches of the saints, the women should keep silence in the churches. For they are not permitted to speak, but should be subordinate, as even the law says. If there is anything they desire to know, let them ask their husbands at home. For it is shameful for a woman to speak in church.

Is Paul saying that women should never be allowed to speak in the assemblies of Christians and that they should always be in positions of subordination in the church? It looks as if he is, doesn't it? And that is indeed the principle that the conservative draws out of this passage.

But in this same "good order" passage Paul says that "any woman who prays or prophesies with her head unveiled dishonors her head" (11:5). Clearly, in the assemblies at Corinth women *did speak* in the form of praying and prophesying, and Paul expresses not a word of disapproval of this. All he says is that they should be veiled when they do it. Thus the conservative picks the 1 Corinthians 14 passage but ignores 1 Corinthians 11. This is what I mean by the pick-and-choose strategy.

But was it perhaps Paul's point in this entire "good order" passage that although women could *speak* in the assemblies, they couldn't speak *with authority?* This interpretation implies that to prophesy is not to speak with authority, which will not do at all; the person who prophesied spoke with authority — the authority of the Lord. The plain fact is that Paul allowed women to speak with prophetic authority in the church at Corinth. What more do any of our ministers do?

There is a little book from the early church called *Didache* ("teaching"), apparently written around A.D. 80. The writer gives a number of instructions for how the Lord's Supper (which he calls "The Thanksgiving") is to be celebrated. At the end of the instruction he says, "But allow the prophets to hold The Thanksgiving as they will." Apparently these prophets traveled from church to church; from this passage it is clear that in the apostolic church they were given *supreme* authority.

The conservatives also follow the selectively-applied-principle strategy when treating 1 Corinthians 14. They interpret Paul as saying that women may never speak in the assemblies of the church nor have any authority there. Yet in almost all our churches, the conservative allows women to be commissioned as missionaries and to teach in church school. Certainly both of these involve *speaking*. And to the reply that these are not cases of speaking in the *official* assemblies, there are two responses: (1) Paul never says that women may speak in unofficial assemblies but not in official ones; he makes no such distinction whatever. And (2), to teach in church school is certainly to exercise authority in the assemblies of the local church. In a Reformed church one scarcely need argue that teachers have authority over their students! Why don't the conservatives agitate for the removal of women from such positions? Again, the selectively-applied-principle strategy.

This is not yet the end of the difficulties with the conservative handling of this "good order" passage. Paul says that women should be veiled, or "if a woman will not veil herself, then she should cut off her hair." He says that "nature itself" teaches this, and "if anyone is disposed to be contentious, we recognize no other practice, nor do the churches of God"

(11:5-16). Now I know of no conservatives in our churches who advocate that women wear veils covering their heads. So once more we find the conservatives practicing the pick-and-choose strategy. They pick up on what's said about the silence of women and ignore what's said about their veils — *in the very same passage.* No doubt there is a temptation to say that the latter is culturally conditioned while the former is not. But Paul does not suggest that the silence-instruction holds for all times whereas the veils-instruction does not. In fact he says that the veils-instruction is a dictate of nature.

In short, I know of no conservative in the CRC who has an interpretation of Paul's "good order" passage that does not follow the two strategies of pick-and-choose and selectively-applied-principle. The use of those strategies, unless based on something more than preference, seriously compromises fidelity to the Scriptures.

Is there an interpretation of Paul in 1 Corinthians that does not suffer from the defects of picking and choosing according to one's taste and of selectively applying principles? I think there is. Paul affirms here that for all time the principle of love holds. Likewise he affirms that when the principle of love is applied to the Christian assemblies, it yields for all time the conclusion that these assemblies should build the people up.

Then Paul applies these abiding principles to the situation in Corinth. He says that they lead to the conclusion that, in that cultural context, men should have short hair and women long hair with their heads covered by veils. He assumes that it is all right for women to pray and prophesy. But he adds that they should keep silence; and he goes on immediately to amplify his point by saying that if they have questions to ask of their husbands, they should ask them at home. If one remembers that women and men almost certainly sat on opposite sides of the church in Corinth, one can see why he says this. All of us would say the same.

To understand in detail why Paul says what he does about veils and hair, we would obviously have to know the practices of the surrounding culture and of the local pagan religions. There is a wonderfully illuminating article on this topic by Richard and Catherine Clark Kroeger in the *Reformed Journal* of June 1978, entitled "Pandemonium and Silence at Corinth." To read it is to feel a flood of light welling over one. But let us move on to consider the passage in 1 Timothy 2:8-15:

> I desire then that in every place the men should pray, lifting holy
> hands without anger or quarreling; also that women should adorn

themselves modestly and sensibly in seemly apparel, not with braided hair or gold or pearls or costly attire but by good deeds, as befits women who profess religion. Let a woman learn in silence with all submissiveness. I permit no woman to teach or to have authority over men; she is to keep silent. For Adam was formed first, then Eve; and Adam was not deceived, but the woman was deceived and became a transgressor. Yet woman will be saved through bearing children, if she continues in faith and love and holiness, with modesty.

Conservatives interpret this passage as saying with great clarity that no woman should ever have authority over any man in the church. But once again the pick-and-choose strategy surfaces: I know of no conservative man in the CRC crusading to have all men raise their hands when praying. Nor do I know of any who forbid their wives and daughters all jewelry. These injunctions are ignored.

Presumably the conservatives, once again, are tempted to say that these injunctions are culturally conditioned. Why else do they ignore them? But they don't want to say the same thing about Paul's injunction against women speaking and having authority. That is supposed to hold for all time. Yet Paul nowhere says that his commands about prayer and jewelry are culturally conditioned whereas those about silence and authority hold for all time.

The conservative might reply that Paul nonetheless appears to ground the command about women not speaking and not having authority in a creation ordinance, whereas he does not appear so to ground the commands about men praying with hands uplifted and women wearing no jewelry. The thought is, thus, that Paul himself appears to give these injunctions a different status.

But now a new problem arises. In the reason he offers, Paul does indeed seem to have in mind a creation ordinance. And since it is a creation ordinance, it is not an ordinance restricted to the church, for of course there was no church at creation. The creation ordinance Paul seems to have in mind is a very general one: no female should ever have authority over any male; or, possibly, no *adult* woman should ever have authority over any *adult* male.

But once again we come up against the conservatives' use of the selectively-applied-principle strategy. For though they wish to use this principle to keep women out of office in the church, there are other perfectly obvious applications of the principle that they do not make. They do not protest against women senators, representatives, governors, mayors, and city council members. They do not argue that we ought not to have women teachers in our colleges and universities. They do not speak out against women as business executives or as members of denominational boards. They do not protest the fact that the Dutch and the Canadians have a queen. And of course they do not suggest that female parents ought not to exercise authority over their male children. All they protest against is this one thing: that women hold office in the church.

In short, I do not see how conservatives can interpret the passage in 1 Timothy without following the pick-and-choose and selectively-applied-principle strategies — neither of which technique can be used in responsible biblical interpretation. I have sometimes heard conservatives argue that Paul is speaking here only about women having authority in the church, not about their having authority in society generally. But that simply ignores his allusion to the creaturely status of men and women.

How then should the Timothy passage be interpreted? I don't know. At least I don't know how all of it should be interpreted. Neither, to the best of my knowledge, does anyone else. I am inclined to think that the commands about silence and no authority are just as much Paul's application of abiding principles to *that particular* cultural situation as are the commands about lifting hands and not wearing jewelry. So I do not follow the strategy of picking and choosing. To know just why Paul issues these commands in that culture, we would again have to know in detail what that culture was like.

Neither do I follow the strategy of selectively applying a principle. The Bible as a whole most certainly does not teach that God wants females never to have authority over males. Just remember: "Honor thy father and *thy mother.*" It does not even teach that God wants adult women never to have authority over adult males. Nor has any Christian tradition ever thought that it taught this.

What is profoundly obscure in this passage as a whole is the *reason* Paul offers for what he says. The reason does indeed *seem* to be his conviction that there is a creational norm to the effect that no woman may ever have authority over any male — though that does not square with the rest of Scripture, nor indeed with other passages in Paul. So I don't know what Paul has in mind here. Neither do I know why he seems to affirm that from Adam's being created first, it follows that men must always have authority over women. As others have pointed out, the animals were created before

Adam; but obviously they do not have authority over humankind. I also do not know what Paul means when he says that women will be saved through bearing children. The suggestion sometimes made — that humankind in general will be saved through Mary's bearing Jesus — seems to me not at all to fit the words. Paul speaks, after all, of *children,* not of *a child.* And neither do I know why Paul says that "Adam was not deceived," since Adam and Eve were both deceived. Some commentators have pointed out that the kinds of things Paul says here can also be found in rabbinical Jewish writings of the time. But that doesn't help us to understand what Paul means.

What should we do when confronted with an obscure text? We should do what we have always done — give weight to the non-obscure ones. *That* is a responsible principle of interpretation. Nobody has ever recommended that the obscure should govern the interpretation of the clear. So let us do here what we have always done. One of the *fundamental* themes of the New Testament is that Christ has come to bring deliverance from every form of bondage and to bring unity where before there was hostility and division. Especially is this the theme of Paul's letter to the Galatians. He summarizes what he says this way: "There is neither Jew nor Greek, there is neither slave nor free, there is neither male nor female; for you are all one in Christ Jesus." It is my firm belief that to keep certain members of the church out of church office just on the ground that they are female is to act disobediently to the Lord of the church. It is to preserve a wall of partition where there should be none. It is likewise my conviction that not to allow women to speak in the assemblies is to refuse to allow them to use fully the gifts of the Spirit of which Paul speaks so eloquently in that same Corinthians passage about good order:

> To one is given through the Spirit the utterance of wisdom, and to another the utterance of knowledge according to the same Spirit, to another faith by the same Spirit, to another gifts of healing by the one Spirit; to another the working of miracles, to another prophecy, to another the ability to distinguish between spirits, to another various kinds of tongues, to another the interpretation of tongues. All these are inspired by one and the same Spirit, who apportions to each one individually as he wills.

And let's not forget this: Paul *did* allow women to speak with prophetic authority in the assemblies at Corinth.

It makes absolutely no difference to me what people in the secular Women's Lib Movement are saying. What I care about is what the Lord of the church and the Spirit are asking of us. I do not see how the conservative position can be held except at the cost of picking and choosing, of selectively applying principles, and of allowing the obscure more weight than the clear. And those are not responsible strategies of biblical interpretation.

So let us together try to put behind us our fears, let us together try to put behind us the insidious effects of the secular movements around us, let us together try to treat the Bible responsibly, and let us together ask sincerely what it means in our day and age that Christ is creating a new humanity in which the distinction between male and female is no longer a wall of partition and what it means that the Spirit pours out on all alike its gifts for teaching, counseling, praying, and preaching prophetically.

Hearing the Cry

What is the upshot of our papers and discussions at this conference on women in the church? Much of it was intellectually fascinating; and that, in my judgment, is something worthwhile in its own right. God did not make us to be just hewers of wood, wearers of clothes, and eaters of food. He also made us to find delight and fulfillment in knowledge. We experienced such delight in these days together.

Nonetheless, we did not assemble for intellectual delight and fascination. What motivated this conference is the fact that a cry is being heard in the church. It is a cry of pain and suffering. It is the cry of women in the church that they are being treated unjustly. It is the cry that this new community which is Christ's body, called to show forth his glory, including then the glory of his justice, is not doing that.

Men must learn to hear that cry for justice. When one group deprives another of just treatment it invariably excuses that treatment by insisting that close scutiny reveals that the oppressed group does not deserve better treatment — that given its nature or behavior, it is already being treated as well as it has a right to expect. One of the saddest of all the results of oppression is that the oppressed group begins to internalize the low esteem that the oppressor has of it. It begins to adopt a low *self-esteem*. One sees this happening in South Africa where many of the blacks, having internalized the whites' opinion of them, believe that they are indeed inferior and ask why God cursed them by making them black. We heard at this conference that when women in the church are made to feel less than fully human, they begin to wonder why God cursed them with being female.

Women at conferences such as this wonder whether they are really adequate. They begin, so they tell us, in paranoid fashion to turn over various episodes to discern whether the men regarded them as not really "up to snuff" as scholars.

The impulse of men in this situation is to become analytic and criticize the *statements* that women make. "Less than fully human? Of course we don't believe that. We believe that you women are just as human as we are. It's unfair of you to accuse us of any such thing." I suggest that the precise formulation is of no importance; the feeling coming to expression is important. Women are expressing the low self-esteem that they have acquired by internalizing the low esteem that they perceive us men as having of them. They are expressing their *doubts of their own self-worth*. Rather than criticizing the particular manner in which the feeling gets expressed, we men have to answer this fundamental question: do we or do we not think that women are equal partners with men in God's creation and kingdom — and, in particular, do we think that they are equally gifted? If we do think that they are equal, we had better listen carefully to a description of the ways in which, in the past and yet today, we indicate otherwise.

But why is the cry coming forth now? We learned at this conference that the cry is not coming forth *just* now. Women in the church have been crying out for more than a century. But the cry has now reached a crescendo. Why?

It is often said that this is just the latest manifestation of an ideology, stemming from the Enlightenment, which says that everybody must be treated as equal and all differentiations rubbed out. The cause, supposedly, lies in the currency of certain *ideas* — academics, of course, always like to attribute power to ideas. Evangelical women, so it is said, are being duped by the ideology of secular feminism.

I think that this reading of the history is almost entirely mistaken. It's true that an ideology of secular feminism is abroad in the land. But Christian women were pleading for justice long before secular feminism was heard of. Rather than presuming that evangelical Christian women have swallowed the ideology of secular feminism, we should listen to what evangelical Christian feminists are actually saying. Women in evangelical churches have swallowed far less of the secular ideology of feminism than men have swallowed of the secular ideology of capitalism.

What has happened is that women who have enjoyed the benefits of universal education have read their Bibles and heard there the message of God's justice and liberation. They have then looked at themselves and noticed that they have been graced with gifts of the Spirit; they have listened carefully and heard the call of God to use those gifts. Then they discover that the church refuses to let them use those gifts, usually without denying that they have them, and refuses to acknowledge that they have heard a call from God. That has pained our women. Right there you have one of the major causes for the crescendo. This cause, as I see it, interacts with another. In the modern West, we have participated in a long social process whereby what sociologists call ascriptivism has been radically diminished. In former times, the social roles that a person occupied were largely determined by factors over which the person had no control. One's position in society was determined by the status and occupation of one's father; by the religion, race, and ethnic identity of one's parents; by one's sex; and so forth. In short, one's social roles were simply ascribed to one. To a remarkable degree this has changed in the modern West, so the social roles we now occupy are determined much more by choice and talent than by ascription. Most of those who complain most loudly about the movement of Christian feminism would themselves be confined to spending their lives as indentured farmers and servants if this vast social process had not taken place.

As ascriptivism diminishes, its remnants prove more infuriating. In our century, two areas have been the focus of controversy: race and gender. Today almost everybody in American society says that people should not be forbidden from certain social roles or assigned to others because of race; many are saying that the same should be true for gender. Yet some in the church say that because certain persons are women, they should be kept out of offices of the church.

My suggestion, in short, is that what has led to the crescendo of voices calling for equal treatment of women in the church is not primarily an ideology, not primarily a cluster of ideas, but rather a social *process* in which we all participate. Failure to notice this makes our discussions socially disembodied. Even if the ideology of feminism disappeared, the pressure would still be there.

We must ask ourselves, then, whether we approve of this diminishing of ascriptivism. We cannot, without hypocrisy, assume that it is good when it yields us benefits and bad when it causes us discomfort. Remember, too, that the breaking down of the walls of ascriptivism has never occurred without struggle and controversy. We now take for granted the right of everyone to be educated; we forget the struggle for this right in the nineteenth century. In my opinion, the message of the Christian gospel gives powerful support to this lessening of ascriptivism and that, as a matter of history, the coming of the gospel into the world contributed to the process.

Let me cast what I have been saying into a slightly different form. As ascriptivism diminished, people asked why such and such differences were relevant to the distribution of social benefits and deprivations. "Why is my being born of a commoner and your being born of a noble relevant to whether we will become educated?" At each point a question of justice was raised; for people are treated unjustly when benefits and deprivations are distributed on the basis of differences that are morally irrelevant. The question that women in the church are raising is a question of justice. There are, indeed, a good many more issues involved than the issue of justice, but justice is basic. Women are not asking for handouts of charity. They are asking that in the church — in the church, of all places — they receive their due. They are asking why gender is relevant for assigning tasks, roles, offices, responsibilities, and opportunities in the church. The gifts of the Spirit are relevant. But why gender? The answer they are given is that this is how God wants it. Immediately it is added that we are, of course, spiritually equal; between men and women there is full spiritual equality. Nonetheless, God does not want women ministers, elders, and deacons. I need not tell you how frustrating it is for women to hear this combination of granting full spiritual equality while insisting on ecclesiastical inequality. What we are dealing with here is again the fundamental question, how is the gospel to be socially embodied in our situation? Over and over the church, when confronted by social realities that are unjust but that it prefers not to change, retreats into spirituality. I notice it in the publicity that I receive from South Africa: the church, so it is said, must stick to spiritual matters. My own denomination, the Christian Reformed Church, to its credit, has traditionally resisted this spiritualizing. True spirituality, it has insisted, is spirituality embodied in life obedience. Yet now, when the issue of women arises, a chorus of voices insists that spiritual equality between men and women must remain purely spiritual; it must not be expressed in the concrete life of the church.

In earlier days, men in the church insisted that women were not equal. They were inferior — made inferior by God. At this conference, we have once again heard some of those embarrassing comments from the great theologians of the Christian church. If women were in fact inferior, then there would be a difference between men and women that would be relevant to the unequal distribution of benefits and deprivations. But nowadays we are in the strange position of those who insist that women must be kept out of the offices of the church also insisting that they are fully equal with men. I have heard some of these people give rousing speeches to the effect that the Spirit distributes its gifts equally while insisting, nonetheless, that no woman may use her gifts as a preacher. Where men in the church once justified the unequal position of women with the insulting claim that God had made them inferior, now they grant that there is no relevant difference between men and women but insist that God demands this inequality of treatment. They defend it, in short, by making God appear utterly arbitrary.

It becomes pivotal, then, that we look carefully at the Bible to see whether it does indeed say that God wants women kept out of church office. Before I turn to that, though, let me comment on one way in which the feminist case should not be argued. Some women appear to make their case by arguing for the abolition of all authority and all hierarchy. All that, they say, is simply the reflection of male power.

I think that is mistaken. I do not see how there can be human society without authority. The Bible, so far from repudiating authority in society, sacralizes some of it; governmental authorities, it says, are ministers of God. Parents have authority over their children, and God has authority over all of us. No diminishing of ascriptivism will change that. My point is not that authority and hierarchy are to be eliminated from thought and practice but that gender is simply irrelevant to the assignment of benefits and deprivations, both within the church and without. In particular, gender is not relevant to the assignment of positions of authority.

I found the biblical studies at this conference very impressive. I judge them to represent a large step forward. Let me offer some overall impressions and some overall advice. First, it seems to have been established fairly securely that, whatever headship means in the New Testament, it does not mean *authority over*. The Greek word for "head," *kephalē*, seems never to have had the metaphorical sense of "an authority." The situation seems to be that though the English word *head* is indeed the literal translation of the Greek word *kephalē*, the English word fits into a very different metaphor system from that of the Greek word. It is a metaphor system in which an authority can be spoken of metaphorically as a head, whereas that was not true in Greek. I also judge it to have been pretty securely established at our conference that whatever *authentein* means in 1 Timothy, it almost certainly does not mean "having authority over."

Second, our discussion reminded me that those opposed to the opening of church offices to women should not be permitted to set the entire agenda of the biblical discussion. We must look at the full sweep of the biblical message, seeing its message of justice and liberation for women. It is important for us to keep before the church the memory of such liberating passages as Acts 2 and Galatians 3. Within this larger affirmative context we must deal with those few, those *very* few, negative-sounding passages in 1 Corinthians and 1 Timothy.

Third, I think I saw emerging at this conference a consensus as to how, in general, the relevant biblical passages are to be read. When we look at the overall sweep of the New Testament, we discern a message of the full equality of men and women in Christ and, thereby, in the church. The male/female distinction is not relevant to the sorting out of roles in the church. What is relevant is the gifts of the Spirit. Nonetheless, the church of the New Testament existed in a social situation that was intensely patriarchal. The message of the apostles was addressed to that society. It was not couched in completely general terms, equally relevant to all societies at all times. The message had social specificity even though over and over we discern elements that leap out of the specificities of that situation and speak to us as well. In Ephesians, for example, Paul speaks the message of the gospel to a patriarchal situation and specifies how men and women in Christ must relate as husbands and wives in that situation. He nowhere says that families must always be patriarchal in character; he is simply speaking the gospel to families that in fact were so. He knew no others. In 1 Corinthians, Paul is concerned with practices that were, in that society, bringing shame and dishonor to the church: women wearing short hair was one, and women speaking in a certain way in a certain situation was another — though the way and situation are not clear to us since in fact Paul allowed women to pray and prophesy in public. Paul does not say that such practices must always be avoided because they will always bring shame to the church. He just says they must be avoided there. In 1 Timothy, Paul is again concerned about shame and dishonor, but also now about heresy in the church, perhaps especially the heresy of Gnosticism. He does not say that in all situations the way to cope with heresy is to silence the women. In the first chapter of Titus, for example, he talks differently.

Suppose that it is along these lines that we must understand these passages. We twentieth-century Christians must then ask one further question, the most important question of all for us. We must ask what is the word of the Lord to us in these passages. Let us not slide into the assumption that there is no word of the Lord to us in them. The fact that Paul was not speaking in socially disembodied fashion but was speaking the word of the Lord to a particular social situation (a social situation profoundly different from ours) does not mean that in what he says there is no word of the Lord to us. Though the word to us is not that we must reintroduce old-fashioned patriarchal families, surely, the Lord nevertheless asks of us mutual submission. Though the word of the Lord to us is not that women must be silent in the church and must be kept out of all positions of authority, surely he asks of us that we not needlessly bring shame on the church. Though the word of the Lord to us is not that we must cope with heresy by silencing our women, he continues to ask that we oppose heresy.

Exactly how one discerns the word of the Lord to us in a biblical passage that is socially specific is a complex question. A rough-and-ready description of what is to be done, though, is that one tries to discern the reason that the biblical writer had for saying what he did, and to continue digging deeper into those reasons until one comes to something that applies to us as much as it did to the people the writer was addressing. Sometimes in doing this we will discover, to our surprise, that the concrete application to our society of those deep reasons will be just the opposite of what it was to that ancient society. In our day, keeping women silent brings shame on the church.

It has been characteristic of the evangelical churches — indeed, of the Christian church in general — to think of the biblical writers as delivering timeless truths unsullied by the particularities of the cosmology, the anthropology, the social outlook, and so forth of the day. Likewise it has been characteristic to overlook the internal biblical structure of centrality and peripherality and to see everything in the Bible as on the same level. And it has been characteristic to resist granting that in the history of the church we discern a deepening of insight into the implications of the biblical message. On all these points, this conference has represented, to my mind, a most important breakthrough. We are moving toward a new, more adequate, more realistic hermeneutic — more realistic in the fundamental sense that it takes with full seriousness the mysterious reality that the word of the Lord comes to us as the word of eminently human beings.

We have asked how we can bring the evangelical churches to see that God's message for women is not one of restriction but of justice and freedom. One immensely important approach is to offer a new and better way of reading the relevant biblical passages — and then, of reading *all* of them. The conservatives have never managed to give a plausible reading of all the relevant passages. I think we saw emerging here at this conference a plausible way of reading all the passages together. Until the evangelical churches have such a new way of reading the passages, I am persuaded that they will continue to wonder whether perhaps after all the Lord of the church does want women kept out of the offices of the church.

But this new way of reading is not enough by itself. In my experience, issues of justice do not seize the hearts of most people until the victims of injustice acquire human faces and human voices. We must allow women to express their cry of pain. We must allow them to function with equality wherever that is permitted so that people will see concretely what they are missing when they do not allow women to use the gifts that the Spirit has granted them.

But even that is not quite enough. My experience in struggling for the rights of the Palestinian people has taught me that Israelis often cannot hear the cry for justice coming from the Palestinians even though faces and voices are right there before them. They cannot hear because they are seized with fear — that the cup of suffering of the Jewish people is not yet full, that over the horizon somewhere is yet another holocaust. The same applies to the issue of women in the church. The reason some cannot hear the cry of women and cannot see the edification that will result from allowing their gifts to be used is that they are seized by the fear that, if they granted the justice of the cry and the benefits of the gifts, their world would change in ways too frightening for them to contemplate. Accordingly, just as I, who speak for the rights of the Palestinians, must stand by the Jewish people in their fear, so you and I, who speak for the full equality of women with men in the family of Jesus Christ, must stand by our fellow Christians in their fear. We must be pastors to them. Only in that way will they be able to hear that in Christ and in the church there is neither male nor female but all are equal.

Letter to a Young Theologian

W e were talking, that morning over coffee, about your future career. You asked me whether I would recommend your going into systematic theology; and if so, what I thought was important to do in it. I gave you only a moderately competent answer. Your questions, after all, were big ones; and though I can't say that I had never thought about them before, still you caught me off guard. Now, after a bit of reflection, I'd like to try again.

I suppose I don't really have to remind you that I'm not a professional theologian. I'm a philosopher by trade. I feel I should mention this because my being a philosopher rather than a theologian will naturally shape my answers to your questions. Also, I'll keep in mind that, as our conversation made clear, you had decided that *if* you would pursue the career of systematic theologian, it would be in the context of the Reformed church of which you are a member. You weren't wondering whether you should pursue it in some nonconfessional ecumenical context.

IT'S MY FIRM IMPRESSION that systematic theology on the American scene has fallen on bad days. I don't really keep up with it; but one thing that strikes me when I do dip into it is that American theologians have become tractarians. They are constantly saying that we ought to have a theology of this and we ought to have a theology of that; but the called-for theologies seem never to appear. I regard such tractarianism as marking a lack of intellectual seriousness.

Then, too, it seems that contemporary philosophy has struck terror into the minds of theologians. I would certainly be the last to argue that philosophy is irrelevant to the work of the theologian. In fact I think it's indispensable. But I find it pitiful that shortly after Whitehead's process philosophy became well known, theologians began declaring that Christian theology must now be harmonized with process philosophy; that shortly after Heidegger's philosophy became well known, theologians began declaring that Christian theology must now be harmonized with Heideggerianism; that shortly after logical positivism became well known, theologians began declaring that Christian theology must now be harmonized with logical positivism. I admire the guts of Karl Barth who thumbed his nose at us philosophers and said "No" to all such one-sided harmonizing.

So it seems to me that if you become a serious systematic theologian working with Christian integrity on the American scene, you'll be rather lonely. While I'm on the topic, though, let me urge you, nonetheless, to maintain the contacts you've already built up with American theologians. Don't become a hole-and-corner theologian. We have enough Reformed theologians who have no interaction with the American theological scene. We who are academics have responsibilities toward many different, overlapping communities. The Reformed theologian has responsibilities not only to the community of Reformed theologians but to the whole community of American theologians as well.

BUT *should* you become a systematic theologian? Certainly. I can't think of anything more worth your becoming. I'm taking for granted that you've already made the decision — as you told me you had — to go into some form of academic work.

I'll give you my reasons shortly. But first let me set something off to the side as *not* my reason. In the Reformed churches it has long and often been thought that the heart of a person's appropriate response to the gospel is the acceptance of certain beliefs. On occasion I have called that view *doctrinalism*. It was, as I look back, the view that I imbibed as a child. Furthermore, in the tradition there was often no distinction drawn between the beliefs that someone as a follower of Christ is obliged to hold and the articulation given those beliefs by the classical Reformed theologians. These were blurred together. So what came out was the conviction that the heart of a person's appropriate response to the gospel is the acceptance of Reformed doctrine — total depravity, unconditional election, limited atonement, and so forth. No doubt if you had put it straight to any one of those doctrinalists, he would have said that *life* is also important. But a member was always far more likely to be put out of the church for denying total depravity than for cheating on his taxes.

Now in that way of thinking, systematic theology is obviously of immense importance. Yet, ironically, that way of thinking has always had the effect of thwarting all fresh and imaginative theological efforts. It's not hard to see why. All such efforts will appear either as revisions of the true gospel or as needless additions. Thus the Reformed churches have always been in the position of canonizing a few theologians, recognizing a somewhat larger group as loyal camp followers, and consigning the others to limbo. If you had put your first question to some Reformed doctrinalist, he would almost certainly have advised you to go into systematic theology, emphasizing its great importance. But he would have expected you to repeat loyally what Calvin said, what Bavinck said, what Berkhof said, with possibly some rearrangement for pedagogical purposes. He would have expected you to hand on, unrevised, classical Reformed theology.

I think this view, that the acceptance of Reformed doctrine constitutes the heart of our faithful response to the gospel, is mistaken on two counts. I agree that faithful followers of Christ are required to hold certain beliefs. God cares what we think. Let's not go down the existentialist road of saying that there is no "propositional content" to the faith. But beliefs are only part of what is required. What is required is obedience *in our lives as a whole*. It is indeed required that we *believe* that Jesus Christ rose from the dead. But so too it is required that we celebrate the supper of our Lord and stand at the side of the poor and the oppressed as friend and defender.

But then, second, I don't for a minute believe that as faithful followers of Jesus Christ we must embrace all that stands in the books of classical Reformed theology, even if it were all true. And I hope you never believe that about any books you yourself may eventually publish. That is to confuse the belief-content of the faith with the elaborate theoretical structure developed by the theologian concerning God and God's relation to humankind and the world. The theologian presumably believes that what he writes is true. But he must also admit that not all of what he writes is required to be believed if one is to be a faithful follower of Christ.

Incidentally, as a reaction against these two mistakes that have been so prominent in our tradition — the mistake of identifying our loyal following of Christ with our assenting to the belief-content of the faith, and the mistake of identifying the belief-content of the faith with Reformed doctrine — there are those in our community who want nothing to do with systematic theology. They regard it as a curse. Such an attitude is just as misguided as the other. I mention it because you had better be aware that your very existence as an imaginative theologian will provoke critics on the left as well as on the right.

MY PRINCIPAL REASON for thinking the work of the professional systematic theologian important goes along the following lines. Systematic theology is unavoidable for Christians. The systematic theology of most of us is rudimentary, piecemeal, and inarticulate; but it's there nonetheless. The calling of the professional systematic theologian is to do more deeply, more systematically, more articulately, what all of us do in our own less-than-competent ways.

We study our Bibles and try to put together what we read there about God and God's relation to human beings and the world. Then we read commentaries, go to church, talk with fellow Christians, and read Christian literature, trying to put all that together with what we had already concluded. And then we read some psychology, some philosophy, some comparative religion, some biology, trying to fit that together with the rest. What emerges is a body of beliefs, a body of theories, on God and God's relation to human beings and the world. What emerges is a systematic theology of an informal sort.

But usually it's rudimentary, not thought-through. Usually it's fragmented, not tied together. Usually it's inarticulate, not expressed with any precision of thought. The professional theologian does the same thing that we all do, but better. His work, as I see it, is not qualitatively different from the hasty efforts of the rest of us. His work, for example, does not mark the incursion of theory where there was none before. Rather, it's an *intensification* of what we all do.

When there are professional theologians working within the community and making their work available to us, then we all benefit, each at our own level. For then we can go to someone for assistance in working out our own framework of beliefs. Naturally the theologian to whom we go for assistance will have to be someone to whom we are willing to listen. But I think that confessional theologians usually exaggerate the degree of acceptance that must exist between them and their audience. Not finding it, they are paralyzed into timidity, inactivity, or privacy. Don't expect everybody to accept you on anything you say, and don't expect anybody to accept you on everything you say. Your contribution to your own confessional community (not to speak here of your wider contribution) will not lie in everybody's just going along with what you say. We laypeople can and will make up our own minds. What we need is assistance in that.

Another way of getting at these matters is to ask what goes wrong in a confessional community when solid and imaginative systematic theology is missing. Many things. For one thing, the community becomes susceptible to a multitude of fads, arising both within and without. A new method of evangelism is proposed, or a new method of counseling; and no one has thought things through well enough to know whether the proposal should be accepted or not. The rapid rise and fall of fads within the church is a pretty good sign that professional systematic theology is not doing its work.

Professional systematic theology is of particular importance in a confessional community within the Reformed tradition — and here, of course, I speak directly to your loyalty and to mine. In great measure what holds the Anglican community together is its common liturgy. In great measure what holds the Roman Catholic community together is its shared authority structure. In great measure what holds the Reformed community together is a certain perception of God's relation to human beings and the world, plus an impulse that flows from that perception to see every legitimate occupation as a calling from God and to seek the reform of the surrounding society. Because a certain mode of understanding is thus at the heart of what holds a Reformed community together, the Reformed tradition has always had a very intellectual tone. For the same reason, systematic theology has always been of great importance in it. Its importance lies in the fact that if we do not have professional systematic theologians within the community who are fundamentally Reformed in their perspective, assisting us in each shaping our own informal systematic theology, that particular contour of beliefs that one might call "Reformed" is bound to fall apart and disappear in most of us. As a matter of fact, I think that is happening in most Reformed churches. Seeing it happen makes me sad. For I believe that the Reformed tradition represents a profound perception of the shape of the gospel and has the promise of continuing to be of great benefit to Christendom and Western civilization. I think the disappearance of good systematic theology is in great measure responsible for the decline. I see in you, and in some other young theologians, the promise of a renascence.

Perhaps here is the place to tuck in my advice that since you see it as part of your calling to enliven the Reformed tradition in the twentieth century, you must become acquainted with that tradition deeply enough so that you can distinguish between what lies at its heart and what constitutes irrelevant accretions picked up over the centuries. Include that in your program of studies.

I WANT TO highlight two implications of what I've been saying. One is that, in your professional work, you must keep an ear open for the perplexities of those of us who are not professional theologians and address yourself to those perplexities. That follows from my having said that the rationale for the work of the *professional* systematic theologian is that he or she gives assistance and guidance to the rest of us. One thing that distresses me about many of our theologians is that they seem strangely unconcerned to give guidance to us nonprofessionals on the issues that vex us. For example, all of us today are concerned — and confused, I might say — about the nature and task of the church. Yet we who are not professional theologians are forced to work out our ideas by ourselves. That is defection from responsibility on the part of our professional theologians. So at the beginning of your career let me say to you as emphatically as I can: part of your calling as a professional theologian will be to listen to us and to address yourself to answering *our* perplexities.

A second implication is that the systematic theology that you produce must be *systematic* systematic theology. That sounds odd. What I mean is this: one of the chief flaws in the systematic theology of us laypeople is that it isn't very systematic. There are theologians around who are interesting to read and sometimes helpful; but many of them are also unsystematic. They are *dabblers*. They do not, with passion and intensity, follow out the consequences of their ideas, probe their foundations, and fit it all together. Such theologians are of little permanent benefit. For really to know whether an idea is acceptable you have to know where it goes, what underlies it, and how it fits together with other ideas. The great contribution of Karl Barth to twentieth-century theology is that he was a passionately *systematic* systematic theologian. After his work we know, very much better than we ever did before, where certain ideas go. To be a *systematic* systematic theologian takes a great deal of intellectual determination and single-mindedness (Latin, *monomania*). It's so much easier to be a genial dabbler. I hope you've got what it takes. I know you do; so instead I say, *cultivate* what it takes.

ALREADY I'VE WRITTEN you a sizeable letter and I still haven't gotten around to what I think it's important for you and others to do in systematic theology. So let me hurry on to that.

(1) Over the years I've come to the conviction that one of the most fateful decisions ever made in the classical tradition of Western theology was to explicate God's relation to time in terms of eternity rather than in terms of everlastingness. God, it's said, is outside of time. The alternative would have been to say that though God is without beginning and without end, and though God is Lord of what takes place in history, yet God's own life incorporates succession. Once the decision is made that God is eternal, vast consequences follow. Then God is immutable, then God does not really respond to the actions of human beings, then God does not do one thing before another — create, say, before sending his Son into the world — etc. The Bible, of course, pervasively speaks of God as acting in sequence. The theologian committed to God as eternal must somehow explain that all away.

I myself have concluded that the classical theologians made the wrong choice, and I have argued the case in some detail in my essay "God Everlasting" (in *God and the Good,* Eerdmans, 1975). When I first delved into the matter, I expected to find a great number of biblical texts that would give trouble for the "God everlasting" position. To my surprise I discovered that there are only two or three texts that are ever cited in favor of the "God eternal" position and that these, when read in context, clearly say not that God is outside of time and unchanging but that God is faithful to God's covenant promises.

(2) More recently I have come to think that an even more crucial stone in the edifice of classical Western theology is the doctrine that God is simple — that within God there are no distinctions of any sort. God's exemplification of any one attribute is identical with God's exemplification of any other attribute; God as such is identical with God's exemplification of any attribute; there is no earlier part of God's history distinct from any later part; etc. What this means, of course, is that the whole categoreal structure with which we think and speak of God does not in fact apply to God. For we of course make and presuppose a multitude of distinctions, unavoidably so. Thus, as I now see it, the doctrine of divine simplicity does not so much function as a distinct doctrine in theology but as a preface to theology. What it says is that none of what follows in the theological discussion is really true. What *is* really true of God is of course never said. It is inexpressible. I think you can easily see why it was that their doctrine of divine simplicity led the classical theologians to formulate a doctrine of analogy when they were discussing our predications concerning God.

Now some have seen it as a mark of piety to say that none of what we say about God can be really true of God. They say that we must humbly confine ourselves to thinking and speaking of God as God has revealed to us that God wants us to think and speak of God; and that we must never suppose that that is how God is. To me, that seems not a matter of piety but of extreme scepticism. And if those who espouse this position *really* hold it, they will also have to say that God does not *really* reveal Godself and is not *really* an object of our worship.

But more relevant is to ask why theologians have held this view. Here one finds the biblical evidence even more meager than it was for God as eternal. The historical truth of the matter, so it seems to me, is that later theologians have followed in the path of the early theologians, and that the early theologians took over from the Greek philosophers the two doctrines of God as eternal and God as simple. It was Parmenides who first thought of the divine along these lines. I think both doctrines must be rejected as incoherent and as unfaithful to the Scriptures. Christian theology must be de-Hellenized.

But for the theologian to reject these doctrines is to commit himself to a massive project of reconstruction, the scope of which I have only hinted at. I myself see the prospect of that reconstruction as both enormously exciting and — I admit — rather frightening. But the outcome, I am persuaded, will be a theology both more biblically faithful and more coherent.

(3) I have also slowly over the years come to see that fundamental to the whole biblical witness is a certain understanding of how God acts — namely, that God acts in great part by human beings acting. By Jesus doing what he did, says Paul, God was reconciling the world to himself. By the prophet saying what he did, says the writer of Deuteronomy, God was speaking. In short, by persons acting, God acts. Yet, in spite of the centrality of this understanding in the biblical witness, theologians have given it little attention. The early Christian theologians began to worry over questions of identity — was Jesus identical with God or not, did he have a nature identical with God's or not? The whole notion of God acting by men acting fell from view. And once again, what they began, others have continued. Here, I think, is a whole rich and important area of theological — and philosophical — investigation.

The implications again are many. I don't see, for example, how we can ever formulate a coherent evangelical doctrine of Scripture without achieving clarity on this matter. For surely the evangelical confession is that by way of Paul saying what he did in his letters, *God* spoke to the Corinthians and speaks yet to us. So, too, the Calvinist understanding of the sermon requires clarity on this matter. For Calvin was of the view that by the minister saying what he says, God speaks.

Thus far I have spoken of various matters that need exploration in the foundations of theology. I have suggested that what is called for is considerable reconstruction. Let me now move to important, but less foundational, matters.

(4) I think the doctrine of election needs to be explored anew. (When didn't it?) As I see it, Reformed theologians have thought of election as God's making persons be and do something. God's producing conversion in a person, say. That conception of election gets expressed in vast stretches of Reformed thought. But in the Scriptures there is another — and I would guess far more prominent — way of thinking of election. Election consists of God's *choosing* a person (or a people) to do or become something. And to such a choice, such a call, there are many biblical examples of the called person saying "No." I don't know where a doctrine of election thus conceived would go. But it seems to me to bear the promise both of being more faithful to the Scriptures than the concept of election as God's making someone do or be something, and of delivering us from a morass of traditional impasses.

(5) I think the relation of creation and redemption must be explored anew. That's pretty vague; unfortunately, I can't do better. In great measure this seems to me to be an issue raised for the theologian not so much by the perplexities of us laypeople as by occurrences in twentieth-century theology. In Barth, for example, there is a systematic reluctance to see redemption as occurring within the context of, and for the fulfilment of, creation. Rather, creation is seen as for the sake of redemption. Barth's greatness, as I earlier suggested, lies in carrying out this idea with astounding single-mindedness and imagination. For example, the basic task of the State on his view is to make the preaching of the gospel possible. Christianity on his view is not a religion but is opposed to all religions; it is a word of God whereas they are all words of men. On his view, when the gospel is preached there are no beliefs, and perhaps not even any concerns, in the auditor to which the preacher can attach his proclamation. And so forth. I don't think that theologians have even begun to work through the issues that Barth raised.

(6) An issue raised for the theologian by the perplexities of us laypeople is the nature and task of the church — whether now you understand the church as the people of God or as the ecclesiastical institution. We are confused about both and about their relation. Consequently we

don't know what form evangelism should take. We don't know what role the church should take with respect to social justice. And we don't know very well whether the church is the company of the committed ones or the covenant community of the baptized ones (believers and their children), or some combination of these.

(7) Last, the church's confrontation with Marxism — and with many other "isms" as well — requires that we begin to develop a theology of history, or as it was traditionally called, of eschatology. Do we as human beings have a role to play in the coming of the Kingdom? If so, what is it? Do only Christians have a role to play, or does everyone? How do their roles differ? Do nations have a role? Are there some favored nations in God's scheme? Do we now have only the promise of a new life and will the Age of the Resurrection for the first time introduce that new life? Or do we already have new life and does the Age of the Resurrection mark its fulfilment? If the latter, what does that mean as to how Christians should be living today? Should they be living in model communities committed to communism of goods and to pacifism?

IN READING OVER this letter I find that I myself can get excited about the prospect of being a systematic theologian today. Actually, I once considered becoming one, as I told you. Now I almost regret having made the decision I did. Almost.

One last point. I suppose some concerned but rather cautious and conservative person will ask why the old Reformed theologians aren't enough for our purposes today. Why something new? Why have I been emphasizing imagination? Well, it's really fairly obvious, isn't it? Over the course of history we come to a better understanding of the difference between biblical Christianity and classical Greek philosophy. Over the course of history new theologies enter the public arena. Over the course of history new concerns and perplexities grip the minds of God's people. That's why theology must always be done anew. That's why imagination is needed.

As ever,
Nick

The Theological Significance of
Going to Church and Leaving and
the Architectural Expression of That Significance

I

Every Sunday for almost two millennia Christians have left their homes, their places of work and recreation, and assembled to perform the liturgy. When the liturgy is finished they return to their homes, their places of work and recreation. Seven days later they repeat this pattern of assembling and dispersing.

The temporal dimension of this familiar yet curious systolic-diastolic pattern invites reflection. What is the significance of inserting this one-plus-six rhythm into the flow of time? But on this occasion I wish to reflect instead on the spatial dimension of the pattern. What is the significance of Christians assembling from hither and yon and then dispersing again? Is the significance of their assembling, perhaps, that they are leaving secular space and entering a sacred place and that, when they disperse, they reverse the process, now leaving the sacred place and re-entering secular space?

For two millennia, Christians have sung, chanted, or recited the Psalms in their liturgies — or as some traditions call them, their *services*. They have sung,

I was glad when they said to me,
"Let us go up to the house of the Lord!"

(122:1)

228

They have sung,

> Who shall ascend the hill of the LORD?
>   And who shall stand in his holy place?
> Those who have clean hands and pure hearts,
>   who do not lift up their souls to what is false,
>   and do not swear deceitfully.
> They will receive blessing from the LORD.
> Lift up your heads, O gates!
>   and be lifted up, O ancient doors!
>   That the King of glory may come in.
> Who is this King of glory?
>   The LORD of hosts,
>   he is the King of glory.

(24:3-5, 9-10)

And they have sung,

> How lovely is your dwelling place,
>   O LORD of hosts!
> My soul longs, indeed it faints,
>   for the courts of the LORD,
> my heart and my flesh sing for joy
>   to the living God.

(84:1-2)

The psalmist sounds like an ancient Athenian talking about ascending the Athenian acropolis to the temple of Athena. If the temple in Jerusalem was the house of Yahweh, Lord of hosts and King of glory, then it would indeed have been a sacred place.

But imagine that an Athenian had been allowed to enter Israel's temple. He would at once have asked, "Where is the god?" The image of Athena was an awesome looming presence in the Parthenon, as were images of other gods in the temples of other Greek cities. But Israel's temple was empty of god-images. The closest thing to an image of Israel's god, while yet not an image at all, were two stone tablets in the inner sanctum, these having been handed down from Moses and containing Yahweh's Ten Commandments to his people. And had our visiting Athenian been there in the crowd at the dedication of the temple in Jerusalem, he would have heard Solomon, its builder, say something in his dedicatory prayer that our visitor would have found paradoxical indeed. After praising Yahweh as unlike any other god in heaven and earth for covenant fidelity, Solomon went on to exclaim, "But will God indeed dwell on the earth? Even heaven and the highest heaven cannot contain you, much less this house that I have built! Regard your servant's prayer and his plea, O LORD my God. . . . Hear the plea of your servant and of your people Israel when they pray toward this place; O hear in heaven your dwelling place; heed and forgive" (1 Kings 8:27). So in what sense is this temple *the House of the Lord* if Yahweh's dwelling place is in heaven? And in turn, in what sense is his dwelling place in heaven if heaven and the highest heaven cannot contain him?

Or suppose that another Athenian, some centuries later, had read around in Israel's writings. He would have discovered that not only did Israel think of Yahweh as too great to be confined to any house on earth. He would also have noticed a certain skittishness about this god that Israel worshipped. In no way would Israel's god allow himself to be fettered. Already at the dedication of the temple Yahweh had warned Solomon that if he, Solomon, did not obey Yahweh's commands and worship Yahweh alone, Yahweh would destroy this House of the Lord that had just been built and turn it into "a heap of ruins" (1 Kings 9:8).

In his wonderful *Theology of the Old Testament*, Walter Brueggemann structures his presentation in terms of Israel's dominant testimony and Israel's counter-testimony. For example, in its dominant testimony Israel celebrates Yahweh's justice; in its counter-testimony Israel complains that God is not acting justly. So too here: the Old Testament preserves for us both Israel's songs about the temple as the House of the Lord and Israel's reminders that God does not dwell in houses made of stone and built with human hands.

The question for you and me as Christians is what we, as people "grafted into Israel," are to make of all this. In his rich and provocative book, *Sacred and Profane Beauty: The Holy in Art,*[1] Gerardus Vander Leeuw suggests that "In the place of the house of God comes now the house of prayer. Man no longer builds a holy place, but rather builds himself a place in which he can pray to God in peace" (p. 199). Vander Leeuw is speaking descriptively here, not prescriptively. And he goes on to observe that even as a description, what he says has to be qualified; reality is more ambiguous. For quite some time now, he says, the Christian church has once more become

1. New York: Holt, Rinehart and Winston, 1963.

the house of God, in which his immediate, miraculous presence resides upon the altar. Even today the Catholic goes to the house of the Lord in the literal sense of the primitive structure. Even the Calvinistic Protestant, who has probably made the prayer of Solomon most thoroughly his own, perceives no contradiction between his sober house of prayer and his beloved hymn in which he sings of an ascent to the altar of God. Along with the name "house of God," the churches of the Reformation, even though they often became almost completely houses of prayer and even places of religious assembly, preserved much of the original power of the house of holiness. (pp. 199-200)

Well and good. But what does this distinction come to, house of God versus house of prayer?

II

I think our reflections on the significance of the assembling-dispersing habits of Christians will be enhanced if we first reflect a bit on patterns of assembling and dispersing generally. One way to think of the built environment is to think of it as consisting of places designated for assemblage and of paths among these assemblage-places. In tribal societies, the great bulk of these assemblage-places were family dwellings. A prominent characteristic of modernized societies is that our assemblage-places come in a huge variety, the variety being the consequence, in good measure, of the different activities that members of society perform in these places and of the fact that the group which assembles in one of these places is usually quite different from that which assembles in another. I assemble with quite a different group of people in the buildings of my university from those with whom I assemble in the building of my congregation; and these groups are in turn both very different from those with whom I assemble in my home. These two sorts of variety are, in good measure, the architectural consequence of the social differentiation that Max Weber famously regarded as one of the defining features of a modernized society.

Consider, then, that sort of assemblage-place in our society that is a home. Where once upon a time a business was a family enterprise and one and the same building housed the home of the family and its business, now most of us leave home to go to work. We leave one assemblage-place, that of the home, and go along architecturally determined paths to another assemblage-place, that of work or school, where typically we never see any of the people with whom we assemble at home.

This transition is customarily thought of as the transition from the private to the public: we leave the privacy of the home and enter the space of the public. This way of thinking is even enshrined, to a considerable extent, in our laws; government is allowed to intrude considerably more into what goes on in public spaces than into what goes on in the private space of the home. A consequence of this is that, as many of our social critics have pointed out, the home is for many wives and children a far more dangerous place to be than is the public space. There is a deep historical irony in this. Traditionally the home was designed not only for protection against the elements but for security against social menace.

I have been hinting at one of the main points I want to make here. Home is understood by us as the space for conducting very different kinds of activities from those we conduct in public. Here children are conceived and reared; here deep bonding takes place; here affection is expressed without worrying about embarrassment or consequences; here meals are eaten together on a more or less regular basis; here family devotions often take place. All very different from what goes on outside. And not only very different. To a considerable extent one has to learn to leave behind one's public activities lest they destroy life in the family. One has to leave one's briefcase at the office. It's appropriate within the shelter of the home to discuss what happened at work and school. But that done, one must then get on to other things.

The traditional architecture of the home both enables and is expressive of the difference between the private activities of the domestic sphere and those activities that take place in a public space. There is a clearly demarcated threshold between inside and outside. There is a firm door with a good lock on it. Inside there are intimate gathering spaces, places for meals, and places for bathing and sleeping. It's true that modernist architecture has in certain ways erased the boundaries between home and physical environment: the environment enters the house and the house extends into the environment. But only visually. No matter how much the line between house and environment may be blurred, at some point one bumps up against glass. It was new glass technology that made modernist architecture possible.

III

Consider secondly that sort of assemblage-place which is a public museum. As the phrase "public museum" indicates, this is a place within the public space. So what is the significance of assembling at the place and within the space of a public museum, and then dispersing into other places within public space or into the private space of the home?

The significance is best revealed by taking note of what I have called, in some writings of mine, the Grand Modern Narrative of the Arts. This is not the occasion to discuss the narrative in any detail; let me mention only what is essential. The Grand Narrative is a narrative concerning the significance of the revolution that took place within the arts in the eighteenth century, when the middle class of Western Europe began to emphasize the importance of art for disinterested perceptual contemplation. The narrative tells the story of this development as the story of progress. After millennia of servitude to purposes extrinsic to art, in the eighteenth century art finally began to come into its own; people began to engage art for art's sake rather than for the sake of purposes extrinsic to art. In the early days of Romanticism this progressivist story got caught up into a yet grander story. The Romantics were the first secular analysts and critics of modernity. Modernity, they said, is fragmentation produced by the spread of instrumental rationality. But the artist who produces art for its own sake is socially other, as is the art thus produced. For the work of art is inherently unified, rather than fragmented; and its rationality is interior rationality, rather than the instrumental rationality that haunts modernized society. Let me quote a passage from one of the earliest Romantics, Karl Philipp Moritz:

> While the beautiful draws our attention exclusively to itself . . . we seem to lose ourselves in the beautiful object; and precisely this loss, this forgetfulness of self, is the highest degree of pure and disinterested pleasure that beauty grants us. In that moment we sacrifice our individual confined being to a kind of higher being. . . . Beauty in a work of art is not pure . . . until I contemplate it as something that has been brought forth entirely for its own sake, in order that it should be something complete in itself.

And here is a passage from another writer of the same time, Wilhelm Wackenroder:

Art galleries . . . ought to be temples where, in still and silent humility and in heart-lifting solitude, we may admire great artists as the highest among mortals . . . with long, steadfast contemplation of their works. . . . I compare the enjoyment of nobler works of art *to prayer*. . . . Works of art, in their way, no more fit into the common flow of life than does the thought of God. . . . That day is for me a sacred holiday which . . . I devote to the contemplation of noble works of art.[2]

Lest you dismiss these passages as nothing more than the somewhat mantic ravings of early Romantics, here are words to the same effect from an early twentieth-century writer, Clive Bell. "Art transports us," says Bell, "from the world of man's activity to a world of aesthetic exaltation. For a moment we are shut off from human interests, our anticipations and memories are arrested; we are lifted above the stream of life." In disinterested contemplation of a work of art we "inhabit a world with an intense and peculiar significance of its own; that significance is unrelated to the significance of life."[3]

So when I enter that assemblage-place which is a public museum I not only enter a place dedicated to a very different sort of activity from the activities of the workplace or the home, namely, the activity of disinterested perceptual contemplation of works of art. I enter a place where, if I am fully to engage in the activity to which this place is dedicated, I must leave behind what Bell calls "the world of man's activity" and allow myself to be "lifted above the stream of life" so as to "inhabit a world with an intense and peculiar significance of its own." In Wackenroder's words, works of art "no more fit into the common flow of life than does the thought of God."

I submit that this is the ideology that museum architecture of the modern period both enables and expresses. The museum has the appearance of a royal palace; some in fact began their lives as royal palaces. One ascends a long flight of steps, and enters through imposing doors. Once inside one finds oneself in a place from which the outside world has been blocked out: lighting is controlled, sounds are hushed, one cannot see out.

2. These passages both come from M. H. Abrams's essay, "Art-as-Such: The Sociology of Modern Aesthetics," to be found in his collection, *Doing Things with Texts: Essays in Criticism and Critical Theory*, ed. Michael Fischer (New York: W. W. Norton, 1989). They are to be found on pages 156 and 157 *of Doing Things with Texts*.

3. The passages quoted come from pages 27 and 28 of Bell's *Aesthetics* (London: Chatto & Windus, 1914).

The only visible intrusion of daily life is those museum shops that have been insinuating themselves into our museums in recent years. The new Getty Museum in Los Angeles might seem at first sight to be an exception to my description. But not really. The ascent is far more dramatic and extreme than the ascent for any other museum in the world. Though the plaza is open to the environment, the city is not present to one but lies before one as a panorama. And with the exception of a few sculptures, the art is housed in five pods, each of these pods being as inward-looking as any traditional museum.

IV

With these reflections as background, let me now turn to our question: what is the significance of the fact that Christians leave those private assemblage-places which are their homes and the assemblage-places in public space designated for work, recreation, art, and so forth, to enter an assemblage-place in which they perform the liturgy—and then, when the liturgy is concluded, leave that assemblage-place and disperse into all those assemblage-places from which they came? Is it right to think of this transition on analogy to the transition between assemblage-places located in the public space and the private assemblage-place of the home, or on analogy to the transition between assemblage-places in which we conduct our ordinary activities and the assemblage-place of the museum in which we inhabit the world of aesthetic exaltation? And if it is right to think of the transition on analogy to one or the other of these transitions, should we think of this particular transition as the transition from assemblage-places located in secular space to a sacred assemblage-place? Is the significance— the *theological* significance now—of going to church, that one leaves secular space and enters a sacred place?

Let me call your attention to the fact that my question is not whether in going to church one enters a sacred *space,* but whether in going to church one enters a sacred *place.* A space is sacred when the shape of the space and the way light pervades the space are *expressive* of the sacred. A great many of the spaces within which Christians conduct the liturgy on Sunday are minimally expressive of the sacred—just as many of those outsized houses being tossed up in American suburbs are minimally expressive of domesticity. Christians meet in storefronts, warehouses, school basements, you name it. My question is whether, nonetheless, the *place* is sacred. Whatever be the expressive character of the space, are Christians entering a sacred place when they enter the church?

Well, what would make a place sacred? Indeed, what is meant in calling a place sacred? Begin here: suppose you were planning a new city somewhere out in an unbuilt environment—like LaFayette planning Washington, D.C. Would it make sense to ask whether there are any sacred places in the area so as to be sure either not to build there or to build only a church?

The paganism of Greco-Roman antiquity—to mention only that form of paganism—recognized many places that were sacred antecedent to building, the most famous being the place in Delphi where fumes of some sort came out of the earth and inspired the Delphic Oracle. Rudolf Otto, in *The Idea of the Holy,* conceptualized the notion of such sacred places with the category of *the numinous.* Human beings have experienced certain places as numinous — or if they did not exactly experience the places themselves as numinous, they found themselves repeatedly having experiences of the numinous in certain places.

The Hebrew and Christian scriptures repudiate all such forms of nature religion. The Old Testament writers speak of Mount Zion as holy. But so far as I know, there is no suggestion that the temple was located on Mount Zion because it was antecedently regarded as a sacred place in the way in which the Greeks regarded Delphi as a sacred place. It was the other way around: Mount Zion was holy because the temple was located there.

It's true that in the thought-world of Judaism and Christianity there are analogues, of a sort, to paganism's conviction that certain places are inherently holy. Mount Sinai is a holy place for both Jews and Christians. And Jesus' purported birthplace in Bethlehem, his purported burial place in Jerusalem, and Mount Golgotha and the Via Dolorosa in Jerusalem, are sacred places for Christians. The antecedent sacredness of these places is what determined the location of the Monastery of St. Catherine at the foot of Mt. Sinai, of the Church of the Nativity in Bethlehem, and of the Church of the Holy Sepulchre in Jerusalem.

But two observations must be made here. First, these places are regarded as antecedently holy by Christians in quite a different way from the way in which paganism regarded certain places in nature as antecedently holy. The place in Jerusalem in which Jesus was purportedly buried is like the Shroud of Turin in which Christ was purportedly wrapped: both are *relics* of some of God's most decisive actions among us. So too, the Via Dolorosa is a relic-place in the same way that a piece of the true cross would be a relic-sliver.

And second, though the three churches I mentioned above are located at places antecedently regarded as holy relic-places, that is not true for the great bulk of Christian churches. There are far too few places regarded by Christians as antecedently holy relic-places for this to be what determines the location of our churches. There are more than I have mentioned; there is, for example, the chapel on the island of Patmos built over the spot where St. John purportedly received his revelations. But all together, far too few.

Now we must take the argument a step farther. Granted that there would be very few churches if we limited ourselves to building churches over places that are antecedently regarded as holy relic-places. But suppose that one is a Catholic of the pre–Vatican II, Tridentine, sort. One will then believe that when a duly qualified priest, in the course of celebrating Mass, pronounces in a duly qualified way the words, *Hoc est,* the bread that he has in hand becomes the body of Christ—literally speaking. If one believes this, then one will view the place where this transubstantiation takes place as a holy relic-place in exactly the same way that Jesus' tomb in Jerusalem is regarded as a holy relic-place by Christians generally. Jesus was bodily present here. This is the point that Vander Leeuw was alluding to in the passage I quoted. It is true, of course, that even for the Tridentine Catholic, the altar in a church will not have the same centrality in the Christian narrative as the tomb of Jesus; but that will be the only significant difference. Perhaps the traditional Lutheran who affirms consubstantiation will also be of the view that once the Eucharist has been celebrated here at this altar, this place is a holy relic-place of the bodily presence of Christ; I am not sure. But all those who do not affirm that in the Eucharist Christ becomes bodily present, literally speaking—this group including most if not all of the Orthodox, many if not most post–Vatican II Catholics, and virtually all Protestants—will not think that this place here is sacred in this way.

So suppose one does not believe that the place in which one is assembled with other Christians on a Sunday morning is sacred in either of the senses I have discussed. It is not located over an antecedently sacred relic-place, as is purportedly the Church of the Holy Sepulchre, nor has Christ literally become bodily present here when the Eucharist was celebrated. In what sense then, if any, might one still think of coming to church as leaving secular assemblage-places to enter a sacred place?

Well, one might think that God is *spiritually* present here in the church building. It is my impression that this has long been a significant theme in lay Christian piety. Going to church is entering the presence of God. But there are few who would be willing to carry this line of thought to its conclusion and affirm that when we leave church, we enter the sphere of God's absence. And in any case, this way of thinking bumps up against Jesus' declaration that where two or three are gathered, there I am with you. Likewise it bumps up against Jesus' well-known declaration to the Samaritan woman. "Our ancestors worshipped on this mountain, but you say that the place where people must worship is in Jerusalem," she says to Jesus, taking him to be typically Jewish in his attitude. Not so, says Jesus. "The hour is coming when you will worship the Father neither on this mountain nor in Jerusalem. . . . The hour is coming, and is now here, when the true worshipers will worship the Father in spirit and truth, for the Father seeks such as these to worship him" (John 4:19-23). Jesus responds to the woman's comment not by saying that the hour is coming when temples will be scattered all about but by dismissing place as having anything to do with the authenticity of worship.

So far as I can see, there is only one other way to understand the idea that when one goes to church, one enters a sacred place. One might hold that the *activities* performed here in this place are sacred activities in distinction from the secular activities that we perform when dispersed. On this view, the sacred-secular distinction is first of all a distinction among kinds of activities and only derivatively a distinction between kinds of places. A sacred place is a place dedicated to sacred activities; a secular place is a place meant for secular activities. The museum would be an analogy. What distinguishes the museum from other places is that it is devoted to the socially-other activity of disinterested perceptual contemplation of transcendent works of art.

There can be no doubt that vast stretches of traditional Christian thought have employed the distinction between sacred activities and secular activities. But a truly astonishing change has occurred in Christian thought and sensibility during the latter half of the twentieth century. There is no esteemed writer in any of the traditions of Christendom— none that I know of, anyway—who would today be willing to affirm that distinction.

We must step carefully here. This does not mean that everybody has now succumbed to what I shall pejoratively call "vulgar reductive Protestantism," according to which our work is our worship. Quite to the contrary. Almost all writers on these matters would argue that there is something unique and important about the actions of the liturgy. The point is rather than none of them thinks that it is right to characterize the distinction between these actions and others as that between sacred actions and secular actions. For the Christian there should be no secular actions.

The challenge to the liturgical theologian is then to find better categories for articulating what is distinct and important about the actions of the liturgy in contrast to all the other actions performed by Christians. On this occasion I will resist the temptation to take a stab at doing this myself. For our purposes here, it is sufficient to affirm that there is indeed something distinct about the actions of the liturgy and that the full-orbed Christian life requires fidelity in both worship and work.

V

A point I made in my discussion of the home is that not only do we customarily conceptualize entering the assemblage-place of the home as leaving public space and entering a private place; it is also important, when in the home, that one guard against allowing one's activities in public space to intrude excessively into the life of the family lest that life be distorted and lose its own integrity. I made a similar point in my discussion of the museum. Not only do we customarily conceptualize entering the assemblage-place of the museum as leaving the space of the workaday world for a place devoted to that version of the *vita contemplativa* which is the engrossed contemplation of works of art; those who embrace the Grand Narrative also think it important that when in this space one put out of mind one's everyday interests so as to engage in disinterested contemplation. Is the counterpart thing to be said about entering a liturgical place? Upon entering, are we to leave all earthly cares behind?

It cannot be denied that this is how Christians have often talked and thought, both in the past and today. Yet even a casual inspection of every Christian liturgy that I have ever come across belies the talk and thought. If the liturgy consisted exclusively of praise of God for what God is as such, plus praise of God for creation and for what was accomplished in Christ, then there would be some plausibility in such talk and thought. But almost every liturgy goes beyond praising God for God's nature, God's creation, and God's redemptive activity in Christ to thanking God for what the worshipers experience in their daily lives. Almost every liturgy includes confession for sins that the worshipers committed in their daily lives; and every liturgy includes intercessions for deliverance from the sorrows of our own daily lives and those of all humanity. In short, not much of the Christian liturgy would be left if we did in fact leave life in the world behind when we crossed the threshold into the place of the liturgy.

VI

Let me summarize. The assembling of Christians on Sunday morning for the performance of the liturgy does not represent leaving secular space and entering a sacred place. It represents entering a place devoted to the performance of the liturgy. The actions of the liturgy are not sacred actions in distinction from secular activities; for the Christian there are no secular activities. And the liturgy cannot be performed if one has left behind all memory of one's daily life. The liturgy requires that one take one's daily life along with one so as to bless God for what has been good in this life, to confess to God one's wrongdoings and those of one's fellow human beings, and to intercede with God for deliverance from all the sorrows of our lives.

The challenge for the architect, then, is to achieve in one building and its environment the two aspects of the liturgy that I have been emphasizing. Beyond creating an environment that enables the liturgy and provides appropriate symbolic and typological resonance, his challenge is to create an environment that is both expressive of the unique character of those actions that comprise the liturgy and expressive of the fact that as we enter the place of the liturgy, we carry with us the thanksgivings, regrets, and laments of daily life, and the fact that, when we disperse, we in turn carry into daily life the guidance and strength, the courage and hope, that we have received.

My own view is that the second of these two challenges will require that our architects give far more attention to the relation of the church to its environment than has been customary, and will require that they provide different modes of entering and leaving the church than is customary. I cannot believe that surrounding the church with a vast sea of asphalt-paved parking and inserting into the building itself tiny ingress apertures is the way to go. But now I am trespassing on the craft of the architect; so best to stop.

The Light of God's Love

L et me preface my meditation with an issue of translation. In the NRSV translation, verse 9 of First John 1 reads as follows: "If we confess our sins, [God] is faithful and just, and will forgive our sins and cleanse us from all unrighteousness." This translation invites the thought that what characterizes God, namely, fidelity and justice, is something different from what God cleanses us from, namely, unrighteousness. But the Greek word translated as "just" is *dikaios,* and the Greek word translated as "unrighteousness" is *adikias.* The preface "a" in Greek means the same as the preface "non" in English; in fact we sometimes substitute the Greek "a" for the English "non" — as in "atemporal." What God cleanses us from is the lack or negation of that very thing which characterizes God. The English translation obscures this identity from us — the identity of that which characterizes God with that whose negation God cleanses us from.

"God is light," says John. In God "there is no darkness at all." No shadows, no dark places. Light everywhere.

A friend of mine, Lee Wandel, teaches Reformation history at the University of Wisconsin. Wandel notes that John Calvin, in a few passages, argues that the best symbol we have for God is light, and the best metaphor, the word "light." Calvin's argument for this position is that light is uncircumscribable. Light has no boundaries that one could draw around, scribe around, circumscribe.

Having noted this claim on Calvin's part about symbolism for the divine, Wandel goes on to argue that Calvin's thought on this matter had a profound influence on Calvinist church architecture. Most of the early

241

Calvinist churches in central Europe were taken over from the Catholics; it's the later churches which the Calvinists themselves built that she has her eye on. The West Church — Westerkerk — in Amsterdam, for example, and the early Congregational churches in New England.

A person familiar with Catholic church buildings will, without even thinking about it, interpret these churches as empty — stripped of statuary, of carvings, of paintings, the whole lot. It's all been tossed into a dumpster. The church is bare. Some Calvinist church historians argue, defensively, that this is an exaggeration. Some carvings do remain, on the pulpit, for example; and there is some decorative painting on panels displaying the Ten Commandments.

True enough, says Wandel; but this misses the point in almost ludicrous fashion. These buildings are not empty but full, chock full, full of something else, of course, than statuary, carvings, and paintings. Full of light, as chock full of light as a building could be before the days of steel framing.

Some fifteen years ago I served on the building committee of my congregation back in Grand Rapids, Michigan. I was on the subcommittee charged with composing the program for the architect — guidelines for him to follow in the design process. As preparation for our work, our subcommittee visited a number of churches that had recently been built to see what ideas we could glean. In almost every case these new churches were dark inside, the darkness usually alleviated with a shaft of light from a light-scoop. To enter them was to enter darkness.

At the time I had not yet met Lee Wandel and had not thought about the significance of the fact that the historic Calvinist churches are chock full of light. Nonetheless, I and my fellow committee members felt in our bones that darkness was all wrong. We told our architect that he had to design a building that gave one the sense of coming into the light upon entering. He succeeded admirably.

If one asks oneself what it is about God that Calvin thought light was the most adequate symbol for, the answer, surely, is God's infinity; the uncircumscribability of light makes it the best symbol available to us for God as infinite. But when John in his First Letter says that God is light, it is not God as infinite that he has in mind but God as love. Out of love God has given us a commandment that illumines our way. And that commandment itself speaks of love. We are to love one another. The one who "loves his brother abides in the light, and in it there is no cause for stumbling," says John. The one who does not love but "hates his brother is in the darkness and walks in the darkness, and does not know where he is going, because the darkness has blinded his eyes."

All readers will be aware of the fact that this theme, of God as shining a light on our path, and of that light as radiating out from Christ, runs deep in Christian Scripture. Matthew quotes Isaiah (9:2) to describe the significance of the coming of Christ into the world:

> The people who sat in darkness have seen a great light,
> and for those who sat in the region and shadow of death
> light has dawned.
>
> (4:16)

And in Luke's Gospel, Zechariah, speaking of the young Jesus, declares that

> the day shall dawn upon us from on high
> to give light to those who sit in darkness and in the shadow of death,
> to guide our feet into the way of peace.
>
> (1:78-79)

But in his First Letter, John is saying something more and something deeper than that the love-command is a light on our path, so that we do not have to stumble and fumble around in the dark wondering how to live and what to do. John introduces that "something more and something deeper" in chapter 4 by declaring that "God is love." Earlier he said that God is light; now he says that God is love. Not only is the commandment to love a light on our path that God out of love gives us; God as love is himself light. God is the light of love.

What's the connection? With his eye on God as love, why would John describe God as light? What do love and light have to do with each other? I daresay that everybody would say that light goes with love and darkness with hatred. Love, we agree, is bright; hatred is dark. But why? Is it possible to discern why we all think that hatred is dark whereas love is bright and light?

Having declared that God is love, John goes on in chapter 4 to say that

> In this the love of God was made manifest among us, that God sent his own Son into the world, so that we might live through him. In this is love, not that we loved God but that he loved us. . . . Beloved, if God so loved us, we also ought to love one another. . . . If we love one another, God abides in us and his love is perfected in us.

Do you see how remarkable this is? God's love for us takes the form of our loving one another. God's love for us is manifested in our loving each other. Earlier John said that God's fidelity and justice toward each of us is manifested in God's forgiving our sins and cleansing us of our wrongdoing. Now he says that God's love for each of us is manifested and perfected in our loving our brothers and sisters. God does not only, out of love, give us the love-command as a light on our path in this dark and confusing world, and our loving one another is not just obedience to a command God has given us. Our love for each other is a manifestation of God's love for us.

I think we can now begin to spy why God as love is light. To love my brothers and sisters is to seek their good, their flourishing. God's love for us radiates out into our seeking the flourishing of each other. Is that not analogous to what is most fundamental about light in our lives? Yes, light illuminates our path. But even more fundamental, light radiates out from the sun to nourish us, to provide the energy without which there could be no life. How better to describe God as love — love radiating out from God onto and into us and from us to the neighbor — than to say that God is light?

You don't need me to tell you that this has been the chapel talk of a professor, not a preacher! I've been asking in professorial fashion what John was saying and why he might have said it. But I do not want these hermeneutical reflections about what John said to be the last word. These reflections were aimed not at replacing what John said, nor at standing in between you and what John said, but at casting light on what he said. John's own gentle injunction must be the last word:

Beloved, let us love one another; for love is of God, and those who love are born of God and know God. Those who do not love do not know God; for God is love. And God is light. God's love is the light that shines onto and into us and through us to the neighbor, sustaining us and making us flourish as does the sun.

Thinking about Church Architecture

Sometimes when a congregation sets about designing and erecting a building to house its Sunday assemblies it thinks in purely functional terms. How big must the sanctuary be to hold the congregation, how high must the pulpit be for people to be able to see the preacher, what rooms are needed in addition to the sanctuary, what can the congregation afford by way of materials, and so forth. Some congregations add to these purely functional considerations the requirement that their building look like a church. If they hire an architect who happens never to have been inside a church, they insist that he take a day to visit some churches in the area so as to find out what churches look like. Almost certainly he will then design for them something with a rather high roof supported by exposed laminated wood beams. If the congregation has quite a bit of money available it's likely that, in addition to the above considerations, they will stipulate the architectural style of the building — gothic, colonial, perhaps contemporary.

I submit that if this is the full extent of the considerations that go into a congregation's choosing a design for its church building, something of prime importance is missing. Buildings speak; buildings are expressive. A building says something. But different buildings say different things. So when a congregation is considering a design for its church building, it should ask whether the building, so designed, will say what it thinks should be said. Will it say what should be said about the congregation? Will it say what should be said about the significance of the congregation's assembling for the liturgy? Will it say what should be said about the character of the liturgy itself, and about the role of God and the people in the liturgy? In short, when choosing a design for its church building, a congregation should think not only functionally but also *theologically* about what it wants its building to say.

I propose putting some flesh on this abstract idea by describing how an actual congregation went about incorporating both functional and expressive considerations into the design of its church building. The congregation happens to be my own, Church of the Servant, in Grand Rapids, Michigan. The design process took place in the late 1980s; the building was built in the early 1990s. I was a member of the committee responsible for formulating an architectural program, for choosing an architect, and for working with the architect in the actual design process. The architect we chose was Gunnar Birkerts, a well-known architect with offices near Detroit who had designed a variety of buildings around the world, including some churches.

I will describe the considerations that went into our formulation of an architectural program without, on this occasion, defending those considerations. My aim here is to illustrate how to think about the design of a church building, not to argue that the specifications we gave to our architect are the best ones or the right ones. Congregations that understand and practice the liturgy quite differently from how COS understands and practices its liturgy should build a quite different kind of building. In my narration I will often use the pronoun "we."

Church of the Servant was formed in the early 1970s; it met for almost two decades in school gymnasia. Its liturgical practices and convictions were thus well in place before it designed and built its own building. There are two worship services every Sunday morning; both include the Lord's Supper as an integral part of the service. At the moment when the bread is to be received and eaten and the wine received and drunk, the worshipers come forward in a succession of groups, each group forming a circle at the front of the sanctuary; the people pass the bread and wine to each other.

This liturgical practice implied an obvious functional consideration: the building had to be designed so that this liturgical practice of going forward, forming a circle, and then returning to one's seat, would not be cumbersome, that it would instead flow naturally. The practice had a less obvious implication as well. It seemed to us that if the number of worshipers was larger than roughly 500, communion would take too long. So we instructed the architect to design a sanctuary that would comfortably seat roughly 500 people. The members of the congregation also get out of their seats to bring their gifts forward at the time of the offering. Our reason for this practice is that this seems to us to fit the liturgical action of the offering far better than everybody remaining in their seats and deacons coming around to "collect." It's worth adding that there is good evidence that bringing one's gifts forward was the practice in at least some of the ancient churches.

Let me now move on to a central item in our architectural program that was a blend of function and expressiveness. The shape of the interior space of a church building, the way in which congregants are disposed in that space, and the location in that space of those who lead the liturgy, all together say something. Consider the typical Protestant church building. The space is a channel, a tube. The roof may be rather high; nonetheless the dominant axis of the space is horizontal. Further, the pews give to this space an unmistakable directionality; the space is arrowed forward, culminating in an elevated platform with a pulpit, perhaps a communion table, sometimes choir stalls. It's no accident that rather often one hears members of such churches refer to the sanctuary as the "auditorium." It is an auditorium. Contemporary mega-churches, with their sloped floors and large platforms, are even more obviously auditoria. The people are assembled to hear a religious message delivered and to listen to religious music performed; the delivery of the message is itself often a performance.

I will refrain from trying to articulate the understanding of the people of God and their liturgy that the typical Protestant church interior reflects. Let me instead say how we at COS understand ourselves and understand what we are doing when we assemble for the liturgy. We understand ourselves as the family of God, brothers and sisters of Christ, assembled around Word and sacrament to worship God, listen to what God has to say to us, and celebrate a meal as a memorial of Jesus. It is we who enact the liturgy; neither the preacher nor the musicians do it for us. We have not come to witness a performance but all together to do something. If this is one's understanding of what takes place in the assembly, it would never occur to one to want a building like the typical Protestant church building, let alone one like a mega-church.

What would one want instead? Well, if one is on the design committee of the congregation one will, first of all, give the architect the challenging task of designing an interior space in which the horizontal and the vertical are balanced, the horizontal dimension reflecting the fact that this is a family, the vertical reflecting the fact that the family has assembled not for a potluck but to worship and listen to God.

Second, one will not want the people lined up in rows but seated in a semi-circle around pulpit and table, with the space shaped accordingly. An obvious question here is, why a semi-circle, why not a circle? Congregations have occasionally built circular buildings with pulpit and table in the middle; I am told that many of the original Huguenot churches in France, now all destroyed, were either circular or octagonal. In my view there are two considerations against such a configuration. It makes preaching extremely difficult; what is the preacher to do, continually rotate? But I also think the expressive significance of a circle is not right; it too strongly suggests completeness. Yes, we are the family of God, the company of the redeemed. But we are still on the way. I think a semi-circle captures this tension architecturally, this duality of "already but not yet," as well as it can be captured.

Third, gathering as the family of God around Word and sacrament requires one or more leaders or presiders — to lead us in the prayers, to read Scripture, to preach, to preside at the Lord's Supper. These leaders or presiders will, naturally, have a position at the center of the semi-circle; and they will have to be somewhat elevated in order that the people can see and hear them? But *how much* should they be elevated? How much should they be separated from the people? Different liturgical theologies and different theologies of ordination will give different answers to this question. Our own answer was that the separation should be minimal. Being appointed to lead or preside over some liturgical action is a special assignment; it does not make one a special human being. Scripture at Church of the Servant is always read by laypeople and the prayers are usually led by a layperson.

Our architect, Gunnar Birkerts, seems to me to have succeeded brilliantly in designing a space that fits this understanding of the assembly as the family of God assembled around Word and sacrament. But only after I have introduced some additional considerations can I explain how he accomplished the most challenging part of the task, that of striking a balance between horizontality and verticality.

Any congregation that plans to construct a building for itself has to make a choice of materials. A rather large number of different considerations go into that choice, including expressive considerations. Different materials "say" different things; marble and stained glass say something different from what cement block and drywall say. In our case, expense was an important consideration; we had a low budget. Many members of the congregation would have argued against expensive materials in any case; but since expensive materials were out of the question, the arguments never had to be made.

Our discussion with Birkerts on this point was fascinating. The issue of materials came up in our first or second meeting. There was a bit of talk about the obvious point, that since our budget was low, the materials had to be ba-

sic. Something inside me impelled me to add, "Your challenge, Mr. Birkerts, will be to use ordinary materials in such a way that the dignity of the ordinary is revealed. You can use steel, provided you use it in such a way that people say, 'I had no idea that steel could be so beautiful.'" Birkerts was quiet for quite some time, looking down; I began to worry, have I insulted him? Then he looked up and said, "I think I understand what you are saying. A dumpy woman can wear silk and still look dumpy; an elegant woman can wear burlap and look elegant. What you want, if I understand you, is an elegant burlap church. Is that correct?" We burst into laughter; he had caught it, exactly.

And that's what the building is: exposed steel framing, sealed concrete floor, cement block, drywall, and a new translucent building material called KalWal, all used with great elegance. The dignity of the ordinary is revealed. It does not have a churchy look.

At a subsequent meeting Birkerts raised another issue pertaining to materials and budget. "Nowadays we can build long spans with steel," he said; "but the longer the span, the more expensive. Will you let me use a post to reduce the length of the span?" Someone replied, "Sure, provided that, when people see it, they don't say, too bad he had to put that post there." I now think that Birkerts was being cunning. There is a post, as we shall see shortly; but it does not function to reduce the length of any span!

At the heart of architecture is not only the shape and size of interior space and how those spaces direct motion within them; also at the heart of architecture is how light pervades those spaces. As preparation for our work, we on the design committee visited a number of recently constructed churches in the area. Almost all of them were dark inside, big swooping roofs coming down low; sometimes there was a light scoop sending a shaft of light onto the front wall. No doubt most people, when they think of church interiors, think of them as dark. We on the committee felt intuitively that this was wrong. In my own case, I had First John 1 ringing in my ear: "God is light, and in God there is no darkness at all. . . . If we walk in the light, as God himself is in the light, we have fellowship with one another."

A few years after the building was built, a Reformation historian friend of mine, Lee Wandel, told me that John Calvin was of the view that the best symbol or image for God is light, since light is uncircumcribable; she has argued, in several papers, that the reason the early Calvinist churches were so light inside is that they were putting into practice this view of Calvin. Whereas a person familiar with traditional Catholic churches "reads" the Calvinist churches as empty, empty of sculpture, empty of images, empty of almost everything, they should instead be "read" as chock full of something else, namely light.

Be all that as it may, we on the committee asked Birkerts to design the building in such a way that a person entering it would have the sense of coming into the light. This too Birkerts achieved brilliantly.

Let me describe how he achieved this; this will enable me also to describe how he achieved a balance between horizontality and verticality. The post that Birkerts said he wanted, in order to shorten the length of the roof spans, is in fact a "tree": a steel column with branches off the branches and branches off those branches. These branches support a translucent peak rising a considerable height above the flat roof, the base of the peak being an irregular octagon. The trunk of the tree goes through the point of the peak and is topped by a cross that one sees outside the building. The tree of life becomes a cross. The entire sanctuary is surrounded at the top by a clerestory made of the same translucent material, KalWal. Even in bright daylight there are no shadows in the sanctuary, not even under the translucent peak.

These design features already produce a powerful sense of coming into the light as one enters the sanctuary. Birkerts heightened this sense by using concrete block of three slightly different degrees of grayness; as one approaches and enters the building, the darkest comes first, the lightest comes last. The wall at the front of the sanctuary, and behind the tree, is drywall painted an off-white; the tree itself, supporting the translucent peak, is a true white.

Not only does the translucent peak contribute powerfully to the sense of coming into the light as one enters the sanctuary; the peak, in conjunction with the tree supporting it, also creates a powerful vertical axis, balancing the horizontality of the spans supporting the flat root. Immediately

in front of the tree are the pulpit, communion table, and baptismal font. The communion circles form around the tree and the liturgical furniture. Communion is around the tree in the light.

One last point must be mentioned. We on the committee agreed that liturgy should be thought of not as a special separate thing that Christians get together to do, but as one pole in the rhythm of assembling and dispersing, and that the building should be designed in such a way as to express this idea. It should have a processional dimension to it, we said. Once again, Birkerts succeeded brilliantly. There are two strong axes, starting from well outside the building, that converge on the tree. From outside one can see along each of these axes straight ahead through the glass doors to the tree; from the tree one can see along each of these axes straight to the outside. One is led from outside in and from inside out.

There are a good many more things that could be said about the building. The building is, for example, handicap-accessible throughout. This was a matter of justice for us, justice for the handicapped. But I trust I have said enough to give the reader some grasp of how to think theologically and liturgically about the expressive qualities of a church building. My aim, let me repeat, has not been to persuade anybody to think theologically and to practice liturgically the same way COS does, nor to encourage others to build copies of its building. My aim has been to encourage congregations, when working on the design for a new church building, to ask not only how their building should function but what it should say, theologically and liturgically.

Thinking about Church Music

I

Throughout the ages, the music of the church has been mingled with tears. Sometimes tears of gladness. A new arrival at Calvin's church in Strasbourg in the early 1540s wrote the following about his experience of first hearing the entire congregation singing psalms to some of the earliest Calvinist tunes:

> For five or six days at the beginning, when I looked on this little company of exiles from all countries, I wept, not for sadness, but for joy to hear them all singing so heartily and as they sang giving thanks to God that He had led them to a place where His name is glorified. No one could believe what joy there is in singing the praises and wonders of the Lord in the mother tongue as they are sung here.[1]

In the *Confessions*, his eloquent and endlessly fascinating address to God, Augustine similarly recalls weeping in response to the music of the church at the funeral of his seventeen-year-old son Adeodatus: "[T]he tears flowed from me when I heard your hymns and canticles, for the sweet singing of your Church moved me deeply. The music surged in my ears,

---

1. Quoted in James Hastings Nichols, *Corporate Worship in the Reformed Tradition* (Philadelphia: Westminster Press, 1958), p. 35.

truth seeped into my heart, and my feelings of devotion overflowed, so that the tears streamed down. They were tears of gladness" (IX, 6). Augustine checked himself from weeping tears of grief over the death of his son — such tears, he believed, were wrong; but he freely allowed himself tears of joy over the music of the church sung upon the death of his son. I need not cite historical examples to make the point: many of those reading this essay will have had the experience of being moved to tears of joy by the music of the church.

The music of the church has also been mingled with tears of grief. When fifty-seven Huguenots from Meaux were led off to the dungeon, they sang the opening of Psalm 79 to the Genevan tune:

> O God, the heathen have come into thy inheritance,
>   they have defiled thy holy temple;
>   they have laid Jerusalem in ruins.
> They have given the bodies of thy servants
>   to the birds of the air for food,
>   the flesh of thy saints to the beasts of the earth.

And when fourteen of them were later led out to execution, they sang on from the same psalm until their tongues were cut out to silence them:

> Why should the nations say,
>   "Where is their God?"
> Let the avenging of the outpoured blood of thy servants
>   be known among the nations before our eyes!
> Let the groans of the prisoners come before thee;
>   according to thy great power preserve those doomed to die![2]

The music of the church has obviously not been mingled with the tears of martyrdom of any of us. Yet for many of us it will have been mingled with tears of grief. Recently a graduate student of mine asked if he could take me out for lunch. We talked for a bit about how his dissertation was going. Then it all came out. A few years back he and his wife had found a lively, committed church where they felt at home. They had become active; and young though he was, he had been elected to the council. Now the church was being split apart and he and his wife were in deep grief. What

2. Ibid., p. 39.

was the problem? Music. A deep conflict had arisen between the pastor and a number of his supporters on the one hand, and a sizeable group of protesters on the other, over the music of the church; and my student was hurt and bewildered by the whole experience. Bright and reflective though he was, he had never thought about church music; he had just experienced it. Now his position of responsibility within the group embroiled in controversy was forcing him to think about it. But he had no idea what to think — no idea even how to go about thinking. How should we think about church music, he asked me, tears in his eyes.

I do not doubt that now and then it is tears of joy that evoke reflection on church music. That young person experiencing for the first time the congregational singing within the early Protestant liturgy in Strasbourg might well have been provoked by his tears of joy into reflecting on this new use of music in the liturgy. More often it is tears of anger, frustration, or grief that provoke the reflection. Either way, we are dealing with passions. I have yet to come across the church member for whom the music of the church is a matter of sheer indifference.

My question is the question posed by my student: how should we think about church music? My answer is simple: we should think of church music as serving the liturgy. I admit there is a bit more to be said than just that. So let me insert the qualifier: we should *primarily* think of church music as serving the liturgy.

A few years back, when we at Yale were looking for someone to fill our position of church music, one of our candidates, a well-known teacher of church musicians, argued that the governing principle of church music should be that God wants the best — by which he meant the *aesthetic* best. In the question period after his lecture it became clear that he did in fact draw the obvious implication, that congregations should be allowed a relatively small role in church music; if one had to let them sing, best to drown them out with powerful organ playing. At the time I happened to be teaching a seminar on the issue of divine impassibility: does God suffer, does God experience grief? I remember thinking the mischievous thought that if what God wants out of church music is the aesthetic best, then, given the state of church music, one has to conclude that God suffers — every Sunday anew! I cite this example to make clear that there are alternatives to the principle I will defend, that we should primarily think of church music as serving the liturgy.

II

As my opening point, I wish to argue that all music, with the rarest of exceptions, is composed or used for the service of something or other. By this I do not mean that all music is produced for some reason or other. That's obviously true. Works of music are not objects of nature produced by one and another natural process. They are human artifacts — the outcome of intentional action on the part of human beings. That, I say, is obvious. What I have in mind when I say that almost all music is composed or used for the service of something or other is that almost all of it is composed or used for some social function.

The reason I emphasize the point is, of course, that this is not how the situation is customarily seen. Ever since the eighteenth century it has been customary for theorists to work with the distinction between music composed and used for the service of something external to itself, and music not so composed and used — between so-called functional music and so-called absolute music. Almost invariably, when this distinction is employed, a comparative evaluation is lurking in the wings: absolute music is higher on the scale of worth than functional music. For when music is freed from the requirement that it be in the service of something outside itself, it is free to follow out its own inherent laws of development rather than having its development shaped and stunted by the requirements of liturgy, the requirements of entertainment, the requirements of national celebrations, or whatever.

This is not the occasion to dig into the ideological and historical origins of this way of thinking about music — and about the arts generally. Let me content myself with observing that by the end of the eighteenth century, the concept and celebration of supposedly absolute music had become intertwined with the emergence of a new cultural paradigm. It was said that if one wants to be a person of culture, of *Bildung* as the Germans called it, you must engage yourself with nonfunctional art: attend concerts, visit galleries, read novels and poetry, admire architecture. The connection established between supposedly nonfunctional art and the cultural elite remains intact to this day. If I confessed in public that I never went to concerts, that hymns and birthday songs were good enough for me, that I never visited museums, that a few mountain scenes on my walls at home were quite sufficient, that I never read novels, that the stories I share with the guys on the job are quite enough, I would immediately be judged as embarrassingly uncultured. No doubt many of those in the hordes who crowd our present-day museum blockbusters genuinely take delight in what they see; it is safe to say, however, that all of them, without exception, are aware of the fact that by attending the Van Gogh exhibition, they are acquiring culture, and that that is seen by our society as a really good thing.

My own judgment on this line of thought is that it is a thicket of theoretical confusion and indefensible elitism. At the heart of it is the claim or assumption that concert hall music, museum painting and sculpture, reading room poetry and fiction, represent *art come into its own,* since the works are presumed no longer to serve a function outside themselves. To get started in thinking about this, consider something not an example of any of the fine arts — a chair, say. The concept of a chair is of something meant to be regularly used for sitting. Chairs can serve other functions than being used to sit on; and things other than chairs can be sat on. Furthermore, chair-like objects can be produced with the intention that they shall never be sat on. Yet it remains the case that the concept of a chair is of something meant for sitting. The concept of a chair is thus *a functional* concept. And when a chair is used as it is meant to be used, one might appropriately say it has then "come into its own" — that is to say, it has then come into its own intended function. A chair used to prop a door open or to provide aesthetic delight in a museum has not "come into its own."

Compare, now, the concept of a chair to the concept of a work of music. The latter, admittedly, is not a functional concept. If one asks what chairs are for, the answer is clear: chairs are for sitting. But if one asks what works of music are for, no similarly clear and unambiguous answer is forthcoming. The concept of a work of music, instead of being a functional concept, is of a sequence of sounds of a certain kind. But — and this is the important point — it does not follow that works of music are not meant to serve some social function. With rare exceptions they surely are. Where they differ from chairs is that they are meant to serve a wide variety of different social functions. The concept of a work of music is thus more like the concept of an item of furniture than like the concept of a chair. Music is multifunctional: some works are meant for one function, some, for another. And as with chairs, they can be used to serve functions for which they were not meant. A Bach cantata can be performed in the concert hall; a Bach fugue, as postlude to the liturgy.

One may say that music performed and listened to in the concert hall nonetheless represents music freed from function. My response is that it represents nothing of the sort. Music in the concert hall is caught up into the social function of contemplative listening for the sake of delight, inspiration, and so forth. Listening carefully to music is doing something with it, putting it to a use. So-called absolute music is just as functional as liturgical music; what makes it different is that it is meant for serving a different function.

Music meant for the liturgy comes into its own when it functions in the liturgy. It is not waiting, longing, to be allowed to come into its own by being freed from service to the liturgy. It is doing what it was meant to do; it has come into its own. By the same lights, music meant for contemplative listening in the concert hall comes into its own when it is listened to contemplatively in the concert hall. It comes into its own when it is put to that use, when it serves that function — not when it serves *no* function, but when it serves *that* function.

That's my case for the conclusion that the distinction between functional and absolute music is a piece of confusion, as is the claim that absolute music represents music come into its own. What remains to consider is the elitism interwoven with this way of thinking. The central issue is now clear. Is contemplative listening a nobler action than all the other things done with works of music — nobler, for example, than any of the things done with music when it functions in the liturgy? I refuse to accept such Platonism. I do indeed want to defend the worth of contemplative listening against those who are dismissive of it. But I reject emphatically the suggestion that the use of music as an object of contemplative listening is nobler than its use for praising God. I would in fact contend the opposite.

III

My thesis, again, is that we should primarily think about church music in terms of its service to the liturgy. I have argued that there is nothing distinctive about church music in its being of service to some social function; that is true of virtually all music, concert hall music included. What is, or ought to be, distinctive about church music is what it is in service to, namely, the liturgy.

But is church music not best thought of as *religious* music? some might ask. I think not. A great deal of the music meant for the concert hall — hence meant to serve the function of contemplative listening — is religious music: Beethoven's *Missa Solemnis,* Brahms's *German Requiem,* and Penderecki's *Utrenja* come to mind. Not only is each of these masterpieces a work of religious music meant for the concert hall rather than for the liturgy; none of them would function at all well within a liturgy. They are too powerful, too overwhelming. Church music and religious music are distinct categories — overlapping, of course, but not coinciding.

To advance our discussion I must now say a word about how I understand liturgy. First, the word itself. To some, the word will evoke thoughts of Orthodoxy, high-church Anglicanism, and pre–Vatican II Catholicism. Those for whom the word has these connotations will think of some traditions as liturgical and of others as nonliturgical, perhaps even of some as *anti*-liturgical.

That is not how I use the word — nor, to the best of my knowledge, how any contemporary liturgical scholar uses it. In my tradition, an Americanized version of the Dutch Reformed tradition, we customarily spoke when I was growing up of what transpired in church on Sunday as "the service" — sometimes, more elaborately, as "the worship service," but usually just as "the service." We spoke of when the service began, of when the service was over, of the language of the service as either Dutch or English, and so forth. That is what I mean when I speak of the liturgy: the liturgy is the service. If the word "liturgy" evokes for you connotations of elaborate rites and rituals, replace it with the word "service."

What we in my childhood meant by "the service" is exactly what the Orthodox mean when they speak of "the divine liturgy." In fact the Greek word *leitourgia*, of which our English word "liturgy" is merely the transliteration, just meant, in classical Greek, a service to the public rendered by a well-to-do individual. Liturgy is public service. The word "service," as used in my childhood to refer to what transpires in church on Sunday, was a precise translation into English of the Greek word *leitourgia*.

It follows that all traditions of Christianity have liturgies. For they all have services. And it makes no sense to speak of some of them as more liturgical than others. They either have a service or they do not; in fact, all of them do.

The question of substance is how we should understand what goes on in these services. A near consensus has emerged among contemporary liturgical scholars on the basic answer to this question. It's a consensus I gladly affirm: *Liturgy is action.* I once had a pastor who insisted to me — "argued with me" would better describe the character of our discussions — that the liturgy, that is, the service, is a sequence of happenings meant to produce a religious experience that he called "edification." For each Sunday he would design a somewhat different liturgy depending on what he judged would prove edifying for the bulk of the congregation on that day. I think I can safely say that no liturgical scholar writing today would accept that way of thinking of the liturgy. Liturgy, to say it again, is action. On that there is now, to the best of my knowledge, universal agreement among scholars.

As to the sort of actions that comprise the liturgy, there is considerably less agreement; on this occasion I must present my own view without doing much to defend it against alternatives. One can see in those from the Lutheran tradition a strong tendency to fit all the actions of the liturgy under the rubric of proclamation; one can see in those from the Orthodox and Catholic traditions a similarly strong tendency to fit all the actions of the liturgy under the rubric of prayer, or more broadly, worship. My own view is that the liturgy properly incorporates actions both of proclamation and of worship; and not only does it properly do so, but every actual liturgy does in fact include elements of both, albeit in different proportions. In Lutheran liturgies one finds elements of worship; in Orthodox and Catholic liturgies one finds elements of proclamation.

Whatever one's view—proclamation, worship, or both—a question one must soon consider is, who is the agent of the liturgical actions, or who are the agents? There is a strong impulse in most contemporary Christians in the West to say the agents of the liturgical actions are the individual human beings assembled: the preacher is the agent of acts of proclamation, the individual congregants are the agents of the acts of worship. Thus, for example, in my own church recently the layperson leading the prayers introduced them by saying, "Will you join me in prayer?"

I think I can safely say that on this point too there is today a consensus among liturgical scholars: none would accept this individualistic answer to the question as to who is the agent, or who are the agents, of the liturgy. The Lutheran inclined to fit the actions of the liturgy under the rubric of proclamation will be inclined to say God is the agent, and/or Christ; it is not the preacher who proclaims the gospel but God by way of the preacher. And the Orthodox and Catholic inclined to fit the actions of the liturgy under the rubric of worship will be inclined to say that the people is the agent, the people being understood not as a collection of individual persons but as *a people*. The person leading the prayers does not invite the assembled individuals to join in on *her* prayer; she leads the congregation in *its* prayer. It is neither *her* prayer that is prayed nor *their* individual prayers but *its* prayer, that is, the people's prayer.

My own view is that the liturgical agent is both of these — both God and the people. I concede that in most liturgies there are a few actions that are the actions of individual congregants — as, for example, when the peace is passed. But for the most part, liturgy is a dialogue between God and God's people. In the assembly, the people of God address God and God addresses the people, back and forth.

Liturgies vary from each other in the specific actions of proclamation and worship they incorporate; they vary even more in the sequence of such actions; they vary yet more in the words and gestures used to accomplish such actions. But we must be careful not to exaggerate the differences. Any outsider to Christianity would discern, beneath the differences in specific actions, sequences, words, and gestures, a remarkable similarity. It is in the Eucharist — the Lord's Supper — that both the actions and the official understanding of the actions diverge most widely.

IV

Suppose you are willing to go along with my suggestion that the primary way to think about church music is to think of it as music in service of the liturgy. And suppose you are also willing to think of liturgy as a sequence of actions — actions on the part of God addressed to the people interwoven with actions on the part of the people addressed to God. Then quite obviously what we want to consider, when we get down to details, is how music can best serve the diverse actions of the liturgy. I think I can best proceed by stating, and all-too-briefly developing, a few relevant principles.

(1) My first principle is that Christian liturgy *calls for* music. The testimony of history speaks so loudly here that belaboring it would be pointless and tedious. It is true that the actions of the liturgy can be performed without the service of music. In some traditions, they are so performed during Lent. So it cannot be said that Christian liturgy *requires* music. It does not. Nonetheless, the testimony of history is that the liturgy cries out for, calls out for, music. The church has always felt that, in ways too mysterious to describe, music profoundly enhances its liturgy. The way to put the point is perhaps this: in its assemblies the church has always found itself *breaking out* into music, especially into song.

Given the pervasiveness of background music in our culture, I think it worth adding that at some points in the liturgy silence is appropriate: neither words nor music. In the liturgy of my own congregation silence occurs at two points: for a few minutes after the sermon, and during the offertory. We conduct the offertory as did the ancient church, by people getting out of their seats and bringing their gifts forward. When we first adopted this practice, the musicians provided some background instrumental music. After a few weeks we asked ourselves why we were doing that; finding no good answer, we stopped. Now there is just the rustle of people moving forward and returning.

(2) A second, more specific, principle is that any action of the liturgy can be enhanced by the use of music. Though this enhancement can consist of background music, what I really have in mind is song and chant: any liturgical action can be enhanced by song or chant. No liturgical actions permit one to dismiss music out of hand as inappropriate. What this implies is that discerning judgment is needed about when to use or not to use music.

Most Protestants operate with the tacit principle that only acts of the people are appropriately served by music, not acts of God. Hence there is no chanting of Scripture or sermon. And today even the Orthodox and Catholics do not chant their sermons. My own view is that most of the time Scripture and sermon are best not chanted; chanting, in my experience, makes them too much an artifact to be admired rather than a message to be received. But what makes me resist saying "never" even about the sermon is a recording I have of the Easter liturgy celebrated in one of the monasteries on Mount Athos. In the liturgy, an Easter sermon of John Chrysostom is chanted by the presider. I find the chanting in this case grippingly celebrative. And Easter, need I say, ought to be celebrative!

(3) My third principle for your consideration is that all the music occurring during the liturgy should be in the service of one and another liturgical action, and that it should be relatively clear to the congregation what that action is. At no point should the liturgy be halted to enable the choir to sing an anthem, or a soloist to render "special music." Mind you, I have no objection to concerts of religious music; my own life has been wonderfully enriched by attendance at such concerts. But the Sunday service, the divine liturgy, is not the occasion for concerts of religious music.

I admit that the application of this principle can get a little sticky. I think that if some action of the people is going to be accomplished by song, then most of the time all the people together should be the singers. My own view, in contrast to the candidate I mentioned for our position in church music, is that the sound of the monotone trying to sing is far sweeter in God's ear than the sound of the professional choir singing religious music with the congregation all listening with aesthetic delight. But I readily concede that the people can normally use some assistance in the form of instruments or choir. Let us be sure, though, that the instruments really do assist the song of the people rather than the song of the people being turned into a *sotto voce* accompaniment to the organ; and let us be sure that the choir really does assist the song of the people rather than the song of the people being turned into a murmuring continuo to the song of the choir.

Not only do I think it appropriate for instruments and choir to assist the singing of the congregation; just as I think it appropriate sometimes for someone to *lead* the people in its intercessory prayer, the leader alone speaking and the people being silent, so I think it appropriate sometimes for a choir to lead the people in its confession, its praise, its thanksgiving, and so forth, the choir singing and the people being silent. What I insist on, however, is that this be practiced and understood as I have just described it. We are not listening in on the choir's praise of God. The choir is not praising God in place of our doing so; nor even, strictly speaking, is the choir praising God *on our behalf.* Rather, we as a people are praising God, being led in our praise, on this occasion, by the singing of the choir.

(4) My fourth principle for your consideration — one I regard as extremely important — is that the character of the music *fit* the liturgical action it serves, and fit the theologically correct understanding of that action.

In my book *Art in Action* I develop at length the concept *of fittingness* I use here; in this essay I will have to be content with offering no more than hints of what I mean. It is probably best to do so by way of examples. Everybody ever asked has agreed with me that an undulating line fits better with tranquility and a jagged line better with agitation; a straight horizontal line fits better with green and a straight vertical line better with red; the interval of a seventh or a second fits better with tension and the interval of an octave or a fifth better with rest; the tritone fits nicely with, say, the demonic — and so forth.

These examples are, of course, abstract: actual paintings come with a thick complex of lines and colors, actual passages of music with a thick complex of melodic lines, harmonies, rhythms, and volumes. But I submit that fittingness applies as much to such complexes of qualities as to the simple abstracted qualities I invited you to consider. If someone who does not know the title listens to Chopin's Funeral March, it might not occur to him to think of it as funereal in character; nonetheless, he would surely think of its character as somewhere in the region of the funereal. No one would think of it as light, gay, and skipping. Though someone who listens to the section called "The Angels" from Messiaen's Nativity Suite might not, in the absence of the title, think of angels, nonetheless, anyone to whom the choice is presented will think it fits archangels much better than cherubim. My own view, in fact, is that if you want to know what archangels are like, listen to Messiaen's piece; then you will know.

Back to the issue at hand: just as the character of a piece of music will typically be more fitting to one emotion than another, so too it will typically be more fitting to one liturgical action than another, and to one way of understanding that action than another way. Some music better befits the liturgical action of confession than the action of praise; and some music better befits a worried, anxious way of understanding confession than a humble but confident way of understanding it. Of course, I concede that distinct ways of performing a passage of music can give it a quite different character — and even that different words connected with the same passage can lend it a quite different character. Witness the difference in how the tune sounds when the words sung are "Baa, baa, black sheep" from how it sounds when the words sung are "Twinkle, twinkle, little star."

I am not an aficionado of contemporary Christian praise music. But on those occasions on which I have been confronted with it, I have found those who use it bafflingly insensitive on this point of fittingness. I also find the words painfully prosaic and sometimes even shudderingly inappropriate. I will not soon forget being confronted, in a service in the Anglican church in Amsterdam that my wife and I attended a few years ago, with a song on the overhead projector whose first line was, "Oh how I appreciate you, Jesus." But on the issue of fittingness, my most unnerving experience occurred at a Christian school convention in Sydney, Australia, where we confessed our sins to a rollicking tune accompanied by a rock band. The only conclusion I could come to is that those who had put these words to that music had never asked the question of fittingness. They thought we ought to confess our sins, they had this tune in their repertoire, so off we went on our clangorous, hard-driving, rollicking confession.

(5) Let me finish with a word about style. I think fittingness, not style, is the basic consideration to be introduced when thinking about music in the liturgy; but once the requirements of fittingness are satisfied, then certain considerations of style do become relevant. Perhaps I should first articulate my assumption that music in many different styles can be equally fitting to a certain action in the liturgy. I have never heard any rock music that struck me as fitting the action of confession; possibly that indicates a deficiency in either my experience or imagination. But certainly music in

the style of Gregorian chant, of Genevan psalm tunes, of Lutheran chorales, and of African American spirituals — to mention only a few — can all be used to set fittingly Psalm 51.

When it does come to choosing style, I think it desirable that the music of the liturgy fit comfortably the ears of participants in the liturgy. Let me explain what I mean by "ears." Any musical culture whatsoever has two sides to it: the objective and the subjective. The objective side consists of the works available for performance within that culture; the subjective side consists of the habits acquired for listening to the music performed. Genuinely listening to music requires more than just the ability to hear; it requires those habits that consist in highlighting some elements and allowing others to recede into the background, recognizing repetitions, noticing harmonic contrasts, being able to pick out melodies, and so forth. Only a very few highly trained specialists will have acquired the ears appropriate for every style of music; most of us in the modern world will have acquired the ears appropriate for a few distinct styles, though only a few.

Back to the principle I propose: it is desirable that the music of the liturgy fit comfortably the ears of participants in the liturgy. I do not mean to imply that the congregation should never be invited to sing or listen to music for which it has not acquired the ears; but it should then be taught how to listen. It should be assisted in acquiring the ears. The liturgy, after all, belongs to the people; it is the dialogue of the people with God, not the performance of some specialists to which the people are invited to listen.

You see the implications. No matter how fond you, the music director, may be of Palestrina and Bach, if your congregation has not acquired the ears for listening to Palestrina and Bach, I do not think it appropriate for you to impose Palestrina and Bach upon them. Wherever the congregation does have the appropriate ears, then by all means do what you can to keep alive the richness of the Christian tradition of church music as well as honoring what is good in the here and now; but if those ears are absent, then it would be wrong for you to alienate the congregation from its liturgy on some such ground as that God wants the best and that Palestrina and Bach are the best. Of course there might be some congregations that have acquired the ears for Palestrina and Bach but not for any music beyond, say, 1900; then give those people Palestrina and Bach.

These last comments of mine describe an idealized situation. I have been talking as if the members of the congregation have all acquired the same ears — not to mention the same preferences. In most of our congregations, that is far from the situation. I will never forget the time a friend took me to visit his home congregation in the village of Karatina, in the Great Rift Valley above Nairobi, Kenya. The congregation was Catholic; the language used was Kikuyu, so I understood not a word of it. When the priest said something, the congregation chanted in response. And when it was time for a hymn, a small percussion band up front set the rhythm and shortly the people joined in. The music was completely unfamiliar to me. The week before I had visited, with the same friend, the Anglican cathedral in Nairobi. There too, when the people began singing, I found it unfamiliar; but invariably, after about five seconds, I recognized a familiar tune sung in a most unfamiliar way. Not so for this village church in Karatina.

Afterward I asked the priest where the music came from. He said when first the new Vatican II liturgy was translated into Kikuyu, the people spoke their responses but that gradually they fell into chanting them. As for the hymn tunes, those, he said, were tunes used at weddings, birthdays, and so forth. I felt a profound nostalgia for a musically unified culture.

That day is past for us. Given the ready availability of radio and CDs and the diversity of musical styles heard on these, the members of virtually every congregation in North America come to church with significantly different ears and significantly different tastes. What is one to do when choosing a style — or styles — for the music of the church? I have no other answer to this difficult question than the answer of charity: I will sing hymns in the style that fits comfortably with your ears and suits your tastes, and I will ask and hope that you treat me likewise.

V

I close by returning to my beginning. When those who occupy positions of leadership in church music grow weary — I do not say "if" but "when" — when they grow weary, I hope they will recall that the music of the church sinks so deeply into our identity as Christian human beings as to bring tears to our eyes. Tears of grief, sometimes; more often, tears of joy. Our tears are existential testimony to how important the music of the church is. The music contributes to our shalom, our flourishing. Yes, the liturgy can be performed without music. But if the liturgy is to be caught up into our shalom, there has to be music. In the new age of God, we will not be reciting the *Sanctus*, but singing it — most of the time, I would guess, to its hair-raising setting in Bach's B minor Mass.

Playing with Snakes:
A Word to Seminary Graduates

T he phrase goes past very smoothly and quickly: "ordained into the ministry of the Word and sacraments." But the undertaking on which you are about to set out, seminary graduates, is awesome. Shortly you will be authorized and enjoined to minister the Word of God to us — to serve our needs, our fears and hopes, with not just a human word but in and through your human words with a Word from Beyond. And to minister the sacraments of the church to us — to serve our needs, our fears and hopes, with not just earthly bread and wine but in and through earthly bread and wine with Sustenance from Beyond, Jesus Christ himself, and with not just earthly water but in and through that earthly water, to serve us with the Cleansing Declaration of God that "I hereby name you, you are one of mine." Awesome! Our support and our prayers are with you.

What can I say on this occasion that won't be terrifying? Well, rather than talking further about the meaning of ordination, let me speak just a bit about an immediate and specific calling, namely, to work with and for children — defending them, befriending them.

You are to be ordained into the ministry of the Christian church in one of the denominations within the Reformed tradition of Christianity. In that tradition, doctrine is important. I think doctrine is important. I know *you* think doctrine is important. Doctrine is *teaching;* and since most people do not find themselves capable of walking around with empty heads, if the church doesn't teach its members anything, those members will fill their heads with something other than the teachings of the church.

I don't propose presenting you with a few doctrines and then urging you to live by them. I propose instead presenting you with an image or two, and then inviting you to see your work through those images. And let me remark here that though the well-formed Christian is one who holds certain doctrines, the well-formed Christian is also one who sees life and reality through certain images. To be a Christian is to live with certain formative images.

What can guide and direct you in your work for children? What can inspire you when the flesh is weary, illumine you when the days are dark? I mean, what *images* can do so?

Recall this messianic passage from Isaiah:

> The wolf shall live with the lamb,
>   the leopard shall lie down with the kid,
> the calf and the lion and the fatling together,
>   and a little child shall lead them.
> The cow and the bear shall graze,
>   their young shall lie down together;
>   and the lion shall eat straw like the ox.
> The nursing child shall play over the hole of the [viper],
>   and the weaned child shall put its hand on the adder's den.
> They will not hurt or destroy
>   on all my holy mountain;
> for the earth will be full of the knowledge of the LORD
>   as the waters cover the sea.
>
>   (11:6-9)

Beautiful! But what does it mean? Animals normally at each other's throats living peaceably together, wolves frolicking with lambs, leopards lying down in meadows alongside kid goats, lions alongside calves and yearlings, bears grazing with cows, lions eating hay with oxen: and then this whole astonishing menagerie being led — led where? — by a little child. While that's going on, a toddler plays over a viper's hole and a four-year-old puts its hand in an adders' den, laughing as the adders all scurry harmlessly about.

The image of the snake runs throughout Scripture. The snake is, in the first place, unclean, loathsome. For it is a misfit, a crossover; it straddles the boundaries established at creation. It is a land animal; but it doesn't move as properly formed land animals do. It doesn't walk or leap; for it has no legs. It slithers. And so, instead of being an expression and indicator of

God's wholeness, God's holiness, it is an expression and indicator of the brokenness that strangely haunts creation. It's unclean, loathsome; image of the unholy. Snakes have to be kept off the holy mountain, out of the holy city.

There are lots of unclean animals. The ostrich is also unclean because it, too, crosses the boundaries established at creation. Though it's a bird, it can't fly. It, too, accordingly, is not an expression and indicator of God's holiness; it, too, is an expression and indicator of the brokenness that haunts creation, of the fact that something has gone awry in this world. But the snake is singled out in Scripture in a way that ostriches are not — nor any other unclean animal. "The serpent," we read, "was more crafty than any other wild animal that the LORD God had made." The snake is the image in Scripture of all that is cunningly hostile to the cause of God and the flourishing of humanity. Not only is the snake unclean: the snake is the image of the enemy. Human beings will strike the head of the snake; the snake will strike the heel of human beings.

In the messianic passage from Isaiah, the toddler plays over the hole of the viper, the four-year-old sticks its hand into the den of adders. The enmity is gone. The snakes don't strike, and the child doesn't attack. There's no hurting or destroying. Instead there's play and processions. And all this takes place on God's holy mountain. There are snakes on the holy mountain. They're still snakes, but they're no longer unclean. They've been incorporated into the realm of the holy. The excluded are now included. Either all along there was something about them that pointed toward the holiness of God or some strange healing has taken place. Or alternatively, the holiness of God is now understood differently, as inclusive rather than exclusive.

Once again, what does it mean? What does the child mean? Why isn't the animal procession being led by an adult? Why the image of a child playing around with the snakes rather than the image of an adult snake handler? Well, the playing is one consideration. There's to be play on the holy mountain. And adults don't play very much; they compete. So we need a child. Perhaps another consideration is that the child is a type of the anti-type, Christ. But in addition to both of those considerations, surely what we have to see in the image of the child is vulnerability — extreme vulnerability. And innocence. I don't mean *moral* innocence; the biblical writers were not Jean-Jacques Rousseau born out of season. I mean "innocence" in the sense of innocent of danger. What makes children even more vulnerable than they are anyway is that they are innocent of danger. With innocent vulnerability the child leads the carnivorous animals; with vulnerable innocence the child plays around with the venomous snake.

On the holy mountain, the child's innocence and vulnerability have, as their counterpart, peaceability. In rearing our children we do our best to diminish their vulnerability and eliminate their innocence. Here on God's holy mountain innocence is appropriate, vulnerability represents no danger. The child is innocent of the dangers of the situation because there are no dangers of the situation. The child has not changed; the child is like all children, innocent and vulnerable. What's been changed is the beasts and the snakes. For the earth is now as full of the knowledge of God as is the sea of water.

And what does that mean: the earth is full of the knowledge of God? To picture an earth full of the knowledge of God, the writer offers us images of a world so altered that we can play and process in vulnerable innocence. What's the connection? Well, "knowledge" here means *acknowledgement*. It's an earth in which God is fully acknowledged. And we know, from a good many other passages in Scripture, that what we have here in this particular passage from Isaiah is a picture of shalom: of human flourishing as God meant it to be. The acknowledgement of God will pervade the earth, making the earth itself holy, when humankind flourishes as God meant us to flourish — when shalom is complete along with the justice that shalom presupposes and incorporates.

We all know that children are not only innocent and vulnerable but that they live in a dangerous world, surrounded by carnivorous animals and venomous snakes. We have all seen the pictures of gaunt starving children in Africa. We have all heard the stories of children abused, battered, abandoned, and tossed into dumpsters. We have all read the statistics about the number of malnourished children in our own wealthy country. Most of us have met children who were religiously, morally, and emotionally malnourished, children who were told nothing of God, given no moral direction, offered no love. Your calling is to do what you can to bring some bit of shalom into the lives of children — to do what you can to bring about, in that way, the acknowledgement of God. It is your calling to do what you can to be a voice for these voiceless ones. It is your calling to struggle to make the world a place in which their innocent, vulnerable playfulness is appropriate. To tame the carnivorous animals, defang the venomous snakes.

Be under no illusion that your efforts will bring about the holy city for children. But likewise, do not despair of making a difference. For it is

God's cause; and God will take both your fumbling efforts and your skillful efforts and use them as building stones for God's holy city.

And do remember, and constantly remind the rest of us, that the child is more than a wearer of clothes, an eater of food, a dweller in houses. Remind us that the child is a creature of dignity, calling for respect. Not an entity waiting to become an adult whereupon it will then be a creature of dignity calling for respect. But already a creature of dignity already calling for respect. For the child is an image of God, an icon of the Holy One. It's a child who has the honor of being appointed to lead the procession.

Leads it where? I asked the question earlier, but gave no answer. The answer, I think, is that the child doesn't lead the procession anywhere; there's no watering hole to which they are headed. Because they're home with their needs satisfied; they're on the holy mountain. This is shalom. So it must be that the procession is a dance; what else? The child, innocent and vulnerable, leads the dance of the reconciled ones.

I invite you to live and work with this image of innocent vulnerable children leading the dance of the reconciled ones and playing with snakes because there's no longer any hurting or killing; for the earth has become holy, full of shalom — the acknowledgment of God.

Part Four

WORLD

Can a Calvinist Be Progressive?

Imagine a person reared in the Reformed tradition who has come to hear the cries of the oppressed of the earth. Imagine, further, that this person has discerned the biblical legitimacy of this cry. With these cries in his ears he has read his Bible; there he has discerned the call of Jesus and the prophets to liberate the captives. Must that person leave the tradition in which he was reared, the Reformed tradition, if he is to respond to those cries and answer that call, perhaps joining those for whom Liberation Theology is their inspiration?

Our twentieth century appears to give to give us ample reason for thinking that he must. Those who oppressed the blacks in South Africa consciously identified themselves as members of the Reformed churches. And among those philosophical frameworks which have emerged within the Reformed tradition in our century, the most prominent has spoken much of law, of creation ordinances, and of cultural mandates, but has said nothing about a liberation mandate.

We must not try to deny this evidence. In our century the Reformed tradition *has* often been oppressive in practice. In our century the Reformed tradition *has* often been conservative in thought. Neither should we try to argue that this oppressiveness in practice and this conservatism in thought are not *true to* the Reformed tradition, that they are a betrayal of the tradition. Whether we like it or not, we shall have to interpret the tradition as including these. And even if we trace such oppressiveness in practice and such conservatism in thought to *outside* influences rather than to impulses deep in the tradition, we shall have to grant that the tradition was at least susceptible to these influences. The contemporary Catholic may not like the old Spanish Inquisition; nonetheless, it emerged from within the bosom of Catholicism and he will have to interpret his tradition so as to take account of that.

The question to ask is whether this oppressiveness and conservatism is all there is to the tradition. The Reformed tradition, like any other, has plenty of shame to its credit. The question to ask is whether it has anything else to its credit. The person from the Reformed tradition who has heard the cries of the oppressed and accepted the biblical call to liberate the captives and secure justice for the poor — is there anything in his own tradition that can nourish his thought and action? It is my own experience that there is.

We can begin with the observation that the Reformed/Calvinist tradition, at least in its youth, was a radical revolutionary force. Indeed, the American political theorist Michael Walzer argues in his book *The Revolution of the Saints* that the first modern political revolutionaries emerged from this tradition. Here I shall not rehearse the evidence. One can find it in any standard history of the English Puritans and in such more general works, in addition to Walzer's, as David Little's *Religion, Law, and Order: A Study in Pre-Recolutionary England* and Quentin Skinner's *Foundations of Modern Political Thought*.

What was the root of that deep and powerful revolutionary impulse in early Calvinism? Max Weber and Michael Walzer attribute it to a psychological impulse: they see it as a way of coping with one and another form of anxiety. Skinner attributes it to a social impulse: the oppression of the Calvinists by Catholics and others led them to take a much more radical revolutionary stance than Calvin, at the beginning of the tradition, was willing to take. My own view is that David Little is much the best guide here. Little attributes the social stance of the early Calvinists to their theological convictions. Of course the Calvinists had anxieties — who does not? — and of course the reflections of Calvinists under oppression were different from their reflections under freedom — whose aren't? But there are many different ways of coping with anxiety and oppression. What turned the thought and practice of the early Calvinists in the direction it took was their religious convictions.

What were those convictions? Let me lay out one line of thought that lies deep in the Reformed tradition. I do not say that this is the only line of thought to be found there. I am myself inclined to think, however, that it is deeper than any other.

When Reformed persons survey this cosmos of ours, and us humans and our works within it, they see goodness. Behind this goodness they see the hand of God. The goodness that they see they interpret as God's gift. They see reality in all its dimensions as sacramental — not sacramental in the weak sense characteristic of Anglicanism, namely, as the sign of God's goodness; but sacramental in the strong sense characteristic of Eastern Orthodoxy, namely, as the *actual manifestation and exercise* of God's goodness. Reformed persons resonate to the biblical theme of God as the one who blesses. They echo the words of God himself in Genesis: "And God saw what he had made; and behold, it was very good." But they go beyond Genesis. For they not only see God's goodness in what God himself has created but they see it also in what humanity has made. Behind the culture we human beings produce and the social institutions we erect Reformed persons see the grace of the Almighty. Sometimes they call it "common grace" (see Calvin's *Institutes*, II, ii, 15).

But when Reformed persons survey reality, including society and culture, they see more than goodness and gift. They also see fallenness, evil, destructive powers, idols. This too they relate to God; namely, as sin, as violation of the will and purpose of God. Typically Reformed persons will relate these two, creation and fallenness, by saying that the good potentials and possibilities inherent in creation have often been turned in wrong directions — in life-squelching, oppressive directions. Reformed persons will always find some goodness left. Yet deep in their consciousness is the awareness of the ravages of sin.

A dialectic of Yes and No, of affirmation and negation — of Yes to God's creation, of Yes but also No to humanity's life in that creation — that is characteristic of the Reformed sensibility.

What is called for, then, is discernment. But not only discernment; also redemptive activity. We human beings are called to struggle for renewal, called to critical creative engagement. We are not just to wait for God to restore God's groaning creation. We are called to cooperate in the *missio dei,* called to be God's coworkers, called to struggle toward making the world holy — always acknowledging, however, that it is God who will have to bring about God's Reign in its fullness. The coming of the shalom of God's Kingdom is divine gift. There is, in Reformed life, a displacement from the emphasis on conversion so characteristic of Anglo-American evangelicals to an emphasis on sanctification, understood holistically.

I suggest, then, that one of the themes characteristic of the Reformed tradition is this interlocking understanding of creation, fall, and redemption. There is a second, closely related, theme. One finds in the Reformed tradition a *holistic* view of sin and its effects, of faith, and of redemption. It is characteristic of many Christian thinkers down through the ages to draw a line between those areas of human existence where sin has its effects and those areas where it supposedly does not. Sin affects our will but not our reason, so it has been said; our values but not our perception of the facts; our technology but not our art. Reformed persons intuitively react against all such line-drawing attempts. They have a profound sense of the pervasiveness of sin — not pervasiveness in the sense that everything is now evil, but pervasiveness in the sense that sin and fallenness are to be found in all facets and dimensions of our existence — in our will, indeed, but also in our reason too; in our values, but also in our perception of the facts; in our technology, but also in our art.

Corresponding to this holistic view of sin is a similarly holistic view of faith and redemption. Faith, trust in God, is not an addendum to our existence, one among other theological virtues. Authentic faith is the fundamental dynamic in a person's life. Authentic faith transforms us, leads us to sell all and follow the Lord. The idea is not, once again, that everything in the life of the believer is different. The idea is rather that no dimension of life is closed off to the transforming power of the Spirit — since no dimension of life is closed off to the ravages of sin. But faith, in turn, is only a component in God's program of redemption. The scope of divine redemption is not just the saving of lost souls but the renewal of life, and more even than that: the renewal of all creation from its groaning.

There is yet a third theme, connected with the preceding ones. Deep in the Reformed tradition is the conviction that the Scriptures are a guide not just to salvation but to our walk in the world; and then, to the *fundamental character* of our walk. They are a *comprehensive* guide. They provide us with "'a world and life view." This theme, of the comprehensiveness of the biblical message for our walk in this world, matches, of course, the holistic view of sin and faith and redemption.

It may help to give an example or two of the complex attitude I have been describing. Music qua music is good, a gift from God. But as we actually find music in our society, it serves both good and bad ends. It is our calling, then, to discriminate between the good and the bad and struggle to promote the good and diminish the bad. We are called to redeem music. In that endeavor, we are to listen to the Scriptures. Such listening will not answer all our questions; it will, though, orient our endeavors. So too politics qua politics is good, a gift from God. As we actually find politics being practiced in our societies, however, it serves both good and bad ends. It is our calling to discriminate between the good and the bad and to struggle to promote the good and oppose the bad. We are called to redeem politics. In that endeavor, we are to listen to the Scriptures. Such listening will not answer all our questions in politics; it will, though, give us orientation.

Two important consequences flow from this complex attitude. In the first place, when compared to the classic medieval attitude it represents a radical turn toward the world. Instead of the contemplative vision of God being the center of thought and practice, grateful appreciation of God's gifts and grateful obedience to God's will are the center. What emerges is what I called, in my book *Until Justice and Peace Embrace,* "world-formative Christianity." Second, what this complex attitude represents is a radical bracketing and dislocation of tradition. Instead of human tradition being our guide, God's Word is our guide. The speech of the Puritan minister Thomas Case to the English House of Commons in 1641 is atypical in its hysterical tone but thoroughly typical in its content:

> Reformation must be universal . . . reform all places, all persons and callings; reform the benches of judgment, the inferior magistrates. . . . Reform the universities, reform the cities, reform the counties, reform inferior schools of learning, reform the Sabbath, reform the ordinances, the worship of God. . . . You have more work to do than I can speak. . . . Every plant which my heavenly father hath not planted shall be rooted up. (Quoted in Walzer, pp. 10-11)

This all remains in a certain way formal. Reformed persons who have heard the cries of the oppressed and discerned the call of God to struggle for their liberation can find, in their tradition, nourishment for reforming thought and action. They can find support for holding social practices and traditions up to biblical critique. But can they also find nourishment for reform in a *liberating* direction? The radical reform instituted by the Afrikaners in 1948 can be seen as a twentieth-century manifestation of the revolutionary potential present in Calvinism from its beginnings. But it was an oppressive reform. Can those of us in the Reformed tradition who long and struggle for *liberating* reform find nourishment in our tradition? Or must we at this point depart?

Here the topic is too vast even for summary. Let me confine myself to pointing out a few of the things that John Calvin himself said about justice, now offering citations where up to this point I have spoken in unsubstantiated generalities. The Reformed person holds that in our reforming endeavors we are to align ourselves with God's will. And it was Calvin's conviction that at the very core of that will lies *human solidarity*. Commenting on Genesis 2:18 — "It is not good that man should be alone" — Calvin writes:

> Moses now explains the design of God in creating the woman; namely, that there should be human beings on the earth who might cultivate mutual society among themselves. Yet a doubt may arise whether this design ought to be extended to progeny, for the words simply mean that since it was not expedient for man to be alone, a wife must be created, who might be his helper. I, however, take the meaning to be this, that God begins, indeed, at the first step of human society, yet designs to include others, each in its proper place. The commandment, therefore, involves a general principle, that man was formed to be a social animal.

In his exhaustive study, *Calvin's Economic and Social Thought*,[1] André Biéler puts the point as follows, citing Calvin's comment on Luke 10:30:

> The primary character of the social order created by God is the *solidarity* that unites all beings one with another. The human race is conjoined together by a sacred bond of community. All are neighbors one of another. . . . We must never wipe out our common nature.[2]

As one would expect, Calvin's vision of an ideal human community places a good deal of emphasis on the religious dimension. Yet he simultaneously and pervasively speaks of its economic dimension.

> Hence we infer what was the end for which all things were created; namely, that none of the conveniences and necessaries of life might be wanting to men. In the very order of the creation the paternal solicitude of God for man is conspicuous, because he furnished the world with all things needful, and even with an immense profusion

---

1. André Biéler, *Calvin's Economic and Social Thought*, trans. James Greig (Geneva: World Alliance of Reformed Churches, 2006), p. 205.

2. What Calvin actually says is stronger, not that we must never wipe out our common nature but that "it is not in our power to blot out our common nature." John Calvin, *Harmony of the Gospels* (Grand Rapids: Eerdmans, 1957), vol. III, p. 61.

of wealth, before he formed man. Thus man was rich before he was born. (Commentary on Genesis 1:26)

Though the family was extremely important for Calvin as a vehicle for the development of a way of life in which our solidarity is acknowledged, in some ways it is economic relationships, rightly structured, that provide an even more significant expression of our social interdependence. As Biéler put it in his earlier book, *The Social Humanism of Calvin,*

> "God has created man," Calvin says, "so that man may be a creature of fellowship." . . . Companionship is completed in work and in the interplay of economic exchanges. Human fellowship is realized in relationships which flow from the division of labor wherein each person has been called by God to a particular and partial work which complements the work of others. The mutual exchange of goods and services is the concrete sign of the profound solidarity which unites humanity.[3]

It is in this context that the proverbial Calvinist emphasis on hard work in a worldly vocation must be placed. Max Weber's interpretation was that hard work, if crowned with material prosperity, was the only sign available to the Calvinists which answered their anxious worry as to whether they were among the elect. What Calvin himself actually said is distinctly different from this speculative interpretation by Weber. Self-initiated hard work in worldly vocations is to be done for the sake of the common good.

> This truly is *ataraxia* (disorder) — not considering for what purpose we are made, and not regulating our life with a view to that end; . . . it is only when we live according to the rule prescribed to us by God that this life is duly regulated. . . . God has distinguished in such manner the life of man, that every one should lay himself out for the advantage of others. He, therefore, who lives to himself alone, so as to be profitable in no way to the human race, nay more, who is a burden to others, giving help to no one, is on good grounds reckoned to be disorderly.

3. André Biéler, *The Social Humanism of Calvin,* trans. Paul T. Fuhrmann (Richmond, VA: John Knox Press, 1961), pp. 17-18.

Because "it is certain that a calling would never be approved by God if it is not socially useful, and if it does not redound to the profit of all," Calvin proposes the notion of *general usefulness* as the standard for evaluating economic performance. He envisions a system of material benefits that are efficiently produced by the dedication and hard work of all employable human beings and that are universally and justly exchanged and distributed, so as to satisfy the basic needs of all and, in addition, to stimulate continued production.

Calvin's idea of property fits within this general framework. Private property is for the general good. "Let those . . . that have riches, whether they have been left by inheritance or procured by industry and effort, consider that their abundance was not intended to be laid out in intemperance or excess but in relieving the necessities of the brethren." Calvin's language on the subject is strong.

> Let us understand that when our Lord wills the life of our fellowmen to be precious and dear in our sight, he shows that, as far as he is concerned, each time we fail to help our neighbor in need, we kill him. For we are not only murderers when we harbor ill will and secretly hate our neighbors: even when we do not help them in their need and do not attempt to engage ourselves in their behalf, when they need our help, we are guilty before God. Therefore, let none of us think that it is only lawful for us to guard what he has; rather, as the principle of charity exhorts us, let us see that we preserve and procure our neighbor's property as much as our own.

In short, justice for Calvin is not secured simply by protecting our neighbor against assaults of various kinds. Justice is secured only if we also see to it that his or her needs are satisfied. Justice, for Calvin, goes well beyond the negative justice of the modern liberal tradition to include positive justice. (At the same time, we must not neglect the contribution of the English Puritans to the struggle for freedoms of various kinds, especially religious freedom.)

Let us dig yet deeper. What is it that undergirds Calvin's repetitive stress on our human solidarity, and his emphatic insistence that our social arrangements — political, economic, familial, whatever — must give adequate expression to that solidarity? The answer is clear. It is his conviction that each human being is created in the image of God. "So man was created in the image of God; in him the Creator himself wills that his own glory be seen as in a mirror"(*Institutes,* II, xii, 6). "God . . . beholds Himself in men as in a mirror" (Sermon on John 10:7).

It is this mirroring of God by each and every human being that ultimately grounds that special love which God has for human beings. "God's children are pleasing and lovable to him, since he sees in them the marks and features of his own countenance. . . . Whenever God contemplates his own face, he both rightly loves it and holds it in honor" (*Institutes,* III, xvii, 6). The thought is clear: God beholds what God has made. God observes that God's human creatures are icons of himself. God observes that they mirror God, that they image God, that they are likenesses of God. In this God delights. God's delight grounds God's love. God delights, of course, in all God's works. But human beings are singled out from other earthlings in that in them God finds God's own perfections mirrored back to himself.

A consequence of the fact that each human being mirrors God is that we as human beings exist in the solidarity of which we have spoken. No more profound kinship among God's creatures can exist than this; nor can such kinship ever be obliterated. Furthermore, each of us mirrors God in the same respects — though some more, some less. Thus we also resemble each other. One could say that we mirror each other. In looking at you and at me, God finds himself mirrored. Accordingly, in my looking at you I discern, once my eyes have been opened, that you mirror God — and more, I discern that you mirror me. I discern myself as in a mirror. I discern a family likeness. As Calvin puts it,

> We cannot but behold our own face as it were in a glass in the person that is poor and despised . . . , though he were the furthest stranger in the world. Let a Moor or a barbarian come among us, yet inasmuch as he is a man, he brings with him a looking glass wherein we may see that he is our brother and neighbor. (Sermon on Galatians 6:9-11)

Calvin grounds the claims of justice in this phenomenon of our mirroring God. The standard picture of Calvin is that obligation, duty, responsibility, and the call to obediencc loom large in his thought; and indeed they do. Yet for Calvin there is something deeper than these. All of us in our daily lives are confronted with other human beings. We find ourselves in the presence of others who, by virtue of being icons of God, make claims on us. Moral reflection can begin either from responsibility or from rights — from the responsibilities of the agent or from the claims of the other. The degree to which Calvin begins from the claims of the other is striking. The pattern is displayed with great insistence in a passage from the *Institutes* (III, vii, 6) of which I will quote only the opening and closing sentences:

> The Lord commands all men without exception "to do good." Yet the great part of them are most unworthy if they be judged by their own merit. Here Scripture helps in the best way when it teaches that we are not to consider what men merit of themselves but to look upon the image of God in all men, to which we owe all honor and love. . . . We are not to consider men's evil intention but to look upon the image of God in them, which conceals and effaces their transgressions, and with its beauty and dignity allures us to love and embrace them.

But how, exactly, does the fact that each of us is an icon of God ground our claim to being treated justly? One would expect Calvin to say at this point that is the *great dignity* inherent in being an icon of God that grounds the claim of the other on me; this dignity calls for respect, and there is no other way of showing the appropriate respect than by treating the person justly. Calvin does speak this way now and then. But his emphasis falls elsewhere. For one thing, he insists that the claim of the other on my love and justice is grounded in the fact that we are kinsfolk, in the deepest possible way, by virtue of jointly imaging God. But there is another way in which the iconicity of the other in my midst grounds his or her claim to love and justice on my part. Commenting on Genesis 9:5-6, Calvin says this.

> Men are indeed unworthy of God's care, if respect be had only to themselves; but since they bear the image of God engraven on them, He deems himself violated in their person. . . . This doctrine . . . is to be carefully observed, that no one can be injurious to his brother without wounding God himself. Were this doctrine deeply fixed in our minds, we should be much more reluctant than we are to inflict injuries.

The thought is striking: God "deems himself violated in their person"; "no one can be injurious to his brother without wounding God himself." And as if to make clear that his speaking thus is not some fancy rhetorical flourish on his part, to be taken with less than full seriousness, Calvin adds that this doctrine "is to be carefully observed." It is to be "deeply fixed in our minds." To inflict injury on a fellow human being is to wound God himself; it is to cause God himself to suffer. Behind and beneath the social misery of our world is the suffering of God. If we truly believed this, says Calvin, we would be much more reluctant than we are to wrong our fellows. To undo injustice is to relieve God's suffering. "God himself, looking on human beings as formed in His own image, regards them with such love and honor that He Himself feels wounded and outraged in the persons of those who are the victims of human cruelty and wickedness."

It is worth adding Calvin's comments on Habakkuk 2:6. Commenting on the cry, 'How long?' in the center of the passage, Calvin says:

> This also is a dictate of nature. . . . When any one disturbs the whole world by his ambition and avarice, or everywhere commits plunder, or oppresses miserable nations — when he distresses the innocent, all cry out, How long? And this cry, proceeding as it does from the feeling of nature and the dictate of justice, is at length heard by the Lord. For how comes it that all, being touched with weariness, cry out, How long? except that they know that this confusion of order and equity is not to be endured? And this feeling, is it not implanted in us by the Lord? It is then the same as though God heard himself, when he hears the cries and groanings of those who cannot bear injustice.

Again the thought is striking. Not only is the perpetration of injustice on one's fellows the infliction of suffering upon God. The cries of the victims are the very cry of God. The lament of the victims as they cry out "How long?" is God giving voice to God's own lament.

For Calvin, the demands of love and justice are grounded not first of all in the *will* of God, which is what much of the Christian tradition would have said; nor are they grounded first of all in the *reason* of God, which is what most of the rest of the tradition would have said. They are grounded in the sorrow and in the joy of God, in God's suffering and in God's delight. If I abuse something that you love, then at its deepest what has gone wrong is not that I have violated your command not to abuse that object of your affection — though you may indeed have issued such a command and I will accordingly have violated it. It lies first of all in the fact that I cause you sorrow. The demands of love and justice are rooted, so Calvin suggests, in what Abraham Heschel, in his great book on the prophets, has called the *pathos* of God. To treat unjustly one of these human earthlings in whom God delights is to bring sorrow to God. The demands of justice are grounded in the fact that to commit injustice is to inflict suffering on God. They are grounded in the vulnerability of God's love for us, God's icons.

Can such themes as these, mined from the father of the Reformed tradition, nourish those of us who have heard the cries of the oppressed and discerned the divine call to liberate the captives? It is not only my conviction but my experience that they can, profoundly so; and that there are many other themes in the tradition which can do so as well. The sad truth is that we in this tradition have allowed many of its creative resources to fall away into oblivion. We remember, as indeed we must, the episodes of oppressiveness; we are fully aware of the themes which nurture conservatism. But there at the beginning of the tradition a profound vision of a just and liberating human society was formulated. In the context of the debate going on in the Western world today, between liberalism and neo-conservatism, it would be worth our while recovering the memory of that vision and reflecting on what, in it, can be of use to us today.

Three years ago this past October I sat in a small courtroom in the village of Malmesbury, near Capetown, South Africa. In the witness box was Allan Boesak. The prosecution for the State accusingly asked him whether his political activities did not go well beyond his call as a minister of the gospel. Boesak straightened himself up, and then, in a clear and loud voice, said, "I belong to a tradition, the Reformed tradition, which confesses that there is not one square centimeter of this world which does not belong under the lordship of Jesus Christ." In those words Boesak tore to shreds the shroud of oppressive conservatism which the Afrikaners had thrown over the Reformed tradition and revealed its liberating potential.

The Moral Significance of Poverty

What is the moral significance of poverty? Is poverty — involuntary, preventable poverty — just unfortunate and regrettable or is there something morally wrong about it?

In the Old and New Testaments, and in a variety of classic Christian theological texts, one finds a preferential option for the poor; more specifically, one finds the view that involuntary, preventable poverty is not just unfortunate and regrettable but is a violation of God-given rights. I wish to look at some of these texts and to argue that there are reasons deep within the Christian interpretation of reality for the presence of this theme in these texts. Its presence there is not accidental.

Some readers will recognize the phrase "preferential option for the poor" as coming from the Latin American liberation theologians. It has become common in recent years for North American Christians to ridicule the notion of a preferential option for the poor in the course of trashing the Latin American theologians for their Marxism. But we must divide the question. Marxism as a social movement has been a disaster; insofar as the liberation theologians have defended it, they have been naive. Or perhaps desperate; they saw the impoverishment of their people as intimately related to the capitalism and wealth of North America and they turned in desperation to Marxism as the only visible alternative. Their defense of a preferential option for the poor is quite a different matter.

That the well-being of the poor and the socially weak is to be the concern of everyone, and one of the fundamental considerations that those with a voice in the governance of society are to use for appraising social arrangements — this is a theme that comes to the surface often and in many different contexts in Scripture. Consider, for example, the well-known description of the good king in Psalm 72:

> Give the king your justice, O God,
>   and your righteousness to a king's son.
> May he judge your people with righteousness,
>   and your poor with justice.
> May the mountains yield prosperity for the people,
>   and the hills, in righteousness.
> May he defend the cause of the poor of the people,
>   give deliverance to the needy,
>   and crush the oppressor.
>
> May he live while the sun endures,
>   and as long as the moon, throughout all generations. . . .
>
> For he delivers the needy when they call,
>   the poor and those who have no helper.
> He has pity on the weak and the needy,
>   and saves the lives of the needy.
> From oppression and violence he redeems their life;
>   and precious is their blood in his sight.

One of the most striking features of this passage is the prominence given, in the appraisal of the good ruler, to whether or not the ruler promotes the cause of the poor and needy. In the words, "May the mountains yield prosperity for the people," one hears the suggestion that though prosperity for the people as a whole is a good thing, it's not something that the ruler can or should bring about. Prosperity of the people as a whole is presented as something that happens, rather than as something that the ruler's policies bring about; the mountains and the hills are enjoined to bring prosperity! We nowadays are inclined to place our hope for general prosperity in political and economic policies formulated by economists and implemented by governments. But even if we revised the psalm to accord with this conviction, the welfare of the poor and the needy would still receive vastly more prominence than would an increase in the gross national product. So too, in the words, "May he judge your people with righteousness," one hears the suggestion that the good ruler will be concerned with justice in all its forms; but immediately the words are added, "and your poor with justice." In short, one of the most fundamental tests for the good ruler is whether he or she is a defender of the poor and the weak.

The subject can also be approached by noticing the pervasive connection in the Old Testament between justice on the one hand, and the welfare on the other hand of those four marginal groups in old Israelite society: widows, orphans, aliens, and the poor. It makes no difference whether it is God's justice that is spoken of or God's injunction to us to act justly. In Psalm 146 it is said of God that God "executes justice for the oppressed," that the Lord "watches over the strangers," "upholds the orphan and the widow." In Deuteronomy 24 God instructs Israel, as part of the holiness code instituted as a memorial of liberation, not to pervert the justice due to the sojourner or to the fatherless and not to take a widow's garment in pledge. Then follow detailed regulations for the care of the poor.

Yet a third way of approaching the subject would be to look at some of the canticles concerning Jesus in the early chapters of Luke's Gospel, at Jesus' self-identification in that Gospel — both to John's disciples and to the worshipers in his first recorded appearance in a synagogue — and, in general, at the actions, parables, and blessings of Jesus. In all of these there is the theme of the outsiders, including the poor, being brought into the community and being honored.

There are yet other approaches that one could take, and each of those could be developed at length. But whatever approach one takes, over and over what comes through is a preferential option for the poor. Over and over the theme is sounded of God's love for the little ones of the world and God's command that they be cared for and honored: the weak defenseless ones, the ones at the bottom, the excluded ones, the miscasts, the outcasts, the outsiders. It is in this framework that one must understand the associations of Jesus with the outcasts of his own society and his positioning of himself among the poor and defenseless ones.

What, more precisely, is the moral significance of poverty in this scriptural perspective? Clearly the presence of impoverished people in a society, when that impoverishment is preventable and not undertaken voluntarily, is treated as a mark against it. Shalom is missing. But is the presence of poverty just one among other social evils, its absence just one among other social goods? Is the impoverishment of a segment of society to be weighed off against, say, an increase in the gross national product? If a society can achieve the latter only at the cost of the former, is it to go ahead and do so?

When it is well-to-do societies that we are dealing with, we need the conceptuality of rights and the violation of rights to capture the moral significance of poverty. To be preventably and involuntarily impoverished is to suffer a violation of one's rights I see no other way of interpreting those strands in the biblical writings to which I have called attention.

Correlative to rights are duties; if I have a right to being treated a certain way, then some person or organization has a duty of some sort to treat me that way. But what exactly the duty is that corresponds to the right, and who or what has that duty, will vary significantly from case to case. If I have a right against you to your treating me a certain way, then you have a duty toward me to treat me that way. But sometimes one has a right to be treated a certain way without there being any one particular person against whom one has the right, and thus without there being some one person who has the duty to treat one that way. If I am drowning in the surf and there are three lifeguards on duty, I have a right to be saved by one or another of the three though not by any particular one; hence no particular one of the three has the duty to save me.

An application of this last point to the issue at hand may be helpful. The presence of preventably and involuntarily impoverished persons in our midst imposes moral obligations on the rest of us. But which obligations are imposed on whom will vary widely. Characteristic of much libertarian argumentation is the assumption that, if the impoverished person in our midst did impose an obligation, then the obligation would be an obligation on the government to make a dole available to the poor. The libertarian then cites evidence for the conclusion that a governmental dole to the poor is injurious to society in general and to the poor in particular. From this he then draws the conclusion that there is no such thing as a right to shelter and sustenance. The point made above, about the relation of rights to obligations, should be sufficient to show how simplistic and fallacious this line of argument is.

It's also important to make a few distinctions among various kinds of rights. Among the rights that we have, some are socially conferred by law, practice, speech, or whatever, whereas others are not so conferred; they are natural rights, grounded in the "nature of things." It was long thought, for example, that the right of certain persons to be monarchs is grounded in the very nature of things, and that persons who have this right have it no matter what revolutionary developments might take place in society.

A second distinction to be made, among the rights that human beings have, is the distinction between what are standardly called *human rights* and all the others. A human right is a right such that the only status one needs to possess the right is that of being a human being. One doesn't have to be any particular kind of human being; one only has to be a human being. The example I gave above, of the purported natural right to be monarch, is obviously not a human right. It's not sufficient to possess the right that one have the status of being a human being.

It is often assumed that human rights are universal — that is, that every human being always has the right if it is a human right. But that seems to me not true. Assume that the right to fair access to adequate means of sustenance is a human right. One doesn't have to be any particular kind of human being to have the right; it's sufficient just to be a human being. But now suppose that one's society is ravaged by drought and that there is no way for outsiders to come to the aid of the society. In that circumstance, one does not have a right to fair access to adequate means of sustenance; one is not being wronged if one lacks such access. Whenever one does have the right, the *status* of being human is sufficient for having the right; but there are *circumstances* in which one does not have the right.

These distinctions are useful for stating what seems to me the best way of interpreting the strands of biblical thought to which I called attention. The right of fair access to shelter, adequate means of sustenance, and decent health care, is a natural human right. One has the right whether or not one's society accords one the right; one has it by virtue of "the nature of things." And the only status one needs to possess the right is that of being a human being; one does not have to be any particular kind of human being. But if one's society is so economically destitute or administratively incompetent as to be incapable of preventing impoverishment, then there may well be people in that society who, in that circumstance, do not have a right to fair access to housing, adequate sustenance, and decent health care.

But is it true that Scripture presents adequate sustenance as a natural human right? Perhaps in the Old Testament it's not entirely clear; with some plausibility it might be argued that it is presented there not as a human right but as a right of members of the Israelite community and of sojourners among them. In the New Testament this limitation — if it was indeed present in the Old Testament — is removed. Hence it is that it was typical of the ancient, medieval, and Reformation theologians to treat the right as a human right.

Consider, for example, this passage from one of the Greek fathers, Basil the Great of Caesarea:

Will not one be called a thief who steals the garment of one already clothed, and is one deserving of any other title who will not clothe the naked if he is able to do so? That bread which you keep, belongs to the hungry; that coat which you preserve in your wardrobe, to the naked; those shoes which are rotting in your possession, to the shoeless; that gold which you have hidden in the ground, to the needy. Wherefore, as often as you were able to help others, and refused, so often did you do them wrong.[1]

Ambrose of Milan, one of the Latin fathers, remarked that "not from your own do you bestow upon the poor man, but you make return from what is his."[2] And with characteristic vividness and acuity, Chrysostom, the great preacher of Antioch and Constantinople, says in the second of his series of sermons on the parable of Lazarus and the rich man:

This also is theft, not to share one's possessions. Perhaps this statement seems surprising to you, but do not be surprised. I shall bring you testimony from the divine Scriptures, saying that not only the theft of others' goods but also the failure to share one's own goods with others is theft and swindle and defraudation. . . .

The rich man is a kind of steward of the money which is owed for distribution to the poor. He is directed to distribute it to his fellow servants who are in want. So if he spends more on himself than his need requires, he will pay the harshest penalty hereafter. For his own goods are not his own, but belong to his fellow servants.

The poor man has one plea, his want and his standing in need: do not require anything else from him; but even if he is the most wicked of all men and is at a loss for his necessary sustenance, let us free him from hunger. . . . The almsgiver is a harbor for those in necessity: a harbor receives all who have encountered shipwreck and frees them from danger; escorts them into its own shelter. So you likewise, when you see on earth the man who encountered the shipwreck of poverty, do not judge him, do not seek an account of his life, but free him from his misfortune. . . .

Need alone is this poor man's worthiness. . . . We do not pro-

---

1. Quoted in Charles Avila, *Ownership: Early Christian Teaching* (Maryknoll: Orbis Books, 1983), p. 66.

2. Quoted in Avila, *Ownership*, p. 50.

vide for the manners but the man. We show mercy on him not because of his virtue but because of his misfortune, in order that we ourselves may receive from the Master His great mercy. . . .

I beg you remember this without fail, that not to share our own wealth with the poor is theft from the poor and deprivation of their means of life; we do not possess our own wealth but theirs.[3]

Finally, to leap some eight centuries, here is what Aquinas says:

Now according to the natural order, instituted by divine providence, material goods are provided for the satisfaction of human needs. Therefore the division and appropriation of property, which proceeds from human law, must not hinder the satisfaction of man's necessity from such goods. Equally, whatever a man has in superabundance is owed, of natural right, to the poor for their sustenance. So Ambrose says, and it is also to be found in the *Decretum Gratiani:* "The bread which you withhold belongs to the hungry; the clothing you shut away, to the naked; and the money you bury in the earth is the redemption and freedom of the penniless." But because there are many in necessity, and they cannot all be helped from the same source, it is left to the initiative of individuals to make provision from their own wealth for the assistance of those who are in need. If, however, there is such urgent and evident necessity that there is clearly an immediate need of necessary sustenance — if, for example, a person is in immediate danger of physical privation, and there is no other way of satisfying his need — then he may take what is necessary from another person's goods, either openly or by stealth. Nor is this, strictly speaking, fraud or robbery.[4]

The teaching is clear: those who find themselves in preventable involuntary poverty have a natural human right to have their poverty alleviated. But let us dig deeper to spy how the fathers were thinking. Why did they believe that there is a natural human right to fair access to shelter, adequate sustenance, and decent health care? How were they thinking?

Underlying their thought was a way of thinking about rights of own-

---

3. Chrysostom, *On Wealth and Poverty,* trans. Catharine P. Roth (Crestwood: St. Vladimir's Seminary Press, 1984).

4. *S. Th.* II-II, q. 66, a. 7, ad. 2.

ership. They all held that a given person's ownership of a given set of goods is always entirely a matter of social arrangement; there is nothing natural about it. My ownership of this Macintosh computer is entirely a matter of social arrangements. John Locke argued that certain rights to specific items of property are natural; no such argument is to be found in any of the classic Christian theologians. As Aquinas puts it, "The division and appropriation of property . . . proceeds from human law."

Given this conviction, the question to be considered is this: what principles ought a society to follow in its distribution of property rights? I am not aware that any of the fathers attempted a general answer to this question. They contented themselves with affirming a more limited, necessary condition of any acceptable arrangement: insofar as possible, the arrangements must assure that everyone's basic needs are met. This is a natural human right. And so it is that we find in the theologians the startling doctrine that the bread, the coat, the shoes, the money of the well-to-do belong to the poor — belong, that is, to those whose needs are not met. An implication of much modern libertarian thought, not infrequently expressed, is that taxation is a form of theft. The position of the church fathers was very nearly the opposite: unshared wealth in the face of poverty is a form of theft.

And why, in turn, did these theologians hold that there is a natural human right to the satisfaction of one's basic needs? They don't say. So let me speculate as to how they were thinking. I think they were assuming that we are one and all called by God to honor our fellow human beings as persons; and that to honor a human being as a person is to prize the enhancement of that person's capabilities for her particular mode of human flourishing, for her particular mode of contributing to the flourishing of others, and for her capacity for self-direction in the use of her capabilities. What else would it be to honor a creature as a person but something like that? But if we allow her basic needs to go unmet, we are undermining those capabilities rather than prizing their enhancement. Something like that, so I suggest, is how they were thinking. We in our pluralistic societies have deep disagreements as to what constitutes human flourishing, and so we have different views about natural human rights. But without a broad enhancement of capabilities, and without the availability of significant scope for self-direction in the use of one's capabilities, there is no human flourishing on anyone's understanding of it. What happens to the person in poverty is the closing down of her capabilities and of her capacity for self-direction.

This prizing of a person's capabilities for flourishing and for contributing to the flourishing of others, and of scope for a person's self-direction, is close to what the Christian tradition has meant by love. Maybe it is the same. And there is nothing more fundamental than love — loving the other person as oneself, placing oneself in the position of the other, striving for the enhancement of her ability to contribute to the flourishing of others just as one strives for one's own.

At some point the Christian church began to see the personhood of human beings as not just a self-contained phenomenon, so to speak, but as constituting a deep similarity to God, an imaging of God. In their personhood human beings mirror God — the personhood of God — more closely and intimately than do any other of God's creatures. Thus, to honor the personhood of another human is to honor the image of God in that person.

This amounts to a great deepening of rights: Given that human beings mirror the personhood of God in their own personhood, one cannot with full integrity honor God without honoring those creatures that mirror God, and conversely; the two come together. Christian theology joins with Christian anthropology in affirming the central worth in reality of personhood. The worship of God and the honoring of a person's rights belong together. And we have already seen that the intuition behind a good many rights, among them the most fundamental, is that to fail to accord a human being his or her rights is to fail to honor and respect the personhood of that human being.

Of all the classical theologians there was none who so intimately related these themes of image of God, love, honoring the personhood of a human being, and rights as John Calvin. But what I find even more fascinating in Calvin is his introduction of yet one more theme at this point — that of the suffering of God. To wreak injustice on a creature who was created by God to mirror God is to wound God's love for that creature. "God himself," says Calvin, "looking on [human beings] as formed in his image, regards them with such love and honor that he himself feels wounded and outraged in the persons of those who are the victims of human cruelty and wickedness." And again, since human beings "bear the image of God engraven on them, [God] deems himself violated in their person . . . no one can be injurious to his brother without wounding God himself. Were this doctrine deeply fixed in our minds, we should be much more reluctant than we are to inflict injuries."

We have come to the end of the road we were travelling. The question I posed was this: when regarded in Christian perspective, what is the moral significance of the poverty which is today not just a massive phenomenon in the Third World but a pervasive presence in the cities of the United States? The answer I suggested was that the moral significance of preventable involuntary poverty is that it is a violation of the person's *natural human rights,* just as surely as physical assault on them is a violation of their natural human rights.

Obviously this answer leaves many questions untreated. What constitutes *fair access* to means of sustenance? For example, is some sort of work-requirement for healthy adults compatible with fair access? I would say it is. What constitutes *adequate* shelter and sustenance and *decent* health care? Won't these differ to some extent from person to person? I would say that they will; and that the true focus of our concern is not that everybody have available to them a dole of a certain size but that certain of their basic capabilities be enhanced and their scope of self-direction in certain ways enlarged. Again, who should be the provider? Should government? If so, what should be the mode of its provision? These questions too I have not considered.

On this occasion I have argued just one basic point: in Christian perspective, a society which tolerates involuntary poverty in its midst when it has the means and skill for its prevention does not even get past the gate of acceptability. Perhaps it is generally a good thing if the Gross National Product of a society increases; in many situations it may even be true that such an increase is necessary for alleviating poverty. But an increase in the GNP is not *sufficient* for the alleviation of poverty.

Since poverty is a violation of rights, the poor person is fully entitled to stand up and demand what is hers by right. She does not have to beg for it; she may demand it. That's what's implied in rights. Further, as Chrysostom emphasized, she is entitled to demand it not on the basis of her good behavior but on the basis of her personhood — this in turn grounding her imaging of God. And if and when she does finally receive what is due her, she does not have to pen letters of gratitude. It will be quite enough for her to breathe a sigh of relief and move forward toward becoming what she can and should become.

Love It or Leave It

Everybody knows what the "it" refers to: Love *America* or leave it.
        I still remember my feeling of anger when first, some months ago, I saw the sign on someone's bumper. I also remember wondering whether I was right in feeling angry. Perhaps, I thought to myself, a good point was being made that I, at least, had not thought about much of late.

The sticker is meant, of course, to be a comment on social protest in our society. On first reading I took it to mean: Shut up or get out; accept America as it is or leave. On that reading of it, the sticker fits in very nicely with a song I heard on my radio the other day. It was called "God Bless America Again"; it naturally reminded me of the song "God Bless America" that was making its rounds about the time of the Second World War. The lyrics of this new song went like this: "Once God blessed America. Now He isn't blessing her any more. Please, God, bless America again. I don't have much book learning, so I don't understand what all these people are complaining about. All I know is that America is like a mother to me. All that I am I owe to her. So, God, bless America again."

What has to be said is that this song, and the bumper sticker interpreted in this way, are expressions of idolatry. They are manifestations of what is, historically, one of our most prevalent American forms of idol worship, namely, worship of nation. The nation, America, is made into something of transcendent worth, beyond criticism, responsible for our very being. Criticism of it is viewed as blasphemous, rather as if a man of Old Israel had mounted demonstrations against Jehovah. The thought is that it's better to leave America than to blaspheme her.

297

When thus understood, the alternative, Love it or Leave it, is an alternative that no one should accept and that no Christian *can* accept. The Christian can never, in Hitlerist Caesarist Stalinist fashion, worship his nation and treat it as transcendent. In every age he will see that the nation in which he lives is corrupt and will not hesitate to say so, nor will he rest from trying to reform it. The contemporary American Christian sees that his nation is spoiling God's earth rather than developing it, that it is frustrating and thwarting human life rather than fulfilling it, that it is lusting after idols rather than listening to God. Thus the contemporary Christian must be among our contemporary dissenters. Or better, among our reformers. If ever he finds himself thinking that America is above criticism, or that all that he is he owes to America, he will not on that account ask God for blessing but rather for forgiveness.

And yet, love it or leave it. For there is a place for love of nation; there is a place in the life of the American Christian for loyalty to America. Nations are certainly not of ultimate worth, but they *are* of worth. In our century at least they provide the only viable context for human life. Thus they merit loyalty. And fallen as America may be, there is no ground whatsoever for thinking that a revolutionary destruction of the fabric of our society will bring a state of affairs better than what we have now. And what is absolutely certain is that neither the Utopia that our revolutionaries long for nor the Utopia that the Christian longs for lies on the other side of social revolution. Thus the Christian is bound to resist those radicals who wish to destroy our nation rather than to work for its reform. To them, and to himself, he must say: Love it or leave it. That is, be loyal enough to this nation to be willing to work for its reform or leave it. And if you leave it, you'll find yourself of course in some other nation. Love *it*, then, or leave it.

Everybody knows what the "it" refers to. But yesterday I saw a bumper on which someone had painted the word "Vietnam" above the words "Love it or leave it."

Reflections on Patriotism

May a Christian be a patriot? That question has been coming to me as an American over and over in this year which marks the bicentennial of the American Revolution.

For me, like many others, patriotism has in recent years become a problematic thing. In my childhood out on the midwest prairies it was different. There I experienced fresh, enthusiastic, uncomplicated patriotism. Each Memorial Day, with the air full of the fragrance of lilacs, our entire village marched or rode in parade to the village cemetery to honor the war dead. The parade was led by members of the American Legion, somewhat out of step, cramped by the tight uniforms of their late adolescence — but always impressive. Before the parade there was a patriotic program in the local high school, the high point being the recitation of Lincoln's Gettysburg Address by an honored school child. One year I was the honored one. As I recited those moving cadences that morning my voice was choked with the emotion, and my skin covered with the goose-bumps, of patriotic exaltation.

I have not recited the Gettysburg Address lately. I do, though, periodically sing "The Star Spangled Banner." I find that when I do, it is not emotions of patriotism that well up within me but feelings of offense at the anthem's militarism and flag-fetishism. Somewhat less often I recite the pledge of allegiance to the flag. When I do, it is not the patriotic promise I am making that is uppermost in my mind but rather the fetishism at the beginning and the hypocrisy of the closing phrase, "with liberty and justice for all."

I KNOW WHY my feelings of patriotism have weakened. Mainly it is because of my fear, even my conviction, that the soul of my nation has become corrupted. Once America held aloft the flame of liberty before the nations. The immigration of millions is testimony to that. True, there was always discrepancy between the ideal and the actuality. Indians, blacks, Catholics, and women have all suffered oppression at the hands of those who professed liberty and justice for all. But in the past one could promote the just treatment of oppressed groups by appealing to the American soul. My fear — and dawning conviction — is that this is no longer true. America is on the way to becoming a nation indifferent to justice at home, committed only to libertarian sensualism; and indifferent to spreading the light of liberty abroad, committed only to shoring up the American experiment by lending support to whatever governments will in turn support us — even, ironically, those which forbid to their own people the very privileges of liberty that they help to keep going here.

The weakening of my feelings of patriotism has led me to explore a line of thought that I should perhaps have explored in any case. Could it be that my membership in the church of Jesus Christ implies that my love for nation should be rooted out of my life? The central component in my identity is my membership in that people which is the church — "a chosen *race*," "a dedicated *nation*," "a *people* claimed by God for his own" (1 Pet. 2:9). This chosen race transcends all nations. For after Pentecost, God's chosen people on earth does not exclude the members of any natural grouping — not Greeks and not Jews, not females and not males, not slaves and not freemen. But neither does it automatically *include* the members of any natural grouping. The church is a presence within each nation while transcendent to all, alien to all while resident in each, "elect from every nation, yet one o'er all the earth."

Does that not mean that my love for the American people should be rooted out of my life? When a person emigrates from one country to another and becomes a citizen of the second, his love is transferred from his native nation to his adopted one. Should it not be so when one joins the church? My people are now the people of the church. It is her joys and victories that lift me, her sorrows and retreats that depress me. The bombs falling on the cathedral of Hanoi are bombs falling on *my* people. The joy of the church in Nigeria over the manifestations of the Spirit is the joy of *my* people.

That is the line of thought I have been led to explore. Many other Christians have explored it before me. But is it on the right track? Is it true that having made the church my people I should no longer embrace America as my nation? Is it true *in general* that having chosen the church as one's people one should no longer embrace as one's people the nation in which one finds oneself?

IN ASKING THIS QUESTION I am not posing the issue of my relation as a Christian to the American *state,* but that of my relation as a Christian to the American *nation.* It's been easy to confuse the two ever since there emerged in the early modern period in Europe a new kind of state — the *nation-state.* This is a state that comprises as its citizens a single people — that is, one of those most comprehensive natural grouping of persons who share a sense of cultural identity (supported normally by a common language). Or alternatively, it is a state that comprises various component peoples but with one of them dominant in the affairs of state. Neither the ancient Roman Empire nor the Holy Roman Empire was a nation-state. But in the modern period the German nation acquired its state, the Italian nation its, the French its, the Dutch nation its state, and so forth.

It's worth noting that the emergence of the American nation-state occurred in the reverse order from the emergence of most other nation-states. There was not here a people who already had a sense of cultural identity and then managed to compose a state with a citizenry coterminous with itself. Quite the contrary. The collection of immigrants here at the beginning had only frail bonds of cultural identity. That situation, though, did not long last, in part because they and their descendants did not want it to last. We who dwell in the United States have wanted to be *one* nation — not just a group of nations under one state. And so the world has seen before its eyes the birth of a nation. Our shared historical experiences under a common government, and our shared dwelling and traveling within this common land, would themselves perhaps have given birth to a nation. But we have taken matters into our own hands. We have forced the birth and nourished the infant by enjoining the use of a common language and by adopting countless stratagems to instill within us a body of shared aspirations and a common way of life. Though we did not begin as a nation, and though we were far from being a nation in the middle of the nineteenth-century torrent of immigration, we have wanted and tried to be one. We have succeeded. There is today an American nation and not merely an American state. And my question concerns my relation to that American *nation,* not my relation to the American state.

In asking about the legitimacy of patriotism I am not asking whether I as a Christian should try to shed the marks of my being an American. For being a patriotic American does not consist in bearing such marks. One can bear them while being thoroughly unpatriotic. In fact I display in all sorts of ways my identity as an American. There is no chance of its being otherwise, unless I go to live in some other land and after a long, slow process of acculturation lose my identity as an American by acquiring some other national identity. There is no such thing as standing before God and among my fellows as *just a* Christian. Always one wears the clothing of some nation.

Further, such national diversity is to be prized. Life in Christ does not stifle but fulfills the potential of humankind. And no single complex of language, clothes, customs, characteristics can adequately express that potential; only all together, in complementary and mutually enriching diversity, can do so. Only if we express our commitment to Christ through distinct cultural forms can the rich diversity of human potential be brought into the Kingdom.

Nor am I asking whether I may work and pray for nations in general, including the American nation. Nations are part of the reality of humankind. As far back as anthropological research can carry us, we find humankind divided into distinct cultural entities. Always and everywhere we find a diversity of peoples. And in our world these nations, these peoples, are important for human life and fulfillment. To the structured social existence that they provide, and to the fulfillment of human potential that they thereby make possible, there is no alternative. Accordingly, Christians work not for the abolition of distinct nations but for mutual understanding and tolerance among nations. Within each particular nation they work to bring it about that that nation fulfill rather than distort and oppress the lives of its members.

So when I ask whether I as a Christian may be a patriotic American, I am not asking whether I may work and pray for the health of the American nation. The church will survive the rise and decline of every nation. But the rise and decline of nations is not on that account a matter of indifference to the church. For in the rise and decline of nations lie millions of tales of human joy and suffering.

Finally, I am not asking whether I may work and pray *especially* for the American nation. For doing that is also not the essence of patriotism. In fact I do bear deeper responsibilities for the health of the American nation than for that of any other. God has placed me here in this country; and it is from this spot that I must do my work. Occupying as I do this particular place in the whole family of humankind, I have a distinct, concrete pattern of responsibilities. To the persons with whom I interact in the course of my life I bear deeper responsibilities than I do, say, to some Argentine of whom I know nothing. Part of my particular, concrete pattern of responsibilities is the special responsibilities I bear for working for the health of the American nation. Still, the acknowledgment of these special responsibilities does not constitute patriotism.

PATRIOTISM IS *love* of country. It consists in *feelings of affection and loyalty* for one's nation. Patriotism enters the picture when someone *loves* one nation above all others — either that one within which he was nourished from birth or that one which he has adopted by choice. My question is whether I as a Christian may feel a special love for the American nation. Is it legitimate for any Christian to *love* his nation above all others — in the sense of feeling special affection for it and loyalty to it?

The roots of patriotism lie in *loving one's own,* feeling at home within some group. The child first feels at home within his family, where he or she first acquires rootage on the face of the earth within the human family. But each of us gradually begins to feel at home within other groups and to love them as our own — larger groups, overlapping and concentric groups. That does not mean that we give up love for family. One can love as one's own both one's clan and one's immediate family, both one's schoolmates and one's church. For the love is in each case grounded and expressed differently.

Perhaps the most decisive expansion *of loving one's own* occurs when one begins to feel at home among a group which is too large and too dispersed to make it possible ever to have face-to-face contact with all the members. A good example is the nation. Such groups might better be called societies than communities. Societies are abstract whereas communities are concrete.

Except for rare periods of emotional frenzy, abstraction cannot sustain a sense of being at home. So if an abstract group is to engender love and devotion it must be *concretized,* related to everyday experiences, tied down to characteristic patterns of life and types of artifacts that will be missed when they are gone. If that abstract group which is the Dutch people is to engender love and devotion to itself, a "Dutch way of life" must emerge. Communities are such that, when one loves them as one's own, one misses both the people and their ways of doing things when gone from them. By that test, many — if not most — families are communities. One does not, however, miss the members of a *society* to which one belongs. Most of them one does not know. But concretized societies are such that, when one loves them as one's own, one misses at least their ways of doing things when gone from them. Nations are like that. The American who travels abroad misses "a good hamburger." Therein is revealed part of what makes him feel at home among his own American people.

This distinction between communities and societies also applies within the church. There, too, one perceives strategies of concretization at work on the part of societies. A congregation (if people feel at home in it) is a community; its members can enjoy face-to-face contact with each other. A denomination is at best a society, something abstract. If it is to engender loyalty it must become concrete in the everyday lives of its members. When a denomination is concretized, so that people feel at home in it and love it as their own, they will miss its way of doing things when away from it. They will not, though, miss its members, for most of them are unknown to any single person. But if one loves one's congregation as one's own, then one misses both the people and their ways of doing things when away. Insofar as different denominations go off and "do their own thing," and insofar as the church in different countries goes off and "does its own thing," the transdenominational and transnational character of the people of God will lack concretization, with the result, in turn, that the members of the church of Christ will not love it as their own and will not feel that the church as a whole is *their* people.

THE QUESTION of the legitimacy of patriotism for the members of that transnational people which is the church can now be set within a larger context. Is it legitimate for Christians to love any group as their own, other than the church as a whole or some component thereof? Is it legitimate for Christians to feel at home in *any* group other than the church? Is it legitimate for them to love their families as their own? Is it legitimate for them to feel at home among their schoolmates? Is it legitimate for them to miss the American way of doing things when traveling abroad?

In a striking passage Augustine answered a rousing no to all such questions:

> Man is not to be loved by man as brothers after the flesh are loved, or sons, or wives, or kinsfolk, or relatives, or fellow citizens. For such love is temporal. We would have no such connections as are contingent upon birth and death, if our nature had remained in

obedience to the commandments of God and in the likeness of his image. It would not have been relegated to its present corrupt state. Accordingly, the Truth himself calls us back to our original and perfect state, bids us resist carnal custom, and teaches that no one is fit for the kingdom of God unless he hates these carnal relationships. Let no one think that is inhuman. It is more inhuman to love a man because he is your son and not because he is a man, that is, not to love that in him which belongs to God, but to love that which belongs to yourself. . . . If we are ablaze with love for eternity we shall hate temporal relationships. Let a man love his neighbor as himself. No one is his own father or son or kinsman or anything of the kind, but is simply a man. Whoever loves another as himself ought to love that in him which is his real self. Our real selves are not bodies. (*Of True Religion*, 88, 89)

It is clear that what underlies Augustine's repudiation of all natural affections is his insistence that the true self of a person is the person's eternal soul. It is for this reason that Augustine insists that we must repudiate insofar as possible all concern for our bodies and all concern for temporal and physical relationships. It's so obvious as to need no arguing that Augustine's dichotomy here manifests more of Plato than the Scriptures. What's important for our purposes, however, is that Augustine has relentlessly drawn out the implications of his Platonist assumptions. We are thereby better able to see the way toward the correct answer to our question.

We human beings are not eternal souls attached for a while to gross and inferior bodies: we are complex physical, social, emotional, spiritual creatures, created good by God in all our aspects. An implication of this is that redemption is not the negation but the renewal of our natures, making possible once again their fulfillment. Supposing Augustine's line of thought to be typical, the contention that my membership in the church requires my feeling at home nowhere else presupposes that redemption requires in large measure the repudiation of creation rather than its fulfillment. It presupposes that the social, physical side of our natures, if not bad, is markedly inferior.

As a whole we have come good from the hand of God with no inferior aspects. Accordingly, our membership in the community of the redeemed does not require us to repudiate our eminently natural overlapping and concentric rootages in the human family on the face of the earth. It does not require the abolition of the natural affection of children for parents and siblings, of students for classmates, of citizens for nations. I rightly celebrate my mother's birthday in a way in that I do not celebrate other birthdays; and I do so whether or not she is a member of the church — though all the more joyfully if she is. I rightly grieve over my father's death in a way that I do not grieve over other deaths; and I do so whether or not he is a member of the church — though with all the more feeling if he is. Did not our Lord weep over Jerusalem? It is in fact the experience of many that in joining the church they are motivated and enabled to work for the *healing* of their broken relationships to their natural families.

The American nation is my parent in the family of nations. It has nurtured me as no other has. In it I feel at home. I embrace it as my own. And I do so as a member of the church which transcends this and all other nations. My membership in the church does not abolish, and does not *require* the abolition of, my patriotism. On the contrary, it strangely bears within itself the potential for healing my broken relationships to my nation.

Yet, though it does not abolish my patriotism, perhaps even renews it, at the same time it profoundly alters it. Now a new and more fundamental loyalty has entered my life with the result that my love of nation is relativized. If ever I was a nationalist, making my membership in the American nation my fundamental loyalty, no longer am I that. Now I find myself sometimes forced, painfully, to choose against my nation. What it asks of me I sometimes cannot grant.

Now, too, I can no longer share fully in the joys and sorrows of my nation. Sometimes what gives my nation joy gives me sorrow. Sometimes what gives it sorrow gives me joy. For now I judge my nation in the light of its service to the coming of the Kingdom. And that alters my assessment of it. The militarism so characteristic of nations, and so pervasively celebrated in their anthems, their rituals, their venerated leaders, I now repudiate. The new growth that sometimes springs up from the burned soil of defeat I now celebrate.

Even the ideals of my nation I do not now entirely share. Some of them I do; but never all. For judged by reference to what promotes the coming of God's Kingdom, the ideals that guide and inspire my nation are tangled mixtures of good and bad. My unqualified allegiance I cannot give.

And now I cast my eyes abroad. Though I nourish my affection for my nation, at the same time I love all peoples, praying and working for their flourishing. I do not allow my affection for my own people to stop my ears and harden my heart to the starving and oppressed cries of others.

So I SHALL CELEBRATE my nation's bicentennial. I shall remain, or become again, a patriot. But it is a transformed patriotism that I shall feel and practice. I am at home in my nation. Yet I am a pilgrim here. My love of country tugs at me. Yet the cords have been loosened.

> The distinction between Christians and other men is neither in country nor language nor customs. For they do not dwell in cities in some places of their own, nor do they use any strange variety of dialect, nor practice an extraordinary kind of life. . . . Yet while living in Greek and barbarian cities, according as each obtained his lot, and following the local customs, both in clothing and food and in the rest of life, they show forth the wonderful and confessedly strange character of the constitution of their own citizenship. They dwell in their own fatherlands, but as if sojourners in them; they share all things as citizens, and suffer all things as strangers. Every foreign country is their fatherland, and every fatherland is a foreign country. *(Epistle to Diognetus, V)*

The American bombs falling on the cathedral of Hanoi and those falling on the Lutheran church in Dresden were falling on *my* people. How do I cope with the tragedy of a member of my people — of my very own people, the church — being inspired by distorted love for his nation and to take up a gun against some other member of my people?

Contemporary Christian Views of the State:
Some Major Issues

What is the nature of the state, and how does it fit into God's ordering of creation?

Once upon a time — until the 1930s to be more exact — one knew what the Catholic, the Reformed, the Lutheran, the Anabaptist, the Anglo-American evangelical, and the Liberal traditions would each say to those questions. Each of the main Christian traditions had worked out its views on the state and built up its rejoinders to those of the others. Each had marshalled its claims to biblical support and its rebuttals of the claims of the others.

That familiar stalemate has now been upset, that comfortable equilibrium destroyed. Catholics have refused on grounds of conscience to enter military service. Reformed persons have argued that the chief function of the state is to make possible the proclamation of the gospel. Lutherans have participated in revolutionary assassination attempts. And Anglo-American evangelicals have publicly enlisted support for McGovern.

There are many reasons for this shifting of positions and mingling of lines. I wish to call attention to just two.

The Christian community came into the twentieth century with the confident belief that all states are ordained by God for the good of human beings and that, accordingly, we are to obey them out of conscientious support for their repression of evil and encouragement of good. Within the community there were disagreements concerning the limits to one's duty of obedience. But these disagreements had a speculative quality, since nobody was actually proposing acts of disobedience. Anabaptists did continue to say that Christians should not actively participate in the functioning of the state; but they were by now saying this very quietly. The only issue still being discussed with vigor was, what is the good that the state should perform and the evil that it should thwart?

Today we are living in the aftermath of Auschwitz, Viet Nam, and the collapse of the Great Society. The political events of our century have shaken us all. We have all undergone reality therapy. Our sanguine attitude toward the state has been destroyed.

A second fundamental reason for the fluidity of our current situation is that important new biblical studies have forced us to reconsider the old lines of exegesis. I have in mind here particularly those studies into the New Testament teaching concerning *the powers* — those elements of reality that, though created by God, continue in demonic fashion to enslave human beings even though they are on the way to being overcome by Christ. The teaching of the New Testament concerning angels, principalities, rulers of this present age, powers, etc., once seemed on the edge of New Testament doctrine, harmlessly excisable from the gospel. Now it seems near the center and astoundingly relevant to our twentieth-century experience. Romans 13, which once looked like a simple statement of God's authorization of the state, with its opening reference to "supreme powers," now looks rather different — and much less simple.

The shifting of old familiar positions induced by twentieth-century political experience has given us all a feeling of insecurity. Guideposts have disappeared. But we would not be true to our calling as God's agents in the world if we dwelt on that feeling. For the shifting of positions provides us with an opportunity such as we have not had for centuries — the opportunity to work out a common Christian doctrine of the state. I do not think it is unrealistic to hope that the traumas of our century will provoke us into something near a common position. My hope is that this paper can make a contribution to that future event, by digging beneath the surface of our disagreements to the basic issues that together we must discuss and by pointing a way out of the impasses that have so long plagued us.

I

The basic issue that political events in our century have posed to Christians is not which candidates to support nor which legislative programs to promote. Today the basic issue is that of the nature of the state itself and its place in God's order. Because of our confusions and disagreements on this point we are in confusion and disagreement about officials and programs. Our experience has made the nature of the state a deeply existential issue for all of us. And that, of course, is why this issue is also at the center of all those theories of the state that have been worked out by contemporary Christian thinkers.

I must offer a word of explanation as to what I mean when I speak of the "nature of the state." I do not mean the complex of features that all states do as a matter of fact display. Nor do I mean the complex of features that are essential to states — those features that something must possess if it is to be a state at all. I mean rather the complex of features necessary to something's being a *properly formed state.* That is what contemporary Christian theories of the state have mainly been about. The question as to the nature of the state is a normative issue.[1]

When I remarked, above, that political events in our century have forced us all to reflect on the nature of the state, what I had in mind was that our century has confronted us not only with the passing of bad legislation and the accession to power of bad officials. It has confronted us with states that have themselves become monsters. Our states have become grossly malformed, their structure seriously misshapen. Perhaps the greatest service we Christians can render the states in which we live is reminding them of what a properly formed state is like.

I dare say that most political theorists would reject with scorn this talk of a properly formed state. Here I cannot enter into a defense. It must suffice to remark, first, that a delineation of the features necessary to a properly formed state is indeed what contemporary Christian theories of the state are centrally about. If you and I today reject this concept, we shall have to work out entirely new lines of thought from those of our predecessors. Second, it is worth remarking that even those theorists most scornful of the concept of a properly formed state operate with counterpart distinctions throughout their lives. Think, for example, of what the botanical taxonomist tells us about, say, the Shingle Oak *(quercus imbricaria).* He does not tell us which features all shingle oaks have in common, nor does he tell us which features are essential to something's being a shingle oak. Rather he tells us which features are necessary to something's being a properly formed shingle oak. He knows very well that there are malformed shingle

---

1. See especially Herman Dooyeweerd, *A New Critique of Theoretical Thought* (Philadelphia: Presbyterian and Reformed Publishing Co., 1957), vol. III, pp. 384ff., 401-2.

oaks and that his description will not wholly fit those. Similarly, all of us in dealing with our pets distinguish between some undesirable action that the animal performs and some malformation in the animal itself. There is nothing apriori absurd about applying counterpart distinctions to the state by delineating the features necessary to a properly formed state.

II

I begin with what all Christians hold in common. States are institutions. While God-ordained, they are actualized by human beings. They are not, like rocks and trees, part of the world in which we are placed by God. They are brought into existence by human activity. Further, they are *governmental* institutions, comprising a structure of governing and governed, of authorities and subjects. And they are *historical* governmental institutions. They are not, like families, foundational to the whole pattern of human historical development. Rather, they arise within the course of human history. They are elements of human culture, appearing at certain points in the development of human societies.

To each state belongs a certain territory, that territory, namely, over whose inhabitants the state in question has the power of the sword. That phrase, "the power of the sword," is of course a metaphor. What the metaphor points to is the fact that states are not only governmental institutions that make demands over certain people, but they back up those demands with coercive power. The state does not permit its members the choice of resigning from membership if they do not wish to obey. The subjects of a given state are those people over whom the state makes demands and over whom it is effective in backing up those demands with its coercive power. And the territory that belongs to a state is then that area over whose inhabitants the state has this power of the sword. In thus having a certain territory that belongs to it, a state is strikingly different from the church.[2]

What is especially worth noting is that one's subjection to the state is

---

2. The *subjects* of a state must be distinguished from its *citizens*. As already explained, the subjects of a given state are those who inhabit the territory belonging to the state. Different from these are the state's citizens, its body politic. I may be the subject of France by virtue of living there, while yet remaining a citizen of the United States. To be a citizen of a certain state is to have certain sorts of claims on that state, recognized by the state itself, which one does not acquire just by virtue of dwelling in the territory of the state and does not lose just by virtue of dwelling outside that territory.

311

not a voluntary matter. Of course one can become a subject of a different state by moving. Yet we are all *born* subjects. This makes the state almost unique among historical institutions. Furthermore, today it is no longer possible to escape being a subject of some state or other. There are no longer any unclaimed lands. The combination of the fact that one is subject to a certain state just by virtue of dwelling within its territory, with the fact that all states have the power of the sword over their subjects, has always troubled the Christian. What is the place of this non-voluntary coercive institution in God's order? And how should we who are members of Christ's body participate in it?

So much, then, all Christians hold in common.

III

Christian thinkers have also believed that a certain proper function belongs to the nature of the state. But it's here that our disagreements begin. While we all hold that the proper function of the state is set by God, we disagree as to what that function is.

If we dig down to fundamentals, there are, I think, three basic views on this matter that have been defended and articulated by Christian thinkers in the twentieth century. These are also, I believe, the views that are most alive as patterns and options in the Christian community today. Of course most of us probably don't have any clear views on the proper function of the state—either that or we have inconsistent views. But these three are the basic views that both pattern our thought in subtle ways and confront us as options when we try to think clearly and consistently. These are the basic types around which our thinking gravitates.

As background it will be convenient to have before us the medieval and traditional Catholic view of Thomas Aquinas. For all three contemporary views have been carved out in opposition to the main features of that traditional view.

Aquinas repeatedly described man as "a social and political animal." What he had in mind by that was, first, that existence in society is necessary if a human being's created nature is to find fulfillment. In that way human beings are *social* creatures, "destined more than other animals to live in community."[3] Second, Aquinas argued that no society can exist unless there

---

3. A. P. D'Entreves, ed., *Selected Political Writings by Thomas Aquinas,* trans. J. G. Dawson (Oxford: Blackwell, 1981), p. 6.

is some government within that society — that is, unless someone has a care for the common good of the society and the others render to him obedience. In this way, human beings are by nature *political* creatures.[4]

Within every body politic there is a whole fabric of institutions. Aquinas thinks of the state as part of such a fabric, as one of the institutions of the body politic. To explain which part, we must first distinguish between religious matters and secular matters. In Aquinas's view, the concern of the state is wholly with secular matters. Religious matters belong within the competence of the church. Second, the state is the topmost of the institutions in the body politic dealing with secular matters. It is the one having supreme authority; all the others fall within the scope of its authority. The proper function of this topmost part of the entire institutional fabric is to care for the secular common good — that is, for the secular good of the body politic as a whole. It does this, in part, by ordering those other social institutions that are properly subordinate to it.

Viewed from our vantage point in the twentieth century, the most striking feature of this view of the state is that it sets so few limits to the totalitarian tendencies of states. Aquinas does say that the proper function of the state is limited to secular matters. And he does say that within the domain of the secular, the proper function of the state is limited to the common good of the body politic. But within the domain of the secular common good, the state may properly act wherever it deems such action conducive to the common good. In many circumstances it may well be bad policy for the state itself to make medical decisions, educational decisions, economic decisions, etc. But if it did so, it would not by virtue of so doing be a malformed state.

A totalitarian state is not necessarily an evil state. Its laws may be good and its administration may be just. Yet biblical reflection and twentieth-century experience have sufficed to convince contemporary Christian political thinkers that a state so near-totalitarian as Aquinas's theory would allow is inherently malformed. Accordingly, contemporary Christian political theories can all be viewed as forged in opposition to the extremely comprehensive scope that the Thomistic theory assigns to the state's proper function. All have tried to formulate limits, structurally comparable to those that Aquinas set with respect to religious matters, to the proper function of the state. All have gone along with Aquinas in saying that the proper function of the state is limited to the common good of the

4. D'Entreves, ed., *Selected Political Writings,* p. 5.

body politic; that is already an extremely important limitation. And all have gone along with Aquinas in ascribing autonomy within its own domain to the church. But all have also attempted to go well beyond this to form a theory in which the proper function of the state is confined to some definite domain within the common good. They have not been content to say that the state differs from all other institutions concerned with the common good in that, except for the church, it is topmost.

IV

Let us begin with the most comprehensive of these contemporary theories — that which I shall call the *law, justice, and welfare view* of the proper function of the state. This view is most characteristically found among Catholics and Liberal Protestants. It is the view to which the Catholic Jacques Maritain gravitates.[5] I shall expound the general view by looking at Maritain's specific version of it.

5. Jacques Maritain, *Man and the State* (Chicago: University of Chicago Press, 1951). Actually, it would be more accurate to say that it is one of the views toward which Maritain gravitates. Maritain's theory is in fact riddled with internal tensions between the traditional Catholic theory and a certain alternative thereto. In the text I expound what I take to be that alternative. But in fact Maritain says that the state has "topmost authority" in secular matters (p. 13); and that "the common good of the body politic demands a network of authority and power in political society, and therefore a special agency endowed with uppermost power, for the sake of justice and law. The State is that uppermost political agency" (pp. 23-24). This conception of the state as the ultimate authority in matters of the secular common good, all other institutions being subordinate in such matters, is obviously the traditional Thomistic conception, and different from the state as properly functioning in only certain *limited aspects.*

Another ambiguity in Maritain's thought that should be pointed out lies in his concept of the *body politic.* He says that a body politic is a *society,* and he says that "supreme authority is received by the state *from the body politic,* that is, from the people" (p. 24). But also he says that the state and the body politic "do not belong to two diverse categories, but they differ from each other as a part differs from the whole" (p. 9), and he then goes on to say that the state "is not a man or a body of men; it is a set of institutions . . ." (p. 12). What is happening here is that a society is sometimes thought of by Maritain as a body of people and sometimes as the complex of institutions of a body of people. Consequently the body politic is also sometimes thought of in the one way and sometimes in the other. This confusion pervades all of Maritain's thought in the book. I think that he does consistently think of the state as an institution, part of the whole fabric of a people's institutions. But given his confused thought about the body politic, sometimes he thinks of a state as a part of a body politic and sometimes as one of the institutions of the body politic. In my discussion, I consistently mean by a body politic, a body of people—specifically, the citizenry of a given state.

Maritain vigorously argues the point that a well-ordered body politic will not be a collection of individuals having just one important institution, the state. Rather, it will to a high degree be what he calls a *pluralistic society*. His own words describe well what he has in mind: ". . . the body politic . . . contains in its superior unity . . . a multiplicity of . . . particular societies which proceed from the free initiative of citizens and should be as autonomous as possible. Such is the element of pluralism inherent in every truly political society. Family, economic, cultural, educational, religious life matter as much as does political life to the very existence and prosperity of the body politic. Every kind of law, from the spontaneous, unformulated group regulations to customary law and to law in the full sense of the term, contributes to the vital order of political society. . . . Finally, the public welfare and the general order of law are essential parts of the common good of the body politic, but this common good has far larger and richer, more concretely human implications . . ." (p. 11). In short, a well-ordered body politic will have within it a large number of institutions each of which has its own distinct domain of proper functioning.

Where is the state in this array of institutions? What is its proper function? Maritain's answer seems to be that the state has a three-fold proper function. For one thing, it is the state's proper function to regulate the activities of members of the body politic — both individuals and societies — by a system of law based on justice and good order. Second, it is the state's proper function actively to promote social justice among the citizens and societies of the body politic. Sometimes when the basic structures of society "are not up to the mark with regard to justice," the state may itself have to step in and provide benefits of one sort and another. But that is malformation. In general, it is the proper function of the state actively to promote the satisfaction of the right to education without itself providing it. Third, Maritain holds that in the area of economics it is the state's proper function to engage in whatever activities are necessary to secure economic welfare.

Even in the domain of economics, however, Maritain wishes to protect his principle of pluralism. He argues that normally it is good policy for the state to promote and support the efforts of business and labor institutions rather than itself to perform the economic functions necessary to the public welfare. He cites the TVA as a good example of what he has in mind (pp. 22-23). Still, he does not hold that the state is necessarily malformed if, for example, it nationalizes certain industries or provides a guaranteed annual income. In the domain of economic welfare, but only in this domain, it is within the state's proper function to act as a service organization.[6]

The main question that must be put to the law, justice, and welfare view of the state is this: What is the rationale for limiting the service function of the state to economic welfare? Is this not a purely arbitrary limitation? What is fundamentally different between the sphere of economics and that, say, of art? To this question Maritain has no answer. The attempt to give a theoretical safeguard against the totalitarian state proves, at least in Maritain's version of the law, justice, and welfare view, to have no structural basis. And this, I think, is characteristic. Those who hold such a view characteristically have no *principle* to offer in objection to the state's becoming a service institution in other domains than the economic. And thereby they have no principle to offer in objection to the state's becoming totalitarian. The chief task for anyone attracted to the law, justice, and welfare view would be to find such a principle.

V

In strong contrast to the law, justice, and welfare view is what I shall call the *law and order view*. This is the most constricted of contemporary

6. Maritain believes that false and pernicious notions of sovereignty are constantly leading the modern state to aggrandize itself and overstep the domain of its proper function. But he also realizes that the modern state is repeatedly placed before the dilemma of either failing in its duty to promote social justice or of overstepping its proper function and itself becoming a service institution in other than the economic domain. Sometimes the only right choice in such situations is malformation. He says,

> As a matter of fact, this primary duty is inevitably performed with abnormal emphasis on the power of the State to the very extent that the latter has to make up for the deficiencies of a society whose basic structures are not sufficiently up to the mark with regard to justice. Those deficiencies are the first cause of the trouble. And thus any theoretical objections or particular claims, even justified in their own particular spheres, will inevitably be considered as but minor things in the face of the vital necessity — not only factual but moral — of meeting the long-neglected wants and rights of the human person in the deepest and largest strata of the human society. (p. 20)

The dilemma is a hard one. For the risk that the state incurs in overstepping its proper function so as to answer the call for social justice is that it will become totalitarian, "not only supervising from the political point of view of the common good (which is normal), but directly organizing, controlling, or managing, to the extent which it judges the interests of public welfare to demand, all forms — economic, commercial, industrial, cultural, or dealing with scientific research as well as with relief and security — of the Body Politic's life" (p. 211).

Christian views as to the domain of the state's proper function. It has been found mainly among Anabaptists and Anglo-American evangelicals — though of course these two traditions differ sharply from each other on the related but distinct issue as to whether Christians may actively participate in that coercive non-voluntary institution which is the state, an issue that, unfortunately, I will not have time to discuss. To give some specificity to the general view, I shall expound it by considering Carl Henry's statement of it in his book *Aspects of Christian Social Ethics,* for this is the view to which Henry quite consistently gravitates.

A theme that pervades Henry's thought is that of abhorrence for the totalitarian tendency of contemporary states. He remarks that "when the power of the State becomes the means for compelling people to do their whole duty, this power can easily be employed to force people to do *what is not their duty at all.*"[7] In his discussion Henry singles out especially two connected causes for the self-aggrandizement of contemporary states: The belief that the state should act out of benevolence toward the desires of its citizens (pp. 154ff.), and the belief that the state can and should be an instrument of social transformation and renewal (pp. 108ff.). He sees these beliefs as the principal culprits behind the encroaching welfare state which "is no longer dedicated to justice and order, encouraging and enforcing human rights and responsibilities under God, but is benevolently bent toward people's socio-economic wants" (p. 169).

Henry is himself deeply convinced that our society needs renewal, as he is that Christians must work for such renewal. But he argues that such renewal will come about if and only if there is a religious change in the hearts of individual persons. Evangelism and not legislation is the road to social betterment. "The reliance on political means to lift all the burdens of mankind . . . is characteristic of contemporary social theory in which secular concerns wholly replace the spiritual. . . . Such secular proposals, while claiming to promote social justice, tend in the long run simply to readjust the existing disorders along new lines" (p. 124). The "aim of the Christian's political activity," he goes on to say, "is not to produce a Utopia, but to preserve justice and promote order in a fallen world" (p. 96). For, he asks rhetorically, "is not the State's obligation in preserving justice to provide what is *due* (as corresponding to the rights of men) rather than to implement *agape* by acts of mercy or love?" (p. 166).

---

7. Carl F. H. Henry, *Aspects of Christian Social Ethics* (Grand Rapids: Eerdmans, 1964), p. 118.

From these quotations it is already clear how Henry views the proper function of the state. The state's proper function is to maintain a system of laws regulating the activities of the members of society, a system of laws that secure good order and protect the rights of the members of the body politic. As he puts it, "The justification of civil law is that it *protects* my rights (and my neighbor's). . . . The role of government is but to declare, to apply, and to enforce rights which are given of God and therefore inalienable. . . . The purpose of law is to prevent one person from injuring another; my rights end and become my duty where my neighbor's rights begin" (p. 92). The same point could be put in terms of justice rather than in terms of rights: The laws must be based on principles of good order and justice. For "justice considers every person a subject of rights and an object of duties . . ." (p. 92).

On reflection this point of view will quite inevitably stimulate the following line of questioning: Do not the members of our society have a *right* to education, to fire protection, to decent medical care, to enough income to live decently if disabled? And so will not a system of laws based on justice secure these rights to the citizenry? Why then should the securing of these rights be prejudicially described as the benevolent satisfaction of wants? But if the state does actually secure these rights, will it not then become what Henry so abhors — namely, a service-state distributing benefits? In short, does not Henry's own principle of justice lead to a vastly more comprehensive state than he wants? No doubt some thinkers have justified a comprehensive service-state by the principle of benevolence. But does not Henry's own principle of justice lead to the same destination by a different road?

I think not, and it's important to see why not. I don't know whether Henry holds that in our well-to-do society citizens have a right to education. But it's clear that even if he does, he does not believe that it is the state's business to provide education. For this is not the kind of right he is speaking of. Henry is speaking of *freedom-rights* — the right to act without coercion in one area or another. Examples of freedom-rights are the right to free assembly, the right to free speech, the right to private property, and the *habeas corpus* right to one's own body. But when we speak of the right to education, we do not mean the absence of coercive threats against getting educated. We do not mean the right freely to pursue an education if one so chooses. We mean rather the right to *receive* an education. Similarly the right of the disabled to a decent income is not the right freely to go about securing such an income for oneself. It is the right to *receive* such an income. Such rights as these are *benefit-rights.* Freedom-rights call for protection. Benefit-rights call for provision. A freedom-right is a claim on everyone to respect that right. A benefit-right is a claim on someone or other to satisfy that right.

When Henry speaks of rights, it is freedom-rights and not benefit-rights that he has in mind. Correspondingly, when he speaks of justice as consisting in establishing a man's rights by securing what is due to him, he has freedom-rights in mind (pp. 154-71). It is not *social justice* but *regulative justice* that he is thinking of. Henry's view is that the atate's proper function is to regulate the activities of its citizens by maintaining a system of laws based on *regulative justice* and good order. It is not the state's proper function actively to promote *social justice,* i.e., actively to promote the satisfaction of benefit-rights. And certainly it is not its proper function itself to dispense services in any area whatsoever. This Henry takes to be the biblical view on the matter: "The Bible," he says, "views government as a means of preserving justice in a fallen and sinful order" (p. 93).

Parenthetically it may be remarked that what I mean by social justice — namely, the satisfaction of benefit-rights — is not to be identified with what has traditionally been called *distributive justice or equity.* Distributive justice consists of treating people equitably in the distribution of benefits or burdens. It does not speak to the issue of whether someone has a right to such-and-such a benefit but only to the mode of distribution of benefits. Social justice, however, consists in the satisfaction of someone's right to some benefit. And the right to some benefit is of course different from the right to be treated equitably if that or some other benefit is to be distributed at all. For benefits may be distributed to which no one has any right. In that situation, distributive justice pertains but social justice does not.

It is worth adding to our discussion of Henry's views that in the course of developing his law and order view of the state, Henry espouses an extremely individualistic view of human society. This is not a necessary accompaniment of the law and order view. The Anabaptist shares the law and order view while holding a non-individualistic view of at least the church. On the other hand, the law and order view does quite inevitably accompany an individualistic view of society. Henry seems to regard all institutions apart from the family, the state, and the church, as purely instrumental and contractual. No other institutions are regarded as having a definite domain of proper functioning. Thus no other institutions are regarded as having independent authority within a definite domain. And so no other institutions are regarded as entering into the fabric of rights and duties. When Henry speaks of rights, he speaks exclusively of the rights of one individual vis-à-vis another (though his discussion assumes the right of the state to the obedience of its subjects).

What should chiefly give us pause before the law and order view of the state is its radical exclusion of social justice from the domain of the state's proper function. It is impossible to read the Old Testament prophets without seeing that it was social justice they were calling for; it was the deprivation of benefit-rights that evoked their denunciation. The Christian cannot possibly regard justice as confined to regulative justice. Of course it is one thing to say this and quite another to say that social justice belongs to the proper function of the state. But still, what reason might be offered for not drawing this conclusion?

Henry's defense is that social justice can be secured only if hearts are changed, and conversely, that it will be secured if hearts are changed (pp. 15-16, 72). But this seems just false. It is true that in a society of sanctified human beings, social justice will flow forth. So too will regulative justice. And we must indeed beware of the utopian heresy that the Kingdom of God will be inaugurated by the state and its coercive devices. But what concerns us here is not the society of sanctified human beings but our mixed society. And it is simply not true that benefit-rights cannot be secured in such a society. The freedom-right to hold private property is protected in our mixed society. And in that very same society the benefit-right to fire protection is secured. The right to fire protection is not secured by conversion of the hearts of human beings but by the very device that Henry suggests cannot be used to secure benefit-rights — by legislative action of the state. It must of course be acknowledged that in our mixed society we will never succeed in fully securing all benefit-rights, neither by legislation nor any other means. But that is scarcely a reason for not even trying to do so. We will also never fully protect all freedom-rights.

St. Paul's statement in Romans 13 that the state is for restraining wrongdoing has sometimes been used to support the conclusion that the state is to be limited to regulative justice. But surely the deprivation of benefit-rights is a matter of wrongdoing, both individual and collective: a matter of perversity, and of dereliction in duty. Amos would never tolerate the suggestion that the deprivation of benefit-rights in Old Israel somehow occurred without wrongdoing on anyone's part. The wrongdoing that underlies social injustice, as well as that which underlies regulative injustice, must be restrained and punished. But what other institution than the state is authorized to exercise the power of the sword over the entire citizenry?

There is no escaping the conclusion that all justice which falls within the common good — social as well as regulative — belongs within the proper function of the state.

But once again we are faced with what now looks like the other horn of an inescapable dilemma: If the state seeks to secure social justice, does it not then become a distributor of services, and that not only in the area of economics but in all other areas as well? And is not a comprehensive service-state inevitably a totalitarian state?

We have here touched on one of the most basic polarities confronting Christians today. We seem to have to choose between blinking our eyes to the deprivation of social justice and acquiescing in the monstrosity of the comprehensive service-state. Some of us choose one way, some the other. Some of us cannot ignore the cry for social justice, so we put up with the evils of the comprehensive service-state. Some of us cannot ignore the evils of the comprehensive service-state, so we put up with the absence of justice. That is our agony. Is there no escape?

VI

There is, I am convinced. To see what it is, we must sketch out the third major view as to the proper function of the state that has been developed by Christian thinkers in our century, what I shall call the *law and justice view*. To the best of my knowledge this view has never been characteristic of any one Christian tradition. It has received its finest expression, however, by two thinkers in the Reformed tradition — Emil Brunner in his book *Justice and the Social Order*, and Herman Dooyeweerd in the third volume of his *New Critique of Theoretical Thought*. I will depend on their expositions in sketching out the general view.

Brunner and Dooyeweerd both express their alarm at the totalitarian state which exceeds the state's proper function — exceeds God's ordering for the state. The thought of both is in good measure shaped by their attempt to work out the limits of the state's proper function. Brunner says that

> The monstrosity which bears the name of the totalitarian state has at last succeeded in reminding us that there are not only primal rights of individuals and of communities, but that there is a just and unjust order of the state itself. The totalitarian state is not, like a

dictatorship, a form of the state. It is the absorption of all institutions and all rights by the state. The totalitarian state is the inevitable consequence of the view that . . . all rights obtaining among the people issue from the state. The totalitarian state must of necessity come into being wherever political thought is centralistic, and all organization is regarded as issuing from above, from state centre.[8]

And Dooyeweerd remarks that

In whatever shape the absolutist idea of the body politic is set forth, it does not recognize any intrinsic legal limits to the authority of the State. This idea implies an absorption of the entire juridical position of man by his position as citizen or as subject of the government.[9]

But at the same time that Brunner and Dooyeweerd express their alarm over the totalitarian tendencies in modern states, both also express their conviction that the state is charged by God with the function of promoting social justice.

Central to the thought of both is the vision of a well-ordered society as being what Brunner calls a *federal society* — that is, a society whose institutional fabric contains a large number of distinct autonomous institutions. Brunner's federal society is obviously similar to Maritain's pluralist society; and it is interesting that there should be this coalescence between Catholic and Reformed thinkers. Yet they cannot be identified, if only because Maritain is hazy as to the nature of his pluralistic society — more hazy than my exposition made him out to be. Maritain clearly thought that the church and the family each have a proper function within a definite domain, and that consequently each has an authority not derived from the state and rights to be protected by the state. But Maritain can be read as saying that all institutions except these are subordinate to the state. His recommendation that the state grant each a considerable degree of independence can be read as having no deeper basis than that this is good policy in most circumstances.

On this crucial issue, Brunner and Dooyeweerd are clear. They hold

---

8. Emil Brunner, *Justice and the Social Order,* trans. Mary Hoffinger (New York: Harper, 1945), p. 134. See also p. 203.

9. Herman Dooyeweerd, *New Critique of Theoretical Thought,* trans. David H. Freeman and William S. Young (Philadelphia: Presbyterian and Reformed, 1953-58), vol. 3, p. 441.

that the institutional fabric of a well-ordered society will contain a great many institutions having a proper function within a definite domain, each of such institutions accordingly possessing both authority in that particular domain and rights that must be respected by the state. The institutions of society are not purely instrumental and contractual. "In the Christian understanding of man," says Brunner, "communities are just as much established in the divine order of creation as the independence of the individual. They are innate in the God-created individual with his capacity and need for completion" (p. 83).

Thus it is not the proper function of the state to make educational decisions for society, nor of schools to make business decisions for society. Each of these God-ordained institutions has autonomy in its own domain, sovereignty in its own sphere. The state too is sovereign. But like every other institution it is sovereign only in its own sphere. Hence

> the standards of justice obtaining in these forms of community are antecedent to the state; they are formed in manners and customs, agreements, contracts, rites and ceremonies, established rights to which, in the first instance, no state pays heed. It is not the state which sets this life in motion, not the state which determines by which rules it shall proceed, not the state which can pronounce on its justice or injustice. . . . The state, in all this, comes late, protecting, preserving, regulating, but not as a creative or constitutive agent. (Brunner, p. 137)

What then is the sphere of the state's action? What is the domain of its proper function? A two-fold one. The state's proper function is to regulate the activities of the members of society — both individual and institutional — by a system of laws based on good order and regulative justice. Second, the state's proper function is actively to promote social justice.

The phrase "actively promote" is crucial here. When at all possible, the state is not itself to provide the services and engage in the activities that will satisfy our benefit-rights. Rather, its function is actively to promote a society containing institutions that can and will satisfy those rights. For in all its actions the state must respect the autonomy, the sovereignty, of the other institutions in society:

> The State may promote the interests of science and the fine arts, education, public health, trade, agriculture and industry, popular mo-

rality, and so on. But every governmental interference with the life of the nation is subject to the inner vital law of the body politic, implied in its structural principle. This vital law delimits the State's task of integration according to the political criterion of the 'public interest,' bound to the principle of sphere-sovereignty of the individuality structures of human society. (Dooyeweerd, pp. 445-46)

Here then we have an escape from the dilemma pressed upon us: how can the cry for social justice be answered without turning the state into a comprehensive service-institution? The state is properly concerned with social justice. Yet insofar as possible it must not itself become a service-institution distributing all sorts of benefits. That would violate the principle of federalism. Its fundamental role in the area of social justice is that of actively promoting a federal society containing non-state institutions that satisfy the genuine benefit-rights of the citizenry.

A real public legal integration of a country and people is, therefore, only possible within the internal limits set by the structural principle of the State-institution itself. This integration can only be accomplished within the juridical limits set by this structural principle to the competence of the body politic, and with due regard to the internal sphere-sovereignty of the other societal structures. Every political theory denying these limits is in principle a theory of the 'power-State,' even though it masks its absolutization of the State's power by a law-State ideology. (Dooyeweerd, p. 441)

VII

This last theory needs a good deal more elaboration than I can give it here — and more than either Brunner or Dooyeweerd have given it. The theory does not imply that the state may not use its taxing powers to support non-state institutions. Nor does it imply that the state may never render anything which can be regarded as a service. For example, the maintenance of a system of good roads is a service justified by the principle of good order — that which makes it possible for the citizens to go about their tasks. And perhaps some benefit-rights are such that it is impossible for anything but the state to satisfy them; perhaps that is true of the right to a decent income if disabled. These and other distinctions call for more detailed articulation. Yet it seems to me that this theory does, in its main lineaments, provide an escape from the dilemma pressing upon us.

Our American legal structure does, to a gratifying degree, recognize the domain autonomy of our many non-state institutions. Insofar as that is true, our legal structure is resistant to totalitarianism. And for that we should be thankful. Yet undoubtedly our state has been moving in the direction of becoming more and more an entrepreneur and a distributor of services in a multitude of areas. For this there are many reasons, some no doubt insidious. Yet it would be wrong glibly to say that, in every case, the right thing for the state to do is to resist itself acting to secure social justice. Brunner states well the predicament to which we as Christians must be sensitive:

> The fundamental Christian realization is that the state has only to intervene where individuals, families, free social groups, the churches, the municipalities, cannot perform their tasks. Any justice created by the state is a makeshift, a substitute for the justice which human society should create of itself. . . . And vice versa, the greater the decline in the moral vigour of society, the more tasks the state must take upon itself, and the greater the expansion of the element of compulsion in justice, the nearer the approach of the totalitarian state. Hence the rise of the totalitarian state is in the first instance quite simply a judgment on the wretched moral condition of modern society. We must not fear to add — a judgment too on the Christian church and its powerlessness to direct the moral forces of society in the sense of the justice of creation. Let us take as an example the welfare work of the state, which has already assumed monstrous proportions. This would not have been necessary if the family in the narrower and wider sense of the word, the social community, the Christian community and the economic community of labour had not so conspicuously broken down. (pp. 205-6)

VIII

We have probed some of the issues involved in the nature of the state. With this as background let us consider, lastly, how the state fits into God's ordering of God's creation.

Christians have traditionally affirmed that the existence of states among human beings is authorized by God, that their existence conforms to God's will for our human condition. But what is the fundamental status of that authorization? Is it part of God's *creation* decrees for the life of human beings, no matter what our condition? Or is it rather part of God's *providential care* for the life of *fallen* humankind?

The Catholic tradition has favored the former view, the Protestant, the latter. Yet, passionate though the dispute has often been, it is hard to avoid the conclusion that there is no genuine issue here. The Catholic emphasizes the fact that the state is a governmental institution in charge, for all the inhabitants of a certain territory, of some domain within the common good. And he rightly insists that the Christian neither views governance in general as an evil or necessitated solely by evil, nor does he view *such* governance thus. The Protestant, on the other hand, stresses the embeddedness of our states within our present fallen age. Our states exact obedience from the inhabitants of a certain area by their power of the sword; and, given our sinful condition, how else could they exact it? And our states maintain a system of laws whose purpose and effect is in large measure to restrain wrongdoing. No one should hold that this is the sole purpose and effect of our laws. In part they have a purely regulative, ordering purpose and function. Still there is no denying that our political structures are in large measure devoted to restraining wrongdoing.

What makes it hard to see any genuine issue here is that the coin of the state simply does have these two faces. The state is a governmental institution responsible for some aspect of the common good of all those who inhabit a certain territory. The Protestant need not deny this, nor need he deny that God's authorization of such an institution can be seen as belonging to God's creational decrees. But the state is also an institution that acts to restrain wrongdoing and does so by exercising the power of the sword. The Catholic will scarcely deny this, nor will he deny that God's authorization of such an institution belongs to God's providential care for a fallen world.

Protestants have sometimes cited Romans 13:1-8 as support for their side in the dispute. And indeed, the only task of the state that Paul mentions in this passage is that of curbing wrongdoing. Governing authority, he says, is "God's servant for your good. But if you do what is wrong, you should be afraid, for the authority does not bear the sword in vain. It is the servant of God to execute wrath [*orgē*] on the wrongdoer." But if we look at the larger context within which this passage is embedded, it becomes clear that Paul is not here offering a general theology of the state but is simply pointing to that task of the state which is relevant in the context.

That larger context begins with Paul saying, "I appeal to you therefore, brothers and sisters, by the mercies of God, to present your bodies as a living sacrifice, holy and acceptable to God, which is your spiritual worship" (12:1); it closes with Paul saying, "Love does no wrong to a neighbor; therefore, love is the fulfilling of the law" (13:10). Paul's comments on the task of the state are set within the context of a discussion of the Christian life.

Within that context, Paul says, at the end of chapter 12 and just before he turns to the topic of the state, "do not repay anyone evil for evil, but take thought for what is noble in the sight of all. . . . Beloved, never avenge [*ekdikeo*] yourselves, but leave room for the wrath [*orgē*] of God; for it is written, 'Vengeance [*ekdikēsis*] is mine, I will repay, says the Lord.' No, if your enemies are hungry, feed them; if they are thirsty, give them something to drink. . . . Do not be overcome by evil, but overcome evil by good" (12:19-21).

Paul's topic at the end of chapter 12 is wrongdoing, specifically, how Christians should and should not respond to wrongdoing and how God deals with wrongdoing. That's why, when he turns to the topic of the relation of God and believers to the state, what he takes note of is that the state is authorized by God to curb wrongdoing. It should be noted that he does not say that it is the task of the state to execute vengeance *(ekdikēsis)* on the wrongdoer; he says that it is the task of the state to execute wrath or anger *(orgē)* on the wrongdoer. Vengeance remains reserved to God.

Perhaps the context not only explains why, when Paul turns to the topic of the relation of God and believers to the state, it is only the state's task of curbing wrongdoing that he mentions. The context may also explain why he abruptly introduces the state into the discussion. If we are told that God enjoins us never to repay evil for evil but instead to overcome evil with good, a rather obvious question is, "And how, then, must we understand and relate to what the state does?"

In short, if one keeps in mind the context within which Romans 13:1-8 is set, it's obvious why Paul mentions no other task of the state than that of curbing wrongdoing. No other task is relevant. The context does not set the stage for a general theology of the state. It sets the context for some comments about the relation of the state to wrongdoing. Paul neither says nor implies that this is the full extent of what the state is permitted to do.[10]

---

10. I have deleted a few pages that followed in the original, since I no longer agree with what I said there.

The Political Ethic of the Reformers

For about a century now it has been characteristic of social historians, looking back at the Reformation, to see in that movement springing forth from the central regions of Western Europe some of the principles and practices that have been most decisive in the shaping of the modern world. One thinks at once of Max Weber and Ernst Troeltsch; but these are just two among many. In the case of political thought and practice, the difficulty of identifying what was new proves equal to the fascination of making the attempt. Many of us feel that new social and political attitudes and practices of abiding significance came to light in the Reformation; yet it proves extraordinarily difficult to put one's finger on them. No doubt the attempts with which we feel most secure are those most limited in scope — for example, Quentin Skinner's tracing of the Reformation movement's thoughts concerning justified revolution, leaving out entirely their revolutionary practices.

In this essay I shall look at some facets of the political ethic of the Reformers. Along the way I too will be constructing a narrative concerning the role of the Reformation in the emergence of the modern world from the medieval. I will pretty much confine myself to the Calvinist wing of the Reformation, however, not so much because I think the role it played is more important in the formation of the modern social world than that of the Lutheran and Anabaptist wings, but because I know more about it. Even so, I have that curious feeling of not having quite put my finger on the essence of what I feel to be different. To the best of my knowledge, nobody has yet made a penetrating and comprehensive study of the political ethic of the Reformers; Ernst Troeltsch remains the one who has come closest to having done so. As a consequence, all those of us who talk about it do so at a risk.

Sometimes the most helpful interpretations of a period are those which are profound but at crucial points mistaken. For such interpretations at least serve the function of being provocative and suggestive. That is how I appraise the remarks of Alasdair MacIntyre about the Reformation in his book, *After Virtue*. So let us begin there. This will take us into a general discussion of the ethic of the Reformers; that done, I will narrow down the focus of our discussion to the political ethic.

MacIntyre argues — correctly in my judgment — that in the European Middle Ages the dominant categoreal scheme for analyzing the moral dimension of our existence was what may be called an *ethic of virtue*. A crucial assumption of this scheme was that we human beings all share a certain essential nature, and that this nature is of such a sort that on account of it we all seek the fulfillment of this nature, such fulfillment being happiness. Our true end, or telos, is that which gives us full happiness; and this is the human good, the good for us *qua* human. Within this teleological scheme, says MacIntyre, "there is a fundamental contrast between man-as-he-happens-to-be and man-as-he-could-be-if-he-realised-his-essential-nature." And "Ethics is the science which is to enable men to understand how they make the transition from the former state to the latter" (p. 50). In this science of ethics — which is a rational enterprise, an enterprise of scientific reason — two topics will be central. The ethicist will instruct us as to our true end, and he will instruct us as to how to get there. As part of this latter, he will teach us what precepts to follow; but perhaps more important, he will teach us what habits of action to cultivate. Such habits of action are the *virtues*. Human morality is present where the virtues are present; it is absent where they are absent. Or perhaps I should say, it is absent in so far as they are absent, for probably they are never entirely absent. Morality is not so much a matter of actions as of the character of persons; the moral significance of actions lies in their being manifestations of persons. And a person has a moral character not on account of performing right acts of will but on account of being virtuous, of having virtues — that is, on account of having acquired the habits that lead toward that telos which is the human good.

From this complex picture MacIntyre singles out three elements as central. "We thus have," he says, "a threefold scheme in which human-nature-as-it-happens-to-be (human nature in its untutored state) is initially discrepant and discordant with the precepts of ethics and needs to be transformed by the instruction of practical reason and experience into human-nature-as-it-could-be-if-it-realised-its-telos. Each of the three elements of the scheme — the conception of untutored human nature, the conception of the precepts of rational ethics, and the conception of human-nature-as-it-could-be-if-it-realised-its-telos — requires reference to the other two if its status and function are to be intelligible" (pp. 50-51).

This ethical scheme, as I have described it following MacIntyre, is the scheme bequeathed to the medievals by Aristotle. The medievals revised the scheme in two important ways without exploding it. They held that our human telos cannot be completely achieved in this world but only in the next; and this, they held, is not accidentally so but grounded in the nature of things. The achievement of our full telos, the vision of God, requires a fundamental alteration of our embodied status. This at once raises the question of whether, conversely, there are not some goods that are available to us here in our embodied status that will be unattainable to us in our disembodied status — the goods, let us say, of finding satisfaction in the practice of farming, of taking delight in the sight of trees and paintings, etc. If so, then there is tension within the human good. In my judgment this is in fact a weak spot in the medieval scheme. Given the distinction between natural and supernatural goods, they emphasized that the goods available to us here in our earthly existence include an inkling of our supernatural good of the vision of God; what they do not emphasize is that among our natural goods are some that we shall have to surrender entirely if we are fully to attain our supernatural good. Of course, they would all have added that the trade-off is overwhelmingly worthwhile.

In any case, because our full telos can be divided up into a natural and a supernatural component, the medievals added to the four cardinal natural virtues of the Greeks — justice, prudence, temperance, and courage — the three supernatural (theological) virtues of St. Paul, faith, hope, and charity.

There is a second revision that the medievals made to the Aristotelian ethical scheme. They viewed the precepts of ethics now not simply as the injunctions or precepts of right human reason concerning how the human telos is to be achieved but as the will of God — specifically, as having the status of the *law* of God for God's human creatures. Accordingly, "to say what someone ought to do is at one and the same time to say what course of action will in these circumstances as a matter of fact lead toward man's true end and to say what the law, ordained by God and comprehended by reason, enjoins" (p. 51). What came along with this revision, of course, was the conviction that wrongdoing is not just error but sin.

What does MacIntyre see as the response of the Reformers to this scheme? He sees them as having kept "the contrast between man-as-he-happens-to-be and man-as-he-could-be-if-he-realised-his-telos" (p. 51), and also as having kept the notion of "the divine moral law" as "a schoolmaster to remove us from the former state to the latter." But, he says, they became sceptical about the powers of reason at two points. They were no longer persuaded that by natural reason we could discern the human telos; revelation was necessary. "Reason can supply, so these new theologies assert, no genuine comprehension of man's true end; that power of reason was destroyed by the fall of man" (p. 51). Perhaps by reason we can still discern much of the *means* to the end; but only by revelation can we discern the end. Second, reason was now also seen as "powerless to correct our passions" (p. 51), powerless to move us from man-as-he-happens-to-be to man-as-he-could-be-if-he-realized-his-telos. What is needed is grace; practical reason does not suffice.

But MacIntyre sees more in the Reformation than this two-fold scepticism concerning the powers of reason. In other passages (not very well integrated with those we have already looked at) he sees here the beginnings of the "interiorisation" of the moral life that becomes so prominent a part of modernity. One facet of this interiorization is that there is a decline in the significance of the virtues in ethical reflection, with a corresponding increase of stress on will and law. That whole complex of dispositions which constitutes a person's virtues and vices, and which in turn go into the making of his character, is seen as one more circumstance external to will of which the will must take account in making its decisions. Indeed, the dispositions of one's character are to be made *subservient* to the will, in the sense that in each case the promptings of one's disposition must be appraised and, in the light of one's appraisal, assented to, or dissented from, by the will. What counts is not good character but right decisions. The correlate of this is God's law for the will, which now is not seen as grounded in our telos but as just the arbitrary dictate of God. Indeed, says, MacIntyre, once the virtues with their positive thrust are removed from prime place in the moral life, the law will tend to be seen as something negative, telling us how to restrain our evil impulses. (And this will be mirrored in the liberal state by laws that restrain the citizens from certain modes of interference with each other.)

As MacIntyre sees it, there is another facet to this interiorization. Not only do acts of will displace dispositions of character in significance, but the self is sharply differentiated from its social roles of father, of butcher, of church member, or whatever. The self is de-roled and placed naked before God. No longer can it plead that it was simply acting as a good hangman acts, that it was simply engaged in the practice of hanging, but now before God it must justify engaging in that practice in that way. Society as it touches him becomes now his responsibility.

MacIntyre appears to see this new way of thinking as the reflection of new social realities. As he sees it, in any social group that deserves the name "society" there will be a significant number of "coherent and complex forms of socially established cooperative activity" to which certain goods are "internal." Farming can be one such activity. Of course farming can be engaged in solely for the sake of some such external good as the making of money — external in the sense that one can just as well achieve this good in other ways. But there are also goods *internal* to farming, goods that can only be achieved by farming — those, say, of efficiently producing socially needed crops, of preserving and even enhancing the fertility of the land, etc. When one engages in farming for such internal goods, one engages in it as what MacIntyre calls a *social practice.* Now given the goods internal to farming, there will be standards that a good farmer meets and that he finds satisfaction in meeting, this then being one more of the goods internal to farming. And second, it will be possible to discern the habits that tend to enable him to achieve the goods. These will be the virtues of farmers. And now what can be said is that MacIntyre thinks that a central element in the traditional concept of a virtue is that a virtue is an acquired disposition the possession and exercise of which tends to enable him to achieve the goods internal to some practice, with the cardinal virtues being those that are necessary to sustain social practices in general. MacIntyre regularly mentions justice, courage, and truthfulness as examples.

Now if a society is to have a rich array of social practices, thus understood, it will have to be a community in which human beings together pursue the human good as they conceive it, rather than merely an arena in which they pursue their private goods or different conceptions of the human good. "It follows," says MacIntyre, that in much of the ancient and medieval worlds, as in many other premodern societies, the individual is identified and constituted in and through certain of his or her roles, those roles which bind the individual to the communities in and through which alone specifically human goods are to be attained; I confront the world as a member of this family, this household, this clan, this tribe, this city, this nation, this kingdom. There is no 'I' apart from these" (pp. 160-61).

It seems to be MacIntyre's thought that by Reformation times a solidary society of the sort I have sketched out — one in which there is a rich array of social practices and in which people jointly pursue the human good as they jointly conceive it — was collapsing; and that the de-roleing of the self by the Reformers and their placement of the self naked before God was in part a reflection of these social realities. (We must also notice the following striking implication of MacIntyre's theory. Morality for him consists in the cultivation of virtues, and virtues find their basis in social practices. In so far, then, as social practices disappear from a group of people, the virtues begin to lack all social basis; and in so far as the virtues lack social basis, morality lacks relevance. It is MacIntyre's view, so far as I can tell, that morality is pretty much irrelevant to modern society. His call is not that we in our society should be moral but that we should work for a society in which morality is once again possible.)

We are now in a position where we can address the question of whether MacIntyre's analysis of the ethical thought of the Reformers is accurate; and let me say, once again, that the benefit of following his analysis is that it enables us to enter the matter at a deep level. Recall the two basic claims that he makes about the Reformers: they asserted the inadequacy of reason either to discern our true end or to move us toward it, and they interiorized the moral life by substituting right will for good character and by stripping the self's identity of its social roles. It should be clear that any movement that interiorizes the moral life will be incapable of developing an adequate social ethic.

If one looks at the practice of the Reformation, particularly of the Calvinist Reformation, it seems flamboyantly false to suggest that the Reformers interiorized the moral life by replacing a concern for good character with a concern for right will. Indeed, what has struck countless observers, Weber only the most famous of them, is the extraordinary *strenuousness* of the Calvinist way of being-in-the-world, the extraordinary attempt to cultivate the right dispositions, to curb our unruly impulses, to discipline our lives. What impressed Weber in looking at capitalism, for example, was that it required a special character-formation of unusual discipline. He then asked who might have been instrumental in producing this type of disciplined character. He thought he saw a similar sort of life in the medieval monasteries; but he wanted to know who brought it into the marketplace. His answer was that it was the Calvinists who above all produced the character-formation which, in disciplined fashion, engages in work in the world. He called it ascetic Protestantism and worldly asceticism.

Michael Walzer, in his book *The Revolution of the Saints*, looks at another phase of the Calvinist character-formation. Where Weber noticed that a certain character-formation is necessary for capitalism and inquired into the origins of that character-formation, Walzer notes that a certain character-formation, also highly disciplined, was necessary for the social radicals and revolutionaries of the day and inquires into its origins. He traces it to the early Calvinists.

I think that both Weber and Walzer are mistaken in their speculations as to which traits in Calvinism gave rise to these disciplined character types. Weber thought it was the Calvinist's way of coping with anxieties over eternal election; Walzer thinks it was the Calvinist's way of coping with anxieties over the threat of social disorder. But be that as it may, I think Weber was right in claiming that the only close analogue to the intensity of character-formation that one finds among the early Calvinists is what one sees in the medieval monasteries. And to the more specific revolutionary character-formation on which Walzer concentrates I think one finds no close analogues in the Middle Ages at all. In short, MacIntyre has gotten things turned completely around.

What, then, about the distancing of the self from its social roles that MacIntyre claims to find in the thought of the Reformers, provoked perhaps by changes in social reality? Here we must tread especially carefully. What is meant when it is said that, in medieval and traditional society, the individual is identified and constituted in and through certain of his or her social roles? Various things, I suppose; but at least the following two: with respect to the majority of social roles, the person's taking up a role has only minor elements of personal choice in it; and second, one raises no questions about the rights and responsibilities traditionally attached to the social role in which one finds oneself. In so far as one's roles are a matter of choice, and in so far as one raises questions about the rights and responsibilities traditionally attached to some role, one is distancing oneself from that role.

Now in the attitude of the Reformers toward social roles it is especially important, it seems to me, to see their thought and practice as emerging from an amalgam of social changes and intellectual reflection. One characteristic feature of that long change from medieval and traditional society to modern is the diminishing of what sociologists call *ascriptivism* — the diminishing of people's having no choice in the social roles they play. This process was well underway by the time of the Reformation. Partly it was underway by virtue of the decline of feudalism and the rise of cities; partly it was underway by virtue of warfare and the refugees produced thereby. It is characteristic of refugee populations that few of their roles are "ascribed" to them. To my mind it is not insignificant that the Reformation at its beginnings was prominent in cities, and that the Calvinist Reformation was prominent in cities with large refugee populations. In medieval times, the social order was seen as part of the nature of things and persons were in good measure born into their social roles; that way of thinking was well on the way to disappearing from the thought of the Reformers. My suggestion is that it was not so much the theology of the Reformers that led them to new views but that the old views no longer looked plausible given the society that had emerged.

One more thing must be said before I draw my conclusion. Given the vast alterations in social order that the Western Europeans were experiencing at this time, not only did the Reformers and others no longer regard social order as part of the nature of things; how could they, when they saw it changing radically before their eyes? They no longer automatically regarded the social order given them as good. They began regularly to criticize that order — not just to criticize the persons filling the various roles in that order, but to criticize the order itself.

I think that in these various ways one does find among the Protestants a certain distancing of the self from its social roles. Roles were increasingly seen as open to choice; and there were emphatic calls for the *reform* of one and another social role. But at once we must say something more. What MacIntyre rightly notices is that among the Reformers, the person was held accountable before God for the roles he played and for what he did in those roles. But there is another side of the story that must also be told: just as the Reformers did not allow the person to hide himself in the thick cloak of his roles as he stood before God, so also they insisted that God required of the person that he take up a structure of roles and cloak himself therein — a revised and reformed structure of roles, if need be. What is relevant here is the Protestant notion of all of us as having a vocation, a calling, a *Beruf,* from God. Perhaps Troeltsch is right, that among Lutherans this tended to be seen as the calling to take up some more or less traditional role and occupation, whereas among Calvinists it tended to be seen as the calling to serve the common good in one's own unique way, leaving it a matter of discernment as to the roles and occupations in which one could best do that. If this distinction was indeed present, one can see why there was more revolutionary ferment among the Calvinists than among the Lutherans.

In any case, we can now see why it was that Protestantism did not in fact lead to the interiorization of the moral life to which MacIntyre is so opposed. Though the person was not *assigned* her social identification, she had one nevertheless. She *embraced* one. She identified herself as a mother, as a Genevan, as a Protestant, and so forth, though now the identification was one of resolution rather than ascription. And as part of that identification, she did cultivate character; she did cultivate the appropriate discipline in her life.

One last point here that I cannot take time to develop. It seems clear to me that the Protestants overwhelmingly tended to see their callings as best carried out in what MacIntyre calls social practices. The Calvinists, at least, found it abhorrent to think that governmental activity was aimed at the external good of exercising power over people or that economic activity was aimed at the external good of making money. MacIntyre sees morality as *presupposing* a society in which there is a wide range of social practices and in which people share in the common pursuit of the human good. The Reformers tended rather to see morality as *enjoining* such a society. One implication of that is that, for them, morality is for all seasons whereas, for MacIntyre, morality is only for those seasons in which society is solidary. Were the Reformers not *right* on this basic issue?

If we would understand in depth what was new in the ethic of the Reformers we must dig yet deeper. I have suggested that it was especially the Protestant notion of *calling* that prevented them from interiorizing the moral life. But that notion of calling was in turn set within a larger perspective. MacIntyre suggests that the Reformers kept the distinction between man-as-he-happens-to-be and man-as-he-could-be-if-he-realized-his-telos, but that they scrapped reason as the link between these and replaced it with revelation. I suggest that the revision of the medieval ethic that the Reformers undertook was more radical than this. They no longer attempted to construct an ethic on the basis of human nature, not even when we get a good fix on that nature from revelation. They no longer think — not at least when they are thinking about morals and ethics — about what will fulfill us. Theirs was not an ethic based on how to achieve happiness. Perhaps MacIntyre had some glimmering of this when he suggested that theirs was not an ethic of virtue.

I think they had two reasons for discarding the medieval framework. For one thing, they believed that our nature was corrupted; it was not just "untutored," as MacIntyre often puts it. It had evil impulses deeply lodged within it. There is within us what Kant called "radical evil." Whatever love of God we may have is all too often mingled with hatred, whatever concern we may have for neighbor is mixed with spite. That, then, is why reason is helpless to discern our true telos. But I think that there was something else at work in the Reformers as well. Partly as the result of the work of the humanists and partly, I want to say, as the result of the work of the Spirit, they were able to read their Bibles with a new freshness. And what they heard there was *Torah:* God's utterance of God's law for our lives. What emerged was a wholly new understanding of the moral life, indeed, of human life. The moral life is not to be thought of in terms of what enables us to reach our true end; the moral life consists rather of obedience to our King — a *grateful* obedience, let me add.

There has been a great deal of discussion concerning the extent to which Calvin thought that there was a moral law available to "natural man," apart from revelation. I think that there can be no doubt that MacIntyre neglects the evidence here. But I also think that that is somewhat beside the point. Calvin's dispute with the medievals was not first of all as to how much of the moral law is naturally available; on that issue they stand on a continuum. The deeper issue was that of how they thought of the moral law. The medievals thought of it as the precepts that lead to the fulfillment of our nature. The Reformers began to think of it as the will of the King which in gratitude we obey.

I suggest that in the Reformation we see the beginnings of a fundamental contrast to the medieval understanding of the relation between God and humankind. The divergence in their ethical understanding is a component in this yet deeper divergence. For the medievals, the salvation for which we long and which is the true end of all humankind is the Vision of God. For the Reformers, the salvation for which we long and which is the true end of all humankind is our participation in the Kingdom of God. The Vision of God versus the Kingdom of God: those are the two contrasting perspectives.

I can begin laying out the differences between the two perspectives by quoting a perceptive passage from H. Richard Niebuhr:

> To call the vision man's greatest good is to make contemplation . . . the final end of life; to put the sovereignty of God in the first place is to make obedient activity superior to contemplation. . . . The principle of vision suggests that the perfection of the object seen is loved above all else; the principle of the kingdom indicates that the reality and power of the being commanding obedience are primarily regarded. (*The Kingdom of God in America,* p. 20)

To understand the medieval perspective of the Vision of God we must recall that the medieval thinker characteristically saw all of reality and life as caught up in a double process of proceeding from God and returning to God. He saw the relation of God to the world as a process of circulation.

All things proceed from God, all are brought about by God. They are all an expression of God, God's self-expression. Furthermore, the medieval was fond of thinking of all reality as arranged in a sort of hierarchical pattern, from better down to worse, from nobler down to less noble — which for him meant from more similar to God to less similar to God. Reality was a great chain of being. Human beings had a higher position in this scheme than, say, ducks; and ducks a higher position than stones. But the medievals also thought that there were levels of superiority within the various 'kingdoms': within the animal kingdom, for example, the lion was king. Likewise they believed that there were natural levels of superiority and inferiority among human beings: those born of royalty are naturally superior to those born of serfs; and men, so they held, are naturally superior to women.

A feature of this picture that is important for us to keep in mind is that the social order was regularly seen as part of this order of nature. God in his heaven, the bishop in his chair, the lord in his castle — to the medieval this was part of the very nature of things. We in the modern world are inclined sharply to distinguish between social roles and the persons playing those roles, We go on to think of these roles as human creations and subject to revision. And as I have already remarked, in our liberal democratic societies we follow the practice of allowing persons, in great measure, to choose for themselves the social roles they will play. The medieval made no such distinction between persons and roles, not very articulately, anyway—an oversight for which he may be excused since in his society there was little looseness between person and role. Hence also the medieval did not distinguish the superiority and inferiority of roles from the superiority and inferiority of persons born to fill those roles. And most emphatically he did not think of social structure as an artifact that had emerged from human volition and was susceptible to revision by new volition. In the Middle Ages there was, for these reasons, little by way of programs of social reform. When confronted with social misery, the response of the medieval was ultimately *avertive:* he turned away toward God. His was a form of avertive religion.

This brings me to the other phase of the dual process that the medieval saw as embedded in life and reality: the phase consisting of the return of creature to God. In effect I have already spoken of this. Every human being, so said Aquinas — and we can take him as typical — orders his life by reference to a goal; and the goal is the same for everybody, namely, happiness. Everyone makes happiness his ultimate desire. It's in what we take happiness to be that we rational creatures differ among each other, and in how we think we can attain it.

True and abiding happiness can be found nowhere else than in the contemplation of God — in the vision of God, if you will. Aquinas understood this vision of God to consist in our grasp of the essence of God, for he thought God to be identical with God's essence. And he held that here on earth philosophical reflection is helpful in a sort of preliminary way in enabling us to grasp some elements of that essence of God.

It will come as no surprise when I now add that the having of a body was seen as dispensable for the attainment of this our true end. Few Christian medievals denied the resurrection of the body. But their emphasis was not on the resurrection; and when they did discuss it, they regularly insisted that the resurrected body would be profoundly different from the bodies we presently have. It would be a spiritual body. Rather than emphasizing the resurrection of the body, they emphasized the immortality of the soul. Disembodied contemplation of God, or spiritually-embodied contemplation, was our true destiny.

In the economy of God, only those who have faith are rewarded with the vision of God; and faith, in turn, is response to revelation. In various ways—but centrally in the Scriptures of the Old and New Testaments and in Jesus Christ — God reveals Godself, that is, God reveals various dimensions of God's nature. Faith is the believing acceptance of the content of this revelation. And if you ask, but doesn't God do more than reveal God's attributes, doesn't God also do various things in history and make clear to us what those things are, the answer of Aquinas, at least, is clear. Yes, he says; but God's deeds are to be understood as *illustrations* of God's attributes. This is incarnational theology rather than redemptive theology. The sacramentalism that accompanies it is a sacramentalism of God's *being*.

In general there was, amongst the medievals, little recognition of the significance of history. God was seen as eternal, outside of time, and consequently immutable and impassive. Revelation, whether in Christ or Scripture, was seen as a manifestation of this eternal God. The historicity of the Scriptures, though certainly not denied, was but dimly acknowledged. And the good sought was release from historicity into eternity.

Perhaps this point, of one's attitude toward history, is as good as any for entering the alternative Christian perspective — call it the Kingdom of God perspective — that was beginning its long process of articulation there in the Reformation. Oscar Cullmann argued, in his well-known *Christ and Time*, that the classic Christian picture of God as outside of time, and of salvation as consisting of escape from time into eternal contemplation of God, is not the biblical picture. In the Bible we are presented with a radically historical picture of our human existence. Rather than time and eternity being the fundamental contrast, the fundamental contrast is that between this present age in which we dwell and that new age toward which we look, the eschaton, to be brought in by God's decisive action of renewal and inaugurated by the resurrection of the body. No prescience is needed to anticipate what a profoundly different perspective this will lead to. It would be a mistake, though, to think that Cullmann initiated this new perspective. Rather, as I see it, he gave the biblical basis for one important element of a perspective that was coming to birth in the Reformation.

Pretty obviously the natural accompaniment of that stress on our hope for a new age is a stress on the resurrection of the body instead of the immortality of the soul. And in fact Cullmann also wrote a famous essay under the title, "Immortality of the Soul or Resurrection of the Dead?" in which he argued that the notion of an immortal soul was a Greek idea, profoundly different from the biblical idea of the resurrection of the dead. Of course this emphasis on resurrection of the body rather than immortality of the soul also fits profoundly with the biblical emphasis on the goodness of creation. God created us as embodied persons and pronounced the work good. If we allow the full significance of that word of approval to sink in, does it not seem strange to hold that the goal of our existence is to be disembodied, or to be only spiritually embodied? Does not such an emphasis imply that, after all, there is something defective about our status as embodied persons?

I have been stressing that this new perspective, of looking ahead to a new age in history rather than up to an eternity which is an escape from history, has as its natural corollary a stress on the worth of our bodily status and on the significance of the resurrection. It also, naturally and unavoidably, has as its corollary a new way of thinking about God. God will now be thought of less as the eternal perfection of goodness, beauty, unity, and truth, lodged at the top of the hierarchy of existence, and more as the One who acts. The mighty actions of God, rather than the glorious being of God, will now come to the fore — as indeed it does in the opening of

Calvin's *Institutes*. God will be seen as an agent within our history as well as the agent who brings about our history. Our celebration of God will now focus on what God has done and not on what God's doing reveals of God's being.

What will also have to be re-thought in this Kingdom of God perspective is the nature and function of revelation. For one thing, revelation will be demoted from the all-embracing, looming importance that it had in the classical Vision of God theologies. There revelation, once creation had occurred, was the principal engagement between God and us. But in the Kingdom of God perspective, God is seen as acting throughout history for the redemption of God's wayward and suffering human creatures. Redemption is here the central engagement. Revelation, apart from that which occurs in creation, is an accompaniment to redemption, whereby God makes clear to us what God asks of us and what God does for us. It is God's will and God's works that are made known to us, rather than God's attributes. And in so far as God's revelation is the manifestation to us of God's will for us, hearing God rather than seeing God will seem the appropriate metaphor. We would not go far astray if we contrasted the two perspectives as the Vision of God's Essence versus the Hearing of God's Word. The appropriate response to hearing God's Word will be grateful obedience. Prominent in the Reformers are these concepts of hearing, gratitude, and obedience.

It will be easy now to surmise how the Christian's attitude toward society will be understood in this perspective. As Niebuhr puts it, obedient activity in the world, rather than contemplation, is here placed in the center. In gratitude we are called to obedient activity in a world that is *God's* world, though indeed, God's *fallen* world. We saw that the Vision of God perspective is a form of avertive religion. The Kingdom of God perspective, by contrast, is a species of *world-formative* religion. Our response to social misery is not to turn away from our social world but rather to seek the reform of that world as an act of religious obedience. The social world in which we find ourselves is fallen. We are called in obedience to struggle for its reform. For this social world is not part of the inevitable nature of things. It's the result of our human volitional endeavors; and it is in principle capable by endeavor of being reformed.

I suggest that the difference between the ethic of the Reformers and the ethic of the medievals is ultimately to be traced to the difference between these two perspectives of the Vision of God versus the Kingdom of God. How much of the Kingdom of God perspective was actually articulated by the Reformers is a good question, into which I shall here not enter. My contention is not that it received its full articulation there but that the beginnings of its articulation are there. It is also my contention that it was because this alternative perspective began to grip them that the Reformers, when confronted with social misery, went beyond the charity that had always been part of medieval life to call for structural analysis and structural reform. Likewise it is my conviction that any social theology adequate for dealing with the miseries of our world will have to be framed within the Kingdom of God perspective. The Vision of God perspective will prove inadequate. Indeed, it is my experience that those who want to resist the call to Christians to respond in structural fashion to the suffering of humanity will invariably retreat, tacitly or explicitly, into a Vision of God perspective, arguing that the church must confine itself to dealing with spiritual matters. You may have noticed that in the Kingdom of God perspective there is no such distinction! There are no higher and lower forms of grateful obedience. In this way too, the Reformers differed from the medievals.

Starting from MacIntyre's claim that the Reformers interiorized the moral life — a claim that I said had to be addressed head-on if we who stand in the line of the Reformers are to have an adequate social and political ethic — my strategy has been to open up wider and wider perspectives on what the Reformers were doing. Let me now reverse directions and say a few words, more specifically, about the political ethic of the Reformers — or actually, about the political ethic of Calvin and the early Calvinists.

Statecraft was for Calvin what MacIntyre calls a *social practice*. Those who engage in it do so, or ought to do so, for goods internal to that practice and not for the sake of such external goods as exercising power over people or amassing wealth. Being a political ruler of one sort or another was for Calvin to occupy an office, to exercise a calling.

And what are the rulers to do? What are the goals of statecraft? What Calvin says on this point is in remarkable continuity with the medieval theorists; I think one looks in vain for any significant difference. The best recent discussion of the matter with which I am acquainted is Harro Höpfl's book, *The Christian Polity of John Calvin* (1982). Calvin regularly says that the duty of the magistrate is to be guided by the will of God in seeking to secure *aequitas* and *humanitas*. Höpfl summarizes this by saying that, on Calvin's view, the business of magistrates "is to enforce both justice and godliness" (p. 189). And what did Calvin see as the point of magistrates forcing on people, by laws and directives, virtue and piety? Höpfl argues that the point was sanctification; "the office of magistrates is to participate in *aedificatio . . .*" (p. 191). Of course Calvin never supposed that laws enforcing the actions of virtue and piety would automatically produce true obedience; but he certainly seems to have held that they would cultivate it.

This view of the business of the magistrate poses for Calvin, as it did for the medievals, the question of how to discriminate the state's area of competence from that of the church. The medievals already found difficulties here. For one thing, the membership of the state was coterminous with that of the church; all citizens were baptized. (I recognize the anomaly of speaking of "states" and "citizens" in Reformation times. I do so for the sake of convenience.) But second, though the impulse of the medievals was to say that the state dealt with matters pertaining to our natural end and the church with matters pertaining to our supernatural end, they in fact wanted the state also to promote the work of the church. For Calvin the difficulties were if anything even worse. Here too the company of the baptized and the company of the citizens were assumed to be coterminous; but now, as I have already suggested, any higher/lower, supernatural/natural distinction will seem inept. When obedience to our King rather than attainment of our telos is the fundamental perspective, distinctions of higher and lower will tend to disappear. But not only was there no clear differentiation between the scope of competence of church and state; also there was as yet little thought of some area of privacy that the state might in principle not invade. I think, then, that Höpfl is substantially correct when he says that "There was, then, no inherent limitation in Calvin's thought on the competence of a magistracy, provided it was godly. On the contrary, there were reasons why the activities of a godly magistracy should become ever more wide-ranging, specific and intrusive" (p. 197).

In short, Calvin's picture of society was still that of all the members together engaged in the pursuit of their common good, as commonly conceived; references to "the common good" are sprinkled all around in Calvin's writings. And the state was to play the crucial role of ordering and enforcing justice, virtue, and piety in that endeavor. The liberal state, whose aim is to regulate the affairs of society so that each of us can pursue our private goods, voluntarily joined with whoever may wish to cooperate with us, was still far in the future. Calvin's conception was still, to use Michael Oakeshott's terms, that of *universitas* rather than *societas*. Such a society was, for Calvin, not a presupposition of morality but an injunction of morality (*pace* MacIntyre).

It is at this point, of course, that we who stand in the line of the Reformers cannot follow them but must engage in serious rethinking. For one thing, the Constantianism that medievals and mainline Reformers both assumed has collapsed — I mean, that arrangement whereby the company of the baptized was coterminous with the company of the citizens. And second, in almost all areas of the world the church itself is deeply fragmented. There is, then, nothing like a common conception of our human good. Our societies are all deeply pluralistic. That has profound implications for the nature of the justice that the state seeks and for the scope of the state's competence.

Let me close by observing that there is another dimension of the political thought of the Reformers to which we can, by contrast, attach ourselves directly. It has been customary in discussions on the political ethic of the Reformers to focus one's attention on what they said about the duties of the magistrate. I think it is the great value of Michael Walzer's book to call to our attention another tremendously important dimension of the movement of early Calvinism: their conviction that it is the duty of citizens to work for reform, even, if it comes to that, to work for revolution. This too must be seen as part of the political ethic of the Reformers. Perhaps I can best communicate the point by quoting a passage from Walzer:

> The Puritan cleric insisted that political activity was a creative endeavor in which the saints were privileged as well as obliged to participate. The saints were responsible for their world — as medieval men were not — and responsible above all for its continual reformation. Their enthusiastic and purposive activity was part of their religious life, not something distinct and separate; they acted out their saintliness in debates, elections, administration, and warfare. . . .
>
> But Puritan zeal was not a private passion; it was instead a highly collective emotion and it imposed upon the saints a new and impersonal discipline. Conscience freed the saints from medieval passivity and feudal loyalty, but it did not encourage the individualist. . . . Indeed, the new spirit of the Puritans can be defined as a kind of military and political work-ethic, directly analogous to the "worldly asceticism" which Max Weber has described in economic life, but oriented not toward acquisition so much as toward contention, struggle, destruction, and rebuilding. Calvinist conscience gave to war and to politics (and if Weber is right to business as well) a new sense of method and purpose. It is this above all that distinguishes the activity of the saints from that of medieval men, caught

up in the unchanging world of tradition, fixed in their social place and loyal to their relatives; and also from that of Renaissance men, pursuing a purely personal ambition. (pp. 12-13)

Need I remark how different this picture is from that drawn by MacIntyre?

Some, like MacIntyre, claim to see in the Reformers the interiorization of the moral life. I have argued that they are seriously mistaken. Others have seen in the Reformers the twilight of that long attempt to use the state as an instrument for advancing a Christian *universitas*. I have argued that this interpretation is correct but myopic. In the political practice of the Reformers it fails to take note of the profound importance of the saintly calling of the political reformer and revolutionary. This, along with that perspective of the Kingdom of God which the Reformers began to articulate, is what those of us who are children of the Reformation can appropriate from our tradition as we struggle for justice and shalom in our day. This is what can inspire and move us as we struggle to incorporate our mission within the *missio dei:* the mission of redeeming humanity from its weight of sorrows and shackles.

Theological Foundations for an Evangelical Political Philosophy

O ur topic can be approached from a number of different directions. A good many Christian theologians have included reflections on government as part of their comprehensive theology. We could develop "theological foundations for an evangelical political philosophy" by engaging in dialogue with some of the more important of these theologians. Since every Christian theology is grounded, more or less directly and in one way or another, in the Christian Scriptures, this approach would lead us sooner or later to Scripture. Alternatively, we could start with the relevant Scriptures and move from there to a theology of the political order. On this occasion I will follow the latter procedure: Instead of starting with theology we will start with Scripture.

Starting with Scripture still leaves options. We could first assemble a large collection of relevant passages and then try to arrive at some synthesizing conclusions. Alternatively, we could take a few central passages and allow them to lead us to others. I will follow the latter procedure.

Nothing much hangs on this particular way of going about things; any of these different approaches would lead eventually to the same issues. My reasons for choosing the approach indicated are that it will prove more efficient, and evangelicals rightly want to be assured that the theologian's appeal to Scripture is not an afterthought but that his or her theology is genuinely rooted in, and inspired by, Scripture.

Paul's Advice to the Roman Christians Concerning the State

It was not obvious to the early Christians what stance they should take toward the institutions of Hellenistic society. The radical quality of Jesus' teaching, combined with the fact that he apparently never addressed the issue with full generality, made it problematic for them how they should relate to the extant domestic, economic, and political institutions. Should they reject those institutions and migrate to some place where they could dwell by themselves, establish alternative institutions, and within those alternative institutions live out the radical way of life taught by Jesus? Or, religious institutions excepted, should they live and act within the extant institutions in the manner of everyone else, contenting themselves with living out the radical way of Jesus within the church? Or, religious institutions excepted, should they live and act within the extant institutions but attempt there to live out Christ's new way? Or — yet a fourth possibility — should they live and act within the institutions of polity and economy in the manner of everyone else, while living out the way of Jesus in their households as well as in the church?

Because the answer was not at once obvious, the apostles and their associates regularly gave the members of the new churches advice on the topic, some of this advice being preserved for us in the New Testament. Two of the most extensive passages are found in Paul's letter to the Christians at Ephesus (5:21ff.) and in his letter to the Christians at Colossae (3:18ff.). In these passages, Paul gives advice to his readers on how they should relate to the institutions of marriage, family, and slave economy. He does not give advice on how they should relate to the political order. By contrast, in Romans 12:19–13:7 Paul gives advice on how to relate to the political order but says nothing about marriage, family, or slave economy.

The question arises whether we should interpret the Romans passage in conjunction with those other passages, on the ground that Paul is giving a unified body of advice and that it may well prove illuminating to read them in the light of each other, or whether we should treat the Romans passage by itself. Ever since Luther, the passages in Ephesians and Colossians have been called *Haustafeln* — literally, "house tables" — on the ground that they give advice concerning the household. Very often, using this name for these passages reflects the interpreter's view that Paul's attitude toward the institutions of the household is significantly different from his attitude toward political institutions.

I think there are two cogent reasons for not adopting this latter approach. In the first place, advice concerning the institutions of the household is not always separated in the New Testament from advice concerning political institutions — which makes it seem likely that what accounts for their separation in Paul is nothing more than the focus of his concerns in the passages in question. The writer of 1 Peter moves seamlessly from advice to his readers concerning their relation to political institutions to advice concerning their relation to household institutions. Let me quote a bit of what he says.

> For the Lord's sake accept the authority [*krisis*] of every human institution, whether of the emperor as supreme, or of governors, as sent by him to punish those who do wrong and to praise those who do right. . . . Honor everyone. Love the family of believers. Fear God. Honor the emperor. Slaves, accept the authority of your masters with all deference, not only those who are kind and gentle but also those who are harsh. For it is a credit to you if, being aware of God, you endure pain while suffering unjustly. . . . Wives, in the same way, accept the authority of your husbands, so that, even if some of them do not obey the word, they may be won over without a word by their wives' conduct. . . . Husbands, in the same way, show consideration for your wives in your life together, paying honor to the woman as the weaker sex, since they too are also heirs of the gracious gift of life. (1 Peter 2:13–3:7)

Second, the pattern of advice given in all the passages mentioned is strikingly similar. Nowhere are Christians urged to go off by themselves to set up their own social institutions. With the exception, of course, of religious institutions, they are to participate side by side with non-Christians in the institutions of their society: marriage, family, economy, and polity. They are to do so with a difference, however, a difference both in how they understand the significance of those institutions and in how they conduct themselves within them. This, as I say, is the structure of the advice given in all the passages, no matter whether it is household institutions that the writer has in view or political institutions. Of course, what we learn from history is that as Christians became more numerous, as they came into positions of power and those already in positions of power became Christian, and as they thought through the implications of Christ's teaching, the institutions themselves began to change.

Let us now have before us Paul's instructions to his readers in Rome concerning their relation to the political order — keeping in mind that this is part of that larger body of advice in the epistolary literature of the New Testament concerning the relation of members of the new Christian movement to extant social institutions. The Romans passage is, of course, one of the great classical passages for Christian reflection on the political order.

> Beloved, never avenge [*ekdikeō*] yourselves, but leave room for the wrath [*orgē*] of God; for it is written, "Vengeance [*ekdikēsis*] is mine, I will repay, says the Lord." No, "if your enemies are hungry, feed them; if they are thirsty, give them something to drink; for by doing this you will heap burning coals on their heads." Do not be overcome by evil, but overcome evil with good.
>
> Let every person be subject to the governing authorities; for there is no authority except from God, and those authorities that exist have been instituted by God. Therefore whoever resists authority resists what God has appointed, and those who resist will incur judgment [*krima*]. For rulers are not a terror to good conduct, but to bad. Do you wish to have no fear of the authority? Then do what is good, and you will receive its approval; for it is God's servant [*diakonos*] for your good. But if you do what is wrong, you should be afraid, for the authority does not bear the sword in vain! It is the servant [*diakonos*] of God to execute wrath [*orgē*] on the wrongdoer. Therefore one must be subject, not only because of wrath [*orgē*] but also because of conscience. For the same reason you also pay taxes, for the authorities are God's servants [*leitourgoi*], busy with this very thing. Pay to all what is due them — taxes to whom taxes are due, revenue to whom revenue is due, respect to whom respect is due, honor to whom honor is due. (Romans 12:19–13:7)

Almost every word in this passage has been the subject of intense and extended controversy. Several of the most important points seem obvious, however. The stance that one is to take toward one's government is the same that 1 Peter enjoins. We are to obey or be subject to our rulers (the Greek verb can mean either of these) "for the sake of conscience." Or to put it in 1 Peter's words, we are to obey or submit to the emperor and his governors "for the Lord's sake." All by itself, Paul's verb, translated in the NRSV as "be subject to," might mean buckling under as a matter of prudence. That interpretation becomes implausible, however, when Paul goes on to say to his readers that they are to obey or be subject not only because of governmental power (wrath), but because of conscience *(suneidēsis)*. Doing what is commanded or required is the *right* thing to do, not merely the prudential thing. What this implies is that "the authorities" have genuine authority, not just power. And so we are to "honor" them — which of course is quite different from merely fearing them. Honor the emperor, says 1 Peter, honor the authorities, says Paul. The Greek word used (noun *timē*, verb *timao)* is the same in both cases as that which Paul uses in Ephesians 6:2 when he instructs children to "honor your father and mother."

What is also clear in both Paul and 1 Peter is the goal, the telos, of government. Its telos, in the words of 1 Peter, is "to punish those who do wrong and to praise those who do right." Paul goes on to describe the relation of God to the telos of government. It is *God* who has instituted or appointed governing authorities for the purpose of punishing wrongdoers and praising or approving those who do good. Government must not be thought of as either some purely human artifact or a work of the devil.

These points, I say, seem obvious; the interpretation of other points will require some work on our part. But before we get to that, another *locus classicus* for the Christian understanding of government must be laid on the table. In the thirteenth chapter of Revelation we get a vivid reminder of the painful fact that government, like everything else in this world, is fallen. Though instituted or appointed by God to punish the wrongdoer and praise the one who does good, government itself becomes a wrongdoer, sometimes to an utterly appalling degree. The great beast of which the passage speaks has traditionally been interpreted as a symbol for Rome at a time of widespread persecution of Christians — most likely under Domitian (81-96 C.E.), though possibly under Nero (54-68 C.E.). The beast has "authority over every tribe and people and language and nation." Everyone "whose name has not been written . . . in the book of life of the Lamb" worships it, saying, "Who is like the beast, and who can fight against it?" The beast utters "blasphemies against God," having been "allowed to make war on the saints and to conquer them." Another beast, this one with horns like a lamb, acts on behalf of the first, making "the earth and its inhabitants worship the first beast." It causes everyone who does not worship the image of the first beast to be killed; and after causing everybody to be stamped with its mark on their right hand or forehead, it orders that nobody without the mark be allowed to buy or sell.

The Old Testament Background
to Paul's Advice

Paul's advice in Romans 12 and 13 was not a bolt out of the blue. Paul was steeped in rabbinic Judaism; and the advice he gives to the Christians in Rome concerning their relation to the governing authorities not only echoes some of the things Jesus said, but directly quotes two passages from the Old Testament and employs two lines of thought prominent in the Old Testament.

The first passage quoted comes from Deuteronomy 32. Let us have it before us in its context. God is speaking:

> Vengeance is mine, and recompense . . . ;
> because the day of their calamity is at hand,
>   their doom comes swiftly.
> Indeed the Lord will vindicate his people,
>   have compassion on his servants.
>
> (Deuteronomy 32:35-36)

For the purpose of understanding Paul's thought, it is worth also having before us a passage to which he may have been alluding without directly quoting: Leviticus 19:17-18. Again, God is speaking:

> You shall not hate in your heart anyone of your kin; you shall reprove your neighbor, or you will incur guilt yourself. You shall not take vengeance or bear a grudge against any of your people, but you shall love your neighbor as yourself: I am the Lord.

The other passage Paul quotes comes from Proverbs 25:21-22:

> If your enemies are hungry, give them bread to eat;
>   and if they are thirsty, give them water to drink;
> for you will heap coals of fire on their heads,
>   and the Lord will reward you.

Those were the passages Paul quoted. Now for the lines of thought that he was employing. Prominent in the witness of the Old Testament is its presentation of God as *loving and executing justice.* Here is just one of many passages that could be cited.

Mighty King, lover of justice,
  you have established equity;
you have executed justice
  and righteousness in Jacob.

(Psalm 99:4)

Justice, as we all know, comes in two basic forms. One form can be called *corrective* justice. Someone has done something unjust, or is alleged to have done something unjust; corrective justice consists of rendering what is due the various parties in that situation. But such justice presupposes a more basic type of justice — call it *primary* justice. In doing something unjust, the person has violated the requirements of primary justice; if there were no such requirements, there would be no such thing as corrective justice. Probably we should hear the psalmist, in the passage quoted above, as alluding to both types of justice, primary and corrective.

Confronted with a violation of primary justice, God "executes justice" or "renders judgment." Such rendering of judgment has two components: God *vindicates* the one wronged and God *pronounces verdict and sentence* on the wrongdoer. Dozens of passages could be cited in which God is described as rendering judgment; the passage just quoted from Deuteronomy, from which Paul quotes, is just one example. God judges that God's people have been wronged, thereby "vindicating" them; and he pronounces and carries out sentence on the wrongdoers. "The day of their calamity is at hand."

God renders judgment both concerning that which transpires within Judah and Israel and that which transpires between them and the surrounding powers. But God also renders judgment on what transpires within and among those surrounding powers. The opening chapters of the book of Amos are the most vivid illustration of the latter point. The prophet, speaking in the name of the Lord, pronounces sentence on Damascus (Syria), Gaza, Tyre, Edom, Ammon, and Moab. The sentence pronounced on Ammon is representative:

Thus says the LORD:
"For three transgressions of the Ammonites,
  and for four, I will not revoke the punishment;
because they have ripped up women with child in Gilead,
  that they might enlarge their border.
So I will kindle fire in the wall of Rabbah,

and it shall devour her strongholds,
with shouting in the day of battle,
   with a tempest in the day of the whirlwind;
and their king shall go into exile,
   he and his princes together,"
  says the LORD.

(Amos 1:13-15)

Having pronounced God's sentence on six of the surrounding powers, the prophet then turns to Judah and Israel (i.e., the Northern Kingdom). The denunciation of Israel is far lengthier than any of the others, and filled with a pathos lacking in the denunciations of the surrounding powers. Israel, along with Judah, has been God's favorite. God delivered them from slavery in Egypt:

"I brought you up out of the land of Egypt,
   and led you forty years in the wilderness, . . .
Is it not indeed so, O people of Israel?"
  says the LORD.

(Amos 2:10-11)

And God gave to them, and them alone, God's Torah:

Thus says the LORD:
"For three transgressions of Judah,
   and for four, I will not revoke the punishment;
because they have rejected the law of the LORD,
   and have not kept his statutes."

(Amos 2:4-5)

The fact that God renders judgment on the surrounding powers implies that even without Torah those nations knew, or could have known, what God's justice required. Amos does not develop the point, but Paul does in a passage near the beginning of his letter to the Christians in Rome. Speaking of Christ's eschatological judgment, he says, "All who have sinned without the law will also perish without the law, and all who have sinned under the law will be judged by the law." By "law" Paul here means Torah. But he continues: "When Gentiles who have not the law do by nature what the law requires, they are a law to themselves, even though they

353

do not have the law. They show that what the law requires is written on their hearts, while their conscience also bears witness and their conflicting thoughts accuse or perhaps excuse them on that day when . . . God judges the secrets of men by Christ Jesus" (Rom. 2:12-16).

This passage has traditionally been cited, though not without controversy, as a biblical basis for the doctrine of natural law. Though the Gentiles do not *have* the law, that is, Torah, they nonetheless are a law to themselves — or better, they are *in themselves* a law. The very same things that Torah requires have been written on their hearts; their conscience bears witness to those things. It is for this reason that God's rendering judgment on their actions, and pronouncing and carrying out sentence, is not unjust; they knew better, or could have known better.

The other theme in the Old Testament that we must recover if we are to understand Paul's thought in Romans 13 is that God's rendering of judgment is in good measure mediated by human beings and human institutions. One mode of mediation was prophetic speech. In the denunciations he uttered, Amos was mediating God's judgment. It was not Amos but God who was pronouncing judgment on Judah, Israel, and the surrounding nations; Amos was simply speaking on behalf of God. But God's judgment was also seen as mediated by judges and rulers. Indeed, God's judgment was more fully mediated by judges and rulers than by prophets — though not more reliably! Prophets were not authorized to carry out sentence; rulers were. In Deuteronomy, God is reported as enjoining Israel to "appoint judges and officials" to "render just decisions for the people" (16:18-20). And from a good many other passages it becomes clear that such judges and officials were to be seen as rendering judgment on behalf of God. Consider, for example, the *locus classicus* description of the good king in Psalm 72:1-2:

> Give the king thy justice, O God,
>   and thy righteousness to the royal son!
> May he judge thy people with righteousness,
>   And thy poor with justice!

No doubt it was Judah's king, and/or Israel's, that the psalmist had in view. But Amos's denunciations of the surrounding nations implies that God also requires of the rulers of the Gentiles that they render just judgment and not themselves perpetrate injustice.

Paul's thought in Romans 13, when placed within this context of its

Old Testament references and antecedents, now seems eminently clear. The task of the ruling authorities is to mediate God's judgment; they have been instituted or appointed by God for this purpose. They are God's deacons, God's liturgetes. Their task is to put a stamp of approval on those who do right and to subject the wrongdoer to wrath, *orgē*— this to be seen as the executing of God's wrath, God's *orgē*. Given the Old Testament background, it seems obvious that what Paul means is that the state is authorized to impose corrective punishment on God's behalf.

In short, in his letter to the Romans, Paul took Israel's understanding of the task of its rulers and applied this understanding to ruling authorities in general. His doing so had antecedents within the Old Testament itself — in the psalmist's praise of God as King of Kings, in Amos's denunciations of the surrounding powers, and so forth.

John reminds us in Revelation that rulers all too often do not do what they were appointed by God to do. Rather than rendering just judgment on God's behalf, they render unjust judgment on their own behalf. They become a terror to good conduct rather than to bad; they affirm and praise the one who does wrong rather than the one who does right. They are no longer God's servants and ministers. Or shall we say that they are *false* servants and *unruly* ministers — that they stand to the true ruler described in Psalm 72 as the false prophet stands to the true prophet?

Paul knew that this is how governments behave. He knew it from the Old Testament; more poignantly, he knew it from personal experience and from his memory of Jesus' crucifixion. So we have to understand him as talking about *properly functioning* government. He is speaking normatively, not descriptively.

As part of God's providential care of humankind, God renders judgment, executes justice. Some of God's judgment is rendered at the end of the ages, some is rendered within this present age; some is direct, some is mediated through human beings; sometimes the mediator is no more than an instrument of God's causality, sometimes God authorizes someone to serve him by carrying out a certain task. Government falls into this last category. As part of God's providential care for humankind God assigns government the task of "executing wrath (anger)" on the wrongdoer, rendering judgment, vindicating those who have been wronged and convicting and carrying out corrective punishment on those who have done the wronging. Note well: Paul does not say that the task of government is to execute vengeance *(ekdikēsis)* on wrongdoers. Vengeance, repaying, is to be left to God (12:19). The task of government is to execute wrath, anger *(orgē)* on wrongdoers.

Government as Part of the Creation Order

But is this approach to our topic, from what Paul and 1 Peter say about the task of government, not too confined? The task of government, they say, is to secure justice in society by affirming those who do right and pronouncing sentence and exercising corrective punishment on those who do wrong. Does this not give us a theology of only one among the several functions of government, namely the juridical function?

My response is that it is a mistake to interpret what Paul and 1 Peter say as relevant only to the juridical function of government. The juridical function cannot be exercised without the legislative function; no laws, no judges. And if those who do right are to be affirmed and those who do wrong convicted and punished, it is not sufficient that the juridical function be exercised properly; the legislative function must also be exercised properly. The laws themselves must be just. It was not a point that escaped the Old Testament writers. They bewail not only unjust juridical decisions but unjust laws.

And now for an important point concerning a just system of law. By virtue of the sanctions it attaches to disobedience to the law, a just system of law discourages wrongdoing and encourages rightdoing. But more fundamental even than this effect of sanctions is the fact that a system of just laws is, as such, a guide toward just action. Law performs an inescapable educative function. The Torah was God's guide for Israel's life until the Messiah arrived.

There is a long-standing debate among Christian thinkers whether government, in God's order of things, is simply a "remedy for sin." There can be no doubt that this is prominent in what Scripture says about the task of government. But just now we have caught a glimpse of something more. A system of just laws not only places inhibitions on our sinful inclination to wrongdoing by instituting a system of sanctions. It also instructs us in what justice requires — and reminds us of what it requires when we become forgetful. In that way, properly functioning government represents God's providential care for us as finite, limited creatures, not just as fallen sinful creatures. Properly functioning government is part of God's providential care for God's creation *qua creation*.

And perhaps the proper function of government even goes beyond justice — beyond establishing and applying a system of just laws. Or so, at least, many theologians in the Christian tradition have suggested; and I agree. I must confine myself to one example. In the last chapter of his *Insti-*

tutes of the Christian Religion, John Calvin develops a theology of government. His emphasis falls on the calling of government to promote justice. But he culminates his articulation of the "appointed end" of civil government by saying that government is meant by God "to promote general peace and tranquility" (IV, xx, 2). He gives an indication of what he has in mind with his remark, a bit later, that civil government "embraces" such activities as seeing to it that "men breathe, eat, drink, and are kept warm . . . when it *provides for their living together'* (IV, xx, 3; italics added). The idea is that it belongs to the task of government to serve the common good — the shalom, the flourishing, of the people. In promoting justice government is already serving the flourishing of the people. And let us not forget the lesson of history, that when governments go beyond promoting justice and aim at serving *what they regard as* the common good, they all too often wreak appalling injustice on the citizens. Nonetheless, I think it is impossible to deny that, in addition to promoting justice, government serves an indispensable coordinating function; and that this coordinating function, when properly exercised, aims at the common good, the general welfare. Zoning regulations and trade agreements, to take just two examples from the contemporary world, are for the welfare of the community.

The points I have been making, about the educative function of law and about government serving the common good in its coordinating activities, have traditionally been put by saying that government belongs, in part, to the "order of creation." There would have been government even had there been no sin. Government represents a blend of God's providential care of God's creation *as created* and God's providential care of God's creation *as fallen.* To which must again be added the point, already made several times, that government is itself also fallen.

Duality

Governmental authority belongs to God's providential care for human beings as the peculiar sort of creatures that we are, and belongs to God's providential care for us as fallen. Romans and 1 Peter instruct their readers on how to live under such authority — when it functions as it ought to function. But their addressees were also members of the church, as are most of those who will be reading this essay. And as such they participated not only within God's creational/providential order but within God's order of redemption. They lived, and we live, at a unique point of intersection of God's order of creation/providence with God's order of redemption. We are both subjects of a state and members of the church.

This duality of the Christian's location in history has been the cause of much perplexity and the subject of much discussion over the centuries. If the church were no more than a club organized for the purpose of conducting religious exercises and evoking religious experiences, there would be no perplexity. The club would often have to fight for its independence from the state. But that would be a political problem, not a source of perplexity.

The church is not a club. The New Testament represents the membership of the church as "elected" rather than self-selecting; and it represents Christ as head of the church. The metaphor of "head" carries a number of connotations, among them being that Christ is the ruler, the lord, of the church. The church thereby has an inherent political dimension. The Christian is a subject of two polities: a citizen of some state subject to its rule, a member of the church subject to the rule of Christ.

Living under two rules need not, as such, cause perplexity. A person holding dual citizenship may well have to negotiate some difficult situations; but there is no particular perplexity produced by having dual citizenship in, say, the United States and Canada, and thus being subject to the rule of both. The root of the perplexity caused by the dual rule under which Christians find themselves is that the rules for how one ought to live as a member of the one institution seem so different from those for how one ought to live as a member of the other. To a good many Christians, the rules have seemed not just different but incompatible.

The root of the perplexity is right there in Romans 12 and 13. Abolish from your lives the tit-for-tat vengeance system, says Paul to his readers. Seek the good of others, even of those who have wronged you; feed them if they are hungry, give them something to drink if they are thirsty. That on the one hand. On the other hand, regard governmental authority as mediating God's justice when it renders just punishment on wrongdoers. And obey its laws and judicial declarations out of conscience and not just prudence.

Down through the centuries many Christians have found this to be exceedingly perplexing advice: What sense does it make to approve the punishment of the criminal at the hands of the authorities while at the same time bringing him love-baskets? The perplexity gained poignancy when, after New Testament times, those in governmental positions began to convert to Christianity and those who were already Christian began to occupy governmental positions. It is one thing to visit the criminal in prison while declaring one's approval of the government's putting him there. It is quite another thing — or so it has seemed to many — for oneself to be the government official who puts him in prison and *then* to visit him there.

An additional consideration of great importance must be introduced at this point. Not only is Christ the head of the church. In this present era it is not God the Father but Christ whose authority is mediated by the state. That is the clear implication of the teaching of the New Testament concerning Christ's authority. At the end of Matthew's Gospel we read that "all authority in heaven and on earth has been given to me" (28:18). All by itself, this could be interpreted as meaning *all authority to teach.* But when we add the following passage from Paul's first letter to the Corinthians, we have to conclude that the authority given to Christ includes political authority: "Then comes the end, when he [Christ] delivers the kingdom to God the Father after destroying every rule and every authority and power. For he must reign until he has put all his enemies under his feet. . . . When all things are subjected to him, then the Son himself will also be subjected to him who put all things under him, that God may be everything to every one" (1 Cor. 15:24-28). To this we can add Ephesians 1:22-23: God the Father "has put all things under [Christ's] feet, and has made him the head over all things for the church, which is his body, the fullness of him who fills all in all."

Christ is not only head of the church but head of the state. The Christian is under the rule of Christ not only in the church but also in the state. The judge who sentences the criminal to jail and acts justly in so doing is thereby mediating *Christ's* authority. Now suppose that the judge is also a member of the church and that, in obedience to Christ's rule of the church, he visits the criminal in jail. What sense does that make? Let it be noted that the perplexity is yours and mine. There is no evidence in Paul's words that he found anything perplexing in the advice he gave to his readers in Romans 12:19–13:7. In Romans as a whole, Paul raises and addresses one perplexity after another; he gives no evidence of finding any perplexity here.

A full discussion of this perplexity would require far more space than I have available to me here. I can do no more than point to what I think is the correct answer. The resolution of the perplexity proposed by most Christian thinkers has involved distinguishing between acting as a private person and acting in one's capacity as the holder of some governmental office or position. When the judge declares someone guilty and sentences him to prison, he is not acting as a private person but in his official capacity, in his own person he lacks the "power" to make that declaration and to issue that sentence. In turn, to act in his capacity of judge is to act on behalf of the state. Strictly speaking, it is the state which makes that declaration and the state which issues that sentence. On the other hand, when the person who occupies the position of judge goes to the prison to visit the man whom he, in his capacity as judge and on behalf of the state, pronounced guilty, he is doing so in his own person. Hence it is that the mainline tradition of the church has seen nothing contradictory in one and the same person faithfully mediating Christ's rule as head of the state by sentencing the criminal to corrective punishment and faithfully following Christ's rule as head of the church by visiting the criminal in prison.

My own view is different. Of course there is a distinction to be made between acting as a private person and acting in some official capacity. But what I find striking in Paul's discussion in the concluding verses of Romans 12 and the opening verses of Romans 13 is that the act of exacting vengeance *(ekdikēsis)* which he forbids to Christians in Romans 12 is not something that, in Romans 13, he describes God as authorizing the state to do. God does not authorize the state to exact vengeance; God authorizes the state to execute wrath or anger *(orgē)*. And I think it not unlikely that, when Paul said this, he was revealing his training in Hebrew scripture. In Leviticus we are told that reproving the neighbor for his wrongdoing is an act of love; failure to do so is to incur guilt on oneself (19:17-18).

Yoder's Alternative

The understanding of political authority that I have articulated, starting from Romans and 1 Peter and moving out from there, is that of the preponderance of Christian theologians. Some would want to add things that I have not mentioned, alter the emphasis, change some of the details, and so forth; but most would agree with the main line of thought that I have laid out. But there have also been theologians whose disagreement would not be over details but over the main line of thought. Probably the most important alternative line of thought is that characteristic of the Anabaptist tradition. And everyone would agree that the most important formulation on the contemporary scene of the traditional Anabaptist understanding is that of John Howard Yoder. So, all too briefly, let me sketch out

Yoder's alternative understanding, the basic source being his now-classic book *The Politics of Jesus.*

I have assigned central position, in the line of thought I have developed, to two New Testament passages, Romans 12–13 and 1 Peter 2–3. Yoder also gives central position to Romans; but he makes 1 Peter subordinate. And whereas I have interpreted Romans in conjunction with other New Testament passages concerning extant social institutions, as well as in the context of Paul's Old Testament quotations and allusions, and in the light of his teaching that all authority has been handed over to Christ by the Father, Yoder interprets Romans through the lens of what the New Testament, and Paul in particular, have to say about "thrones and dominions and rulers and powers" (Col. 1:16) — usually now just called "powers" for short. In Colossians 2:15, for example, Paul says that God "disarmed the rulers and authorities and made a public example of them, triumphing over them in [the cross]." The Greek word translated here as "authorities" is *exousiai.* It is the same word that is translated as "authorities" in the opening of Romans 13.

So what is Yoder's understanding of the New Testament teaching concerning the powers? The powers, Yoder says, are the intellectual, ethical, religious, political, and social structures that give order and stability to human existence. Though supra-individual, we need not think of them in personal or angelic terms. They "were created by God" *(Politics,* p. 142). For "there could not be society or history, there could not be humanity without the existence above us of religious, intellectual, moral, and social structures. *We cannot live without them" (Politics,* p. 143).

Though created good, these "powers have rebelled and are fallen. They did not accept the modesty that would have permitted them to remain conformed to the creative purpose, but rather they claimed for themselves an absolute value. They thereby enslaved humanity and our history.... To what are we subject? Precisely to those values and structures which are necessary to life and society but which have claimed the status of idols and have succeeded in making us serve them as if they were of absolute value" *(Politics,* p. 142). "Our lostness consists in our subjection to the rebellious powers of a fallen world" *(Politics,* p. 144). Prominent among the fallen rebellious powers to which we are enslaved is the state.

How are we to understand the fact that even after Christ's crucifixion and resurrection, there remain such fallen powers as the state? We are to understand it as a sign of God's providential care for humankind in this time of the divine patience *(Politics,* p. 149). Recall that these structures, including political structures, are *necessary* for human existence; they provide the *order* without which there could not be human existence. "Even tyranny . . . is still better than chaos" *(Politics*, p. 141). Had God abolished these structures, God would thereby have abolished human existence. "Our lostness and our survival are inseparable, both dependent upon the Powers" *(Politics*, p. 143).

This perspective both yields and is based upon a very different reading of Romans 13 from that which I have articulated. We are not to obey the state because it issues legitimate commands that place us under obligation; we are simply to subject ourselves to it, in the way that Russians subjected themselves to Stalin. The state is not the servant or minister of God in the sense that it mediates God's authority; it is simply an instrument of God's causality. And though there is some wavering on the point in some of his later essays, in *The Politics of Jesus* Yoder states unambiguously that "the function exercised by government is not the function to be exercised by Christians. However able an infinite God may be to work at the same time through the sufferings of his believing disciples who return good for evil and through the wrathful violence of the authorities who punish evil with evil, such behavior is for humans not complementary but in disjunction. Divine providence can in its own sovereign permissive way 'use' an idolatrous Assyria (Isaiah 10) or Rome. This takes place, however, without declaring that the destructive participation in it is incumbent upon the covenant people" *(Politics*, p. 198).

A response that does justice to Yoder's thought would require an essay of its own. Yet the reader will rightly expect that I not move on as if Yoder had said nothing worth paying attention to. So let me express my difficulties with Yoder's position, in good measure in the form of questions. What I have to say will be much too brief and undeveloped to persuade the convinced Yoderian. It may, though, serve to locate some of the basic issues.

Paul, as we have seen, quotes from and alludes to a rich Old Testament body of teaching concerning the role of government in God's providential order; I think that we impose an untenable breach between the New Testament and the Old if we ignore this background. The role of government, according to Israel's witness, is not just to secure order and stave off chaos; its role is to promote justice. Paul echoes this. He does not say that God appointed or instituted governmental authority to secure order. He says that God did so in order that wrongdoing would be curbed and punished and rightdoing thereby affirmed. The corollary of this is that when Paul says that the governing authorities are deacons or liturgetes of God, we must understand him as meaning not merely that they are instruments of divine causality (Assyria) but that they are mediators of divine authority. Thus it is that Paul says we are to obey or be subject "not only because of wrath or anger *(orgē)* but also because of conscience" and that 1 Peter says we are to do so "for the Lord's sake." And let us recall the point made earlier, that the Greek word that both Paul and 1 Peter use for the honor that we are to pay to government is the very same word that Paul uses in Ephesians to describe the honor that children are to give their parents.

An additional point is the following. Yoder describes a fallen power as something that "harms" and "enslaves" us, something that "absolutizes" itself, makes us serve it as if it were of "absolute value," demands from us "unconditional loyalty," something to which we are "unconditionally subjected." Now consider Paul's language: Rulers "are not a terror to good conduct but to bad." Can Paul plausibly be interpreted as talking about one of Yoder's fallen powers? I don't see how.

It is said by some critics of Yoder that he has no doctrine of creation or providence; everything is Christology. That seems to me not correct. The issue pivots rather on his understanding of the fall. States, he says, are *fallen powers.* As one reads along, it gradually dawns on one that what he means is not that states *act unjustly under the influence of "powers";* he means that states are themselves fallen powers. And by this he means, in turn, that they are themselves *intrinsically evil powers.* Necessary, but intrinsically evil. An analogue would be the view that the fall of humankind consisted not in human beings *acting wrongly under the influence of powers,* but *themselves becoming intrinsically evil powers.*

Obviously this is not Paul's teaching when it comes to human beings; quite the contrary. And I find no textual evidence that his teaching was any different when it comes to social institutions. From his *Haustafeln* it is obvious, for example, that he did not regard the social institutions of marriage and family as intrinsically evil powers to which we must submit on pain of creating total chaos. Of course Paul thought that there were plenty of things that go wrong in marriages and families; but he did not think of those institutions as themselves intrinsically evil powers. We would need very clear evidence indeed if we were to understand what Paul says about the institution of government differently.

Last, is there really the intrinsic conflict that Yoder suggests between willing the good of someone and imposing corrective punishment on him or her? To move to the theological plane: Is there really the sharp dichotomy that Yoder suggests between Christ's authority in the church and his authority in the state? Yoder speaks of the authorities as punishing "evil with evil" and of employing "wrathful violence," contrasting this with the believing disciples who return "good for evil." But this is Yoder's description, not Paul's. Paul does not say that authorities do "evil" to the wrongdoer, nor does he mention violence. What he says is that the authorities pronounce judgment *(krima)* and execute anger *(orgē)* on the wrongdoer, this latter meaning, so I have argued, applying corrective punishment. And it is clear, not just from Romans 13 but from the book of Romans as a whole, that Paul most definitely did not regard corrective punishment as "doing evil" but rather as the exercise of justice.

Earlier I used the example of a judge who imposes sentence on a criminal and then visits the criminal in jail. Consider now a parent who punishes her child for some infraction — the family being a social institution, one among those necessary structures that Yoder regards as fallen powers. I take it to be an extrapolation from Paul's thought that it is in the parent's "office" of parent, not in her own person, that she rightly imposes corrective punishment on the child. Is there anything incompatible between the parent's loving the child and also imposing corrective punishment? May she not even impose the punishment *out of love?*

The Application to Us

In addressing the Christians in Rome, Paul was speaking to people who had no voice in government; his instructions were for mere subjects. The empire of which they were subjects was presumably not yet the murderous and totalitarian regime that the writer of the Apocalypse was familiar with. Had the empire fallen to those depths, Paul's advice surely would have been different. Rather than talking about the proper function of political authority and the relation of its subjects to such authority, he would have instructed his readers on how to relate to a regime that had departed so far from God's purpose as to have lost its legitimacy.

You and I are not mere subjects. By virtue of our right to vote, to mention nothing else, all of us have a voice in our government. And a good many of us are government functionaries. So what would Paul have said had he been addressing us?

He would have said everything he did say: Obey or be subject to the authorities, pay the taxes they justly assess rather than questioning their authority to raise taxes or trying to evade one's taxes, honor and respect their positions rather than bad-mouthing them, remember that their calling is to be servants and ministers of God mediating God's judgments. All this Paul would have said. But he would have said something more as well.

The main burden of what he would have added is that it is your and my calling as people who are citizens and not mere subjects to encourage the state to live up to its task of promoting justice and serving the general welfare. When all around are saying that the state is nothing more than an arena for negotiating power relationships, the Christian will never weary of insisting that the task of the state in God's creational and providential order is to promote justice and serve the common good. The Christian will not conform to the world by organizing power blocks to negotiate special favors for Christians or anyone else.

Perhaps the principal way in which Christians of the modern world have called the state to its proper task is by initiating and supporting efforts to set structural limits to the scope of state authority, so as thereby to diminish the risk of overreaching by the state. But before I identify some of the forms these efforts at limitation have taken, let me call attention to two ways in which, in addition to overreaching, states fail to fulfill their proper calling — ways all too frequently overlooked.

The state often fails in its task of promoting justice by overlooking or refusing to acknowledge the occurrence of injustice, insisting on calling it something else instead or insisting that the injustice in question is none of its business. Sometimes this happens because the state is in the grip of some ideology: the ideology of private enterprise, the ideology of nationalism, whatever. Often it happens because the state is in the control of rich and powerful persons who see to it that they remain free to go about their unjust ways. In such situations it is the calling of the Christian to denounce the ideologies, bring the injustice to light, name it for what it is, namely injustice, and insist that the state not shirk its task. The state fails in its God-given task not only by doing too much but by doing too little.

In this identification of injustice, the Christian will be guided by what may be called *the biblical contour of justice*. The contour of justice that the biblical writers had in mind is very different from that to be found, say, in Plato, and from that to be found in libertarian writers of the twentieth century. To mention just one point: whereas the impoverished and the alien are prominent in the biblical contour of justice, they are invisible in both Plato's contour of justice and in the contemporary libertarian contour.

Second, though the state fails to promote justice when the judiciary is so corrupted that it knowingly pronounces the wrongdoer innocent, it also

fails to promote justice when, after vindicating the innocent and convicting the wrongdoer, it metes out punishment that is inequitable, excessively
harsh, humiliating to the point of being dehumanizing, incompatible with
respecting the wrongdoer as a person made in the image of God. The
Christian will insist that punishment always be of such a sort as to be compatible with visiting the wrongdoer in prison and giving him food and
drink.

And now for some of the ideas that have emerged from the seedbed of
the Christian tradition for securing a duly limited government, some being ideas for the internal structuring of government, some being ideas for
restraining the tendency of government to aggrandizement. In saying that
these ideas emerged from the seedbed of the Christian tradition I mean to
suggest that not all of them are to be found, as such, in Scripture. Though
John of the Apocalypse was confronted with a government that was ag-
grandizing to an appalling degree, neither he nor any other biblical writer
proposed, for example, a division of powers within government so as to
make such overreaching less likely in the future. I should add that in saying
that these ideas emerged from the seedbed of the Christian tradition, I do
not mean to suggest that they did not have other roots as well; on this occasion I simply want to highlight their Christian roots.

(1) The most important idea, and also the one that emerged first, was
the idea of government as the rule of law rather than as the will of the sovereign. The idea of law as opposed to sovereign will is omnipresent in the
Old Testament. The king is to see to it that God's judgments are mediated
to the people, these judgments being known to the king and his judiciary
from their knowledge of God's law, whether in the form of Torah or in the
form of the writing on one's heart. And the mediation is to take the form
of a body of historically posited law that enshrines God's law, along with a
judiciary that interprets and applies that law. Such law transcends the personal will of rulers and abides amidst their coming and going. Furthermore — this is crucial — the rulers and the judiciary are themselves to be
subject to this law.

(2) A second development, strictly speaking an aspect of the first but
worth singling out for special attention, was the rise of constitutionalism.
A constitution lays down a system of government by providing for various
"offices," specifying the conditions under which persons are entitled to enter those offices and required to leave them, and specifying the scope and
limits of the "powers" and privileges attached to those offices. In its sharp
differentiation of persons from offices, in its making the holding of office a

matter of procedure rather than of power or happenstance, and in its setting of limits to what a person is authorized to do in office, a constitution goes beyond the rule of law as such. Furthermore, a constitution typically makes the revision of most of these stipulations far more difficult than the revision of ordinary law.

Constitutionalism did not arise as an intellectual force until late medieval times; nonetheless, I think there can be no doubt that the core idea was there already in Paul's instructions to the Roman Christians and in the Old Testament line of thought to which he was giving expression. Only those in authority are authorized to impose corrective punishment. The old vengeance system, in which private parties take it on themselves to pay back the wrongs done them, is to be abolished.

(3) A third development, strictly speaking a development within constitutionalism but again worth singling out for separate attention, was the emergence of the idea that government should be so structured that there is a division of powers — in particular, a division of legislative, judicial, and executive powers. The most influential argument in favor of a division of powers was apparently the argument from human sinfulness. The temptation of those in power to expand their power is among the strongest and most dangerous temptations to which human beings are subject. Best then to specify a division of powers in the constitution, thereby setting up a system of checks and balances. The result will often be postponement, compromise, inaction, lack of clarity, and so forth; but better those flaws than the totalitarian beast of Revelation 13.

(4) A fourth development has been the slow working out of the implications of the idea that the human person, on account of being an image of God, is of such worth that he or she must never be violated. The view of government held by most Christians in medieval times was that it was the task of government not just to promote justice but to cultivate moral and religious virtue in the subjects; the magisterial Reformers perpetuated this view. It is my own judgment that this view comes closer to the views of Plato, Aristotle, and the other philosophers of pagan antiquity than it does to the views of the biblical writers. But be that as it may, every reader is aware that this view of the task of government resulted in appalling cruelty. Those who did not have the approved moral or religious views, or did not exhibit the approved moral or religious virtues, were exiled, tortured, burned at the stake, beheaded.

As I read the history of the matter, the conviction slowly sank in that whatever may be the worth of cultivating moral and religious virtue, it cannot come at the price of such violation of the person. Such cruelty is incompatible with recognizing the worth of the person as an image of God. It was in good measure from this conviction that there emerged the rights and liberties of the limited democratic state as we know it today — especially the right and liberty to worship God according to the convictions of one's own conscience.

(5) Closely connected to the preceding is the emergence of the idea of natural human rights as a protection against tyrannical government. I am aware that some have argued in recent years that the idea of natural human rights emerged not from the seedbed of the Christian tradition but from the supposedly individualistic philosophies of the late medieval nominalists and the Enlightenment philosophers. My own view is that the history here is mistaken. When such great church fathers as Chrysostom and Ambrose declared that if the poor person has no shoes, then the shoes in the closet of the wealthy person *belong to* the poor person, not by virtue of any extant laws but simply by virtue of the fact that he or she is an impoverished human being, they were expressing in their own way the idea of natural human rights.

(6) Though the last development I have in mind has been less influential than the preceding, in my judgment it is no less important. In both Catholicism and Dutch neo-Calvinism of the latter part of the nineteenth century there emerged the idea that the scope of state action is to be limited not only by the requirement that the state not violate the individual person nor allow other persons or institutions to do so, but also by the requirement that the state not absorb into itself the manifold institutions of civil society. Rather than absorbing them, the state is to confine itself to seeing to it that the demands of justice are satisfied, both by how these institutions interact with each other and by how they treat their members.

Abraham Kuyper, the most creative and influential of the Dutch neo-Calvinists, developed the point by arguing that the emergence of social institutions, each with its own authority structure, is part of God's providential care for humankind and for its progress over the course of history. The authority of the various institutions of civil society is not delegated to them by the state but exercised directly before the face of God by each of them. The totalitarian temptation of the state to absorb all competing authority structures and turn them into branches of the state must thus be vigorously resisted. The state is but one authority structure among many — albeit unique in that it is the court of last resort for society as a whole in the promotion of justice and the rendering of just judgment.

Other Issues

There are many elements of a comprehensive evangelical political philosophy that I have not had time to discuss. I have not discussed the limits of our obligation to political obedience; I have simply taken for granted that there are such limits. There is no obligation to obey the ravenous state of Revelation 13 when it demands that we worship it; our duty is to refuse to obey. Neither have I discussed the limits on what Christians may do when functioning in some governmental office. All too often Christians in government assume that there are no such limits — either that, or they assume that the limits are so wide that it's not worth taking note of them. In government one just does what everybody else does: tells lies, bears false witness against one's opponents, pursues power, goes to war for nationalistic reasons, and so forth. These are both exceedingly important issues. My not having discussed them is not to be construed as implying otherwise.

One final remark. The reader must also not conclude from the foregoing that the state is the only institution that has the task of rendering just judgment by establishing a system of just laws and applying those justly. All institutions render this sort of judgment, and all must do so justly. Other institutions do so, however, in the course of carrying out their primary task of providing education, organizing recreation, manufacturing computers, investing funds, or whatever. It would be a calamity if just judgment were exclusively the province of the state. When just judgment is being rendered by the various institutions of civil society, the state is required to "keep its nose out of" their affairs. What is unique about the state is that rendering just judgment is among its *primary* tasks and that it is entitled to use strong coercive measures in carrying out that task.

Basic Theses

In conclusion, let me state some theses concerning government that a broad range of evangelicals can agree on — acknowledging that, at some points, those representing the Anabaptist tradition would disagree.

1. Government is not a merely human creation, nor is it a work of the devil. As part of God's providential care for humankind God assigns government its task.
2. The task assigned by God to government is twofold: to promote jus-

tice, both primary and corrective, and in its coordinating activities to enhance the common good.

3. Government, thus understood, belongs both to God's providential care for us as creatures and to God's providential care for us as fallen.

4. When government acts as it ought to act, it acts with genuine authority. That authority is to be understood as not merely human but as mediating Christ's authority.

5. The corollary of the exercise by government of genuine authority is that its subjects are obligated to obey that authority.

6. Among the things that governments are authorized to do is apply corrective punishment to wrongdoers — provided that the punishment is itself of a just sort.

7. Though government, along with such other social institutions as marriage, family, and economy, is instituted by God as part of God's providential care for human beings as creatures and as fallen, government, along with these other institutions, is itself fallen. That is to say, government and other social institutions never fully carry out the tasks assigned them by God.

8. Though not every failing on the part of government — or any other social institution — justifies disobedience, all too often governments do fail to such a degree that disobedience is required. The starkest examples of such obligatory disobedience are those cases in which government demands that something other than God be worshiped.

9. Christians may serve in the offices of government; in doing so, they are mediating the rule over the state of that very same Christ who is the ruler of the church.

10. When the Christian occupies some governmental office, he or she must not be guided by customary practice but by the God-assigned task of government: to promote justice and the common good.

11. It is the duty of the Christian always to call his or her government to its proper task. Especially is this true for those of us who have some degree of voice in our governments.

12. Such calling of government to its proper task will ordinarily include proclamation. But whenever possible, it will also include the promotion of governmental structures that make it less likely that the government will fail in, or violate, its task.

13. Christians will honor and respect government; they will not talk and act as if government has no right to exist. And they will support government by paying taxes. They will not talk and act as if government,

in assessing taxes, is forcefully taking from its subjects "their money." Financial support is *owed* government.

Bibliography

Aquinas, Thomas. *On Princely Government (de regimine principum)*. In R. W. Dyson, ed. and trans., *Aquinas: Political Writings*. Cambridge: Cambridge University Press, 2002.

Calvin, John. *Institutes of the Christian Religion*. Translated by Ford Lewis Battles. Philadelphia: Westminster, 1960.

Chrysostom, John. *On Wealth and Poverty*. Translated by Catherine P. Roth. Crestwood, NY: St. Vladimir's Seminary Press, 1984.

Kuyper, Abraham. *Calvinism: The Stone Lectures 1898-1899*. New York: Fleming H. Revell, n.d.

O'Donovan, Oliver. *The Desire of the Nations*. Cambridge: Cambridge University Press, 1996.

O'Donovan, Oliver, and Joan Lockwood O'Donovan. *From Irenaeus to Grotius: A Sourcebook in Christian Political Thought 100-1625*. Grand Rapids: Eerdmans, 1999.

Tierney, Brian. *The Idea of Natural Rights: Studies on Natural Rights, Natural Law and Church Law 1150-1625*. Atlanta: Scholars Press, 1997.

Yoder, John H. *The Politics of Jesus*. Grand Rapids: Eerdmans, 1972.

Has the Cloak Become a Cage?
Love, Justice, and Economic Activity

In Baxter's view the care for external goods should only lie on the shoulders of the "saint like a light cloak, which can be thrown aside at any moment." But fate decreed that the cloak should become an iron cage.

Max Weber

"History is irreversible," says the French socialist Lucien Goldmann in his *Philosophy of the Enlightenment*, "and it seems impossible that Christianity should ever again become the mode in which men really live and think" (Goldmann 1973, 82). The choice for humanity is now between the "bourgeois individualism" of capitalism, which Goldmann sees as spiritually empty in its devotion to morally neutral technical knowledge, and socialism, which he sees as an immanent, historical, and humanist religion committed to the creation of a new community. The choice, he observes, is a painful one, since the spiritual emptiness of capitalism is balanced by the violation of individual conscience characteristic of socialism as we know it. But the possibility of a transcendental faith shaping history is probably over; and, in any case, "the 'judgement of history' has passed Christianity by. Diderot's argument that modern society makes it impossible for anyone to give a genuinely Christian character to his whole life is more valid than ever today. The more sincere and intense the Christian life of modern man, the more it becomes a purely inward, psychological 'private matter' deprived of all influence on life in society" (82).

In what follows I want to consider whether these haunting words of Goldmann are true. I will follow Goldmann in speaking mainly about Christianity. It is clear from Goldmann's words that he regards what he is saying as true for "any transcendental faith shaping history" — Judaism, Christianity, Islam, whatever. The day of all such faiths is over; in the modern world, "transcendental faith" is a "psychological 'private matter' deprived of all influence on life in society." But my discussion will be more focused if I concentrate on just one religion, leaving it to the reader to draw out the analogues. I shall choose the religion that I know best: Christianity. And I shall speak only about the economy. Goldmann's thesis is that Christianity is without formative impact on all spheres of public life; even from the comments quoted, however, it's clear that he himself regards the economy as central.

Goldmann is of course following in the footsteps of Max Weber. Weber is notorious for his thesis that religion, specifically Calvinism, and more specifically yet, Puritanism, made a crucial causal contribution to the emergence of capitalism. Weber assumed that for capitalism to emerge in any part of the world, a victorious struggle against the "traditionalism" already in place had to occur. One characteristic feature of traditionalism is the presence of a wide variety of ethical prohibitions against a wide variety of economic transactions; for capitalism to emerge, these must be removed and be replaced by a rationalized legal system whose centerpiece is laws enforcing the sanctity of free contracts made between non-deceiving parties, and the view must gain currency that all that is ethically prohibited is deceiving or coercing one's contracting partner and breaking one's contract. A second feature of what Weber had in mind by "traditionalism" was explained by him in these words: "A man does not 'by nature' wish to earn more and more money, but simply to live as he is accustomed to live and to earn as much as is necessary for that purpose. Wherever modern capitalism has begun its work of increasing the productivity of human labour by increasing its intensity, it has encountered the immensely stubborn resistance of this leading trait of pre-capitalistic labour" (Weber 1958, 60). The structure of a capitalist economy is that of "the rational utilization of capital in a permanent enterprise and the rational capitalistic organization of labour" (58); for this structure to become operative, people must acquire the habit of working whether they have to or not, just to make (more and more) money.

The "traditionalism" from which capitalism initially emerged was the Christianized traditionalism of Western Europe. Accordingly, Weber asked how the *unnatural* character formation necessary for the workings of this virtually *amoral* system emerged from Christianity. What makes of the question a puzzle is that the traditional ethic of Christianity was an "ethic of brotherliness." Weber's famous answer was that the Puritans provided the crucial link, with respect both to the unnaturalness and the amoralism. Weber interpreted the Puritans as saying that the roles allotted us by the capitalist economy are to be seen as our divine callings; accordingly, we are to work devotedly in accord with the imperatives of the system. We serve God by working hard at making money and investing for profit. The Puritans, on Weber's interpretation, took the roles offered them by the capitalist system and propounded the audacious claim that, no matter how "unbrotherly" one's action in these roles might be, we are nonetheless called by God to play these roles. It is God who calls us to hard work in these hard-hearted roles for the impersonal goal of making money!

Now that the system is in place, however, it reproduces itself without the aid of this or any other religious basis:

> Since asceticism undertook to remodel the world and to work out its ideals in the world, material goods have gained an increasing and finally an inexorable power over the lives of men as at no previous period in history. Today the spirit of religious asceticism — whether finally, who knows? — has escaped from the cage. But victorious capitalism, since it rests on mechanical foundations, needs its support no longer. . . . The idea of duty in one's calling prowls about in our lives like the ghost of dead religious beliefs. Where the fulfilment of the calling cannot directly be related to the highest spiritual and cultural values, or when, on the other hand, it need not be felt simply as economic compulsion, the individual generally abandons the attempt to justify it at all. In the field of its highest development, in the United States, the pursuit of wealth, stripped of its religious and ethical meaning, tends to become associated with purely mundane passions, which often actually give it the character of sport. (Weber 1958, 181-82)

Weber's thesis about the causal contribution of Puritan religion to the emergence of capitalism in the West is much contested by historians; by contrast, his view about the nature of economic behavior within capitalism is the orthodoxy of modern economists. With more than a touch of irony in his prose, the economist Amartya Sen, in his recent book entitled

On Ethics and Economics, gives this characterization of the view that most of his fellow economists hold of their discipline: "Perhaps the economist might be personally allowed a moderate dose of friendliness, provided in his economic models he keeps the motivations of human beings pure, simple and hard-headed, and not messed up by such things as goodwill or moral sentiments" (Sen 1987, 1).

The church and its representatives continue to pour forth pronouncements on economic life. Some of these are critical of what transpires in the economy; some are legitimating. Some are aimed at motivating people to continue doing what they are already doing; some are aimed at motivating people to change what they are doing. Materialism is condemned, charity is urged, stewardship is praised, the dignity of work is celebrated, God is thanked for blessings received and petitioned for blessings hoped for. But all of this noise makes no difference. The economy as a whole proceeds exactly as if none of these preachments had ever been made; and individual believers *do* function and *must* function within the economy just like everyone else, each pursuing his or her interests. No longer can anyone give "a genuinely Christian character" to his or her economic life.

I want to consider whether this Weberian picture is correct; and I want to consider whether it is correct on two levels. Is it true that Christian ethical convictions have become irrelevant to our *motivations and dispositions* as we engage in economic activity in a capitalist system? And is it true that Christian ethical convictions have become irrelevant to our *appraisal of the social outcome* of our economic activity?

Christianity applauds a wide array of motivations and dispositions. But it does not regard the motives and virtues that it applauds as a mere grab bag. It sees them all as organized, in one way or another, around a core motive and virtue: that of love or care. So we can conveniently ask the first of our two questions this way: Is care irrelevant to economic activity within our modern capitalist system?

And how shall we pose our question concerning appraisal of the social outcome? Most of us who are academics in the West manage to work and play without coming into contact with impoverished people. Nonetheless, the plight of the poor has been brought to the attention of those of us who read liberation theology by the insistent presence of the poor in those works and to the attention of all of us by our public media. So I propose balancing the extreme generality of our question about the relevance of care to economic motivation and disposition with a somewhat more limited and focused question at this point. I shall retrieve from the Christian tradition a principle concerning justice to the poor, and then ask whether that principle has any relevance to appraising the social outcome of our modern capitalist economy. As it turns out, the principle I have in mind, though it emerges from principles deep in Christianity and was affirmed by prominent thinkers and influential preachers throughout most of the history of Christianity, is now almost forgotten. So let's begin by retrieving that principle.

The Rights of the Poor

Well along in the stately, unperturbed fugal discourse of his *Summa Theologica*, Aquinas, after arguing that theft and robbery are always *mortal* sins, adds this provocative clarification:

> In cases of need all things are common property, so that there would seem to be no sin in taking another's property, for need has made it common. . . . Since . . . there are many who are in need, while it is impossible for all to be succored by means of the same thing, each one is entrusted with the stewardship of his own things, so that out of them he may come to the aid of those who are in need. Nevertheless, if the need be so manifest and urgent, that it is evident that the present need must be remedied by whatever means be at hand (for instance when a person is in some imminent danger, and there is no other possible remedy), then it is lawful for a man to succor his own need by means of another's property, by taking it either openly or secretly: nor is this properly speaking theft or robbery. (*S. Th.* II-II, q.66, a.7, *resp.*)

> It is not theft, properly speaking, to take secretly and use another's property in a case of extreme need: because that which he takes for the support of his life becomes his own property by reason of that need. (II-II, q.66, a.7, *ad* 2)

The most striking point in this passage is, of course, the remedy that Aquinas permits: when no other recourse is available, it is morally permissible for the extremely impoverished person to take what he or she needs for sustenance from the person with plenty. Aquinas adds that "in a case of a like need a man may also take secretly another's property in order to succor his neighbor in need" (II-II, q.66, a.7, *ad* 3). On this occasion, however, I am less interested in Aquinas's permission of this remedy, striking though it is, and more interested in his understanding of the evil to which "taking" is a permissible remedy.

In the course of his comment, Aquinas speaks about the *duties* of the better-off toward the poor: "Each one is entrusted with the stewardship of his own things, so that out of them he may come to the aid of those who are in need." But Aquinas does not content himself with speaking about the duties of the better-off; it's not even his main point here. His main point is about the *rights,* the *claim-rights,* of the poor. It's true that he doesn't use the word "rights." But the thought is there nonetheless. The suggestion one rather often hears — that the concept of rights is a modern invention — is patently false. If some parcel of food that you need for your survival is in the legal possession of someone else who does not need it for his survival, then it's yours, in the sense that you have a morally legitimate claim on it. And if, to exercise this right, it's necessary for you to *take it,* whether "openly or secretly," then that's permitted, since you would only be taking what is morally yours — that is, what you have a morally legitimate claim to. An implication is that should the better-off person *offer it* to you, that is not to be regarded as an act of charity on his part — not, at least, of supererogatory charity — but as an act of extending to you what you have a morally legitimate claim to — extending to you what is yours by (moral) right.

Underlying Aquinas's discussion is the assumption that we all have a natural right to access to means of sustenance — genuine and fair access. Perhaps it's possible to act in such a way that one forfeits this right. And no doubt the right is a *situationally conditioned* right in the sense that if one finds oneself in a situation so appallingly bad that no means of sustenance are available, then one doesn't have a morally legitimate claim to means of sustenance. Furthermore, what a given person needs for sustenance may, though available, be so exotic and expensive that satisfying this right would infringe on the rights of others; the right may be, in that sense, *defeasible.* And of course it's not just obvious what is to count as a means of sustenance: food that nourishes, of course; but what degree of avoidable toxicity is allowable without rights being violated? Neither here nor elsewhere does Aquinas go into these matters. Nor does he reflect on better and worse arrangements for securing our common human right to genuine and fair access to means of sustenance. These issues are of course important. On this occasion, however, I must set them all off to the side and concentrate on Aquinas's fundamental assumption: we human beings all have a *natural right* to genuine and fair access to means of sustenance.

In all his work, Aquinas thought of himself as *interpreting* the tradition handed on to him; there's no note of the modern hubris of beginning over. So too here. Aquinas cites the words of Ambrose, embodied in the Decretals: "It is the hungry man's bread that you withhold, the naked man's cloak that you store away; the money that you bury in the earth is the price of the poor man's ransom and freedom." He might also have cited the following words of Ambrose: "Not from your own do you bestow upon the poor man, but you make return from what is his" (from Avila 1983, 50). And he might have cited the following words from Basil of Caesarea:

> Will not one be called a thief who steals the garment of one already clothed, and is one deserving of any other title who will not clothe the naked if he is able to do so?
>
> That bread which you keep, belongs to the hungry; that coat which you preserve in your wardrobe, to the naked; those shoes which are rotting in your possession, to the shoeless; that gold which you have hidden in the ground, to the needy. Wherefore, as often as you were able to help others, and refused, so often did you do them wrong. (from Avila 1983, 66)

As usual, however, it was John Chrysostom who stated the point most vividly — and in this case also with the greatest acuity:

> This also is theft, not to share one's possessions. Perhaps this statement seems surprising to you, but do not be surprised. I shall bring you testimony from the divine Scriptures, saying that not only the theft of others' goods but also the failure to share one's own goods with others is theft and swindle and defraudation. . . .
>
> Just as an official in the imperial treasury, if he neglects to distribute where he is ordered, but spends instead for his own indolence, pays the penalty and is put to death, so also the rich man is a kind of steward of the money which is owed for distribution to the poor. He is directed to distribute it to his fellow servants who are in want. So if he spends more on himself than his needs require, he will pay the harshest penalty hereafter. For his own goods are not his own, but belong to his fellow servants. . . .
>
> The poor man has one plea, his want and his standing in need:

do not require anything else from him; but even if he is the most wicked of all men and is at a loss for his necessary sustenance, let us free him from hunger. . . . The almsgiver is a harbor for those in necessity: a harbor receives all who have encountered shipwreck; and frees them from danger; whether they are bad or good or whatever they are who are in danger, it escorts them into its own shelter. So you likewise, when you see on earth the man who encountered the shipwreck of poverty, do not judge him, do not seek an account of his life, but free him from his misfortune. . . .

Need alone is the poor man's worthiness; if anyone at all ever comes to us with this recommendation, let us not meddle any further. We do not provide for the manners but for the man. We show mercy on him not because of his virtue but because of his misfortune, in order that we ourselves may receive from the Master His great mercy. . . .

I beg you remember this without fail, that not to share our own wealth with the poor is theft from the poor and deprivation of their means of life; we do not possess our own wealth but theirs. (Chrysostom 1984, 49-55)

Down through the ages, the church has often spoken to the well-to-do of their *duty* to see to it that the poor have access to means of sustenance — probably more often than it has spoken of the *right* of the poor to such access. In the passages quoted the talk is all about the rights of the poor. The talk is not about the *moral guilt* of the well-to-do who fail or refuse to make such means of sustenance available but about the *moral injury* to the poor who do not enjoy what they have a right to.

The line of thought underlying this strand of Christian ethical reflection was clearly articulated by Aquinas in the same article that I have already cited. "According to the natural order established by Divine Providence, inferior things are ordained for the purpose of succoring man's needs by their means," says Aquinas. Aquinas does not take this as implying that all private property arrangements are wrong — not even that all allotments of *means of sustenance* to persons as their private property are wrong. Instead, he takes it to imply that private property arrangements must satisfy a certain condition if they are to be in accord with natural moral law. Nothing in natural moral law specifies which property is to be assigned to whom; "the division and appropriation of property . . . proceeds from human law." But if the property arrangement we select is to be in accord with natural law, we must keep in mind that since "man's needs have to be remedied by means of [inferior things] . . . , whatever certain people have in superabundance is due, by natural law, to the purpose of succoring the poor."

The contrast with the main tradition of modern liberal thought, with its near-exclusive emphasis on negative rights and civil liberties, is stark. Nonetheless, in spite of the fact that John Locke was indisputably the great founding father of modern liberalism, the line of Christian thought to which I have pointed was still alive in Locke. It's true that he spends no time developing the thought that there is a natural human right to genuine and fair access to means of sustenance; his attention was elsewhere. But the acknowledgment is unmistakably there at the very beginning of the chapter entitled "Of Property" in his *Second Treatise:*

> Whether we consider natural *reason*, which tells us that men, being once born, have a right to their preservation, and consequently to meat and drink, and such other things as nature affords for their subsistence: or *revelation*, which gives us an account of those grants God made of the world to Adam, and to Noah, and his sons, it is very clear that God, as King David says, *Psal* cxv.16. *has given the earth to the children of men;* given it to mankind in common. (§25)

Taking for granted these two classic Christian themes, that we all have a natural right to means of sustenance and that God has given the world to human beings in common, the question that drew Locke's attention was how it can be that "any one should ever come to have a *property* in any thing." What he will "endeavour to shew," says Locke, is "how men might come to have a *property* in several parts of that which God gave to mankind in common, and that without any express compact of all the commoners." Most of the Christian tradition before Locke would have assumed that the answer to this question would lie in the origin of the fundamental elements of a particular society's legal arrangements concerning property. From Locke's discussion it becomes clear, however, that he is assuming that property rights are not simply a matter of "human law." He is assuming that although the earth was given by God to human beings in common for their sustenance, nonetheless each normal adult human being has a *natural moral right* to certain items of property and not to others; he wants to know how that comes about.

His ingenious and influential answer, as we all know, begins with the claim that "every man has a *property* in his own *person:* this no body has any right to but himself" (§27). Although the plants and minerals of the earth have been given by God to all of us in common, *my body* has not been given to everyone in common; it belongs only to me, by natural moral right. But Locke does not linger over this dark saying, that by natural right we each have exclusive title of possession to that particular human body which is ours. Instead, he moves on to claim that it follows that by natural right each person also has exclusive title of possession to the *bodily labor* that he or she engages in: "The *labour* of his body, and the *work* of his hands, we may say, are properly his." And from this Locke infers, in turn, that each person, by natural right, has exclusive title of possession to whatever, from the common stock of nature, he puts the imprint of his labor on:

> Whatsoever then he removes out of the state that nature hath provided, and left it in, he hath mixed his *labour* with, and joined to it something that is his own, and thereby makes it his *property.* It being by him removed from the common state nature hath placed it in, it hath by this *labour* something annexed to it, that excludes the common right of other men: for this *labour* being the unquestionable property of the labourer, no man but he can have a right to what that is once joined to. (§27)

What is important to notice, for our purposes, is that Locke's opening affirmations lead him at once to attach two conditions to one's right to that which bears the imprint of one's labor; the metamorphosis of Locke's thought into standard modern liberal thought required forgetting these two conditions.[1] The first condition is that, in Locke's words, "there is enough, and as good, left in common for others" (§27). And the second condition is that, "of those good things which nature hath provided in common, every one had a right (as hath been said) to as much as he could use, and *property* in all that he could effect with his *labour;* all that his *industry* could extend to, to alter from the state nature had put it in, was his. He that *gathered* a hundred bushels of acorns or apples, had thereby a *property* in them, they were his goods as soon as gathered. He was only to

---

1. It might be thought that Locke himself, as his discussion proceeds, forgets this opening affirmation of our natural human right to means of sustenance. Not so. To cite just one piece of evidence: Late in his discussion, in §183, Locke says that "the fundamental law of nature being, that all, as much as may be, should be preserved. . . ."

look that he used them before they spoiled, else he took more than his share, and robbed others" (§46).[2] "Nothing was made by God for man to spoil or destroy" (§30; cf. §37).

In the "state of nature," if an area became heavily settled, then by compact "the several *communities* settled the bounds of their distinct territories, and by laws within themselves regulated the properties of the private men of their society, and so, *by compact* and agreement, *settled the property* which labour and industry began" (§45; cf. §38). In a somewhat similar way, one can contract one's labor to another (§85). But it was Locke's argument that such compacts and contracts presuppose that we each have a natural moral right to certain things — specifically, to our labor and to that which bears its imprint.

What about a society in which money — that is, nonperishable items whose value is exchange rather than use — has been introduced? To such items, the proviso "No more than one can use" simply lacks application. What holds in this case is rather the following:

> Gold and silver, being little useful to the life of man in proportion to food, raiment, and carriage, has its *value* only from the consent of men, whereof *labour* yet *makes*, in great part, *the measure*, it is plain, that men have agreed to a disproportionate and unequal *possession of the earth*, they having, by a tacit and voluntary consent, found out a way how a man may fairly possess more land than he himself can use the product of, by receiving in exchange for the overplus gold and silver, which may be hoarded up without injury to any one. (§50)

The flow of Locke's argument is surprising indeed, not to mention obscure and controversial at many points. He begins with the conviction that we each have a natural right to our labor and to that which bears its imprint, subject to qualifications which flow from the conviction that God

---

2. The passage continues thus: "If he . . . bartered away plums, that would have rotted in a week, for nuts that would last good for his eating a whole year, he did no injury; he wasted not the common stock; destroyed no part of the portion of goods that belonged to others, so long as nothing perished uselessly in his hands. Again, if he would give his nuts for a piece of metal, pleased with its colour; or exchange his sheep for shells, or wool for a sparkling pebble or a diamond, and keep those by him all his life, he invaded not the right of others, he might heap up as much of these durable things as he pleased; the *exceeding of the bounds of his just property* not lying in the largeness of his possession, but the perishing of any thing uselessly in it" (§46).

has given the world to all of us in common for our sustenance. By the end it turns out that just by using the monetary system of our economy and consenting to the property laws of our society we have bartered and contracted away what we possess by natural right, so that now we rightly possess pretty much all and only what our economy and laws say we do. About this culmination of his argument, however, Locke is at pains to say that there are some things which no one can rightly be thought to have disposed of by agreement or contract; and among those is one's natural right to the means of self-preservation:

> [The legislative] power, in the utmost bounds of it, is *limited to the public good* of the society. It is a power, that hath no other end but preservation, and therefore can never have a right to destroy, enslave, or designedly to impoverish the subjects. The obligations of the law of nature cease not in society, but only in many cases are drawn closer, and have by human laws known penalties annexed to them, to enforce their observation. Thus the law of nature stands as an eternal rule to all men, *legislators* as well as others. The *rules* that they make for other men's actions must, as well as their own and other men's actions, be conformable to the law of nature, *i.e.* to the will of God, of which that is a declaration, and the *fundamental law of nature being the preservation of mankind,* no human sanction can be good, or valid against it. (§135)

This passage leaves no room for doubt that the long Christian tradition to which I have pointed — that there is a natural human right to means of sustenance — was still alive in Locke. Though Locke's account of property rights was in many ways innovative, he continued to affirm the ancient Christian teaching that a morally acceptable system of property arrangements must honor this right. The notion that the moral significance of involuntary avoidable poverty is that the poor have somehow failed in their duties, or that the well-to-do have failed fully to implement their duties of almsgiving, is not to be found in Locke.

Is Care Irrelevant?

About ten years ago now I served — quite amazingly — as a philosophical consultant to the Herman Miller Furniture Company in Zeeland, Michigan. Max de Pree, the executive officer of the company, had invited an architect, a physician, a journalist, a furniture designer, a theologian, and me to an all-day session with him and about five of the top officers in his company. At the beginning of the day he posed ten questions that he wanted us to discuss, in whatever order we wished. He asked us not to concern ourselves with trying to say things that we thought would be useful to the company; he wanted the discussion to take whatever shape it wanted to take. I remember three of the questions. "What is the purpose of business?" Some of his younger executives were saying that the purpose of business was to make money. He himself didn't believe that; but he wanted to talk about it. Second, he wondered whether there was "a moral imperative," as he called it, for companies to produce products of good design. And third, he wanted to discuss whether it was possible to preserve what he called "intimacy" in a large company.

In the course of the discussion it became clear what de Pree himself regarded as the purpose of business. The purpose was twofold: to produce products that serve a genuine need and are aesthetically good, and to provide meaningful work in pleasant surroundings for those employed in the company. He added that these purposes had for a long time shaped his operation of the company.

Now it seems to me that these two purposes are, or can be, an expression of love or care — that is, both consist in seeking to promote the well-being of the other. It became clear in the course of the discussion that it was de Pree's religious commitment — specifically, his Christian commitment — that had led him to embrace these goals. He saw his operation of the company as an exercise of care — though he didn't use that word. His own case, at least as he presented it, was a case of "transcendental faith" shaping economic activity.

Was he prevaricating? Or was he deluded?

One would think he was if one adhered to the view of human motivation that Amartya Sen, in the book I cited, attributes to his fellow modern economists. Let us look into that view a bit. And since the generalizations and observations by a highly skilled economist like Sen about the views of economists carry more weight than those of a non-economist like myself, let me make liberal use of Sen's helpful and pointed discussion.

Sen observes (Sen 1987, 12) that the view typical of modern economists, that human beings are motivated by the desire to maximize self-interest, is typically arrived at, or supported, by two moves: the identification of actual behavior with rational behavior, and the identification of rational behavior with the attempt to maximize self-interest. There are some economists who give an alternative characterization of rational behavior — namely, as behavior that exhibits internal consistency of choice. But if that is how rational behavior is identified, the claim that actual behavior is rational behavior does not yield the conclusion that ethical considerations play no role in determining motivations in economic behavior; accordingly, for our purposes here, we can set this alternative characterization of rational behavior off to the side. It may be added that the characterization of rational behavior as consistent-choice behavior is not, as a matter of fact, at all plausible. Sen makes the relevant point: "If a person does exactly the opposite of what would help achieving what he or she would want to achieve, and does this with flawless internal consistency . . . , the person can scarcely be seen as rational, even if that dogged consistency inspires some kind of an astonished admiration on the part of the observer" (13).

As to the majority's characterization of rational behavior, why, Sen asks, "should it be *uniquely* rational to pursue one's own self-interest to the exclusion of everything else? . . . To argue that anything other than maximizing self-interest must be irrational seems altogether extraordinary. The self-interest view of rationality involves *inter alia* a firm rejection of the 'ethics-related' view of motivation. Trying to do one's best to achieve what one would like to achieve can be a part of rationality, and this can include the promotion of non-self-interest goals which we may value and wish to aim at" (15). "Universal selfishness . . . as a requirement of *rationality* is patently absurd" (16). In short, the typical economist's way of getting to the conclusion that people always try to maximize their self-interest — by identifying actual behavior with rational behavior and rational behavior with behavior aimed at maximizing self-interest — will not do.

But may it be the case that though the argument is bad, the conclusion is correct? Or, more cautiously, may it be the case that, however human beings act in general, this is how they act in economic matters? "Does the so-called 'economic man,' pursuing his own interests, provide the best approximation to the behaviour of human beings, at least in economic matters?" (16). It appeared to de Pree that his motivations in the operation of his company were not confined to the attempt to maximize his self-interest. Have economists discovered something about human nature which makes it clear that de Pree was mistaken about that?

Apparently not. "While assertions of conviction are plentiful," says Sen, "factual findings are rare" (18). He adds, "Sometimes the alleged case for assuming self-interested action seems to be based on its expected results — arguing that this would lead to efficient outcomes. The success of some free-market economies, such as Japan, in producing efficiency has also been cited as some evidence in the direction of the self-interest theory. However, the success of a free market does not tell us anything at all about what *motivation* lies behind the action of economic agents in such an economy. Indeed, in the case of Japan, there is strong empirical evidence to suggest that systematic departures from self-interested behaviour in the direction of duty, loyalty and goodwill have played a substantial part in industrial success. . . . [We] are beginning to see the development of a whole range of alternative theories about economic behaviour to achieve industrial success, based on comparative studies of different societies with different prevalent value systems" (18-19).

Max Weber's reasons for holding to the view that a capitalist economy is an autonomous sphere of human action to which ethical considerations are irrelevant were more subtle than those of the modern economists Sen has in mind. Weber was not of the view that human motivation, *by nature,* is exclusively self-interested — quite to the contrary: "The magical and religious forces, and the ethical ideas of duty based upon them, have in the past always been among the most important formative influences on conduct" (Weber 1958, 27). Weber's thought ran along the following lines: every society can be thought of as offering to its members various roles for them to play; among the roles that European feudal society offered to its members were those of lord and serf. Prominent among the roles Western society offers are those of entrepreneur and employee.

These roles of entrepreneur and employee are different in a number of ways from the roles offered by medieval society. First, they are *economic* roles, whereas the roles of lord and serf had, at best, an economic *dimension.* Between us and medieval Europe lies the social sectoring of which Weber makes so much.

Second, the roles of lord and serf were *ethically infused.* To play the role of lord or serf was not just to act in a certain typical and coherent way but was to see oneself, and be seen, as subject to a specific cluster of *requirements* with respect to one's fellow human beings, the fulfillment of these being enforced and reinforced by social expectations. To have the role of serf was to be required to spend a high proportion of one's time laboring for the lord of the manor; to have the role of lord was to be required to provide protection and security to one's serfs. These requirements were, for the most part, not legal requirements. But neither were they merely instrumental requirements — that is, causal conditions for achieving one's goals. They were *moral* requirements, matters of duty and right. And in good measure they were not just *general* moral requirements pertaining to all persons in all roles whatsoever; rather, a specific ethic was attached to a specific role. To occupy a certain station in life was to be subject to a specific set of duties and enjoy a specific set of rights.

By contrast, the role of entrepreneur in a capitalist society is defined not by a particular configuration of rights and duties to other members of society but by the goal of operating an enterprise for profit; and the role of laborer in a capitalist society is likewise defined not by a particular configuration of rights and duties to other members of society but by working for contracted wages. In place of person-to-person rights and duties defining one's station in life, there is the impersonal goal of making money, be it in the role of entrepreneur or in the role of worker. An *ethic* of personal relations has been replaced by a *calling* to work for that impersonal thing called "money." All that's left by way of an ethic — that is, by way of duties to one's fellow human beings — is the ethic of contract.

Third, no matter what roles a society offers to its members, those members have to learn to play those roles. They have to acquire the requisite character formation, the requisite "ethos," the requisite complex of cognitions and abilities and dispositions. That was true for medieval society; it remains true for modern society. But here too Weber saw a difference: the roles of entrepreneur and laborer require vastly more discipline, more "rationalization," than the roles offered by medieval society — that of monk and nun excepted! Our capitalist economy is not the whole of our modern life, however; and the fact that such a character formation is necessary for the working of the economy does not imply that the same is needed for the totality of life in modern society, nor does it imply anything about human nature — other, of course, than that human nature is sufficiently malleable to submit to such formation.

Getting a capitalist economy to emerge out of the seedbed of traditionalism required a special impetus; supposedly the early Protestants, with their preachments about working with religious devotion in one's calling, provided that special impetus. But as mentioned earlier, now that the system is in place, it perpetuates itself by rewarding disciplined pursuit of wages and profit and by punishing other modes of behavior. Other behavior still occurs, of course; but over the long haul it gets snuffed out by the competition of the marketplace.

Let me quote Weber himself:

The impulse to acquisition, pursuit of gain, of money, of the greatest possible amount of money, . . . exists and has existed among waiters, physicians, coachmen, artists, prostitutes, dishonest officials, soldiers, nobles, crusaders, gamblers, and beggars. . . . Unlimited greed for gain is not in the least identical with capitalism, and is still less its spirit. Capitalism . . . is identical with the pursuit of profit, and forever *renewed* profit, by means of continuous, rational, capitalistic enterprise. . . . We will define a capitalistic economic action as one which rests on the expectation of profit by the utilization of opportunities for exchange, that is on (formally) peaceful chances of profit. (Weber 1958, 17)

The earning of money within the modern economic order is, so long as it is done legally, the result and the expression of virtue and proficiency in a calling. . . . This peculiar idea, so familiar to us today, but in reality so little a matter of course, of one's duty in a calling, is what is most characteristic of the social ethic of capitalistic culture, and is in a sense the fundamental basis of it. It is an obligation which the individual is supposed to feel and does feel towards the content of his professional activity, no matter in what it consists. . . . Of course, [we do not] . . . maintain that a conscious acceptance of these ethical maxims on the part of the individuals, entrepreneurs or labourers, in modern capitalistic enterprises, is a condition of the further existence of present-day capitalism. The capitalistic economy of the present is an immense cosmos into which the individual is born, and which presents itself to him, at least as an individual, as an unalterable order of things in which he must live. It forces the individual, in so far as he is involved in the system of market relationships, to conform to capitalistic rules of action. The manufacturer who in the long run acts counter to these norms, will just as inevitably be eliminated from the economic scene as the worker who cannot or will not adapt himself to them will be thrown into the streets without a job.

Thus the capitalism of today, which has come to dominate economic life, educates and selects the economic subjects which it needs through a process of economic survival of the fittest. But here one can easily see the limits of the concept of selection as a means of historical explanation. In order that a manner of life so well adapted to the peculiarities of capitalism could be selected at all, i.e.

should come to dominate others, it had to originate somewhere, and not in isolated individuals alone, but as a way of life common to whole groups of men. This origin is what really needs explanation. (Weber 1958, 53-55)[3]

I think we can all agree that there are profound insights in Weber's analysis. All who lament one and another aspect of American society — its materialism, its acquisitiveness, and so forth — ought to take Weber's analysis with utmost seriousness. It is the habit of intellectuals to attribute socially pervasive phenomena such as materialism and acquisitiveness to the influence of certain ideas. Weber invites us to consider instead that materialism and acquisitiveness may be promoted by the character formation produced by, and required for, participation in our capitalistic economy.

But does Weber's analysis give any reason for concluding that Max de Pree was either deluded or prevaricating in stating that among the goals that guided him in the operation of the Herman Miller Company were those of providing to his employees worthwhile work in a pleasant environment, and of providing to his customers products that satisfy their genuine needs and are aesthetically good in design? I fail to see that it does. Weber reminds us that unless the Herman Miller Company turns a profit and unless there are persons available who will work for the wages it offers,

---

3. Cf. Weber 1958, 72-73: "At present under our individualistic political, legal, and economic institutions, with the forms of organization and general structure which are peculiar to our economic order, this spirit of capitalism might be understandable, as has been said, purely as a result of adaptation. The capitalistic system so needs this devotion to the calling of making money, it is an attitude toward material goods which is so well suited to that system, so intimately bound up with the conditions of survival in the economic struggle for existence, that there can today no longer be any question of a necessary connection of that acquisitive manner of life with any single *Weltanschauung*. In fact, it no longer needs the support of any religious forces, and feels the attempts of religion to influence economic life, in so far as they can still be felt at all, to be as much an unjustified interference as its regulation by the State. In such circumstances men's commercial and social interests do tend to determine their opinions and attitudes. Whoever does not adapt his manner of life to the conditions of capitalistic success must go under, or at least cannot rise. But these are phenomena of a time in which modern capitalism has become dominant and has become emancipated from its old supports. But as it could at one time destroy the old forms of medieval regulation of economic life only in alliance with the growing power of the modern State, the same, we may say provisionally, may have been the case in its relations with religious forces. Whether and in what sense that was the case, it is our task to investigate. For that the conception of money-making as an end in itself to which people were bound, as a calling, was contrary to the ethical feelings of whole epochs, it is hardly necessary to prove."

it will go out of existence. Of course de Pree knew that. And the Herman Miller Company was in fact making a profit; it was successful. But instead of setting profit-making as the all-consuming goal of his economic endeavors, de Pree viewed profit-making simply as a condition that must be satisfied if he and his company were to serve employees and customers in the way he desired. As he put it to me once, "you don't live to breathe, you breathe to live."

At some point in the future he might be forced to make some difficult choices. The competition might prove such that, for the company to continue to make a profit, it would have to make the work less fulfilling or its environment less pleasant, or would have to skimp on good design or produce items that, in de Pree's view, did not satisfy any genuine need. But that is no reason for concluding that ethical considerations *did not in fact* motivate his actions. And the case of Japan, to which Sen referred, makes clear that concern for the welfare of one's workers is not always, given one's competition, an affordable luxury; sometimes it "makes good business sense."

What's also true is that the love or care that came to expression in de Pree's actions was, as it were, extra-systemic in origin. Whereas to learn the role of lord was to learn one's moral rights and duties vis à vis one's serfs, it can scarcely be said that to learn the role of entrepreneur in a capitalist economy is to learn one's moral rights and duties vis à vis one's workers and customers. One has to learn those elsewhere. But of course the important point is not *where* they are learned but *whether* they are learned. Perhaps there are good reasons for supposing that the "ethos" of capitalism endangers the moral life whereas the "ethos" of feudalism promoted it; but if so, that then is the point to make, rather than that the capitalist system snuffs out ethically motivated action.

Capitalism, says Weber, "is identical with the pursuit of profit, and forever *renewed* profit, by means of continuous, rational, capitalistic enterprise. For it must be so: in a wholly capitalistic order of society, an individual capitalistic enterprise which did not take advantage of its opportunities for profit-making would be doomed to extinction" (Weber 1958, 17). The claim of the last sentence is correct: the enterprise in a capitalist economy that does not turn a profit is doomed, sooner or later, to extinction — unless it is in some way "propped up." Hence it is also true that the pursuit of profit is an essential component in the defining structure of a capitalist economy. But it does not follow that all entrepreneurs — not even all *successful* entrepreneurs — are motivated in their economic activity just by the prospect of profit. There is no reason to question the appearance: ethical considerations play a prominent role in the economic activities of many entrepreneurs, sometimes even at the cost of what unadulterated self-interest would call for. Lest too idealized a picture emerge, let me add that motives and emotions such as jealousy, spite, and vindictiveness also play a role, also sometimes at the cost of what unadulterated self-interest would call for.

Is Justice Irrelevant?

Let us now move on to our second topic, the appraisal of the social outcome of a given capitalist economy. Are moral categories, such as that of *justice*, irrelevant to such appraisal? More particularly, are *religiously grounded* principles making use of the category of justice — such as the one I retrieved from the Christian tradition — somehow irrelevant to such appraisal?

Here I fail to see any support for this view that has even the pretense of plausibility. In each of our modern democratic polities we the citizens do in fact appraise the social outcome of our capitalist economies; and in each of them influential groups of citizens do in fact take steps to alter, or to try to alter, that outcome so that it becomes, in their judgment, more desirable, the most obvious of these steps being the passing of laws of various sorts. Libertarians argue that the outcome would be better if we refrained from all such attempts at manipulation; but of course their argument presupposes that influential citizens do in fact manage to alter the social outcome of the economy. It's true that modern economies confront us with difficult problems of "steerage" — to say the least! But steerage does, in fact, occur all the time.

Often the appraisals of outcome that motivate attempts at steerage make no use of moral categories; politicians aim just at increasing the GNP or at increasing the wealth of what they identify as their group. But that scarcely shows the irrelevance of moral appraisal and of morally guided attempts at steerage. In particular, I fail to see anything about a capitalist economy which renders irrelevant that ancient Christian principle of justice: every human being has a natural right to genuine and fair access to adequate means of sustenance. So far as I can see, the fact that this principle is seldom embraced, and rarely used, as a principle for appraisal of social outcome or as a guide for attempts at steerage has nothing at all to do with the fact that ours is a capitalist economy. Something else has led to its demise, and to our almost exclusive concern, when it comes to rights, with negative rights and civil liberties. Perhaps it's true that in the modern Western world Christianity is more a shaper of inward life and private relations and less a shaper of economic life in particular, and of public life in general, than was previously the case in the West. But if so, that is due more to the religious and convictional pluralism of modern Western society than to the fact that our economy is capitalist.

Rethinking Weber

Weber's overarching theory of modernization was that the essence of modernization is located in two related phenomena. It is located, in the first place, in the emergence of *differentiated spheres* — specifically, in the emergence of the differentiated *social spheres* of economy and state, along with household, and in the emergence of the differentiated *cultural spheres* of science, art, law, and ethics. The effect of this differentiation is that modes of thought and activity that once were subject to extraneous demands are now free to follow their own autonomous internal "logic." Previously art was intertwined with other cultural and social phenomena and in their service; now the artistic sphere has been differentiated from the other spheres of thought and action, liberated from their extraneous demands, and set free to follow its own internal dynamics so as to come into its own. Previously economic activity was intertwined with other social and cultural phenomena and in their service; now the economic sphere has been differentiated from other spheres of thought and action, liberated from their extraneous demands, and set free to follow its own internal dynamics and come into its own. So too for *Wissenschaft*, for politics, and so forth.

The essence of modernization is located, secondly, in the spread of rationalized thought and action within these spheres. Just as the fundamental dynamic of action without a modern, capitalist economy is the rationalized pursuit of profit, so the fundamental dynamic of action within our modern, bureaucratic states is rationalized administration, and the fundamental dynamic of *Wissenschaft* is rationalized pursuit of the facts. In the words of Weber's famous speech entitled "Science as Vocation," "The fate of our times is characterized by rationalization and intellectualization and, above all, by the 'disenchantment of the world.' Precisely the ultimate and most sublime values have retreated from public life either into the transcendental realm of mystic life or into the brotherliness of direct and personal human relations" (Weber 1946, 155).

We are all fated, says Weber, to work within the differentiated spheres of modern society and culture as if placed within a calling rather than as applying an ethic. To speak for a moment of the calling of those who labor in *Wissenschaft*, "one cannot demonstrate scientifically what the duty of an academic teacher is. One can only demand of the teacher that he have the intellectual integrity to see that it is one thing to state facts, to determine mathematical or logical relations or the internal structure of cultural values, while it is another thing to answer questions of the *value* of culture and its individual contents and the question of how one should act in the cultural community and in political associations. These are quite heterogeneous problems. If he asks further why he should not deal with both types of problems in the lecture-room, the answer is: because the prophet and the demagogue do not belong on the academic platform. . . . I am ready to prove from the works of our historians that whenever the man of science introduces his personal value judgment, a full understanding of the facts *ceases*" (Weber 1946, 146).[4]

The view that embedded within *Wissenschaft* is a relentless value-free "logic" impervious to ethical and religious values, and that all who choose the "calling" of teacher or researcher must submit to that logic or be tossed out as prophet or demagogue, today seems less and less plausible to more and more of us. I submit that we ought to be just as skeptical of those counterpart claims of Weber concerning the economy. Religious commitments and ethical concerns have not disappeared from art, nor from politics, nor from academic learning, nor from the economy. There is, admittedly, something compellingly gripping in the icy melancholy of Weber's elegant picture of differentiated sectors each relentlessly playing out its own internal autonomous meaningless logic on a disenchanted world, with religion consigned to the mystical and the privately personal. The truth is much more messy. Religious commitment and ethical concern

---

4. "The task of the teacher is to serve the students with his knowledge and scientific experience and not to imprint upon them his personal political views. It is certainly possible that the individual teacher will not entirely succeed in eliminating his personal sympathies. He is then exposed to the sharpest criticism in the forum of his own conscience. And this deficiency does not prove anything; other errors are also possible, for instance, erroneous statements of fact, and yet they prove nothing against the duty of searching for the truth" (Weber 1946, 146).

shape economic activity under capitalism very differently from the way they shaped it under the "traditionalism" that is Weber's ever-present foil to capitalism; but they continue to shape it. It is those differences, then, that we must study — rather than assuming present-day absence and studying to see how absence emerged from once-upon-a-time presence. Possibly it is also true that religious commitment and ethical concern shape economic activity less under capitalism than they did under "traditionalism." But do we know that?

Bibliography

Avila, Charles. 1983. *Ownership: Early Christian Teaching*. Maryknoll: Orbis Books.

Chrysostom, St. John. 1984. *On Wealth and Poverty*. Translated by Catharine P. Roth. Crestwood: St. Vladimir's Seminary Press.

Goldmann, Lucien. 1973. *The Philosophy of the Enlightenment: The Christian Burgess and the Enlightenment*. Translated by Henry Maas. Cambridge: MIT Press.

Sen, Amartya. 1987. *On Ethics and Economics*. Oxford: Basil Blackwell.

Weber, Max. 1946 [1906]. *From Max Weber: Essays in Sociology*. Translated and edited by H. H. Gerth and C. Wright Mills. New York: Oxford University Press.

_____. 1958 [1904-5]. *The Protestant Ethic and the Spirit of Capitalism*. Translated by Talcott Parsons. New York: Charles Scribner's Sons.

Justice, Not Charity:
Social Work through the Eyes of Faith

I. The Charter of Christian Social Work

From near the beginnings of Christianity, the speech of Jesus in Matthew 25 about the Great Assize, as it was traditionally called, has been seen as the grand charter of Christian social work.

Though the passage is familiar, it will be important to have it before us; here it is in the translation of the New Revised Standard Version (NRSV). It's my judgment that the NRSV mistranslates the Greek at two crucial junctures; but we'll get to that later. It might be asked why I use the NRSV translation if I judge that it is a mistranslation. The answer is that every other translation currently available mistranslates the Greek at the same two points.

> When the Son of Man comes in all his glory, and all the angels with him, then he will sit on the throne of his glory. All the nations will be gathered before him, and he will separate people one from another as a shepherd separates the sheep from the goats, and he will put the sheep at his right hand and the goats at the left. Then the king will say to those at his right hand, "Come, you that are blessed by my Father, inherit the kingdom prepared for you from the foundation of the world, for I was hungry and you gave me food, I was thirsty and you gave me something to drink, I was a stranger and you welcomed me, I was naked and you gave me clothing, I was sick and you took care of me, I was in prison and you visited

me." Then the righteous will answer him, "Lord, when was it that we saw you hungry and gave you food, or thirsty and gave you something to drink? And when was it that we saw you a stranger and welcomed you, or naked and gave you clothing? And when was it that we saw you sick or in prison and visited you?" And the king will answer them, "Truly I tell you, just as you did it to one of the least of these who are members of my family, you did it to me." Then he will say to those at his left hand, "You that are accursed, depart from me into the eternal fire prepared for the devil and his angels; for I was hungry and you gave me no food, I was thirsty and you gave me nothing to drink, I was a stranger and you did not welcome me, naked and you did not give me clothing, sick and in prison and you did not visit me." Then they also will answer, "Lord, when was it that we saw you hungry or thirsty or a stranger or naked or sick or in prison, and did not take care of you?" Then he will answer them, "Truly I tell you, just as you did not do it to one of the least of these, you did not do it to me." And these will go away into eternal punishment, but the righteous into eternal life. (Matthew 25:31-46)

I share the view that this passage can be seen as the grand charter of Christian social work. English-speaking people of the modern world almost always misinterpret it, however. They interpret Jesus as talking about charity, and they understand charity as pitted against justice. They understand Jesus to be saying that in practicing charity toward the unfortunates of society, we are treating Jesus himself with charity. I find it beyond reasonable doubt that the passage is not about charity but about justice. Jesus is saying that to fail to treat the naked, the hungry, the imprisoned, and so forth with justice is to wrong Jesus himself.

The context within which those who heard Jesus would have interpreted his words was, of course, the Hebrew Scriptures. So let me begin my argument for how the passage should be interpreted there. The writers of the Old Testament speak often about justice. And, as many commentators have noted, one of the most striking features of their talk about justice is that the presence or absence of justice in society is regularly connected with the fate of the widows, the orphans, the aliens, and the poor. Some or all of the members of this quartet regularly get special attention when justice, *mishpat,* is under consideration in the presentation of the original legal code, in the accusations by the prophets of violations of the code, and

in the complaints of the psalmist about violations. There is nothing remotely like this mantra of the widows, the orphans, the aliens, and the impoverished in John Locke's discussion of justice in his *Second Treatise*, nor
is there anything remotely like it in the discussions of justice by Plato, Aristotle, or Kant.

Let me cite just a few passages from the many that could be cited. In
Deuteronomy 24:17 Moses enjoins the people, "You shall not deprive a resident alien or an orphan of justice; you shall not take a widow's garment in
pledge." In Deuteronomy 27:19 the priests call out, in a ritualized cursing
ceremony, "Cursed be anyone who deprives the alien, the orphan, and the
widow of justice"; to which the people say, "Amen." In Isaiah 1:17, the
prophet says

> Seek justice,
>   rescue the oppressed,
> defend the orphan,
>   plead for the widow.

And in 10:1-2 he excoriates those

> who make iniquitous decrees,
>   who write oppressive statutes,
> to turn aside the needy from justice,
>   and to rob the poor of my people of their right,
> that widows may be your spoil,
>   and that you may make the orphans your prey!

The widows, the orphans, the resident aliens, and the impoverished were
the *bottom ones* in Israelite society, the *low ones*. That's how Israel's writers
spoke of them. Whereas you and I tend to use the metaphor of a circle and
to speak of such people as outsiders or on the periphery, Israel's writers
gravitated toward the metaphor of up and down. These people were at the
bottom of the social hierarchy. Israel's writers regularly describe rendering
justice to them as "lifting them up." Given their position at the bottom of
the social hierarchy, they were especially vulnerable to being treated with
injustice — vulnerable to being "downtrodden," as our older English
translations have it, vulnerable to being excluded from community. They
were *the quartet of the downtrodden and the excluded*.

A question we all want to ask is why Israel's writers placed so much emphasis on the downtrodden when talking about justice. You will find a number of explanations in the literature — as indeed you will find attempts by some writers to overlook or deny that there is any such emphasis. On this occasion I will have to forgo engaging the alternative explanations and simply present my own.

Israel's writers were not indifferent to attacks on the person and property of well-to-do persons and those who enjoyed social esteem; I could cite a number of passages to this effect. So that's not the explanation. It's the following. It's a truism that for any society whatsoever, those with the least social power and esteem are the most vulnerable to injustice, and hence the most likely actually to be suffering the most grievous forms of injustice. The basic reason for this is that robbery and assault are *events* or *episodes* in the lives of the wealthy or empowered. If the robbery is of a wealthy person, the robbery is an episode in a life that otherwise is usually going quite nicely. By contrast, it's likely that the *daily condition* of those without power and esteem is unjust. Widows are also victims of burglary and assault; episodes of injustice occur in their lives too. But in addition to such episodes, the *condition of their daily existence* is all-too-often unjust. Injustice pervades their lives in a way that it typically does not for those at the social top.

Add to this fact about society the aim or concern underlying the declarations about justice and injustice in the Old Testament. Discussions about justice can occur in the context of a variety of different aims and concerns. One's aim might be to set forth the basic social structure of a fully just society. Or it might be to discover the social and psychological causes of one and another kind of injustice in some actual society. Neither of these theoretical aims would require special attention to the plight of the vulnerable low ones in society. But suppose that one's aim is the practical aim of advancing the cause of justice in one's society. Then one has to make priority judgments. One has to decide where lie the greatest injustices and the greatest vulnerabilities in society, and focus one's attention there.

I suggest that it was because the concern of Israel's writers was practical rather than theoretical that the quartet of the downtrodden looms so large in their writings. What they say about justice and injustice occurs within the context of an imperative that they had heard from Yahweh and that they then announced to their fellows: seek justice, undo the bonds of injustice. Israel's religion was a religion of salvation, not of contemplation — that is what accounts for the mantra of the widows, the orphans, the aliens, and the poor. It was not, be it noted, a religion of salvation *from this earthly existence;* it was a religion of salvation *from injustice* in this earthly existence.

Now look once again at the passage on the Great Assize with which I began. Jesus speaks in the passage of being hungry, thirsty, naked, a stranger, sick, and imprisoned. It is of course the impoverished who are typically hungry, thirsty, and naked. So we can condense the list to the poor, the alien, the sick, and the imprisoned. It's hard not to see this as a variation on the Old Testament quartet of the downtrodden. The only item that might raise a question is the sick. Everybody, it may be said, gets sick. Yes indeed. But not all who are sick get no visitors. The sick Jesus has in mind are the lonely sick, the forgotten sick.

Now let me bring another well-known New Testament passage into the picture. Shortly after he began teaching and preaching in public, Jesus attended the local synagogue on a Sabbath and was invited to read from scripture and comment on what he read. "The scroll of the prophet Isaiah was given to him," says Luke, who tells the story. "He unrolled the scroll and found the place where it was written":

> The Spirit of the Lord is upon me,
> because he has anointed me to bring good news to the poor.
> He has sent me to proclaim release to the captives
> and recovery of sight to the blind,
> to let the oppressed go free,
> to proclaim the year of the Lord's favor.

Jesus then "rolled up the scroll, gave it back to the attendant, and sat down." "The eyes of all in the synagogue were fixed on him," says Luke, expecting him to say something. What Jesus then said is that "today this scripture has been fulfilled in your hearing" (Luke 4:17-21).

What are we to make of this self-identification? Well, the first thing to note is that in his report of what transpired in the synagogue, Luke conflated two Old Testament passages, one from Isaiah 58 and one from Isaiah 61. The former speaks of God's demand for justice:

> Is this not the fast that I choose:
>   to loose the bonds of injustice,
>   to undo the thongs of the yoke,
> to let the oppressed go free,
>   and to break every yoke?

Is it not to share your bread with the hungry,
and bring the homeless poor into your house;
when you see the naked, to cover them,
and not to hide yourself from your own kin?

(Isaiah 58:6-7)

The latter passage promises the deliverance and restoration of God's people by the anointed one:

The spirit of the Lord God is upon me,
because the Lord has anointed me;
he has sent me to bring good news to the oppressed,
to bind up the brokenhearted,
to proclaim liberty to the captives,
and release to the prisoners;
to proclaim the year of the Lord's favor,
and the day of vengeance of our God. . . .

(Isaiah 61:1-2)

The import is unmistakable. Jesus identified himself in the synagogue as God's anointed one, the Messiah, whose vocation it is to proclaim good news to the poor, the blind, the imprisoned, the oppressed — in short, whose vocation it is to proclaim that justice for the downtrodden and the excluded is on the way. Isaiah's examples of the downtrodden and the excluded are somewhat different from the standard Old Testament examples of widows, orphans, aliens, and the poor, just as Jesus' examples in the speech about the Great Assize are somewhat different. But there can be no doubt that the examples in each case are illustrations of those who are typically downtrodden and excluded. And there can be no doubt that the Old Testament writers and Jesus regarded the lifting up of the downtrodden and the incorporation of the excluded as the first priority in the undoing of injustice and the bringing of justice.

We are now at the place in our discussion where I can point to the mistranslation in the NRSV translation of Jesus' speech about the Great Assize. Let me say, once again, that the NRSV is not peculiar in this regard; to the best of my knowledge, every English translation currently available in bookstores mistranslates the Greek in the same way. I am not "picking on" the NRSV; overall, I judge it to be the best of our contemporary English translations.

Jesus addresses those at his right hand and says that they fed him when he was hungry, gave him something to drink when he was thirsty, and so forth. What the NRSV calls "the righteous" then ask, when did we do this? And the entire passage concludes with the statement that those on the Lord's left hand will go away into eternal punishment whereas "the righteous" will enter eternal life. My contention is that the English word "righteous," twice occurring, is a mistranslation of the Greek. The Greek word is the adjective *dikaios.* In both cases, the Greek adjective *dikaios* should have been translated with our adjective *just.* It is the *just* who ask when they did what Jesus says they did; it is *the just* who will enjoy eternal life. The just receive this reward for they did exactly what Jesus and the Old Testament say justice requires; they sought to undo the condition of the downtrodden and the excluded.

I am assuming that justice and righteousness are not the same thing. Righteousness is a personal character trait; justice is a normative social condition. The righteous person is the one who has the personal character trait of righteousness. The just person is the one who struggles to bring about that normative social condition which is justice. The Greek word *dikaios,* in the linguistic milieu of the New Testament, could be used to mean either what our word "righteous" means or what our word "just" means; it was ambiguous in that regard — though I should add at once that somewhere along the line our word "righteous" acquired negative connotations and those connotations would not have been part of what was meant by *dikaios.* Our modern English word "upright" comes closer to catching the meaning of *dikaios* than does our word "righteous."

In any case, since *dikaios* could mean either *upright* or *just,* context has to determine how we translate its occurrences in the New Testament. Given the context that I have presented to you, there can be no doubt that Jesus in Matthew 25 is talking about justice, not about justice-blind or justice-transcending charity. The story of the Great Assize is not about charity but about justice. Jesus is not saying that in extending charity to his downtrodden and excluded brothers and sisters, we treat him with charity; he is saying that in rendering justice to them we render justice to him, and that in treating them unjustly we treat him unjustly. Jesus calls these people the "least." To wrong the social least is to wrong Jesus himself.

I began by remarking that the Matthean passage about the Great Assize has long been taken as the grand charter of Christian social work. I said I agreed with that tradition, provided the passage is rightly interpreted. The passage, so I have now argued, is about justice. It says that to alleviate the condition of the social least is to render them what justice requires. It is not to go beyond justice into the realm of charity and benevolence; it is to render to them what justice requires. To fail to come to their aid is not simply to fail in charity or to be less than fully righteous; it is to wrong them. And the passage gives a truly awesome significance to wronging them: to wrong the social least is to wrong Jesus Christ himself.

To take this passage as the grand charter of Christian social work is thus to take justice as the fundamental category for such work. Not everybody that the contemporary social worker deals with fits under the categories of the downtrodden and the excluded. Some are victims of natural disasters, some are victims of disease, and so forth. Perhaps not all the poor that Jesus and the biblical writers spoke of were downtrodden either. Some may have been the victims of natural disasters. This inclusion, however, does not cloud the issue. The fundamental question that the social worker asks in each case is: what does justice require?

II. The Rights of Creatures Made in the Image of God

What is justice? On this occasion I must be extremely brief in my answer to this question. I have developed everything that I say here at considerable length and in considerable detail in my book *Justice: Rights and Wrongs.*

My impression is that most Americans today, when they hear of justice, think of *meting out* justice. They think of retributive justice. A good rule of thumb for listening to our politicians is that if the politician is talking about justice, assume that he or she is talking about prisons. Some Americans, when they hear about justice, think a bit more broadly than this; they think about the justice system in general. They think not only of meting out justice, but also of what precedes that, namely, rendering justice in cases of conflict and determining whether an accused is guilty of the accusation.

To equate justice in general with either meting out justice or with rendering judgment is a serious mistake, however. Meting out justice and rendering judgment deal with what justice requires when injustice has occurred or when someone charges that it has occurred. But if meting out justice and rendering judgment become relevant when injustice has occurred or is said to have occurred, then there has to be another kind of justice and injustice than that of meting out justice and rendering judgment. There has to be that kind of justice which has been violated or is said to have been violated. There has to be that kind of justice which has broken down or is said to have broken down. Call that kind of justice *primary justice.* Only when primary justice has broken down or is said to have broken down do rendering judgment and meting out justice enter the picture.

What I am calling *primary* justice is often called *social* justice. My reason for calling it *primary* is not that I am against calling it social — not at all — but to highlight the fact that this kind of justice is basic. Unless there were this kind of justice, there could not be the kind of justice that apparently most people think about most of the time, namely, retributive justice.

When I said that justice is the fundamental category for Christians in social work, what I had in mind was not only corrective or retributive justice, but justice in general: primary and corrective justice both. The social worker will of course attend to the ways in which her clients are the victims both of crime and of the criminal justice system. But she also will go beyond that and seek to render to them primary justice.

And what, in general, do I take justice to be? Justice has to do with rights. Justice is present in social relationships insofar as people are enjoying what they have a right to. The dark side of enjoying that to which one has a right is being wronged; to be wronged is to be deprived of that to which one has a right. Thus we could also say that justice is present in social relationships when no one is wronged. You may recall my paraphrase of what Jesus says in the Great Assize speech: to wrong the social least is to wrong Jesus himself.

In my view, a right is always a right to be treated a certain way by one's fellows — or in the limiting case, by oneself. That's why I said earlier that, in distinction from the personal character trait of righteousness, justice is a normative social relationship. It is further my view that one's right to be treated a certain way by one's fellows is grounded in what respect for one's worth requires: if respect for my worth requires that I be treated in such-and-such a way by my fellows, then I have a right to such treatment.

Rights have been getting a bad press in recent years from both Christians and others. Rights-talk, so it is said, reflects a self-centered, possessive, individualistic picture of society in which everybody is always talking about what he or she is entitled to rather than about what they ought to be doing and what the loving thing to do would be. I well remember a dear friend of mine standing up after a talk I had given in favor of rights and saying, with quivering voice, "Nick, nobody is entitled to anything; it's all grace!"

But that is mistaken. I acknowledge that rights-talk can be abused and often is abused; but name me the kind of talk that is not abused. The battered wife is abused by the love-talk of those who say she should accept her abuse out of love for her husband; benevolence-talk was abused by the Afrikaners who talked of the benevolence they showered on the workers living in huts in their backyards.

The "other" comes into my presence bearing claims on how I treat her, and I come into her presence bearing claims on how she treats me, for we are both creatures of worth. Rights-talk is for talking about that reality.

And let there be no doubt that we are creatures of worth, all of us. The writer of Psalm 8 can scarcely contain himself when he thinks about our exalted status. Convinced that we human beings have been singled out from all other earthlings for divine attentiveness and love, he asks, "Who are we, that God is thus mindful of us?" The passage is often interpreted as if the psalmist's answer to his question was "We're nothing, we're worthless, just dirt and dust." That is not his answer. His answer is that we are created just a bit lower in the cosmic scale of worth than divine beings, or angels. The theme is picked up by Jesus at various points in the Gospels when he speaks of human worth. "Consider the ravens," Luke reports him as saying, "they neither sow nor reap, they have neither storehouse nor barn and yet God feeds them. Of how much more value are you than the birds!"

III. Rights and Duties Rather Than Freedom

My discussion thus far is in-house. I have argued that justice rather than charity should be the basic category of the Christian in social work. But the main alternative perspectives that you face in doing social work are not alternative Christian perspectives but secular perspectives. I have decided on this occasion to focus on how social work looks through the eyes of faith rather than on how it does *not* look. If I were to analyze the secular alternatives, what I would argue is that almost all of them, so far as I can tell, operate in one way or another with the ideal of freedom. The goal is liberation, empowerment. I have just read a wonderful book by Joseph E. Davis, *Accounts of Innocence: Sexual Abuse, Trauma, and the Self*.[1] In the book Davis tracks the emergence of the diagnosis of the sexually abused person as

---

1. J. E. Davis, *Accounts of Innocence: Sexual Abuse, Trauma, and the Self* (Chicago: University of Chicago Press, 2005).

the innocent victim of a trauma, with one of the goals of treatment being to get the person to accept this narrative of what happened to her. Here is part of what he says in his summary:

> According to the plot of the mediating narrative as it has unfolded in the victim account and survivor story, the pathological secret has been identified, and its effects progressively overcome. The hold of the past on the client has been broken; she has been freed from who she was, freed from the wrong story, freed from encumbering relationships, and has the power to become someone new. (p. 207)

My difficulty with all accounts that take freedom as the basic category is that there are some things that a given person should be freed from and some that she should not be freed from, and some things that a given person should be free to do and some that she should not be free to do. Freedom and empowerment, though often exceedingly important, cannot be basic. Rights and duties, justice and obligation — these are basic.

IV. Focusing on the Worth of the Other

What difference does it make whether the social worker employs rendering justice as the basic category for understanding and directing what she does rather than, say, the category of carrying out her obligations or the category of bestowing charity? My answer is that to employ the category of rendering justice is to place the worth of the other in the forefront of one's attention. It alerts one to her worth and to what respect for her worth requires of one. Thereby it also alerts one to violations of her worth, to the wronging of the other. What I have in mind here by "worth" includes not only the worth we have *qua* human beings — the worth the psalmist and Jesus were speaking about — but also the particular worth we each have: the worth of accomplishment, the worth of character, and so forth.

When thinking of what one is doing in terms of carrying out one's obligations, one does not focus on the worth of the other. One focuses on oneself, the agent, not on the object of one's agency. One focuses on one's own rectitude or guilt, not on whether the object of one's agency is being wronged. And depending on how one thinks of obligation and responsibility, this can be an exceedingly impersonal way of thinking. All too often in the Christian tradition it has been impersonal — especially, I would say, in my own tradition, the Reformed or Calvinist tradition. Responsibility is conceived in terms of conformity to law. One's attention is focused on whether one's own actions and those of others conform to law. That a person or human being has been wronged falls out of view.

When we employ the category of benevolence or charity for understanding and guiding what we are doing we likewise do not focus on the worth of the other — not, at least, if it is the justice-blind love that is regularly recommended by theologians as *agapē,* rather than the justice-alert love of which, so it seems to me, Scripture speaks. Justice-blind love, charity, benevolence, thinks not in terms of the worth of the other but in terms of her well-being. It seeks to enhance her well-being. All too often such benevolence or charity comes across as smothering; not infrequently, as oppressive and demeaning.

If I think only in terms of enhancing your well-being and not at all in terms of what respect for your worth requires of me, then I will see myself as justified in imposing all sorts of hard treatment on you if I think such treatment has the potential of greatly enhancing your well-being. One can understand why Hannah Arendt once remarked that the problem with Christians in politics is that they love too much. Further, if I see myself as treating you with love, charity, benevolence, rather than with justice, it is not unlikely that I will also think of myself as morally superior and will expect gratitude for my generosity. It happens all the time.

Do not misunderstand. I am not saying that the category of doing what one ought to do is irrelevant for the social worker, nor am I saying that the category of charity is irrelevant. I am asserting that the categories of responsibility and of charity, when employed without attentiveness to justice, all too often produce distorted, oppressive, and offensive ways of acting. Attentiveness to justice and injustice means attentiveness to the worth of the other and to all the ways in which she can be wronged. What makes such attentiveness especially important for the social worker is the discrepancy of power typically present in the situation. It is easy for the social worker to wrong the already wronged and suffering person.

V. Victims of Injustice Rather Than Unfortunates

Those who insist on thinking of social work in terms of bestowing charity rather than rendering justice will also insist on describing the clientele of the social worker as *unfortunates;* to describe them as downtrodden and excluded would be to think of them as victims of injustice and thus to give the game away. As I mentioned earlier, some of them are indeed unfortunates; they have been assaulted by natural disasters or disease. So let it be conceded that some of the clientele of the modern social worker are unfortunates. Though failing to make available to them what they need for a decent existence is a rupture in justice, not merely a shortfall in charity, that which makes them needy is not itself a case of injustice. Nonetheless, a striking feature of the biblical writers and of Jesus is how little inclined they are to use the category of the unfortunates when thinking about the needy of the world, and how powerfully inclined they are to use the category of the downtrodden. In their eyes, the needy of the world are in great measure victims of injustice.

Thus justice and injustice operate on two levels in the thought of Jesus and the biblical writers. What I have been arguing up to this point is that Jesus and the biblical writers do not think of rendering assistance to the needy of the world in terms of charity but in terms of justice. What I am now saying is that they do not primarily think of the needy of the world as unfortunates but as victims of injustice.

The implications are as unsettling as they are clear. If it is unfortunates that one is dealing with, one simply treats the victims as justice requires of one. Or in those cases in which technology holds out some promise of forestalling similar unfortunate episodes, one both treats the victims as justice requires of one and promotes the technology. But if one is dealing with victims of injustice, then treating the victims as justice requires itself requires that one do what one can to eliminate the unjust treatment. Hence it is that the passage in Isaiah which Jesus read or referred to spoke not only of sharing one's bread with the hungry, bringing the homeless poor into one's house, and clothing the naked, but also of loosing the bonds of injustice, undoing the thongs of the yoke, letting the oppressed go free, and breaking every yoke. One not only tends to the victims of injustice but looses the bonds that make them victims.

I trust that I do not have to belabor the implications. Christians in social work will see their task as going beyond aiding the victims of misfortune and injustice to struggling to loosen the bonds of injustice. Rendering justice to the victims of injustice requires going beyond aiding victims to attacking the victimizers — be they individual persons, social organizations and institutions, or whatever. Whether or not one wants to call the struggle against injustice *social work* or something else is, of course, a purely linguistic matter. In any case, Christians in social work are called not only to alleviate the distress of the downtrodden but to become their advocates against those who oppress them. The entire Christian community is called to join them in this; but I do think that you who are social workers are peculiarly able, by virtue of your work, to inform, guide, and inspire the rest of us.

VI. The Almost Impossible Position of the Christian Social Worker

I recognize that if what I have been saying is correct, then many Christian social workers will find themselves in an almost impossible situation — and not only Christians in social work but other social workers as well. It appears to me that a good many supporters of so-called *faith-based initiatives* on the part of the federal government are hostile to the employment of social workers by the government. Perhaps the hostility of some is due entirely to the fact that, in their judgment, government does a poor job of social work while other organizations, in particular faith-based organizations, do a much better job. But it appears to me that there are others for whom that is not the source of their hostility. Even if the government did a better job of social work than any other organization or institution, they would still be opposed to government-sponsored social work. Their reason, so far as I can tell, is invariably that social work as they see it consists of bestowing charity rather than rendering justice; and they see government as having no business bestowing charity on people. In their opinion, taxing people to bestow charity is flat wrong. The business of government is justice, not charity.

I am in near-agreement with that last point, that the business of government is justice — though I feel compelled to add that those who argue in the way I have indicated often seem to have no difficulty whatsoever with the government bestowing charity on the powerful and the wealthy. I do think that government is sometimes entitled to go beyond justice and regulate the life of the citizenry in such a way as to enhance the common good. But that exception aside, I agree that the fundamental business of government is justice.

I trust I have said enough, however, to show that the remainder of this argument is flatly unbiblical. The argument turns a blind eye to some of the most fundamental themes in Christian Scripture. Social work is not bestowing charity; social work is rendering justice. It belongs, thus, to the business of government. It does not follow, indeed, that government must itself be the institution that sponsors social work. What does follow is that government must see to it that social work gets done. How it best gets done will differ from time to time and place to place. Here in the United States, the judgment has been that a mix of private and public institutions is best.

And now I can highlight what I called the "almost impossible situation" of the Christian social worker. The Christian social worker, I said, will not be content to come to the aid of victims of injustice but will also struggle to loosen the bonds of injustice and give guidance to the rest of us in behaving and thinking similarly. Unfortunately, the government will seldom be pleased to have its employees speaking out against injustice, unless, of course, it be injustice off in the distance somewhere, in Nepal, Uzbekistan, and the like. The government strongly prefers that its employees shut up unless what they say fits with government policy.

My view of the situation is in fact somewhat more cynical than what I have just said would indicate. I think a good deal of what the government wants out of its social workers is that they will contain the discontent that arises over the injustice of government policies. The Bush administration has not concealed the fact that its tax policies have heavily favored the very rich, that they have shifted the tax burden to the middle and lower classes, and that the number of U.S. citizens living below the poverty line has increased over the past five years. The official defense it offers for these tax policies is that they, when combined with the administration's spend-and-borrow policy, are necessary for "growing the economy." I think it's clear that in fact the administration's tax policies have nothing whatsoever to do with the state of economy. No matter what the economy does, whether it grows, declines, or remains steady, a tax policy that favors the rich will remain in place.

The big danger involved in advancing such a policy in a democracy is of course that the non-rich, and in particular the poor, will rebel. The unspoken task assigned to the social worker is to insure that that does not happen.

VII. Christians in Social Work Stand at the Near End of a Long Tradition

I close by calling attention to something of great importance that I have not done and that I lack the competence to do. My discussion of social work through the eyes of faith has been entirely synchronic. I have said nothing about the long venerable tradition of Christian social work. And let there be no doubt that it is a long venerable tradition, going back to late antiquity when Christians acquired a reputation for their aid to the poor, through the Middle Ages when the bishops were responsible for the poor, on into early modern times when orphanages were founded in many European cities, and on into the nineteenth century when Christians were active in abolition and the Salvation Army was founded. I have been told that present-day textbooks on the history of social work pretend that there was no tradition of Christian social work and locate the beginnings of social work with some secular activists in the 1820s and 1830s. I find this secular bowdlerizing of the history of social work academically irresponsible and morally reprehensible.

One of the most important contributions that the historians among us can make to Christians in social work is telling the story accurately; and as part of that accurate telling, recovering the memory of the tradition of Christian social work. You who are Christians in social work today may sometimes feel that Christian reflections on social work are only beginning. What that story would show is that, far from that being the case, you stand at the near end of a long and rich tradition. Knowing that tradition could not fail to inform, inspire, and encourage all of us in our attempt to uncover and describe how social work looks when seen through the eyes of faith.

AFTERWORD

An Interview with Nicholas Wolterstorff

In October, 2003, David Schelhaas interviewed Wolterstorff for
Perspectives. *Following is an edited version of the interview.*

*Q: We are sitting here a few miles from the rural towns in Minnesota and
Iowa where you were born, grew up, attended church, and went to high
school. It's more than fifty years now since you graduated from high school.
For all that time you have been a member of the Christian Reformed Church,
and for much of it you have been directly connected to it through Calvin College. Would you comment on what you find most notable about the CRC you
grew up in, and then on how things have changed?*

Good question, but not easy to answer. What I would say, looking back, is
that in 1949 when I graduated from high school, the CRC had a strong
sense of its denominational identity. Perhaps too strong; its sense of identity led it to be very chary of all ecumenical organizations — especially of
the National Council of Churches and of the World Council of Churches.
It eventually consented to join the National Association of Evangelicals,
but even that was controversial. It did not see its calling in the world as requiring ecumenical engagement, except with its parent church back in the
Netherlands.

The CRC, like all churches in the Reformed and Lutheran traditions, is
a confessionally-oriented church of continental origins. Furthermore, in
1949 the CRC still had a clear memory of its Dutch origins. That made it
rather unlike the Reformed Church in America. This memory of its Dutch
origins came about because the bulk of the emigration of Reformed people from the Netherlands in the first decades of the twentieth century went
into the CRC rather than the RCA. Also the big surge of emigration after

413

WW II from the Reformed churches in the Netherlands went, for the most part, into the CRC. Thus it was that the CRC not only had a strong sense of being a confessionally-based church but also a strong sense of being an immigrant church. The switch from Dutch services to English services occurred in my own lifetime.

In the intervening fifty-three years between now and the year I graduated from high school, these two characteristics of the CRC have weakened. Its memory of its Dutch origins has weakened drastically. Probably most members of the CRC today know that the denomination has Dutch origins; but those origins have now become little more than a matter of bemusement and a vague sense of ethnic identity — a reason to visit the Netherlands when one takes a trip to Europe. The memory of Dutch origins was long aided by CRC theologians and philosophers studying at the Free University of Amsterdam; that is now completely over.

Second, any confessionally-based denomination of European origin has a very hard time in America. It doesn't fit into the American mentality. Its ecclesiastical structure is relatively weak compared to the Orthodox, Catholic, and Anglican churches. And it's not part of the American mentality to organize one's religious life around a classical, historic confession. So I think those two developments — the fading memory of Dutch origins, and the oddity of a confessionally-based denomination in America — have caused the CRC to have a much weaker sense of its identity than formerly, and consequently a much weaker sense of its difference from others than was true fifty-three years ago.

Q: Before we talk about what the CRC in particular, and the Reformed tradition in general, should do as they move into the next century, perhaps you could identify some of the fundamentals of the Reformed tradition as you see them.

The Reformed tradition is a tradition of Christianity that emerged out of the Swiss Reformation in the 1540s. Its identity is in part determined by the confessions that were framed in the mid-1550s — the Heidelberg Catechism, the Belgic Confession, the Scotch Confession, and so forth. But deeper than that, in my judgment, is a certain style of life, a certain way of living in the world. Some would speak here of a "world and life view." Thereby they are getting at the right thing; but to think of it as a *view* is too limited. The style of life includes a view, indeed; but as a whole, it's a certain way of living in the world before the face of God.

Let me try briefly to characterize what I see as that Reformed lifestyle.

I was at a family reunion this morning; and it became clear to me, as I listened to my cousins talk, that the Dutch and American pietist traditions have had a significant influence on my extended family. But one of them offered an extempore prayer at the beginning of a worship service we had that included some such words as these: "Make us faithful in our entire lives — every inch of our lives," going on from there to say something about the Lordship of Christ and about serving in the Kingdom. In those few words, which I dare say were, for the one who offered the prayer, both formulaic and meaningful, one hears something close to the essence of what I regard as the Reformed tradition.

It's a style of life that gives prominence to the conviction that God is Creator; hence it is that we give thanks to God for the goodness of all that surrounds us. Second, it incorporates a deep and powerful sense of the fallenness of all things, this understood in such a way that there is a strong impulse to resist all attempts to draw lines in the sand and then to claim that human fallenness occurs on this side of the line but not on that side. Fallenness runs throughout our entire existence — indeed, throughout the cosmos. Corresponding to this comprehensive view of sin is then an equally comprehensive view of faith and salvation.

In short, I think that at the heart of the Reformed tradition is a passion for totality, for wholeness, for integrity, for not allowing life to fall into bits and pieces, for constantly asking, "What does my faith — what does the gospel of Jesus Christ — have to do with this and what does it have to do with that?" And then never being content with the answer, "Nothing!" That's my interpretation of the tradition. There are others who think the heart of the tradition is a certain set of theological convictions; indeed, one regularly comes across people outside the tradition who think the essence of the Reformed tradition is the doctrine of predestination. My answer is that, Well yes, when I was growing up, predestination was there all right. But I don't recall ever hearing any sermons about it. It was not at all as up front as people outside think it must be.

I have learned very recently that the notion that predestination is at the heart of the Calvinist tradition comes from nineteenth-century German scholars. In the mid-19th century, German scholars were preoccupied with trying to find the essence of this or that social or cultural phenomenon — the essence of Christianity, for example, as opposed to the essence of Judaism or Islam. And then, within Christianity, the essence of Calvinism, of Lutheranism, of Catholicism, and so forth. It was in the context of this endeavor that these scholars settled on the notion that the essence of

Calvinism is predestination. I found this bit of history fascinating. That Calvin held a doctrine of predestination was of course well known from Calvin's own time; but that that doctrine constitutes the core, the essence, of the Reformed tradition, is something else again. It's worth adding that the classic Catholic and Lutheran traditions also embrace the doctrine of predestination — worked out in only subtly different ways.

In short, I think the view that the doctrine of predestination is the essence of the Reformed tradition is a serious distortion. And to speak more generally, though doctrine is important to the tradition, it is by no means the whole of it. Those people within the tradition who think that doctrine is at the heart of the tradition are, as one would expect, constantly getting into theological arguments with each other; a little bit of doctrinal variance here or there means that one is departing from the essence of the tradition. It's my view, to say it yet again, that the heart of the tradition is not theology but a certain, difficult-to-describe, way of being in the world before God, in which the notion of totality and wholeness is central.

Q: The fixation of some people on confessional purity has caused a lot of heartache and dissension over the past twenty to thirty years in the CRC, over issues like the infallibility of Scripture and the ordination of women. The question I have then is, if we take this view of living our lives as a whole before the face of God as the essence of being Reformed, how important is it to hold onto doctrine purity?

For one thing, I believe that God forgives us for theological mistakes as well as for other mistakes; so I have never felt the sort of religious anxiety that some people seem to feel over making an error somewhere along the line in one's theology. They seem to think God won't forgive them for this, though God will apparently forgive them for all kinds of other faults. Beyond that, I think some folks have mislocated what's important in doctrine. For example, I completely fail to see why anyone would think that keeping women out of ecclesiastical office is central to the Christian gospel; to think that it is central is, to my mind, a deep distortion.

On the other hand, if you think, as do many in the liberal tradition, that Christianity is simply the finest flowering of the human religious imagination rather than a response to God's action — if you remove from your understanding of Christianity the great biblical narrative of God as Creator, Redeemer, and Consummator — then you have lost not only the essence of the Reformed tradition but the essence of Christianity. So I think that doctrinal convictions are of fundamental importance to the identity of the Reformed tradition. My point is that our controversialists have tended to focus on the peripheral doctrines rather than the central doctrines, and have treated doctrine as if it were everything. We sing Luther's hymn about the church prevailing against all the powers of hell; but many act as if it will only prevail if we get all our doctrines right. It's a misplaced religious anxiety.

Q: You have written frequently about worship, and you have also written extensively about Christians doing justice in the world. It occurred to me recently — I was reading one of those powerful passages in Isaiah about true worship — that doing justice is worship. So maybe there's a natural connection between your focus on worship and justice!

I have thought for some time about writing a book on liturgy and justice; in fact I have written some chapters for it. Whether I actually take the time to finish it, I don't know. So yes, worship and justice are closely connected. The best image I have for expressing the connection is the image of a heartbeat: systolic and diastolic. The church assembles and it disperses. In both its assembling and its dispersing it is living before the face of God, but in two different ways. There's a radical element in the Reformed tradition that has downplayed what goes on in the assemblies; your work is your worship, it's said. And then there is the reverse tendency, less strong in the Reformed tradition, I would say, of radically downplaying the significance of our lives as Christians when dispersed and of elevating the significance of the life of the church when assembled.

For me, the two belong together. Worship in the assemblies is of deep importance, and doing justice and struggling for shalom when dispersed is of equal importance. Anybody who comes along and says the one is more important than the other, or that the one just serves the other, is in my judgment misguided. You can't have a heartbeat without having both the systolic and the diastolic phases. The systolic is not more important than the diastolic, nor vice versa.

Q: Then let's talk for a few minutes about worship in the assembly. I guess I see our culture today — popular culture — as powerfully influencing how we worship. There's the need for entertainment in worship; people gathered for worship have to be entertained. Maybe you can comment on how you think worship should be done in this culture.

I just finished teaching a seminar at Calvin College, sponsored by the Luce Foundation, on Liturgy and the Arts. It was maybe the best teaching experience I have ever had. The members of the seminar went from a Catholic priest on one end to a member of the Assemblies of God on the other. They also represented a number of different disciplines: two from architecture, two from music, one a composer, a person from literature, one from philosophy, a theologian, and so forth. On the last day of the seminar I brought in two young practicing architects, working mainly in church architecture; they took us through what they as architects understood the medieval tradition to have been, the Reformed, and so forth, on up to the seeker-type churches of the present day. Then they concluded by claiming that what they now saw in their practice is a new type of church member emerging, people who don't want to go back to the old kind of church but who also want nothing to do with gigantic seeker-type churches. They want intimacy; any group over four hundred is too big. And they are certainly not after performance. So changes seem to be in the air.

But let me just say that I think there is something profoundly wrong, theologically and symbolically, in departing from the ancient Christian tradition of assembling on the Lord's Day, the day of the Resurrection, to celebrate, pray, confess, and so forth, and instead to assemble for Christian worship — if one does so at all — on a Wednesday evening. I say this because, as I understand it, Sunday in the big seeker-type churches is very explicitly aimed not at the faithful but at those who are seekers; the goal is to make Sunday attractive to them. And since the religious seekers are Americans, what emerges is performances, on the assumption that Americans like performances. The whole thing seems to me to betray a painful refusal to identify with the church of all ages. So I have come to think that my major problem with these seeker-type churches is their lack of Christian memory, indeed, their resolute rejection of Christian memory. As to the new music — yes, some of it is awful. Not all of it; some of it has legitimacy, even though it's not to my taste. What's most disturbing to me is not the music as such but the Christian amnesia, the sense that we have to forget all that our forebears did. I think that's ultimately the worst part.

Q: To put it positively and to give advice to the next generation, would you say, hold on to the old Christian traditions and do not let them go?

Yes, without being, I hope you understand, a stick in the mud. I have come to think (maybe I'm reflecting my age!) that one of the most important tasks for the Christian college, the Christian scholar, and the Christian community, is to keep alive the memory. Over and over I come across people of all sorts who don't even have a memory of their forebears in the faith, or if they do, they deliberately neglect and ignore all that they did and act as if they're beginning Christian existence anew. I think it is an important task for the Christian community in general, and for its scholars and leaders in particular, to keep alive, both for the Christian community and for the world as a whole, the incredibly rich inheritance of the Christian church — its music, its philosophy, its painting, its architecture, its theology, its ethics, its political and economic reflections — to stop thinking and acting as if we are beginning anew.

Q: You just mentioned the Christian college and the Christian scholar. It's been twenty years since you gave that address at Wheaton College in which you said something like this: "A Christian college is an arm of the body of Christ in the world, and its focus now (though you stress the importance of holding on to the earlier phases) should be the training of students to reform society." I am wondering if perhaps you see that happening more and more at Christian colleges that you visit.

Let me first talk about why I said that, and then about what I now think about what I said — twenty years later. I have always thought that Christian collegiate education should be oriented towards the lives and not just the minds of its students. Early in my career I thought, as do most academics, that the way to achieve this is for philosophers, literary scholars, and so forth, to give students the theoretical and historical stuff and then send them forth. "OK, now apply what you've been taught." Then that began to seem to me completely implausible. Human beings don't operate by just getting certain abstract ideas in their heads and then, lo and behold, applying them — or even knowing how to apply them. They need bridges, models, and so forth. In saying this, I am assuming that the calling of the Christian in the world does include doing what one can to alter the social structures that one finds around one so that they come closer to what they should be, and fail less abysmally when they do fail. I was concerned with that; hence it was that I said that Christian colleges should be oriented towards helping their students to live lives in which they find ways to reform or alter the fallen structures of society. I still believe that.

What did not come through very well in that speech was my conviction that we in the Christian colleges must keep alive the memory of the rich inheritance that we have been bequeathed. In our attempt to heal the economic and political structures and practices within which we find ourselves, we must allow ourselves to be instructed by the memory of Christian economic reflections rather than thinking of ourselves as beginning anew, by the memory of Christian political reflections, and so forth.

One more thing. Christian colleges, like all academic institutions in the West, give secondary status to any discipline in which you use your hands. Since you have to use your hands to play piano or violin, in every college or university that I have ever come across in North America, practicing musicians have a secondary status to the music theorists and the music historians. The same goes for painters, and all other practicing artists. Likewise the business departments have secondary status to pure economics, and so forth. Whether we identify this as a kind of Gnosticism or as a kind of Platonism, I think we have to face up to the fact that it has no Christian justification whatsoever.

Part of the calling of the Christian college is to identify the fundamental form-giving sectors of contemporary society, and then to teach for life in those sectors. Instead what customarily occurs in colleges and universities is that you have courses in the ethics of this or that — medical ethics, business ethics, and so forth. Usually this amounts to quandary ethics. That is, students are invited to face up to various sorts of quandaries that will confront them if they go into medicine, business, and so forth, and to figure out what's to be done in those quandary situations. Well sure, quandaries do arise, and one ought to think and talk about those; but I suggest that the more important thing to do in the Christian colleges is think about the whole *practice:* of American business, medicine, recreation, and so forth, and to give students guidance for life in these practices, so that they can actually go out and function as both reformers and conservers. Both reformers and conservers, I say. Though many things should be changed, some should be conserved. What's needed is critical discrimination.

Q: Since you have mentioned reforming business, perhaps you could comment on the horrible business climate right now, with CEO's of corporations like Enron and WorldCom and others engaged in flagrantly illegal and immoral activities. The irony for me is that these two especially — the CEO's from Enron and WorldCom — are Sunday school teachers.

Yes, and not just Sunday school teachers in the past. They were teaching Sunday school simultaneously with doing the illegal stuff.

Q: Yes, so do you think that if a genuine Reformed perspective, as you have described it, were part of a business person's mentality and ethos, this kind of thing would not happen?

It would be less likely to happen. A journalist friend of mine related to me his experience of calling up one of the Enron executives who was well-known for being a Christian, having a long conversation over the phone with him, and finally saying, "Well, what do you see your faith as having to do with your business practices?" The executive said, "What do you mean? I don't see that it has anything to do with it." The idea seems to be that one's life has two compartments, each insulated from the other: you do business as business is done, and you teach Sunday school as Sunday school is taught.

As you maybe know, my businessman hero is Max DePree, former head of the Herman Miller Corporation. Some years back Max had me, a philosopher, along with a few other people, over to the Herman Miller offices as what he called "consultants." Not a customary experience for a philosopher, to be asked to be a consultant for business. I was a bit apprehensive, but I accepted, partly because I was intrigued. When the day came, there were five or six of us outside consultants in the room along with Max and some of his own top executives. Max led off the discussion by saying that he had some questions that he would like us to discuss. I remember some of those questions as if it were yesterday. One was this: "What is the purpose of business?" "What do you mean, Max?" "Well, some of my new young executives are saying that the purpose of business is to make money. I don't believe that, but I would like to talk about it," said Max. At once I thought, "My goodness, I expected to feel like a fish out of water, but these are philosophical questions that Max wants us to talk about. I feel at home." Eventually Max got around to stating what he himself thought was the purpose of business. "To serve the genuine needs of the customer and to provide a satisfying place of work for the employees." I was both stunned and delighted. The relevance of the anecdote is that Max is from the Reformed tradition, a devoted member of the RCA in Holland, Michigan. The view he expressed was the Reformed tradition at its best. If American business leaders had that vision — business is called to serve the genuine needs of the customer and to provide a satisfying place of work for the employees — we would not have these scandals.

Q: As I look at students today in the Christian colleges, and at the Christian church in America, I see tremendously affluent people and churches. I find this sort of scary. It's hard to be a rich Christian, I suspect. We live in a world where poverty grows constantly, and where there's just terrible need. I'm wondering if you have any sort of advice to church people, and to the young people who come to Christian colleges, about the American system of acquisitiveness and about commitment to the larger truths. You have written eloquently somewhere that Western Christianity is not the be-all and end-all of Christendom.

Yes, that last is an important part of the answer to your question. It's important to open up the student body and faculty of the Christian colleges to the rest of the world, to show them that American Christianity is only part of the mosaic of Christendom, not the source of all light. I have a colleague at Yale, Lamin Sanneh, who teaches missiology. Lamin grew up in The Gambia in Africa; he converted from Islam to Christianity when he was eighteen. Lamin is an incredibly eloquent spokesman for what he calls "world Christianity." His point is that we have to put behind us the picture of Christianity as something that arose in the West, spread out from there by the missionary movement, and now, outside the West, consists of missionary outposts. "Yes," says Lamin, "the Western missionary movement is the ultimate source of Christianity in much of the world. But in most of the world Christianity is now thoroughly indigenous — just as Western Christianity is now indigenous even though it too originated from the activities of missionaries." The relevance of his point is that you and I must now *listen* to these people and incorporate their voices, their music, their art, their thought, into a new world Christianity. In thus listening, we will not merely be hearing our own voices being reflected back to us.

I think one of the great challenges for the Christian college today is to promote and give expression to world Christianity. If we succeed at that, we will find ourselves thinking about American business within a totally new context.

It's Tied Together by Shalom

In January, 2010, Jason Byassee, of Faith and Leadership, *interviewed Wolterstorff. What follows is an edited version of the interview.*

Q: You've written about Christian colleges as institutions that ought to educate for shalom. Why is it important that schools are not merely academic but that they contribute to the flourishing of communities around them?

As a young philosophy professor at Calvin College, I was involved in curricular revision. About two years after I got there, I began arguing that the entire curriculum of the college needed revision. To this day I am astonished that the senior professors did not just silence this brash newcomer. Instead I became chair of a curricular revision committee. That made it important for me to figure out what holds a curriculum together. You have the sciences, the humanities, and arts, my own passion, justice, and so forth. What holds it all together? Eventually it occurred to me that what can hold it all together is the Old Testament category of shalom. This usually gets translated in our English translations as "peace," as does its equivalent in the Greek of the New Testament, *eirēnē*. But "peace" is a very weak translation of what the writers had in mind. What they had in mind was flourishing in all its dimensions. That's what a Christian college should be about. Not just planting thoughts in people's minds, not just preparing them for professional positions, but encouraging and equipping them to become agents of human flourishing, of shalom.

Q: Is that a model that churches and other Christian institutions besides colleges can also aim for?

Absolutely. When the Scriptures talk about love, and enjoin us to love our neighbors as ourselves, an appropriate question to ask is, "What is the goal of this love? What does it aim at?" It seems to me the answer is that the goal that love seeks is the flourishing in all dimensions of one's fellow human beings. I spoke earlier of my efforts to help shape a curriculum. Wholly apart from that, after a decade or two of teaching and writing I found that I had acquired a number of deep concerns — art, justice, and liturgy prominent among them. And I found myself asking, what integrates these, what unites them? Or are they just separate components in my life that have little to do with each other? I could not accept such fragmentation. I came to see that it was the category of shalom that united them. These are all aspects of human flourishing. The Christian gospel, at bottom, is an answer to the question, how can we human beings flourish?

Q: Why is it important that leaders of institutions, who can live pretty sheltered lives, go out of their way to be in touch with human beings who suffer?

A crucial part of shalom is justice; you can't have shalom without justice. You may con people into thinking that they're doing OK, that they are flourishing. But if they are suffering from injustice, if they are being wronged, then even if they think that are doing OK, they are not fully flourishing. So in teaching students, parishioners, and so forth to seek shalom, a crucial part of what Christian institutions should be doing is alerting people to the ways in which their neighbors, and humankind in general, are being wronged.

I myself was plunged, almost accidentally, into two deep situations of injustice, namely, that of the blacks and coloreds in South Africa before the revolution, and that of the Palestinians. I did not go out seeking these as causes; the injustice came to me, in episodes that I won't now describe. These were for me eye-openers. In the classic Protestant sense of a call, I felt that I had been confronted with a call from God to speak up for these suffering people. That naturally led me to ask why I had previously been unconcerned with these two situations, and with others like them. I had read about both situations; but reading about them did not move me. What moved me was seeing the faces and hearing the voices of the victims. It was this that changed me.

I think that I was not peculiar in this regard but that the same is true for other human beings. If we just read about situations of injustice, they remain, for most of us, an abstraction. Television can help. The pictures of the victims of the earthquake in Haiti are far more effective than news-print. But most effective of all is to hear the actual voices and see the actual faces. So if a Christian institution is to equip and energize its students, its parishioners, whoever, to seek justice, it has to find a way to have the voices heard and the faces seen — either by our going to them or by their coming to us.

Q: I am struck by the Reformed tradition's particular gift of being articulate about institutions: why they should be founded and tended, and what good they effect in the world.

I think that's true. It is typical of the Reformed tradition to care not only about individuals but also about institutions — though why that is typical of the tradition, I'm not sure. In my own case I was certainly reared, for example, to think in terms of the church and not just in terms of a group of Christian individuals getting together. The health of institutions — educational institutions, ecclesiastical institutions, institutions of all sorts — has been a crucial concern of the tradition.

Growing up in an Americanized version of the Dutch Reformed tradition, as I did, I absorbed the idea that being loyal to, and supportive of, institutions is a fundamental Christian responsibility. The loyalty involves criticizing them when they deserve criticism. We in the Reformed tradition have often been pretty good at holding their feet to the fire. But the sense that institutions are the enemy is completely alien to the tradition. I hear a good number of Americans now talking about government as if it were the enemy; suspicion is everywhere. This is totally alien to me. You hold the feet of politicians to the fire, make them act responsibly; you don't regard them as the enemy.

Q: Even with the cases of injustice that were so formative for you, in South Africa and Palestine?

Yes, there too. You don't get rid of government; you work for its reformation.

Q: Much of your recent work has been devoted to art. For you, institutions make artistic ability and craftsmanship possible.

That's right. Every now and then one comes across the Romantic image of a teenager being filled with music or poetry and going up into the attic to write it out in solitude. It almost never happens that way. Instead we have long traditions of writing poetry, long traditions of musical composition; and young people are inducted into these traditions. There are a few cases of folk artists who have not had teachers but have picked it up on their own. But those are the exceptions. And to get to your question: these traditions of artistic composition require an institutional base.

Q: In your observation, what makes for faithful and successful leadership?

To be a good leader one has to tap into the aspirations of the people that one is leading. One cannot just impose; one has to listen, find out what the people aspire to, and then put those aspirations together into some sort of coherent unity. The leader enhances some aspirations, demotes others, and then unites them in such a way that the people feel that they own this vision. That done, the leader figures out ways of getting there.

Leaders of causes are always tempted to do it differently. They find their institutions unruly; so they ignore the aspirations of the people and impose their own rules, so as to get the people to follow the leader's vision. Or sometimes they don't even do this; they just impose order, or try to.

It's crucial that the leader find language that the people can own, about which they can say, "This is indeed what we are after, though we never saw it quite this way." In listening, the leader will listen to more than the sheer words that the people are uttering; he will listen to the undertone. And he will listen to everybody. There will always be talkative people in the group. A good leader listens not just to the talkative ones but also to those who sit off to the side and don't say anything.

Q: Why is craft important to you?

I grew up in a family of craftspeople. One of my grandfathers was a cabinetmaker in Utrecht, the Netherlands; I still have some of his hand tools. My father was a cabinetmaker. My mother made beautiful rugs. I have done woodworking; my sons all do woodworking. It's in our genes.

My father was not in it for financial success. I have sometimes described his attitude like this: when financial success threatened, he succeeded in averting it. People needed cabinets; that's why he did it. And he loved wood. He loved different kinds of wood. He collected exotic woods, and used them when the occasion arose. I can see him yet, rubbing his hands across a piece of wood that he loved. He taught me reverence for wood, letting the wood talk back, as it were. Wood at some point says, "Look, I don't want you to do this to me. You are violating me. I wasn't meant to be treated in this way." I learned from my father to listen to wood. And I learned from him craftsmanship, doing it right, not cutting corners.

Later, when I tried to explain to students how to write a philosophy paper, I would use the metaphor of craftsmanship. A good philosophy paper has original ideas; but it also needs to be crafted. You can't just ooze big ideas. I would say to my students, "The dovetails have to be tight." I would then see them looking around at each other as if to say, "Dovetails? What's he talking about?" Most of them had no idea what a dovetail was. Initially I tried to explain the metaphor. But that proved too complicated. So later I eliminated the reference to dovetails and just spoke about craftsmanship. Craftsmanship is for me an image for how philosophy papers ought to be written.

Q: You taught with a remarkable group of faculty at Calvin: Alvin Plantinga, Richard Mouw. What was it about the institution that made it possible for your department's work to be better than the sum of its parts?

In the late 40s and early 50s, when I was a student at Calvin College, we had some charismatic philosophy professors, Harry Jellema and Henry Stob. They didn't write much; but they taught us to see the importance of philosophy. It wasn't just a game; it was about more than clever techniques. So when Al, Rich, I, and others were together as young professors at Calvin in the 60s and 70s, we met every Tuesday afternoon throughout almost the entire calendar year. We got the registrar never to schedule any courses for us from 2 to 4 on Tuesdays. We all participated in a discussion of the work of a member of the department.

Members of the department would distribute in advance essays or book chapters that they were working on. We would then go through these essays or chapters with care. The strategy was to ask whether anybody had something to say about the overall structure and idea of the paper. Then we would go through it page by page. It was a blend of "You didn't get it quite right here" and "This page is really good." It was often tough love. What made it possible and fruitful, even though we worked in different areas of philosophy, was that we not only liked and respected each other but were engaged in the common project of thinking and writing philosophy as Christians. None of us was a prima donna.

When I went to Yale people said to me, "Why don't you reproduce what you had at Calvin?" I thought about that for a while. But within six months it became clear to me that that was impossible. Yale was and is filled with prima donnas. Most of them are not willing to read someone else's work unless it directly pertains to their own. It was congenial. But it was not collegial in the way it was at Calvin.

Q: What did Yale teach you about institutions of theological education?

Before I went to Yale, I had never taught in a seminary or divinity school, nor had I ever been a student in one. From my casual acquaintance with them, they seemed to me either flakey or oppressive. Yale was neither of those.

Yale Divinity School, like most divinity schools and seminaries, has a four-fold division of academic areas. Biblical studies, theology, ethics, history, and so forth are taught in Areas 1, 2, and 3; liturgy and preaching are taught in Area 4. Almost immediately upon arriving at Yale it became clear to me that within this division into areas there was an implicit pecking order: Area 4 was at the bottom. The people in Area 4 "merely applied" the important things that were done in the other areas. This attitude irritated me intensely, even though I was located in one of the supposedly important areas.

Then I happened to read a book by a Belgian monk, Jean LeClercq, titled *The Love of Learning and the Desire for God.* LeClercq's topic was learning in the medieval monasteries. This was a revelation for me. I was well acquainted with the theology and philosophy of the medieval universities; but I knew nothing about the learning practiced in the monasteries. What became clear to me, when I was reading LeClercq's description of monastic learning, was that this was not mere application of what was taking place in the universities but an alternative theological tradition with its own integrity. It was theology shaped by the need to give guidance and formation to a certain community. Call it "formation theology," in contrast to "school theology."

Once one sees that in the monasteries there was an alternative tradition of formation, then almost immediately it occurs to one that that this tradition is not only to be found in the medieval monasteries. The church fathers were in good measure practicing formation theology, as was Calvin in Geneva. Calvin never had a university position; his efforts were devoted to giving shape to the unruly city of Geneva and, beyond that, to the emerging reformation of Europe. So too Gustavo Gutiérrez in Lima, Peru, is doing for-

428

mation theology. He too has never had a university position; his concern is to give guidance to the community for which he is responsible. In short, there is a long, rich, honorable tradition of formation theology.

I think it would be really interesting for seminaries and divinity schools to introduce students to this tradition of formation theology in so-called Area 4. We would read what Bernard said to his fellow monks, what Calvin said to the Genevans, what Gutiérrez has said to the people in Lima. And then we would ask what those who will be responsible for the life of a congregation in contemporary America can appropriate for their situation from what we have learned from our reading. If that's what happened in Area 4, if the embracing context for the teaching of liturgy, preaching, counseling, and so forth, was formation theology, it would never occur to anybody to think of the people in Area 4 as "merely applying" the important things learned elsewhere. The studies in this area would have their own integrity.

How My Mind Has Changed:
The Way to Justice

Autobiography does not come easy to me. I grew up in a community of Dutch Reformed immigrants in a tiny farming village in southwest Minnesota. The ethos of the Dutch Reformed was never to call attention to oneself, to be modest in all things, never to brag or boast, never to toot your own horn. If you have done something well, let others say so; don't say it yourself. The Minnesota ethos was always to understate. If someone compliments you for some fine job you have done, either say "Thanks" and let it go at that or say "Yeah, not bad I suppose." If a fellow student asks how you did on your report card and you got all A's say, "Done worse." Of course, lying is out. So if you have never done worse, if you have always gotten all A's, say, "Seen worse." Autobiography feels awkward, self-conscious, indecent, rather like exposing oneself in public. But I will do my best.

I

That immigrant Dutch Reformed community in which I grew up was poor. Its poverty was not grinding poverty; but almost all families were poor. And it was egalitarian; people were treated alike. Had there been any wealth to be ostentatiously displayed, the community would firmly have disapproved of such display. Much later I learned about Max Weber's thesis, that the origins of capitalism are to be found in the ethos of early Calvinism; the Calvinists, so said Weber, regarded financial success as a sign of God's favor. The attitude of my father was the exact opposite. He automat-

430

ically assumed that if someone in the community was beginning to accumulate substantial wealth, that was not to be attributed to God's favor but to shady dealing.

Behind Weber's interpretation of early Calvinism was his belief that "double predestination" was prominent in its ethos; finanancial success was regarded as the sign that one was numbered among the elect, so Weber thought. I dare say that double predestination was prominent in the Dutch Reformed ethos of the seventeenth century. But I myself don't recall ever hearing it preached or taught. It was something that we young people pestered our ministers about in catechism classes. The ministers all seemed uncomfortable and defensive when the topic came up; this encouraged us to press on in pestering them. The image of God that I picked up was not the image of an arbitrary tyrant but an image of majesty and awesomeness.

If double predestination was not prominent in the version of Calvinism in which I was reared, what was? If asked as a teenager, I would probably have spouted some folklore about what differentiated us from the German Catholics and Norwegian Lutherans surrounding us there in Minnesota — and from the Presbyterians in our town whom we called "Americans." It was not until I was a student at Calvin College that I came to self-understanding.

Doctrine and theological discussion have always been prominent in the Dutch Reformed tradition. But the professors who inspired me at Calvin College were not theologians. Though they were very good at discussing theology when the occasion arose, they did not spout doctrine. They had imbibed the mentality and spirituality of Abraham Kuyper, the Dutch theologian and activist of the last three decades of the nineteenth century and the first two of the twentieth; what they instilled in us, their students, was Kuyper's neo-Calvinism.

If I had to put into as few words as possible what that mentality and spirituality were, it would go something like this: God's call to those who are Christ's followers is to participate in the life of the church and to think, feel, speak, and act as Christians within the institutions and practices that we share with our fellow human beings. We are not called to go off by ourselves somewhere to set up our own economic practices, our own political institutions, our own art-world, our own world of scholarship; we are called to participate within our shared human practices and institutions.

But we are not to participate within these practices and institutions like everybody else, then adding on our Christian faith. Christian faith is not an add-on. There is no religiously and morally neutral way of participating in these practices and institutions. Everybody participates as *who they are;* and whatever else each of us may be, we are creatures who have convictions about God and the world, about life, about the good and the right. Those convictions shape, in subtle and not so subtle ways, what we do when we participate in those shared practices and institutions. To this must be added the obvious fact that there is no consensus among human beings on those matters; we disagree on matters of religion and morality, we disagree, disagree profoundly, in our comprehensive perspectives. Thus it is that the Christian participates, or should participate, *qua* Christian, just as the naturalist participates *qua* naturalist and the humanist, *qua* humanist. The practices and institutions are shared; but the way in which we participate in them is not neutral but pluralist.

That was the vision that we as students at Calvin College in the 1950s were taught. When it came to the life of the Christian in scholarship, the vision was encapsulated in the Augustinian-Anselmian formula, "Faith seeking understanding." Not faith added to understanding, but faith seeking understanding. What Augustine and Anselm meant by the formula is that the Christian scholar is called to transmute what already he accepts on faith into something that he now *knows* and no longer merely *believes.* What our teachers meant by the formula was that the Christian scholar is called to participate in the academic discipline of, say, psychology, in such a way that she sees through the eyes of faith the reality the psychologist studies. This does not mean that everything there looks different to her from how it looks to those who are not Christian. Enough that *some* things look different. It's all a far cry from the habit, common among Christian academics, of developing theologies of this and of that, theologies of psychology, theologies of aesthetics, etc. A theology of aesthetics is *about* aesthetics; it is *meta*-aesthetics. That's different from looking at aesthetic reality through the eyes of faith.

Note that nothing has been said about constructing proofs for God's existence, about collecting evidence for the reliability of Christian Scripture, and so forth. Our teachers had no interest whatsoever in evidentialism: no interest in evidence, more evidence, yet more evidence. It's not that they explicitly opposed evidentialism; they simply showed no interest in it. They took for granted that one did not have to have proofs and carefully assembled evidence to be entitled to be Christian. I took a course in which we worked through the first twenty or so "questions" in Aquinas's *Summa theologiae.* We studied Aquinas's "five ways" in depth and at length. Never did our teacher suggest that our Christian faith did or should hang on one or another proof for God's existence turning out to be both sound and persuasive to all rational human beings.

This "Kuyperian" vision which I imbibed in college has remained mine throughout my life. I have tried in some of my writings to articulate the vision itself in far more detail than my college teachers ever did; recent developments in philosophical epistemology have been of great aid in that. And I have been pushed, nudged, and jolted to work out the vision in directions that I was not at the time inclined towards. My life in scholarship has been the opposite of the classic German professor — I caricature — who at the age of 25 has a vision for a fifteen-volume system and hopes that his death will roughly coincide with the completion of the final volume. But the vision itself has remained steady — no reversals, no conversions, no dramatic changes of mind.

And it has stood me in good stead over the years. It helped me when I bumped up against logical positivism in my philosophy graduate studies at Harvard. A central part of the positivist position was that every attempt to say anything about God is without meaning. Since my faith was not based on proofs, I did not find myself worried that this contention of the positivists had undermined the proofs. Instead I found myself standing back with something like calm bemusement. I discerned that the deep-lying conviction which led the positivists to say what they were saying was that modern natural science is the only road to human progress. I found this totally implausible. Thus not for a moment did I believe that the positivists had uncovered the objective truth of the matter and that I either had to give up my Christian faith or figure out how to accommodate it to the truth now once and for all delivered by the positivists. I have always found jumping on and off academic bandwagons, all too common among my fellow Christians in the academy, to be unseemly, even disgusting.

II

Now for some of the pushes, nudges, and jolts. After finishing grad school, I taught for two years in the philosophy department at Yale. I then returned to my alma mater, Calvin College, to teach in the philosophy department there. In September, 1975, Calvin sent me to participate in a conference at the University of Potchefstroom in South Africa. Potchefstroom is not far from Johannesburg; the university at the time was run by the

Doppers, a theologically conservative version of the Dutch Reformed tradition in South Africa. There were quite a few Dutch scholars present at the conference, a few of us from Canada and the U.S., both blacks and whites from other parts of Africa, and Afrikaners from South Africa along with so-called coloreds and blacks.

The Dutch were very angry at the Afrikaners over apartheid and very knowledgeable about it; so they exploited every opening they could find to express their anger. The Afrikaners were very angry at the Dutch for being so angry at them, and exploited every opening they could find to say so. After about a day and a half of this angry back-and-forth, neither party had anything new to say. It was then that the so-called blacks and coloreds from South Africa began to speak up, more quietly than the Dutch and the Afrikaners. They spoke movingly of the ways in which they were daily humiliated and demeaned, they described what the apartheid system was doing to their people, and they cried out for justice.

The response of the Afrikaners took me completely aback. They did not contest the claim of the blacks and coloreds that they were being treated unjustly. Instead they insisted that justice was not a relevant category. The relevant category was love, charity, benevolence. They proceeded to tell stories about the ways in which they exhibited charity toward blacks and coloreds. They gave Christmas gifts to the blacks living in their back yards, passed on used clothing to the children, etc. And they argued that it was not self-interest but benevolence that motivated the entire system of apartheid. The overall aim was to allow the eleven or so different nations (peoples) in South Africa each to find its own identity. That would be impossible if they were all mixed through each other; they had to be separated. That was the grand goal of apartheid. The Afrikaners concluded by saying that they felt hurt that blacks and coloreds so seldom expressed gratitude for the charity extended to them. Turning to the blacks and coloreds in the conference, they pleaded, "Why can't we just be brothers in Christ and love each other?"

Scales fell off my eyes. What I saw, as I had never seen before, was benevolence being used as an instrument of oppression. I felt called by God, in the classic Protestant sense of *call,* to speak up for these wronged and suffering people, and to speak up for justice.

Two and a half years later, in May of 1978, I attended a conference on Palestinian rights on the west side of Chicago. I never learned why I was invited, and I have never understood what it was in myself that led me to attend. But I did. There were about 150 Palestinians present, emphatically identifying themselves as Palestinians, not as Arabs who just happened to live in Palestine. Most of them were Christian. They poured out their guts in flaming rhetoric, rhetoric too hot, I subsequently learned, for most Americans to handle. They too spoke of the ways in which they were daily demeaned; they spoke of how they had been dispossessed of their land in 1948 and of how that dispossession was continuing. And they too issued a call for justice. Again I felt that I had been called by God to speak up for these wronged and suffering people, and to speak up for justice.

I have tried on a few occasions to put into words why it was that I was so moved by this cry for justice coming from South Africa and from the Palestinians. I had opposed the Vietnam War. But I had not been affected in the same way; and I had not thought much in terms of justice. Let me here forego any attempt at self-understanding and just say that being confronted by a call from God to speak up for these and other wronged people and to speak up for justice has profoundly shaped my subsequent life. I have spoken up in opposition to apartheid; I have spoken up for the Palestinians. And the topic of justice has become more prominent than any other in my writing. In 1983 I published *Until Justice and Peace Embrace;* in 2008 I published *Justice: Rights and Wrongs.* I am presently bringing to completion a manuscript on the relation between love and justice that I am tentatively calling *Justice in Love.*

Handed down to us from antiquity are two comprehensive imperatives. One, coming to us from both Greco-Roman antiquity and Jewish-Christian antiquity, is the imperative to do justice; the other, coming to us only from Jewish-Christian antiquity, is the imperative to love one's neighbor as oneself. These two imperatives do not display on their face how they are related. Hence it is that the topic of the relation between love and justice pervades the literature of the West. Prominent in discussions of the topic is the theme of tension. Love sometimes does injustice, or appears to do so; justice is sometimes unloving, or appears to be so.

From the time I first began speaking and writing about justice, I have encountered this theme of tension in the response of my fellow Christians. Not in all of them, of course; but in many. Almost invariably it's because they have learned to interpret the New Testament as saying that in the teaching and life of Jesus, love has supplanted justice. Justice is outmoded Old Testament stuff. When I explain how I think of justice, the resistance becomes even more pronounced. I think of justice as grounded in the honoring of rights; a society is just insofar as the rights of its members, and of the society itself, are honored. A society is just insofar as no one is wronged. I remember a dear friend standing up in the question period after a talk I had given on justice and saying, with quavering voice, "Nick, nobody has any rights; it's grace all the way down!"

In the manuscript I just mentioned, *Justice in Love*, I wrestle with this theme of tension between love and justice, and with the interpretation of the New Testament which holds that love there supplants justice. Malformed love does indeed come into conflict with justice. But well-formed love incorporates doing justice; justice is the ground floor of well-formed love. To delete justice from the Bible is to have very little left; that holds for the New Testament as well as the Old. And as to the claim one often hears, that the idea of rights is alien to Christianity, that the idea was invented by secular thinkers of the Enlightenment and carries possessive individualism in its DNA, I say, to the contrary, that recent scholarship makes indisputably clear that the idea of natural rights was explicitly and prolifically employed by the canon lawyers of the 1100s and again by leaders in the early Reformed tradition. Rights are what respect for worth requires; and in the opening chapter of Genesis we learn that God created us as creatures of great worth. The idea of human worth, and of rights as constituted of what respect for that worth requires, are jewels bequeathed all humanity by the Hebrew and Christian Scriptures.

III

On June 12, 1983, I received news that our 25-year old son, Eric, had been killed the day before in a mountain climbing accident in Austria. Nothing has so changed my life as that news. My life was at once divided into before and after. After I had recovered a bit from the shock, I decided to look for some books that might help me in my grief; that's what scholars do, they read books. I found almost all of them unbearable. They were about Grief, capital "G," or about Death, capital "D," or about The Grief Process, capital letters. My problem was not with Grief; my problem was that I was in grief. My problem was not with Death; my problem was that Eric had died. I did not have questions about The Grief Process; I was grieving, and found standing back to think and talk about The Process obscene.

My own small book, *Lament for a Son*, which I wrote within the year after Eric's death, is not about Grief, not about Death, not about The Grief Process. It's not *about* anything. It's a *cry of* grief. I tried to be honest, not to say things that were expected of me even if I didn't believe or feel them.

There's a lot of silence in the book, the silence of empty white space on the page. There are a lot of questions in it. A friend told me that there are almost as many sentences that end with question marks as with periods; I take his word for that. And a lot of it is image and metaphor, as when I said that sorrow was no longer the islands but the sea.

Eric's death changed my life. But did it change my mind? Did it change how I think? I had not much thought about grief previously. I had no occasion to do so — or better, I had not taken occasion to do so. But now, in various of my writings, I have looked at how we in the West, both Christians and non-Christians, deal with grief. What has struck me is how prominent is the strategy of *dis*-owning grief, either by doing one's best to get over it or by denouncing it as sinful. I could not and cannot disown my grief; that for me would amount to disowning Eric. I loved him. If he was worth loving when alive, he is worth grieving over when dead.

And as for the theodicies produced by my fellow philosophers and by theologians, what now strikes me is that almost all of them are greater-good theodicies. For the sake of the greater good, God decided to allow some human beings to die young and some to suffer long and deep. I cannot accept this. What I find Scripture saying is that God wants each and every one of God's human creatures to flourish until full of years. Did Eric's death serve some greater good? I refuse to think in those terms. My problem comes with that *each and every.* Eric did not live until full of years. Something has gone awry in God's world. I don't know why that is. I live the unanswered question. My writing out of these thoughts has been piecemeal and intermittent; I haven't known how to do better.

IV

I have written a good deal about art over the course of my career, not because philosophy of art was a chapter in some system that I was developing but because art intruded itself, begging for attention. And I have written a good deal about liturgy, because liturgy intruded itself, begging for attention. To explain how these intrusions went would be to sound variations on a theme that I have now already sounded twice. My thinking has in good measure been from outside in rather than from inside out, and all the while the basic framework has remained intact. So rather than spinning off additional variations of the theme, let me bring these reflections to a conclusion.

The "Kuyperian" vision that I sketched out earlier presupposes that at the core of the Christian life is a dialectical "Yes" and "No." A "Yes" to God's creation, and to all that is good in human creation; a "No" to all that is non-loving and unjust in what we human beings say and make and do. Christian existence requires Christian discrimination, along with the ability and willingness to say "This is good" to what is good and the courage to say "This must not be" to what is bad — the courage to say "This must not be" even when one is unable to say how it can be undone.

My reflections over the years on justice, grief, and other topics, have led me to the sad conclusion that the ability of present-day American Christians to make Christian discriminations and to act courageously on those discriminations has been grievously impaired.

Rampant in the American church today is the gospel of prosperity; preachers tell their congregations that what Jesus wants for them is earthly happiness and financial success; if they believe in Jesus, those will come their way. So what am I to do with my grief over Eric's death? Am I to conclude that if I believed more firmly in Jesus I wouldn't be bothered by his death? Or what am I to do with my father's suspicion of wealth, conclude that either he didn't believe in Jesus enough or was insufficiently fond of money? I can scarcely find words to express my revulsion for a Christianity of this sort. We worship one who had nowhere to lay his head and who was obedient unto death, death by judicial execution. And now you tell me that this same Jesus wants us all to seek worldly happiness and financial success? I don't understand it.

And as to public life, what I hear many of my fellow Christians say and do is equally painful. When they get into politics, they all-too-often demean their opponents and tell lies with the worst of them; their only goal seems to be power for themselves and their cohorts. When they talk about national affairs, they talk about growing the economy, not about justice to the downtrodden. Yes, health insurance for all is expensive. But in a wealthy society like ours, surely every creature created in God's image and redemptively loved by God has a right to fair access to decent health care. When they talk about international affairs, they talk about national interest, not about what justice requires. Whether torture is useful is controversial. But the question for those of us who are Christians is not whether it is useful but whether is it compatible with a human being's God-given dignity to torture that person. Justice is up-front in Scripture. In the thinking and doing of many of my fellow Christians today, it is nowhere to be found. Love and justice weep.

Acknowledgments

"The Grace That Shaped My Life," in Kelly James Clark, ed., *Philosophers Who Believe* (Downers Grove, IL: InterVarsity Press, 1993).

"Trumpets, Ashes, and Tears," *The Reformed Journal* 36:2 (February 1986): 17-22.

"The Tragedy of Liturgy in Protestantism," *Christianity and Crisis* 44:6 (April 16, 1984).

"Justice as a Condition of Authentic Liturgy," *Theology Today* 48:1 (1991): 6-21.

"Liturgy, Justice, and Holiness," *The Reformed Journal* 39:12 (December 1989): 12-20.

"If God Is Good and Sovereign, Why Lament?" *Calvin Theological Journal* 36:1 (April 2001): 42-52.

"Why Care about Justice?" in David A. Fraser, ed., *Evangelicalism: Surviving Its Success* (St. Davids, PA: Eastern College, 1987), pp. 156-67. Slightly revised version, "Why Pursue Justice?" *The Reformed Journal* 36:8 (August 1986): 11-14.

"Justice in Shalom," from N. Wolterstorff, *Until Justice and Peace Embrace* (Grand Rapids: Eerdmans, 1983), pp. 69-72.

"The Wounds of God: Calvin's Theology of Social Injustice," *The Reformed Journal* 37:6 (June 1987): 14-22.

"Lest Your Brother Be Degraded in Your Sight," *The Reformed Journal* 21:9 (November 1971): 3-4.

"An Evening in Amman," *The Reformed Journal* 32:7 (July 1982): 3-4.

"Death in Gaza," *The Reformed Journal* 38:2 (February 1988): 2-5.

"The Troubled Relationship between Christians and Human Rights" (unpublished talk given at the Silver Anniversary of the Center for the Study of Law and Religion of Emory University School of Law, October 24-26, 2007).

"Six Days in South Africa," *The Reformed Journal* 35:12 (December 1985): 15-21.

"Seeking Justice in Hope," in Miroslav Volf and William Katerberg, eds., *The Future of Hope* (Grand Rapids: Eerdmans, 2004).

"When Did We See Thee?" *The Reformed Journal* 19:9 (November 1969): 2-3.

"The Bible and Women: Another Look at the 'Conservative' Position," *The Reformed Journal* 29:6 (1979): 23-26.

"Hearing the Cry," in Alvera Mickelsen, ed., *Women, Authority, and the Bible* (Downers Grove: InterVarsity Press, 1986), pp. 286-94.

"Letter to a Young Theologian," *The Reformed Journal* 26:7 (September 1976): 13-18.

"The Theological Significance of Going to Church and Leaving, and the Architectural Expression of That Significance," unpublished.

"Thinking about Church Architecture," unpublished.

"Thinking about Church Music," in Charlotte Kroeker, ed., *Music in Christian Worship* (Collegeville, MN: Liturgical Press, 2005), pp. 3-16.

"Playing with Snakes: A Word to Seminary Graduates," *Perspectives* 13:5 (May 1998): 10-11.

"Can a Calvinist Be a Progressive?" *Gereformeerd Theologisch Tijdschrift* 88 (1988): 249-58.

"The Moral Significance of Poverty," *Perspectives* (February 1991).

"Love It or Leave It," *The Reformed Journal* 20:2 (February 1970): 3.

"Reflections on Patriotism," *The Reformed Journal* 26:6 (July/August 1976): 10-13.

"Contemporary Christian Views of the State: Some Major Issues," *Christian Scholar's Review* 3:4 (1974): 311-32.

"The Political Ethic of the Reformers" — unpublished essay, and undated — but, I would guess, from the 1970s.

"Theological Foundations for an Evangelical Political Philosophy," in Ronald J. Sider and Diane Knippers, eds., *Toward an Evangelical Public Policy* (Grand Rapids: Baker Books, 2005), pp. 140-62.

"Has the Cloak Become an Iron Cage? Charity, Justice, and Economic Activity," in Robert Wuthnow, ed., *Rethinking Materialism: Perspectives on the Spiritual Dimension of Economic Behavior* (Grand Rapids: Eerdmans, 1995), pp. 145-68.

"Justice, Not Charity: Social Work Through the Eyes of Faith," *Social Work and Christianity* 33:2 (Summer 2006): 123-40.

"An Interview with Nicholas Wolterstorff," *Perspectives* (November 2002 and December 2002).

"It's Tied Together by Shalom," *Faith and Leadership* (March 2, 2010).

"How My Mind Has Changed: The Way to Justice," *The Christian Century* 126:24 (December 1, 2009): 26-30.